History, Historians,
& Autobiography

History, Historians, & Autobiography

JEREMY D. POPKIN

THE UNIVERSITY OF CHICAGO PRESS

CHICAGO AND LONDON

JEREMY D. POPKIN is professor of history at the University of Kentucky and author of six books, including *A Short History of the French Revolution*.

The University of Chicago Press, Chicago 60637
The University of Chicago Press, Ltd., London
© 2005 by The University of Chicago
All rights reserved. Published 2005
Printed in the United States of America

14 13 12 11 10 09 08 07 06 05   1 2 3 4 5

ISBN: 0-226-67543-2 (cloth)

Library of Congress Cataloging-in-Publication Data

Popkin, Jeremy D., 1948–
    History, historians, and autobiography / Jeremy D. Popkin.
        p. cm.
    Includes bibliographical references and index.
    ISBN 0-226-67543-2 (cloth : alk. paper)
        1. Historians—Biography—History and criticism.   2. Historiography.
    3. Autobiography.   I. Title.
    D13.2.P66 2005
    907′.2′02—dc22

                                                    2004022006

This book is dedicated to my fellow historians, living and dead, who have enriched our understanding of human experience through their autobiographies and memoirs.

CONTENTS

ACKNOWLEDGMENTS

THIS PROJECT ABOUT historians' life stories has had a long life of its own and owes much to the comments, thoughts, and advice of many friends and colleagues. For their willingness to discuss their experiences in writing about their own lives with me and their reactions to earlier versions of my work on this topic, either in person or by correspondence, I am grateful to a number of the historians whose works are included in these pages: Martin Duberman, Evyatar Friesel, Peter Gay, Alfred Grosser, Gabriel Jackson, Michael Kammen, Peter Kenez, Walter Laqueur, Brij V. Lal, Gerda Lerner, the late George Mosse, Henry May, Gaines Post Jr., Charles Roland, Arthur Schlesinger Jr., and Hans Schmitt, and to Maurice Kriegel for talking to me about his late mother Annie Kriegel's autobiography. Two leading scholars of autobiography, Paul John Eakin and Philippe Lejeune, have been especially encouraging of my work and have provided many valuable comments on the project as it has developed, and Doug Munro has filled in many gaps in my knowledge of historians' autobiography in the South Pacific. Thanks to Ted Schatzki, James Albisetti, and Mark Summers for detailed comments on particular parts of the project, as well as to the anonymous readers for the University of Chicago Press, the *American Historical Review, History and Memory, French Historical Studies,* and *Biography,* where earlier versions of some of this material have appeared. I am grateful to audiences at the 1997 American Historical Association conference, the European University Institute, the Institut d'Etudes politiques, the conference "Perspectives on Holocaust Studies" at Middle Tennessee State University in 1996, the conference "Family Histories and the Holocaust" at the University of California–Santa Cruz in 1997, the 2000 annual meeting of the Association for Jewish Studies, the National Humanities

Center, the Huizinga Institute in The Hague, and the history departments at Vanderbilt University and Mills College, for perceptive questions and innumerable bibliographical references. My wife and fellow historian, Beate Popkin, has repeatedly pressed me to clarify many of my ideas, and my parents, Richard and Juliet Popkin, have provided continuing encouragement for my work. Research for this project has been assisted by a fellowship at the National Humanities Center in 2000–2001 and by support from the University of Kentucky's College of Arts and Sciences and the University of Kentucky Research Foundation. Some material in this book has appeared previously, in different form. An earlier version of the introduction appeared as "Historians on the Autobiographical Frontier," *American Historical Review* 104 (1999): 725–48. A version of chapter 8 appeared as "Holocaust Memories, Historians' Memoirs: First-Person Narrative and the Memory of the Holocaust," *History and Memory* 15 (2003): 49–84; reprinted by permission of Indiana University Press. Portions of the text appeared in "*Ego-histoire* and Beyond: Contemporary French Historian-Autobiographers," *French Historical Studies* 19 (1996): 1139–67; copyright 1996 by the Society of French Historical Studies; all rights reserved; reprinted by permission of the publisher. I am grateful for permission to reuse those passages here. Although this project could never have been completed without the encouragement and advice of many others, the arguments and conclusions advanced here are strictly my own responsibility.

SOME YEARS AGO, at the start of a sabbatical, I was browsing in a bookstore in a small German town when a curious volume caught my eye. It was a translation of autobiographical essays by several prominent French historians, members of my own profession. Perhaps because I was then at a point in my own life and career when I was pondering the meaning of my occupation, this discovery piqued my curiosity. Informally, academic historians spend a great deal of time reliving high and low points of our professional lives and speculating about the connection between personal experiences and research interests in the lives of our colleagues, but I had never read a contemporary historical scholar's life story. To be sure, I knew of the existence of Edward Gibbon's memoirs, and I had once read *The Education of Henry Adams*. But those two texts belong to another age. Their authors were independent men of letters rather than modern professionals employed, as most of us are, in large bureaucratic institutions. Their autobiographies have long been part of the canon of literary classics, their status so lofty as to deter imitation rather than encouraging it. What had inspired these contemporary historians to write about their lives? Did their memoirs have any broader implications for the understanding of the past, or for the understanding of the art of autobiography itself?

The French volume whose German translation I had spotted, *Essais d'ego-histoire*, led me to other publications by twentieth-century French historians; reading these French texts led me to ask whether historians in other countries had written similar works. Browsing library shelves, exploring catalogs, and talking to colleagues, I turned up an ever-increasing number of autobiographical works by professional historians. As I followed these leads, I also discovered the existence of a stimulating literature on the nature and significance of autobiography, and I quickly found myself caught up in the works of James Olney, Philippe Lejeune, Paul John Eakin, Elizabeth Bruss, Patricia Meyer Spacks, and many others. This book is the outcome of these unplanned explorations, which have taken me across disciplinary boundaries and into places I never imagined I would visit.

In analyzing the phenomenon of historians' autobiographies, I will be dealing with issues that have attracted little attention in the historical discipline and with many books that are relatively unknown, even to students of autobiography. There are, to be sure, a few exceptions. Edward Gibbon's *Memoirs* is often considered to be the first great modern autobiography in English literature, and in a widely publicized poll at the end of the 1990s, *The Education of Henry Adams* was chosen as the single most important nonfiction work published in the United States during the twentieth century. Among the contemporary historians' autobiographies discussed here, a few, such as Jill Ker Conway's elegant memoir of her childhood in southwestern Australia, *The Road from Coorain,* Saul Friedländer's haunting recollection of his childhood during the Holocaust, *When Memory Comes,* and, in Germany, Hermann Heimpel's marvelous evocation of a turn-of-the-century childhood, *Die halbe Violine,* have achieved the status of minor literary classics. Carlos Eire's recollections of his childhood in pre-Castro Cuba, *Waiting for Snow in Havana,* won a National Book Award in 2003. Others, like the gay historian Martin Duberman's *Cures* and Peter Gay's *My German Question,* can be seen as significant statements about the experience of groups these historians belong to: homosexuals in late twentieth-century America in Duberman's case, German Jewish refugees of the Hitler era in Gay's. The French historian Philippe Ariès's life story is a memorable and often surprising portrait of a man whose work influenced scholars around the world. Those willing to tackle Annie Kriegel's massive self-portrait will learn much about the French Resistance in World War II and the French Communist Party in the years after the war. The Australian historian Manning Clark's portraits of his parents, his childhood, and his career provide important insights into the development of that country's national identity. Some historians' autobiographies, such as Carolyn Steedman's *Landscape for a Good Woman,* a dual portrait of the author and her mother, have stimulated critics of the genre to formulate new ideas about the boundaries of autobiography itself.

Although many of the autobiographies discussed here deserve a wider audience, my purpose is not to claim that the majority of them are neglected masterpieces of first-person writing. Although I myself have found something of interest in each of these stories, even the most awkwardly narrated ones, I recognize that historians' skills as autobiographers, which bear little relationship to their standing as scholars, run the gamut from exceptional to abysmal. Some of these stories are redeemed by a single memorable anecdote, others by the exotic nature of the life story they relate. A few have the awful fascination that comes from watching a disaster unfold: one reads on, unable to tear oneself away from the spectacle of an intelligent person unconsciously doing so much damage to him- or herself. Like Philippe Lejeune, the leading French critic of autobiography, I have learned to appreciate the struggles of those who are least effective in putting their lives down on paper as much as, sometimes more than, the achievements of those for whom words seem to come easily. I have also come to recognize that my interest in these texts reflects my own special relationship to the stories they tell. I do not entirely agree with James Olney, one of the pioneers of contemporary autobiographical criticism, when he writes that "as readers we go to history, as to philosophy, to autobiography and poetry, to learn more not about other people and the past but about ourselves and the present,"[1] but I do recognize that as a historian myself, I am being made to reflect on my profession and my own life each time I read another historian's memories.

My feeling of personal connection to even the most remote of these autobiographical texts also owes something to a family connection with the genre of autobiography. Both my grandmother, the novelist Zelda Popkin, and my father, the historian of philosophy Richard H. Popkin, published accounts of their own lives, and one of my sons recently experimented with creating a weblog, a personal diary posted on the Internet. As a child, I was fascinated to discover that my grandmother's book included a sentence about me: more directly than anything else I read, this made me aware that the names we encounter in the pages of a book can be those of real people. From my present perspective, I can see this experience as a demonstration that autobiographical writing has effects on readers' lives, even if, as in this case, it serves only to convince a young person of his own importance. As I grew older, I also learned to understand the meaning of some of my other relatives' comments that *Open Every Door* was my grandmother's "greatest work of fiction."[2] Although they meant the remark disparagingly, my relatives succeeded in raising one of the critical questions in the study of autobiography. When my father decided to write about his life, he involved our whole family in difficult discussions about how much he should reveal about the motives behind his scholarship and the personal circumstances that had shaped his career. Would candid accounts of his strong religious impulses and his struggle with manic depression undermine the credibility of the scholarship to which he had devoted his life? In the end, he decided that it was more important to give an honest depiction of his experiences, as the title he chose, "Warts and All," suggested.[3] Listening to my father weigh the issues involved in a professional academic's decision to write about his own life taught me much that has proved relevant to this study of historians' autobiographies.

To justify this effort to interest others in the subject of historians' auto-biographies, however, requires a demonstration that these issues have a broader significance. In my view, when historians turn to the genre of auto-biography, their projects raise important questions about the nature of history and the potentialities of autobiography itself. The purpose of this essay is, then, to explore the relations between these two ways of narrating and preserving the past. Although there has been extensive writing on both history and autobiography, the questions I am addressing remain relatively un-explored, particularly from the perspective of the historical discipline. Ex-amining them will contribute both to a better understanding of the nature of history and its complicated connections to individual experience and to a better understanding of the genre of autobiography. The commonalities be-tween history and autobiography are too great to allow historians to pretend that the research protocols of our discipline insulate us from the influence of subjectivity and that we look down on the authors of autobiographies from some higher plane of knowledge. The entire modern historiographi-cal project of recapturing the past *wie es eigentlich gewesen war,* as it really was, owes much to the example of autobiography, with its claim to unite the stories of external circumstances and internal thoughts and feelings.

My analysis of the relations between history and autobiography falls into two parts. In the first two chapters of this book, I explore the problem from a theoretical point of view. Chapter 1 looks at the ways in which his-torians have traditionally regarded autobiographical materials and consid-ers how literary critics' new interest in autobiography that has developed since the 1970s affects historians' attitudes toward the genre. Autobiogra-phy challenges the historian because it serves as a reminder that there are other ways of understanding and narrating the past besides those conse-crated by our profession. Reading autobiography reminds us of the possi-bilities we give up when we subscribe to the canons of our discipline; it also serves to remind us why we make those sacrifices and brings out with un-usual clarity the special virtues of historical writing. For the autobiographer, an understanding of the discipline of history may be of less importance. Autobiography is not an academic specialty with its own turf to protect; autobiographers are free to pay as little or as much attention to the historical context of their stories as they choose, and their success is rarely a matter of how careful they have been in doing so. For readers and critics of autobiography, however, it may be useful to think about the relationships between these two forms of narrative, and their respective strengths and limitations.

In chapter 2, I explore how autobiography might fit into the theories of narrative proposed by three important contemporary thinkers, Hayden White, Paul Ricoeur, and David Carr. These authors have largely confined their discussions to the genres of history and fiction. Bringing autobiography into the picture demonstrates that their analyses, penetrating as they are, do not exhaust the subject and that a full understanding of the relationship between narrative and understanding requires consideration of other forms of narrative besides the two they have highlighted. I thus explore the possibility of making distinctions among history, autobiography, and fiction that are based on internal criteria and not simply on the traditional historians' claim that history is unique because it is based on verified facts. I also propose a basis for answering the claim of more recent literary critics that autobiography (and potentially history as well) can simply be assimilated to fiction on the grounds of that all narratives are texts, rather than transparent representations of some reality outside themselves.

In the remaining chapters of this book, I turn to a particular family of publications in which historians have had to confront these issues: the autobiographies written by historians themselves. Although few historian-autobiographers have reflected at much length on the significance of their enterprise for the wider understanding of history, and even fewer have been conscious of what philosophers or literary theorists have had to say about these issues, these authors have had to wrestle with the problem of how to be true to their professional commitment to the study of the past while presenting their personal memories. Although their literary merit may be modest, these autobiographical texts are thus of considerable theoretical interest for the comprehension of autobiography. A few of these works have caught the attention of literary critics, but as a group, the first-person accounts of professional historians, along with many other examples of "ordinary" autobiography, have been consigned to near-invisibility within autobiography studies. To be regarded as "ordinary" and therefore not worthy of analysis is the fate of autobiographies by authors who write a more or less standard prose, without literary pretensions but also without the savor of popular speech. It is also the classification inflicted on autobiographies that tell stories of lives lived in "ordinary" circumstances, not the "extreme situations" that literary critic Nancy K. Miller finds highlighted in many of the commercially successful autobiographies of the late twentieth century.[4] Almost by definition, professional historians can neither achieve the kind of publicly recognized success that would justify a celebrity memoir nor claim the kind of marginality that would qualify their writings for the status of nonfiction *Notes from Underground.* Autobiography is theoretically a democratic kind of literature, but in fact not all life stories are treated equally, either by academic critics or by the general public. Historians' life stories are almost always at risk of falling into the category of books deemed uninteresting by both these sets of readers.

This essay will attempt to rescue historians' autobiographies from the limbo of ordinariness and show that there are many reasons why this body of literature is of interest. The historian-turned-autobiographer ought to be able to combine the virtues of both of these ways of narrating the past. Every historian knows the frustration of painstakingly putting together the story of some past event and still feeling, when all the documents have been wrung dry and every detail fitted into place, that something is missing: a sense of what the protagonists were thinking and feeling, of what their actions meant to them. For this reason, some historians have always imagined autobiography as the ideal form of history. The autobiographer can describe the past from the inside, filling in the dimension of motives and reactions that the outside observer can never fully know. On the other hand, it is easy to imagine that the historian as autobiographer could bring special insight to the latter genre. Shouldn't historical training provide autobiographers with an ability to put their life into perspective, to distinguish what was truly unique about them and what was shared with others who lived in the same time and place? Isn't the historian's critical training the ideal safeguard against the tricks of memory that bedevil autobiographers?

The hopes that the intersection of these two genres have sometimes generated indicate the importance of the questions each raises about the other, and the theoretical interest of bringing them together. In analyzing the autobiographical productions of historians, I will be dealing with a variety of issues. In the tradition of modern autobiographical scholarship, my discussion will touch on all three of the elements incorporated in the word *autobiography: autos,* the portrait of the author's self that emerges from such a text; *bios,* the narrative of a life that it contains; and *graphe,* the writing of the text itself.[5] To begin with, chapter 3 surveys the corpus of historians' autobiographical writing, and especially the way it has developed since 1980. This chapter deals with a number of questions: What are the common characteristics of historians' autobiographies? Which historians publish their autobiographies, and what does this pattern of publication say about the structure of the community of professional historians? Are there distinctive traditions of autobiographical writing by historians in different countries? In chapter 4, I offer readings of two historians' autobiographies that have been singled out from the rest of this literature and awarded the status of literary classics, Edward Gibbon's *Memoirs* and *The Education of Henry Adams,* putting these two texts in the broader context of historians' autobiographical writing. Self-consciously designed by their authors to stand comparison with the great classics of the autobiographical tradition, such as Augustine's and Rousseau's *Confessions,* these two works nevertheless prove to have important connections with the more humble memoirs of other historians. To a greater extent than critics have realized, Henry Adams's work is also a critique of Gibbon's depiction of the historian's life. *The Education of Henry Adams* thus provides a dramatic demonstration of how one historian's published life story can affect the lives of his professional successors.

In chapters 5 and 6, I look at two aspects of historians' autobiographies that are central to the larger issue of academic autobiography. The theme of a young person's discovery of his or her vocation is a traditional one in autobiographical writing; chapter 5 considers how this issue is dealt with by authors who came to devote themselves to the relatively abstruse pursuit of historical writing. How does one make a significant story out of such a process, and what insights does historical training bring to the understanding of the role of family background, schooling, and historical context, on the one hand, and individual character, on the other, in determining its outcome? Explaining to lay readers what constitutes the work life of a modern academic is a more daunting challenge than narrating the birth of a vocation. Chapter 6 considers how those historians who have written about their career have tried to meet this challenge, and the significance of the difficulties they have encountered from the point of view of understanding how work in general is viewed in modern life.

In chapters 7 and 8, I turn to what historians have written about the historical events they have lived through. It is surely no accident that the largest single group of historians to have written about their own lives are men and women whose lives were directly affected by the great dramas of the mid-twentieth century, particularly World War II, the ideological struggles of that epoch, and the Holocaust. Historians offer their own special insights into the experience of the war, in which a generation of distinguished scholars, including William Langer, Richard Cobb, John King Fairbank, A. J. P. Taylor, Jürgen Kuczynski, René Rémond, Keith Sinclair, H. Stuart Hughes, and Howard Zinn, were personally involved. A significant number of historians tell of lives vitally affected by engagement with ideological movements of the Left or the Right during that era. French historians who were at one time members of the Communist Party, including Annie Kriegel, Emmanuel Le Roy Ladurie, and Alain Besançon, provide important examples of how the age-old theme of the author's emergence from sinful error, the central thread of Augustine's *Confessions,* appears in contemporary settings. More recent historians' memoirs show that political and ideological commitments have continued to affect the lives of professional scholars even after the end of the age of mass movements. Recent historians' memoirs have come from scholars involved in changing the place of women in university life, from some of those engaged in the struggle for civil rights and African American studies, and from authors personally affected by changing attitudes toward sexuality.

The memoirs of historians who had to leave Hitler's Europe, such as Peter Gay, George Mosse, Walter Laqueur, and Susan Groag Bell, to which I devote the eighth chapter of this book, often deal with another traditional autobiographical theme: exile and what personal identity means in lives lived in many different languages and environments. They also provide a case study of historians writing memoirs in the shadow of a larger body of first-person literature—the narratives of death-camp survivors—that has come to have a major impact on the historical understanding of the Holocaust and has thereby demonstrated the power of autobiographical witness. This chapter is thus related to the one that follows, in which I look at contemporary historian-autobiographers who have deliberately set out to test and expand the parameters of autobiographical writing in general. The narrative experiments of historians such as Saul Friedländer, Luisa Passerini, Ronald Fraser, Carolyn Steedman, Inga Clendinnen, Martin Duberman, and Donald/Deirdre McCloskey raise questions about the autonomy of the narrative self and the possibility of autobiographical writing that also incorporates the voices of others. In my conclusion, I return to the central themes of this book: what are the relations between autobiography and history, and what has historians' autobiographical writing contributed to the literature of personal life writing?

The fascination of autobiography as an object of study comes not only from the variety of issues it raises but also from its ability to connect ordinary human experience and deep theoretical questions. A protean genre, autobiographical writing escapes from the limits of academic disciplines and reaches a general audience that most history writing, as well as most literary criticism and most philosophical analysis, does not. At the same time, autobiography strikes most of us as a more accessible form of writing than fiction: we are all capable of telling some kind of story about our own life, even if we never put it down on paper. Historians who become autobiographers are often seeking an opportunity to write in plain language, to connect with readers beyond the circle of their academic peers, and to demonstrate the uniqueness of their personal experiences. In reading their productions as a collective corpus and subjecting them to academic analysis, I may be doing a certain amount of violence to their projects; I certainly recognized myself when I read the critic John Sturrock's comment, "If we accept that the property rights of all autobiography lie inalienably with the author, then what the theorist is set upon is an act of expropriation, or of dismemberment."[6] In another sense, however, I hope to have rendered these authors the justice of showing that their efforts have a significance that they themselves may not have realized.

In reading these texts, I have been primarily interested in them as examples of autobiographical writing rather than as sources for history or biography. My training as a historian makes me acutely aware of the risks one would run by accepting as gospel truth everything these autobiographers have written about themselves, but evaluating their completeness and factual accuracy has not been my main concern. No doubt many of them contain passages that would not stand up to rigorous examination. My own father is the (unnamed) protagonist of one entertaining anecdote in George Mosse's recollections of his years at the University of Iowa, for example, and he vigorously contests Mosse's version of the story. Were I seeking to clarify this particular issue, I could use my researcher's skills to dig out the records that would establish whether Mosse was ever in serious danger of having to serve as the coroner of Johnson County.[7] For the purposes of this project, however, I will follow the example of the modern literary scholars of autobiography and concern myself more with the ways historian-autobiographers have structured their narratives, the themes they have emphasized, the styles in which they have written, and the reflections they have made on their autobiographical projects than with how accurate their self-portraits are or what aspects of their lives these authors may be deliberately trying to conceal. My main goal is to contribute to the understanding of autobiographical literature and its relationship to history, rather than to write biographies of the authors discussed here.

The Australian historian-autobiographer Manning Clark liked to invoke a phrase from one of his favorite historical authors, Thomas Carlyle, to the effect that scholars of the past need to view their subjects with "the eye of pity." It is a notion that has often come to my mind in reading the literature analyzed here. It would be easy to dismiss the majority of historian-autobiographers, as unsympathetic reviewers frequently do, for having written books that fail to meet the standards of the most brilliant literary memoirs, for having told stories lacking in drama, significance, or general appeal, and for reflecting an exaggerated sense of their author's importance. In reading this literature, however, I have been more impressed by the evident seriousness with which almost all these authors have approached their autobiographical project and their unmistakable effort to say something of significance about their life and times. I have not judged all these autobiographical efforts to be equally successful. I have been moved by some, bored, exasperated, or outraged by others. But I have tried to extend to all these authors the courtesy of reading what they have written with attention and with the aim of understanding what they were attempting to accomplish. Like all autobiographers, the historians discussed here have tried to grapple with a question that concerns us all: what is the meaning of our individual existence, so ephemeral and uncertain? Or, as the biblical citation one of the authors discussed here chose as an epigraph puts it, "Who am I? and what is my life?" (1 Samuel 18:18).[8] I consider my professional colleagues' struggles with these questions as deserving of respect as anyone else's.

CHAPTER 1   History and Autobiography

History is the study of the past. But is history the only way in which the facts about the past can be set down and made public? That is the question historians confront when they consider the genre of autobiography. Autobiography, like history, claims to tell true stories about past events. Like history, autobiography is usually presented in the form of a chronological narrative. To be sure, there are many differences between history and autobiography. History deals with collective time and collective experience, aspires to the status of objectively verifiable knowledge, and posits a separation between the historian/author and his or her subject matter. Autobiography adopts the arbitrary time frame of the individual life and the perspective of the individual, is inherently subjective, and derives its claim to authority from a presumed identity between author and subject. Historians see themselves as adding bricks to a collectively created edifice of knowledge that grows more complete over time; autobiographers engage in individual enterprises to which, by definition, no one else can contribute and which cannot be continued after their death.

Despite these differences, the fundamental connection remains: autobiography is often defined as an individual's history of his or her own life. Admitting the closeness of this relationship is awkward for historians, however, as the *Calvin and Hobbes* cartoon reproduced here, with its suggestion that both history and autobiography are merely convenient fictions, indicates. Acknowledging the relationship between history and autobiography means embracing a relative who can never hope to qualify for the status of an academic discipline, a form of *Wissenschaft*, and who also carries on a

Calvin and Hobbes © 1993 Watterson. Reprinted with permission of Universal Press Syndicate. All rights reserved.

longstanding and all-too-public flirtation with pure fiction. Autobiography by its very nature is thus something of a scandal for the historian, and history's campaign to be recognized as a science in the nineteenth century was built in part through an effort to discredit first-person narrative. Even in the nineteenth century, however, there were some historians who succumbed to the temptations of autobiography and wrote about their own lives. As the twentieth century drew to a close, this practice became increasingly common, one sign that the taboos concerning autobiography within the tribe of historians were weakening.

This tentative reconciliation between history and autobiography has coincided, however, with another dramatic development in the life of life writing. Since the 1970s, autobiography, long spurned by literature scholars almost as firmly as it was by historians, has suddenly been publicly embraced and given a place of honor in the family of literary genres. Once dismissed as one of the "simple literatures of fact," a type of writing with no claim to the status of creativity, autobiography is now hailed as an art form fit to be studied alongside that most prestigious of narrative genres, the novel. Psychologists probing the human mind have added their own contribution to this debate by showing that there is no straightforward record of life events encoded in the brain that can simply be transcribed to produce an autobiography. Summing up recent research in this field, Daniel Schachter writes of memory in terms not far removed from those used by literary critics: "Memory is a central part of the brain's attempt to make sense of experience and to tell coherent stories about it. These tales are all we have of our pasts, and so they are potent determinants of how we view ourselves and what we do."[1] Autobiographical memory, in other words, is a creative artist. The study of autobiography or life writing is now a recognized field in its own right, interdisciplinary in nature although dominated by literary critics, with its own scholarly journals and conferences. As they consider ending their family quarrel with autobiography, historians have to recognize that their relative may not be all that eager to rejoin the clan, especially if such a reconciliation means straining the intimate relationship that has developed between first-person narrative and the novel. Does taking autobiography into the historical family also mean accepting fiction as a blood relative?

An analysis of the relations between history and autobiography thus has important implications for the understanding of both genres, as well as their connections to creative literature. As Laura Marcus, one of the most acute scholars of life writing, has put it, "Autobiography is itself a major source of concern because of its very instability in terms of the postulated opposites between self and world, literature and history, fact and fiction, subject and object. In an intellectual context in which . . . these are seen as irreconciliably distinct, autobiography will appear either as a dangerous double agent, moving between these oppositions, or as a magical instrument of reconciliation."[2] For historians, taking autobiographical writing seriously means acknowledging an alternative approach to narrating the past, one that cannot simply be dismissed as fiction; for autobiographers, recognizing that a first-person narrative will be read as history as well as for their success in portraying their own personality and memories imposes a sense of responsibility that may not always be comfortable.

As I have already indicated, this investigation has been prompted in part by a recognition that the relationship between history and autobiography is not merely a theoretical one: a growing number of historians have also become autobiographers. It is true that some historians have also written novels, but there is a significant difference between the usual conduct of historian-novelists and that of historian-autobiographers. Historical scholars who turn to fiction frequently publish their stories under a pseudonym: they wish to maintain a clear distinction between what they write as history and what they write as fiction. Perhaps the most famous example is Henry Adams, who was both one of the great American historical scholars of the nineteenth century and the author of a classic autobiography: it was only after his death that the public learned that he was also the author of the anonymously published novel *Democracy,* one of the most vivid depictions of public life in the Gilded Age.[3] Historians who publish memoirs, however, almost always do so under the same name they have used for their historical works. They thus acknowledge a connection between their personal history and their professional projects and between history and autobiography. Few of these historian-autobiographers have explicitly addressed the theoretical issues raised by the coexistence of these two genres, but their practice shows that they do not see as much separation between historical writing and life writing as members of the discipline normally recognize between history and fiction. Nevertheless, the autobiographical texts that historians have written do often reflect some sense of difference between these two genres. Whether these texts have theoretical aspirations or not, they thus pose theoretical problems.

Although the analysis offered here argues that the relations between history and autobiography are unique, because of their common claim to capture the truth about the past, historians are not the only academics to engage in life writing. Other scholarly disciplines, too, have their privileged connections with autobiography: literary scholars may be especially conscious of the genre's inextricable involvement with language, psychologists and philosophers can apply their insights into the phenomena of memory and consciousness, and sociologists bring their awareness of the way in which individual lives are shaped by group affiliations. This study is therefore just one case study of the larger phenomenon of academic autobiography and the many issues it raises. From the point of view of the growing field of autobiography and life-writing studies, academic autobiography is an important issue. Throughout the Western world, professional academics have become an increasingly visible part of the autobiography-writing population. As academic research has become more specialized and, even in the humanities, harder to communicate to a general public, first-person writing has permitted scholars as diverse as the sociobiologist Edward O. Wilson and the professor of French literature Alice Kaplan to explain some of the issues in their field to nonspecialist audiences.[4] But academic autobiography also tends to separate its practitioners from the other members of their discipline and is sometimes seen as a violation of the norms of scholarship. Among other things, autobiographies escape the normal processes of peer review. By asking what functions autobiography performs in the community of historians, this essay will raise questions that concern all academic disciplines.

In the beginning, history and autobiography were not sharply distinguished. Herodotus's writings incorporate a good deal of his own experience, and Thucydides mentioned his own role in the Peloponnesian War. Certainly neither author saw his personal involvement in the events he chronicled as a problem or a disadvantage. In the famous passage in which he explains the sources of his information, Thucydides seeks to win his readers' trust by insisting that he has recorded only what he had seen or what he has been told by participants and eyewitnesses. Although his narrative tells us little about him, we can infer that he must have spent much of his life either fighting in the war or seeking out those who had participated in its great events; his history is also implicitly his autobiography. As historical writing developed in the medieval and early modern periods, it continued to be closely associated with first-person narrative, and particularly with the political memoir. As Pierre Nora has shown in the case of France, chroniclers who had been directly involved in events, such as Philippe de Commynes and the Cardinal de Retz, were for a long time accepted as the best historians of the episodes they had lived through.

Only in the first half of the nineteenth century—ironically, a period when the European public was inundated with memoirs about the revolutionary and Napoleonic periods—did the new definition of history as an academic discipline requiring specialized training and with the mission of creating a scholarly historical memory of the national collectivity force a clear separation between the two genres. Memoirs were reduced to the status of mere sources. "From the day when history was transformed into a critical balance sheet and ultimate tribunal, the privileged position of memoirs vanished," Nora writes. "It fell to historians to collect sources and to provide a definitive judgment of past events, while it was the role of the actors in history and the servants of the state to bear witness and to furnish a detailed account of their responsibilities."[5] Despite the common impulse to understand and make sense of the past and of the experience of living in time that underlies both history and first-person narrative and the close connections between them, the discipline of history as it has developed since the early nineteenth century has generally sought to keep a clear distance between its productions and autobiographical writing, even the autobiographical writing of historians.

The wall between history and autobiography has been constructed largely from the historians' side. As history separated itself from literature in the nineteenth century and sought to establish its claim to the status of a scientific discipline, apprentice historians were taught to subject all documents to rigorous criticism. Who made this document, when, where, and for what purpose? Above all, the historian was to be on guard against the biases of those who had produced the records from which the past had to be recreated. No category of document seemed more full of these biases than memoirs and autobiographies, whose authors were quite explicitly trying to tell the story of the past from their own particular point of view. The fact that memoir literature had long shared the function that scientific history now sought to monopolize—recording past events and transmitting them to posterity—made it a special target for historians, a competitor that had to be discredited in order to establish the claims of the historical discipline on a firm basis. Historians were thus taught to treat first-person writing with particular suspicion.

The classic French manual on historical method by Charles Langlois and Charles Seignobos summed up the lessons that nineteenth-century positivist historians passed on to their twentieth-century successors. Its authors warned students to distrust any author who "made such statements as he thought likely to give the reader the impression that he . . . possessed qualities deserving of esteem." The critical historian would also be on guard against "the natural tendency . . . to trust writers more readily when they have talent, and to admit statements with less difficulty when they are presented in good literary form."[6] Autobiographies, which normally justify their authors and which tend to be written with more attention to style than the average historical document, obviously fell under these strictures. A prominent mid-twentieth century historian, G. Kitson Clark, rated "the memoirs and autobiographies written by eminent persons" as "the least convincing of all personal records" and pointed to Daniel Defoe's novels as examples of how difficult it can be to distinguish first-person testimony from outright fiction.[7] At best, autobiographies were to be treated as sources, that is, as raw material out of which historians might, by applying careful critical methods, extract some actual knowledge about past events. In this relationship, the historian's superiority to the autobiographer was taken for granted: by virtue of the historian's identification with a recognized scholarly discipline, he or she was to sit in judgment on the autobiographer's production, deciding which parts of it could be regarded as reliable and which were to be condemned as self-serving or ill-informed.

As historians were setting out to emphasize the distinction between what they wrote and the personal writings of memoirists and autobiographers, some of the latter were also redefining the nature of autobiography in such a way to distance it from history. Jean-Jacques Rousseau's *Confessions* exemplifies this process. Although Rousseau situated himself precisely in space and time, writing, "I was born in Geneva in 1712," he had no interest in playing historian and claiming to distinguish those characteristics that made the time in which he had lived unique. Many events of historical significance occurred during Rousseau's lifetime, but his personal narrative offers hardly any insights into them. Its purpose is at once more limited—to tell the story of the author's private life—and more universal: it would serve, Rousseau claims, as "a standard of comparison for the study of man."[8] Since the story in the *Confessions* is that of Rousseau's innermost experience, his "heart," it is by definition a story that only he could tell, and it could not be verified or disproved on the basis of external evidence. It is true that Rousseau claims to have "set down the good and the bad with equal frankness," thus identifying himself with the standards of honesty and objectivity that scientific history would claim for its own. In the same paragraph, however, he admits that he has on occasion "made use of some harmless ornament . . . to fill in a blank caused by my defective memory; I may have assumed something to be true that might have occurred, but never what I knew to be false."[9] He thereby separates himself from the methods of history and associates himself with the realm of imaginative literature, opening the door to those who would read his *Confessions* as a novel rather than a document. Autobiographers who followed in Rousseau's wake distinguished themselves from historians by claiming to reveal a purely private and subjective truth, one beyond the reach of historical investigation.

Although this assignment of history and autobiography to distinct and separate spheres has been generally accepted ever since the first half of the nineteenth century and has become a structural feature of professional training for academic historians, occasional dissenting voices have challenged it. In her essay *The Gender of History*, Bonnie Smith has called attention to the persistence even in the positivist nineteenth century of an alternative tradition of "amateur" history, frequently written by women, that often incorporated personal and subjective elements. Amateur historians focused on the "low" topics related to private life that were also the stuff of autobiography, rather than the "high" politics on which male academic historians concentrated.[10] From within the academic establishment, the most ambitious attempt to reconnect history and autobiography was part of an explicit reaction against the positivist tendency of nineteenth-century science: the German philosopher Wilhelm Dilthey's effort to construct a distinctive basis for the human sciences would distinguish them from the natural sciences by rooting them in human experience. Building on insights from earlier thinkers such as Vico, Dilthey claimed that we can understand human actions in a way that we cannot comprehend the workings of molecules and planets, because we can put ourselves in the place of the actors and, extrapolating from our own consciousness, achieve an intuitive grasp or *Verstehen* of what was in their minds.

Autobiography occupied a special place in Dilthey's argument. It was, he wrote, "the highest and most instructive form in which the understanding of life confronts us."[11] In autobiography, "the self grasps the course of its own life in such a way as to bring to consciousness the basis of human life, namely the historical relations in which it is interwoven."[12] The reason for this special status is that the man who explains his own life "is the same as the one who created it. A particular intimacy of understanding results from this. The person who seeks the connecting threads in the history of his life has already, from different points of view, created a coherence in that life which he is now putting into words." The fact that autobiography is necessarily selective and influenced by hindsight did not strike Dilthey as a disadvantage; instead, these features of memory were part of what gave autobiography meaning and brought it closer to history. "The future has corrected [the autobiographer's] illusions about the significance of certain moments," he wrote. Selectivity and the construction of connections between life events allowed the autobiography to be something more than a simple reproduction of experience: "Between the parts we see a connection which neither is, nor is it intended to be, the simple likeness of the course of a life of so many years, but which, because understanding is involved, expresses what the individual knows about the continuity of his life."[13]

For Dilthey, autobiography was thus a genuine source of knowledge; indeed, it was the highest form of insight into human experience. It was also the basis of all historical understanding. All individuals, including historians, engage in autobiographical reflection on their life, even if this never takes written form. And such reflection "makes historical insight possible. . . . It alone enables us to give life back to the bloodless shadows of the past." As he put it, "The autobiography can, ultimately, widen out into a historical portrait; this is limited, but also made meaningful by being based on experience, through which the self and its relation to the world are comprehended. The reflection of a person about himself remains the point of orientation and foundation."[14] For Dilthey, then, the great autobiographies were the highest expressions of historical understanding, and only those who were capable of understanding their own lives in such perspective were capable of understanding history, because only they had fully understood that "we are first of all creatures of history, before we become observers of history, and only because we are such creatures, can we become such observers."[15]

Dilthey's ideas have greatly influenced the literary study of autobiography. Georg Misch, the early twentieth-century German scholar whose massive study of autobiographical writing in the ancient and medieval periods is still the most thorough examination of the subject, had been Dilthey's student and was also his son-in-law. Autobiographical scholars of the second half of the twentieth century have a less personal connection to Dilthey, but even those who have turned to autobiographical texts for special insights into the lives of workers and other marginal groups can be seen as adopting what Marcus calls a "democratised version" of his claim that first-person records are the most direct windows into historical experience that we have.[16]

Few historians have fully endorsed Dilthey's claim that autobiography provides greater insight into human experience than history, but in recent decades some have taken a more positive view of what historians can learn from autobiographical material. In a pioneering article published in 1976, Kenneth Barkin argued that "the historian is frequently more akin to the autobiographer than is usually admitted. The latter is, after all, an historian whose subject matter is his own life." Historians, he claimed, are just as susceptible as autobiographers to letting their knowledge of how events turned out influence their reconstruction of the past. Furthermore, Barkin contended, changes in the questions historians were asking dictated a less suspicious attitude toward autobiographical materials. The interest in "history from below" that had emerged strongly around 1970 needed to take into account the "feelings and prejudices" of historical actors, and first-person writings were often rich sources on such issues. Writing at a time when social history was heavily identified with the statistical interpretation of quantitative evidence, Barkin saw the study of autobiographies as a way of understanding the "lives of real people as interpreted by those people rather than by generalization deduced from the study of groups." He thus anticipated the critique of "grand narratives" and structuralist models that developed after 1980. Barkin also suggested that historians could usefully adopt some of the methods of literary critique in studying autobiographical texts. "Analysis of style and how a writer organizes his life will reveal a great deal about his basic conceptual categories," he wrote.[17]

Barkin's article foreshadowed many of the ways in which a number of historians would use autobiographical materials over the following two decades. Autobiographical texts have come to be seen as valuable sources for social and cultural history, particularly in contexts where historians are more interested in the attitudes and assumptions that structure autobiographical authors' writings than in the factual claims they make about their lives. As James Amelang has written in his study of artisan autobiography in early modern Europe, "The increasing acceptance of such writing as a source points to important changes in history and the social sciences . . . above all, a renewed interest in individual experience—and representations of that experience—as keys to understanding larger social patterns and groupings."[18] In the preface to her recent study of the making of American identity in the early republic, Joyce Appleby reiterates the traditional concerns that "autobiographies can obscure as much reality as they reveal," that they are inconveniently novel-like, and that they "usually emphasize individual choices while minimizing the powerful structuring forces of law, property, and custom." But, she continues, "while historians are taught to be suspicious of self-presentations, they ignore the information at a loss. Autobiographies are an unparalleled source of clues about sensibilities— the most evanescent of cultural phenomena—as well as of the values and interpretations that constructed reality for a given generation."[19] She thus joins a growing number of contemporary historians in both the United States and Europe who have made first-person texts central to important historical projects, including Natalie Zemon Davis, Rudolf Dekker, Daniel Roche, and Mary Jo Maynes.[20]

This embrace of autobiographical materials has not been universal among historians, however, and it is always tempered by a fear of finding that the truth claims of autobiographical accounts cannot be sustained. The controversy about Pulitzer Prize-winning American historian Joseph Ellis, who admitted in 2001 that he had "misled his students at Mount Holyoke College into believing that he was an airborne soldier in Vietnam when in fact he never served in Vietnam," is just one of several incidents that have reinforced historians' continued concerns about the slipperiness of autobiographical claims. Ellis had not made these claims in print, only in the classroom and in interviews. Nevertheless, other university historians reacted strongly to his conduct, which, one critic said, undermined all historians' "claim to speak and write about the past with legitimacy." Conversely, the biographer Edmund Morris, who had created a stir of his own a few years earlier by publishing a book about the life of Ronald Reagan in which he included fictional passages, seized on the Ellis case to insist that "all human communication, outside of the driest exchanges of statistical and other scientific data, involves a certain amount of story-telling—which is to say, creative license."[21] Morris's assertion was calculated to exacerbate most university historians' worst fears about autobiography and its tendency to meld into fiction.

The Ellis controversy is only one of several that have highlighted this issue. In the 1980s and 1990s, many American college teachers assigned the Guatemalan Rigoberta Menchú's memoir in courses on Latin American and women's history, because of its powerful evocation of the oppression of an indigenous people. In 1999, however, an American critic set off an international controversy when he charged that the book "is not a literal account of her life," and it now seems accepted that, while the general picture of injustice Menchú paints is accurate, some of the specific experiences she attributed to herself and members of her family did not happen as described in her book.[22] Scholars of literature reacted to this controversy by arguing that *I, Rigoberta Menchú* needed to be understood not as a literal autobiographical account of a single person's life but as an example of a different kind of literature, *testimonio* or testimony, in which the experiences of different members of an oppressed group might be conflated to create a symbolic narrative, and some made a point of insisting that they would continue to assign the book in college classes.[23] Historians, however, generally appear to have concluded that the factual inaccuracies in the book render it unsuitable for classroom use.

Controversies over the status of first-person accounts have been even more heated in the area of the Holocaust, where such narratives have come to be far more widely read than the work of scholarly historians. Much attention has been devoted to the case of Binjamin Wilkomirski's *Fragments*, an account of a child's experience in the death camps that received wide publicity after its release in 1995 but that now appears to have been a fabrication by an author who was not Jewish and had never been in Nazi-held territory.[24] Some historians, however, particularly the French Holocaust scholar Annette Wievorka, have criticized the attention paid even to indubitably genuine eyewitness accounts. In her essay *L'ère du témoin* (The Age of the Witness), Wievorka warns that emotion-laden firsthand accounts can obscure the importance of the historian's effort to "establish the facts and try to give them a meaning" through analysis. The attraction of the reliance on memoir is that it seems to "give history back to its real authors, those to whom it belongs: the actors and the witnesses who tell it 'live,' for today and tomorrow." But, she writes, there is a "tension between the witness and the historian, a tension, perhaps a rivalry, and, indeed, even a struggle for power which one finds at the heart of current debates about contemporary history, but that one finds in other fields as well, when individual expression comes into conflict with scholarly discourse." When historians examine Holocaust memoirs, she claims, they learn not to rely on them for "information on specific events, places, dates, figures, which turn out to be, with metronomic regularity, false." More important, the vision of the Holocaust communicated in memoirs

> addresses itself to the heart, not to the mind. . . . This vision makes the historian uneasy. Not that he is indifferent to the suffering, that he has not himself also been overwhelmed by tales of suffering, and fascinated by some of them. But because he realizes that this juxtaposition of stories is not a historical account, and that, in a sense, it cancels out the historical account. How can one put together a coherent historical account if it has to be constantly opposed to another truth, that of individual memory? How can one incite people to reflect, to think, to be rigorous when feelings and emotions invade the public arena?[25]

As Wievorka's critique shows, historians remain sensitive to the danger that autobiography's different way of recounting the past may displace the more sober, analytical procedures of history. Relying on first-person accounts as sources is acceptable as long as the historian can judge them from the outside. Having to rely entirely on an autobiography or a memoir for information about a significant episode of the past still makes most historians uneasy, however. The historical researcher longs for other evidence: archival documents, letters, diaries or journals, at the very least other memoirs and autobiographies referring to the same event. In other words, the historian refuses to read an autobiography as a self-sufficient text; instead, he or she strives to bring personal narrative into an intertextual relationship with other evidence, to decenter it, and thus implicitly to question its truth claims. The recent historians who have employed autobiographical evidence have often worked with large numbers of comparable texts, in order to avoid being misled by the possibly idiosyncratic nature of any one document; their arguments are frequently presented in the form of statistics, the antithesis of the individualizing projects represented by their sources. In other cases, an autobiographical narrative becomes the center of an exercise in "microhistory," in which the historian's ingenuity in unearthing obscure archival documents to provide context for the first-person document often overshadows the original source itself.

The autobiographies that have found favor with historians are also, in general, those that are unpretentious and devoid of aesthetic claims; the qualities that make them of interest become evident only through the historian's commentary and analysis. Philippe Lejeune, the leading French analyst of autobiography, has suggested that the enthusiasm that developed in the 1970s among historians, sociologists, and general readers for the life stories of peasants and workers, autobiographers who belonged to "a culture defined by the exclusion of writing," came in part from the opportunities such texts provided to their commentators. "The writer, who has often taken the initiative to create a story which otherwise would remain concealed in silence, appears like a mediator between two worlds, almost like an explorer." Lejeune devoted one of his essays to the case of a worker's oral history that had been widely read in France: the writer who created the published text had—in violation of the procedures accepted by professional oral historians—erased the original tapes and discouraged interviewers from contacting her subject, thereby turning his story into her property.[26]

When historians are confronted with "literary" autobiographies such as Rousseau's *Confessions*, other strategies for maintaining the distinction between scholarship and first-person writing come into play. Since the authors of these works are generally famous writers, it is most often biographers who deal with them; historians striving to chronicle collective experience almost automatically set aside texts that are too well written, on the grounds that they cannot possibly represent widely shared perceptions. The biographer of a celebrated autobiographer is usually driven to take a critical view of such a text. To concede that one's subject had already given an honest and complete narrative of his or her life would leave the biographer with little to do. More often, historically trained biographers treat such texts as artful attempts to disguise, distort, and evade important truths about the subjects' lives. At best, the historian or biographer may concede to the autobiographer's production an aesthetic superiority, admiring it as a work of art even as he or she replaces its account with a properly documented narrative. Such a concession is, of course, yet another way of keeping autobiography in its place. By emphasizing that autobiography's value depends on its artistic qualities, the historian-critic stresses that genre's ties to fiction and the realm of imagination, the antithesis of scholarly history.

For all of the historical discipline's wariness of autobiography, however, historians cannot entirely cut their ties with this alternative form of past-centered narrative. Autobiographies and memoirs may be classified as dubious sources for historical research, but they are sources nonetheless, and often irreplaceable ones. Try as the historian may, he or she cannot avoid acknowledging that autobiographers were present at the events they describe and that they may be able to claim a certain authority in recounting them that the historian can never duplicate. Furthermore, what the autobiographer claims to do by inherent right is what the historian laboriously seeks to accomplish by roundabout means: to describe the experience of the past from the inside, in its emotional as well as its objective dimensions. The historian hesitatingly suggests what it might have been like to be a slave before the Civil War or to have been in the trenches during World War I; the memoirist *knew*, even if the historian comes along to raise doubts about the details of an account or to wonder whether it represents a typical experience.

Autobiographers, for their part, are inevitably also engaged in writing history, both because such authors claim, justifiably or not, to give true narratives about past events and because no life story can be completely detached from the collective experience of the author's time—in other words, from history. But the relationship between the two genres is not symmetrical. Unlike historians, autobiographers need not insist on the separation between the two forms of writing. Some see themselves as having an advantage over historians, because they experienced the events they write about directly; others adopt a pose of humility and offer their recollections as simple footnotes to historical accounts; those of a third group choose to regard themselves as historians, no more and no less. Furthermore, autobiographers write in a tradition, but they are not part of a structured intellectual community as historians are, and they may or may not feel obliged to help define their genre's boundaries and distinguish it from other forms of writing. To write an autobiography is not to associate oneself with a profession. Concern about the relationship between the two genres thus comes primarily from the side of history. Practicing autobiographers go about their business with varying degrees of consciousness of autobiography's relationship to history, but for the most part they exhibit little anxiety about the issue. Autobiographical authors have a wide choice of how much historical context to provide for their stories, and many of the classics of the genre, such as Rousseau's *Confessions,* can be read with almost no reference to any history but the author's own.

AUTOBIOGRAPHY AND LITERARY THEORY

Until recently, the theorists of autobiography have also shown relatively little interest in the connections between the genres of history and autobiography, as compared to the concern they have had with the relations that bind autobiography and fiction. The great blossoming of contemporary autobiographical criticism associated with the work of pioneering critics such as James Olney and Philippe Lejeune in the 1970s was based on making the question of the historical truth of autobiographical texts a secondary issue.

Albert Stone, another student of the genre, describes the process as "this Long March of autobiography and its critics away from facts, history, and the referential function of language."[27] In a curious way, the literary critics who have made autobiography a major subject of interest over several decades have taken over the historical discipline's traditional attitude toward the genre, but in a positive sense rather than a negative one. It is precisely because these critics now read autobiographies as imaginative re-creations of the past, full of subjective elements and artistic devices, rather than as simple factual chronicles, that such texts can be seen as works of art, embodying intricate authorial strategies as worthy of analysis as those in novels.

It is not easy to sum up the implications of recent developments in autobiographical theory for the understanding of the genre's relationship to history, because the critics of autobiography themselves have taken conflicting positions regarding its nature. Laura Marcus has argued that the instability of all definitions of autobiography is part of its fascination. "The conceptual category and the class of written products it encloses remain unstable, and the coining of neologisms around the neologism 'autobiography' continues to the present day," she writes.[28] The French critic Georges Gusdorf, whose 1956 article "Conditions et limites de l'autobiographie" was a starting point in moden theorizing about the genre, saw autobiography in its modern, secular form as one of the defining characteristics of the modern European culture that emerged at the end of the eighteenth century. It was at this moment, in Gusdorf's view, that the private life of the ordinary individual came to be seen as having a real importance of its own. Autobiography, he contended, has an existential function: "it recomposes and interprets a life in its totality." Consequently, it is not "an objective and disinterested pursuit" of the factual truth about the past but "a work of personal justification." Positivist historians had been right: "the original sin of autobiography is . . . one of logical coherence and rationalization." But this original sin also makes autobiography "a work of art, and the literary devotee, for his part, will be aware of its stylistic harmony and the beauty of its images. . . . The literary, artistic function is thus of greater importance than the historic and objective function." What is more, autobiography gives unique insight into the way individuals defined themselves and understood their own experience. "This secret structure is for him the implicit condition of all possible knowledge in every order whatsoever," Gusdorf concluded, "hence the central place of autobiography, especially in the literary sphere." Autobiography is nothing less than the key to "the effort of a creator to give the meaning of his own mythic tale."[29] Gusdorf exemplified a tendency in literary criticism, as Marcus has noted, to see autobiography as "the 'purest' form of a literature of consciousness." For these critics, "autobiography becomes the site upon which subjectivity will be saved, and saved for literature." [30]

Although the pioneering character of Gusdorf's analysis is generally acknowledged, nearly every aspect of his argument has been called into question in more recent theoretical discussions. Most of this criticism has come from scholars who shared Gusdorf's interest in autobiography, but there have been a few dissenters, most notably the deconstructionist literary theorist Paul de Man, who in 1979 published a ringing denunciation of the effort to classify autobiography as a literary genre. Such an enterprise, he claimed, "does not go without some embarrassment, since, compared to tragedy, or epic, or lyric poetry, autobiography always looks slightly disreputable and self-indulgent in a way that may be symptomatic of its incompatibility with the monumental dignity of aesthetic values." The problem, as he saw it, was not that autobiography was merely referential: he insisted that such texts could not in any event communicate "reliable self-knowledge." Since the whole enterprise of autobiography was based on the false pretense that it could do so, however, it was basically a dishonest undertaking. "Autobiography veils a defacement of the mind of which it is itself the cause," he concluded.[31] In view of the biographical revelations about de Man's endorsement of anti-Semitism during World War II that surfaced a few years after the publication of this essay, it has been easy to see his attitude as a self-serving attempt to justify his silence about his own life. De Man's essay also reflects, however, the tenacious survival of what the French critics Philippe Lejeune and Jacques Lecarme have called an "anti-autobiographical ideology" among defenders—even deconstructionist defenders—of the notion of "pure" literature. As Lejeune has remarked, "Autobiography is disdained by all those who are sure they know what real art is." [32]

Rather than leading to a complete rejection of autobiography, however, deconstructionist and postmodernist critiques of Gusdorf's approach to the subject have usually challenged his premises but have shared his positive attitude toward the genre. Gusdorf assumed that the proper function of autobiography was to reveal a coherent individual self; critics influenced by deconstructionism and feminism have launched a "challenge [to] the notion of the humanist and essentialist self at the center of the autobiography" and protested that "the emphasis on individualism as the necessary precondition for autobiography is . . . a reflection of privilege, one that excludes from the canons of autobiography those writers who have been denied by history the illusion of individualism."[33] Gusdorf's assertion that true autobiography emerged only in Europe at the end of the eighteenth century has been challenged as well, both by scholars who find examples of the genre earlier in the European past and by others who reject his claim that the phenomenon is unique to European civilization. Gusdorf's reference to an autobiographical canon defined by famous authors such as Rousseau, Johann Wolfgang von Goethe, and John Stuart Mill has been another focus of controversy. Lists made up of only white European males "must be seen as participating in the cultural production of a politics of identity, a politics that maintains identity hierarchies through its reproduction of class, sexuality, race, and gender as terms of 'difference' in a social field of power," Leigh Gilmore has written.[34]

On the other hand, autobiography, or, more generally, life writing, has come to be seen as one of the vehicles through which hierarchies of domination can be challenged. "In rethinking autobiographical narratives in terms of the politics of difference, scholars have necessarily developed a critique of Western individualism and the expectation that narrative lives conform to dominant cultural models of identity. They have also challenged theories that posit a universal woman—implicitly white, bourgeois, and Western—and that presume to speak on her behalf," feminist critics Sidonie Smith and Julia Watson write.[35] Finally, the identification of autobiography with relatively compact and structured narratives has been disputed: as part of "a move away from privileging 'high' literary forms and toward the reading of all kinds of cultural production as textual," critics have found expressions of the autobiographical impulse in diaries, letters, newspaper articles, drawings, and photographs.[36]

In *Touching the World: Reference in Autobiography*, published in 1992, Paul John Eakin, one of the most influential American students of autobiography, summed up the situation created by the blossoming of literary theory about autobiography in the 1970s and 1980s: "In the last twenty years, the pervasive initiative has been to establish autobiography as an imaginative art, with special emphasis on its fictions. This shift in perspective from fact to fiction has been accompanied by the poststructuralist critique of the concept of the self (autobiography's principal referent) and of the referential possibilities of language."[37] Eakin himself was one of those who had contributed to this development. In his earlier work *Fictions in Autobiography: Studies in the Art of Self-Invention*, whose title alone indicated his position, Eakin had written "that autobiographical truth is not a fixed but an evolving content in an intricate process of self-discovery and self-creation, and, further, that the self that is the center of all autobiographical narrative is necessarily a fictive structure."[38] Patricia Meyer Spacks had earlier argued that the roots of the novel and the modern autobiography were so closely entangled that the two could barely be distinguished: writers of both "necessarily depend upon artifice—shaping, inventing, selecting, omitting—to achieve their effects . . . [and] both communicate vital truths through falsifications."[39] James Olney, although he questioned whether any definition of autobiography as a genre was even possible, suggested that the key element in any autobiographical text was the master metaphor chosen by the author to represent his or her life, metaphor being by definition a departure from literal reality.[40]

If the notion of the coherent self is dismissed as inherently fictional, and if language is inherently incapable of communicating information about a world exterior to itself, then an autobiographical narrative can hardly be a vehicle for the representation of reality, at least in the sense in which historians understand that term. It is true that not all poststructuralist and postmodernist critics welcomed the promotion of autobiography to the status of fiction. Although literary critics of the 1970s and 1980s frequently argued for the close relationship of autobiography and fiction, most were reluctant to abandon completely the effort to distinguish between these two forms of narrative. But if simple referential truth was not to be the criterion of autobiography, how was the distinction to be maintained? Philippe Lejeune made the most important effort to find a firm basis for it when he proposed his theory of the "autobiographical pact," an implicit contract between author and reader. Lejeune defined autobiography as a "retrospective prose narrative written by a real person concerning his own existence, where the focus is his individual life, in particular the story of his personality," distinguished from fiction because "the *author*, the *narrator*, and the *protagonist* must be identical."[41] As Laura Marcus has argued, Lejeune's emphasis on the importance of the authorial name on the title page was an effort "to avoid both an approach to autobiography based 'on an externally established relation between the text and what is outside it' and one based solely on 'an internal analysis of the functioning of the text.'"[42] Around the same time, Elizabeth Bruss proposed a similar but more detailed version of "rules" that could be used to define autobiography. Like Lejeune, she emphasized the importance of the claim that the author "share[s] the identity of an individual to whom reference is made via the subject matter of the text."[43]

Even though they used similar language in defining the rules of autobiography, Lejeune and Bruss parted company over the nature of the genre's truth claims. Lejeune did assert that autobiographies are *"referential* texts" which, "exactly like scientific or historical discourse . . . claim to provide information about a 'reality' exterior to the text," but the definition of referentiality that he offered was not one that most historians would be prepared to accept. The factual accuracy of the details in an autobiography "has no essential importance," he wrote. "What matters is less the resemblance of 'Rousseau at the age of sixteen,' represented in the text of the *Confessions,* with the Rousseau of 1728, 'such as he was,' than the double effort of Rousseau around 1764 to *paint:* 1) his relationship to the past; 2) this past such as it was, with the intention of changing nothing within."[44] Autobiography thus yields true information, not about the author's past but about the way he or she chose to represent that past. The one historian-autobiographer who seems to have read Lejeune's essay interpreted this to mean that autobiography's "value as a source of historical insight is very limited" because it "shed[s] more light on the state of mind of the author when he wrote his recollections than on the events when they actually occurred." Dissatisfied with this conclusion, this author "tried to forget quickly all I learned about the theory of autobiography—which was not too difficult."[45]

Bruss's version of the autobiographical pact shows, however, that it can be understood as having implications that might reassure historians. Like Lejeune, she stressed the importance of the fact that the author's name in an autobiography is asserted to refer to a real person, one whose "existence . . . is assumed to be susceptible to appropriate public verification procedures." Furthermore, she took it to be a rule of autobiography that "a claim is made for the truth-value of what the autobiography reports—no matter how difficult that truth-value might be to ascertain, whether the report treats of private experiences or publicly observable occasions." Most important, "the audience is expected to accept these reports as true, and is free to 'check up' on them or attempt to discredit them." Autobiography invites critical scrutiny, using techniques that might be those of the private detective or, potentially, the historian. It is true, however, that Bruss went on to offer the autobiographical author an escape clause. "Whether or not what is reported can be discredited, whether or not it can be reformulated in some more generally acceptable way from another point of view," a text could be taken as autobiographical rather than fictional provided that "the author purports to believe in what he asserts."[46] With this emphasis on the autobiographer's sincerity, Bruss opened the door to a range of subjective speculation that threatened to undermine the usefulness of the rules she had just articulated for building a bridge between autobiography and history.

The autobiographical criticism of the 1970s and 1980s thus offered many new approaches for the understanding of the genre, but most of these served to widen the apparent gap between autobiographical and historical insight. The 1990s saw something of a reaction against the full-fledged identification of autobiography with fiction often made during the 1970s and 1980s and a reassertion of the importance of the historical element in the genre. Two of the most forceful statements along these lines are those of Paul John Eakin and the Australian critic David McCooey. In *Touching the World,* Eakin reminds readers overly intoxicated by the idea of auto-biography as a form of fiction that "the notion that an account of an individual's life can provide access to history has always been a major assumption behind much of the literature of autobiography"; if authorial intentions count for anything, this aspiration must be taken into account. In order to make his point, however, Eakin has to plead for a redefinition of history on the part of its professional practitioners: historians, he insists, have to accept the presence of elements of fiction, not only in autobiography but in historical writing as well. As he says, "my concern with the agency of the imagination and the presence, consequently, of fiction in these texts will seem to discredit their documentary potential as sources of referential fact." Furthermore, "my interest in the individual's constructed relation to history will seem irrelevant to those who conceive of history exclusively in terms of collective experience." Eakin's concentration on language also involves difficulties for historians. "Historians understandably prefer to think of language as a conveniently transparent medium," he writes, but "there is . . . no getting around the fact that when we write history, we make it talk." For Eakin, even Hayden White, whom most historians regard as having gone overboard in emphasizing the constructed nature of historical narratives, has been too traditional in retaining the notion that there is some way of writing about the past—the impersonal language of the annalist—that is devoid of fiction and close to "historical reality." Autobiography can be seen as a form of history once historians are prepared to accept "the fundamental paradox of a referential art: the simultaneous acceptance and refusal of the constraints of the real."[47] For Eakin, then, recognition of the historical element in autobiography implies acceptance of the notion that historical writing itself is inherently paradoxical, in that its ability to describe reality depends on accepting the necessary presence of subjective and fictional elements. This formulation would still strike most historians as asking more than history as a discipline can concede.

In his *Artful Histories: Modern Australian Autobiography,* published in 1996, David McCooey has also offered a number of arguments for distinguishing autobiography from fiction and linking it more closely with history. The "'universalist' model" that assimilates all narrative to the realm of fiction "ignores the fact that autobiographies are still written and read as such," he contends, returning to Lejeune's emphasis on the role of readers' expectations in defining what constitutes an autobiography and echoing Eakin's position. In any event, history itself is not the simple fact-based form of narrative that literary theorists often refer to; the notion that historical texts can never be definitive is now generally accepted by historians themselves. The fact that both autobiographies and histories structure events in narrative form is not proof that they are distorting reality, for human reality is necessarily constituted in narrative form. In McCooey's view, the differences between autobiography and fiction are at least as important as their similarities. One of these differences is that "fiction cannot be verified; autobiography, however, is an inherently discursive act of writing. Like other forms of history, it is a form of testimony and as such it is not autonomous in the way fiction and poetry are. It is a social form of writing (and thus a moral one) and open to all the checks and limitations of testimony." More explicitly than Eakin, McCooey thus takes seriously historians' concern with documentation. To be sure, not everything that autobiographers write is necessarily true, but "the fact that autobiographers lie . . . distinguishes them from novelists," as he puts it: authors of fiction cannot be judged by this criterion.[48]

McCooey also emphasizes the moral responsibility inherent in the fact that writing autobiography involves telling the stories of others along with those of the author: "The 'characters' of autobiography refer to real people, and therefore the autobiographer is just as accountable for the interpretation of those people's stories as for the interpretation of his or her own."[49] This point, which is also stressed in Eakin's *How Our Lives Become Stories: Making Selves,* implies that like historians and unlike novelists, autobiographers are not free to invent as they please. The only way they can justify their readiness to tell others' stories is by accepting an obligation to be as truthful as possible and to acknowledge, at least implicitly, that their stories are subject to verification, and to criticism if they turn out to be distorted. Whereas Eakin tries to reconcile history and autobiography by referring to

Hayden White's conflation of history and fiction, McCooey draws on the work of David Carr, a philosopher in the phenomenologist tradition who has argued that narrative structure is an inherent feature of all human experience, and not, as White would have it, an artificial pattern imposed on raw historical data.[50] Carr's approach, which will be discussed at greater length in chapter 2, is clearly closer to the conventional practices of historians than White's. McCooey's approach demonstrates that autobiography can be discussed in literary terms without necessarily having to be defined as a form of fiction. He nevertheless, and for good reason, stops short of claiming that autobiography is the same thing as history. Among other things, for example, McCooey does not fully confront the dilemma posed by autobiographies that probably are highly unfair to characters portrayed in them but that nevertheless attract us because of the brilliance of their writing and the depth of the portrait they provide of their author. Edmund Gosse's *Father and Son* is an example: the fanatically religious father Gosse describes no doubt saw himself as a true servant of God, not the alternatively monstrous and comic figure Gosse so memorably constructed.

Historians' increased willingness to consider autobiographical materials as legitimate sources and autobiographical critics' renewed appreciation of the importance of the genre's documentary function have thus brought history and autobiography closer together, but tensions between them remain. To return to the family-reunion metaphor with which this chapter began, at moments of tension each party to this uneasy reconciliation is still ready to bring up unpleasant facts about the other. For historians, autobiography's past behavior reveals an incorrigible willingness to sacrifice documentable truth to the imperatives of telling a good story. Cases such as the Ellis, Menchú, and Wilkomirski affairs serve as reminders that autobiographical literature cannot easily be assimilated as a form of history. Scholars of autobiography, on the other hand, imply that historians threaten to spoil the relationship by retreating into hypocritical denials of the necessarily fictional characteristics in their own narratives. Claims that history is or should be an objective science, which were frequent in the mid-twentieth century, are rarely articulated nowadays, as Peter Novick documented in his study of American historians' changing views on this issue.[51] But the research methods that historians continue to teach their students are those of a skeptical discipline bent on separating truth from untruth. History and autobiography may be fated to live together as members of the same extended family, but like many family relationships, theirs will continue to be fraught with tension and a certain amount of distrust.

CHAPTER 2

Narrative Theory, History,
and Autobiography

The evolution of critical thinking about autobiography since 1970 has
clearly complicated the relationship between history and autobiography. It
is no longer possible to judge first-person writings solely in terms of their
factual accuracy, but at the same time historians are, for good reasons, reluctant to embrace the notion that their discipline should resolve its concerns about the fictional elements in autobiography by accepting the claim
that history, too, is as independent of reality as is fiction. Can historians
accommodate themselves to the idea that what we write is in some ways
related to these other forms of narrative, while at the same time retaining
a clear sense of what makes history distinctive? And would such a framework provide a way of understanding the relationship between history and
autobiography?

HAYDEN WHITE'S CHALLENGE TO HISTORIANS

One way of answering these questions is by looking at the debate over the
nature of historical narrative opened by the publication of Hayden White's
Metahistory in 1973 and continued in the work of philosophers Paul Ricoeur
and David Carr. In turning to these authors, and especially to the latter two,
I am following in the footsteps of a number of the leading critics of autobiography. Philippe Lejeune, for example, has seen in Ricoeur's analyses a
hope for "going beyond the antinomy of truth versus fiction" and has suggested that autobiographical theory may be entering "the Ricoeur years."
Laura Marcus considers Ricoeur's work as "of particular relevance to autobiography," and Paul John Eakin has put Ricoeur and Carr together because

of their common insistence that narrative is a fundamental aspect of human experience.[1] Historians, however, while they generally have some familiarity with White's main ideas, have paid less attention to Ricoeur's and Carr's writings. For example, Robert Berkhofer's *Beyond the Great Story: History as Text and Discourse,* an important contribution to discussions of narrative and history published in 1995, includes more than twenty index entries for White but only two for Ricoeur and no reference to Carr.[2] This emphasis on White's version of narrative theory has given historians an incomplete notion of what such approaches might have to contribute to historical understanding and, in particular, to the relations between history and autobiography.

More than any other work, *Metahistory* has forced historians to confront the narrative nature of historical writing and the question of the relations between history and literature. Published in 1973, White's work appeared at a moment when graduate students in history were being urged to learn statistics and computer programming so that they could help transform history into "cliometrics." White proposed to take a completely different view. "I will consider the historical work as . . . a verbal structure in the form of a narrative prose discourse that purports to be a model, or icon, of past structures and processes in the interest of *explaining what they were by representing* them," he announced.[3] In an article published a few years later, White was even more explicit in assimilating history to fiction. Historians, White complained, had shown "a reluctance to consider historical narratives as what they most manifestly are—verbal fictions, the contents of which are as much invented as found and the forms of which have more in common with their counterparts in literature than they have with those in the sciences." He had little patience with colleagues "who believe that they are doing something fundamentally different from the novelist by virtue of the fact that they deal with 'real,' while the novelist deals with 'imagined,' events." And White did not see why his propositions should cause problems from the point of view of the historical discipline: "To say that we make sense of the real world by imposing upon it the formal coherence that we customarily associate with the products of writers of fiction in no way detracts from the status of knowledge that we ascribe to historiography. It would only detract from it if we were to believe that literature did not teach us anything about reality."[4] In short, White took the position that all forms of narrative are, in a sense, equally fictional, although he also argued that to call a narrative fictional does not necessarily imply that it is incapable of conveying truth.

White has not explicitly addressed the status of autobiography in his theoretical writings, but it seems clear that the arguments he has developed about the narrative character of history and its similarity to fiction apply equally to autobiography. Like history, autobiography would be the product of a particular emplotment imposed on the facts of an individual's life, and the possible presence of fictional elements in an autobiographical account would be of no more concern to White than their presence in historical writings would be. White's tendency to subsume all forms of narrative under the category of fiction has been attractive to many of the literary theorists of autobiography, who have used it to justify their assimilation of autobiography to fiction. Even in the context of the argument he makes for the referential value of autobiography, an argument that also draws on Ricoeur and Carr, Paul John Eakin cites White repeatedly and endorses his claim that "history writing is inevitably a literary practice and history itself a cultural fiction." Eakin's main criticism of White is that the latter, in the literary critic's view, has remained too wedded to the notion that there are objective facts, even if their meaning depends on the narrative structure in which the historian embeds them. For Eakin, even the dry annotations of a chronicle are "constructed" and not simply reflections of reality.[5] James Olney's *Metaphors of Self*, which appeared one year before White's *Metahistory*, reflects a similar point of view. Olney asserts that "the writers of history organize the events of which they write according to, and out of, their own private necessities and the state of their own selves. Historians impose, and quite properly, their own metaphors on the human past." Olney's purpose in making this claim was to efface the distinctions between history and autobiography, so that the annexation of the latter to the domain of literature would necessarily involve the annexation of history as well. "As readers," he wrote, in a passage I have quoted earlier, "we go to history, as to philosophy, to autobiography and poetry, to learn more not about other people and the past but about ourselves and the present."[6] In other words, the boundaries between different forms of writing are illusory: in the final analysis, all are equally fictional and autobiographical.

If one accepts the virtual merger of history and fiction under the category of narrative proposed by White, the problem of the relations between history and autobiography would be relatively insignificant. If historical narratives could be described as "verbal fictions," and if the distinction between fact and invention were indeed irrelevant, it would be hard to find a convincing reason for putting autobiographical narratives in a different category. White's approach renders historians' traditional concerns about the subjectivity of autobiography irrelevant, since in his view historical narratives, too, necessarily incorporate a subjective or ideological element.[7] The categories of emplotment that White borrowed from Northrop Frye's *Anatomy of Criticism* had originally been developed to describe narratives about individual characters, and there was no reason they could not be applied to autobiographical texts as well as historical ones.

White's assimilation of history and fiction—and, implicitly, autobiography—has been strongly appealing to literary critics, but it has been much less attractive to practicing historians. As historian Richard Vann has written in a study of White's impact, "There is an undercurrent of satisfaction among White's literary readers to see history among the mighty cast down from their seats. Its epistemological privileges and scientific pretensions seemed to be exposed; literature's truth claims were at last taken as seriously as those of history." While literary theorists have frequently cited White's work as evidence of a change in mentality among historians in general, however, historians have virtually read him out of the profession, as Vann's study of citations to *Metahistory* has demonstrated. When White's book first appeared, it was fairly widely discussed among practicing historians. Over the years, however, most members of that discipline have lost interest in White's theses, while references to his work among philosophers and literary scholars have risen.[8]

Mainstream historians' objections to White have usually focused on the claim that his argument undermines the referential character of history and makes it impossible to discriminate between true and false accounts of the past. He has been accused of opening the door to, among other things, negationist denials that the Holocaust took place. White has defended himself against these critiques by insisting that while history necessarily takes the form of narrative, historians' narratives must be constructed on the basis of verified facts. His critics have responded by questioning his assumptions that facts stand outside of the narratives in which they are emplotted and that an event of the magnitude and complexity of the Holocaust can be put in the same category as a physical occurrence such as the Lisbon earthquake.[9]

This type of debate has limited significance for the understanding of autobiography. Although autobiographical narratives are presented as veridical, by their very nature they frequently contain assertions—about the narrator's state of mind or emotions at the time of the events described, for example, or about private interactions with persons no longer living—that cannot be documented. More important for our purposes are the efforts that have been made to preserve White's insights about the central role of narrative in history while finding some ground for distinguishing history from fiction. Because they suggest either that not all narratives are the same or that narrative is not necessarily associated with fiction, these arguments—most notably those of Paul Ricoeur and David Carr—have important implications for the understanding of autobiography and its relationship to history.

PAUL RICOEUR'S *TIME AND NARRATIVE*

The philosopher Paul Ricoeur's lengthy essay *Temps et récit* (*Time and Narrative*) deals with many issues, but it is in part an attempt to incorporate some of Hayden White's insights while providing a framework in which historical narrative can be distinguished from fiction. That Ricoeur intended *Time and Narrative* as a response to White and the danger that White's approach tends "to erase the frontier between fiction and history" is made clear not only in the work itself but in several of Ricoeur's subsequent writings.[10] In *Time and Narrative* Ricoeur makes only a few comments about autobiography, but in several subsequent publications, particularly *Oneself as Another,* he addresses the issue of life narratives more directly; his work is therefore more fruitful for thinking about autobiography than White's. Ricoeur, a philosopher in the phenomenological tradition, starts by addressing a fundamental question that White answers affirmatively without much discussion: do narratives, of any kind, constitute a form of knowledge? Ricoeur's answer is positive. According to Ricoeur, narrative, in all its forms, serves a fundamental purpose in human life: it is the way in which we attempt to understand the relationship between time and human life. "I see in the stories we make up the most important means by which we give shape to our confused, undefined and, in the final analysis, incommunicable experience of time." Narrative is thus a form of knowledge, indeed the only form of knowledge human beings can have about the phenomenon of living in time. Whereas White highlights the fictional character of historical narrative, Ricoeur emphasizes the notion that fiction itself communicates knowledge, having in common with history the mission of displaying "the temporal character of human experience." The phenomenon of time may have an existence independent of human minds, but "time becomes human time to the degree that it is articulated in the shape of a narrative; in return, a narrative has meaning to the degree that it portrays the characteristics of temporal experience."[11]

Although Ricoeur does not comment on the significance of this fact, his discussion of philosophical efforts to understand time starts with an auto-biographical text: Augustine's *Confessions*. "What then is time? Provided that no one asks me, I know," Augustine wrote,[12] thus making him, Ricoeur claims, the first to fully articulate the paradoxes of time. In his efforts to grapple with this question, Augustine recognized human time as a phe-nomenon in the mind or soul rather than an objective reality (Ricoeur, *Temps et récit,* 1:21–53). But time is not merely a human construction, and Ricoeur next turns to Aristotle to show how it can be analyzed as a cosmo-logical phenomenon, external to human beings. Aristotle is equally impor-tant to Ricoeur, however, because of his analysis of literature. Ricoeur sees in Aristotle's doctrine of *mimesis* or imitation the key to the human enter-prise of using narrative to represent the experience of living in time through the making of stories. Ricoeur insists that *mimesis* is not merely the passive imitation of an element present in experience before it is cast in the form of a story: the making of a representation is an active process that "creates something" distinct from what is represented by introducing a plot or struc-ture. "The craftsman of words does not create things, he creates only quasi-things, he makes up 'as-ifs.' In this sense, the Aristotelian term of *mimesis* is the emblem of this separation which . . . marks the literariness of literary works" (1:59, 76).

   In the second half of his first volume, Ricoeur takes up the challenge of establishing the narrative character of all historical writing, even the mod-ern forms of it that explicitly attempt to escape from this framework. He also takes on the Anglo-American philosophers of history of the mid-twentieth century who attempted to establish the scientific character of historical knowledge. Although the French historians of the *Annales* school tried to write a history from which individuals and ephemeral "events" were ban-ished, Ricoeur argues that their works still incorporated a narrative struc-ture, even if its protagonists were what he labelled "quasi-personages" or col-lective entities such as peoples, nations, or civilizations. Furthermore, while these historians attempted to define a notion of temporality—Fernand Braudel's famous *longue durée*—divorced from ordinary human experience, they could not escape their dependence on notions of time derived ulti-mately from that experience (1:255). As for the efforts of philosophers such as Carl Hempel to establish that historical knowledge can be cast in the cat-egories of the natural and social sciences and to eliminate history's depen-dence on narrative and events, Ricoeur asserts that they ended in failure: historical truths could not be formulated as scientific rules (1:172–73).

   Although Ricoeur classifies both history and fiction as forms of narrative, he distinguishes himself from White by insisting that the distinctions between them are as important as their commonalities. He gives credit to White for having made clear the central importance of emplotment in the making of historical narratives: "Emplotment is much more than one level [of the construction of narratives] among others: it is what establishes the transition from recounting to explanation" (1:239). But Ricoeur wants "to do justice to the specificity of historical explanation *and* to show that history nevertheless remains part of the domain of narrative" (1:318). History deals with events that actually took place—Ricoeur shares with White the assumption that such events can in fact be identified—and this gives history "an air of realism that no literature, even if it calls itself 'realist,' will ever equal" (1:123). In the third volume of *Time and Narrative,* he goes further in differentiating historical from fictional narratives by showing that the former depend on "specific *tools of thought,*" namely "the calendar, the idea of the succession of generations . . . , and finally and above all, the reliance on archives, documents, and traces" (3:153). These tools serve as ways of mediating between personal and collective experience, and their use gives historical narratives characteristics that are not shared by fictional ones.

Calendar time, Ricoeur argues, is something defined by human beings, not a feature of the universe, but it is also supraindividual, independent of individual consciousness. Through it, individuals are given a way of locating themselves in time and thus of making sense of their lives. In recognizing that calendar time is an essentially arbitrary human invention, achieved by choosing some foundational event and measuring forward and backward from it by the use of units of measure that are also human inventions, we are able to understand the relationship between human experience and the vast scale of cosmological time. It is historical narratives, and not those of fiction, that fill in the space created by calendar time and give it texture and specificity. Because all historical narratives can be situated relative to one another by reference to the common time grid provided by the calendar, the narratives produced by different historians fit together to form a larger picture in a way that fictional narratives do not.

The notion of the succession of generations, and the distinction between contemporaries, predecessors, and successors, is history's way of linking experience to the biological dimension of human life. It is also a way of differentiating human experience: each generation confronts a unique set of circumstances. The consciousness of belonging to a particular generation provides a mediation between the long sweep of calendar time and the purely interior time-consciousness of individual experience (3:161, 163).

The succession of generations is the mechanism by which human beings achieve their first consciousness of the passage of time. As they become aware of their place in their family, children learn that they are part of a group that existed before they were born and that they will help continue into the future. Older family members pass memories along to newer generations, thus creating a first level of historical consciousness (3:168). Finally, historical narratives are based on documents or traces, evidence created at the time of the events to which they bear witness. To be a document, the trace must be capable of being assigned a calendar date. It must also be something that can be observed in principle by any investigator and thus locatable "in that *public* time that makes all private experiences of duration commensurable" (3:171–72, 179, 181).

Through his definition of historical narratives as stories characterized by organization according to calendar time, by an awareness of the succession of generations, and by reliance on datable traces or documents, Ricoeur succeeds in doing justice to their particular character and differentiating them from their fictional counterparts. Historical narratives must all, in principle, be capable of being fitted into a single temporal framework: we can determine which events were prior to others and which were simultaneous. Fictional narratives need not be situated precisely in the common time defined by the calendar, and there may not be any way to locate one temporally in relationship to another. In any event, fictional narratives do not complement or extend each other: Dickens's England is not a territory to which one can travel from Balzac's France, but a separate universe altogether. Nor can we arrange the characters of fiction in a succession of generations, linked to each other temporally or biologically. And, of course, fictional narratives need not make reference to any kind of documentation. This does not mean that fiction is irrelevant to the understanding of human experience: for Ricoeur, it is fiction that permits "the exploration of the non-linear aspects of phenomenological time, which historical time conceals because of its envelopment in the grand chronology of the universe" (3:191). The two forms of narrative are both part of a larger whole, a "grand scheme of narratology," that constitutes one of the most important ways in which human beings make sense of the world (2:230). But each makes a distinctive contribution to this process.

Throughout most of his analysis, Ricoeur treats history and fiction as the only two significant forms of narrative; he thus leaves open the question of whether he sees autobiography as falling under one or the other. That autobiography is relevant to his discussion Ricoeur concedes, although he deals with it only incidentally in *Time and Narrative.* "It would not be out of place to speak of it in the perspective of a refiguration of time brought about conjointly by history and fiction. That is the best place that autobiography could be assigned in the strategy of *Time and Narrative*," he remarks in a footnote in his second volume, the only explicit reference to the genre in the first nine hundred pages of Ricoeur's opus (2:133n). One can see that autobiography shares features with both of the forms of narrative that Ricoeur concentrates on. Like history, autobiographical narratives can be situated in calendar time, and we can compare their accounts of events with those in other narratives—both autobiographical and historical ones—in a meaningful way, whereas it does not make sense, to cite an example that Ricoeur analyzes at length, to ask whether there are other accounts of the fictional character Hans Castorp's stay in the sanatorium that we can compare with the one in Thomas Mann's *The Magic Mountain.* Autobiographical narratives certainly situate their protagonists in a chain of generations: an autobiography with no references to the author's parentage is hard to conceive.

There is, to be sure, a question about the relationship between autobiography and documentation. Autobiographers claim to be describing events that actually happened, and they may, like historians, make reference to traces and documents to bolster their assertions. As we will see, this is a common characteristic of historians' autobiographies, but it is by no means exclusive to them. Even Jean-Jacques Rousseau consulted his old correspondence in writing his *Confessions.* Mary Karr, author of *The Liars' Club,* a best-selling contemporary American memoir celebrated because it seems as vivid as good fiction, thanks her mother, who "did research for me," and her sister, who "confirmed the veracity of what I'd written."[13] As we have seen, the autobiographical critic Elizabeth Bruss made the possibility of verification an essential element of her version of the "autobiographical pact."[14] The difficulty is, however, that autobiographers are by no means obligated by the rules of the genre to construct their narratives solely on the basis of such documentation. They are entitled to rely on their own memories, even if these cannot be otherwise verified. In fact, one of the characteristics often cited to differentiate "real" autobiography from other genres, such as memoirs, is precisely the depiction of events, such as the author's inner thoughts and feelings at specific moments in the past, that are inherently unverifiable on the basis of other sources. Autobiography—which is this respect differs not only from history but also from biography—is thus not fully assimilable to Ricoeur's framework for history.

Just as it shares many, but not all, of the characteristics Ricoeur assigns to historical narrative, autobiography also shares features with fiction without merging with it. Although autobiographical narratives can be inserted into the framework of calendar time, the autobiographer shares with the novelist the prerogative of exploring the inner experience of private time that Ricoeur sees as the essence of fiction. The autobiographer can also draw on the resources of fiction, freely creating dialogue and emphasizing dramatic incidents for the purpose of showing character in action. Nevertheless, autobiography cannot simply be merged with fiction, for reasons that Ricoeur's analysis makes clear. The fact that autobiography *claims* to speak about real personages and to refer to the common time of historical narrative creates a disjuncture, even if these claims can sometimes be disproved through historical research.

It is thus evident that autobiography poses problems for Ricoeur's overall analysis of narrative. Not only does the binary division between history and fiction have an eminently respectable pedigree, going back to Aristotle, but it also provides a clear and orderly division of responsibilities between the two master forms of narrative. History is the narrative form of the public world, of intersubjective experience; it provides the common framework that makes social life and the formation of "imagined communities" possible.[15] Fiction is the form of narrative that reflects private experience and validates its importance. Readers' engagement with fictional texts brings these expressions of private experience into the public domain and thus enables fiction to escape the danger of solipsism. Ricoeur appears to have achieved an elegant and balanced synthesis that avoids subordinating history to fiction, as White's argument tends to do. But if autobiography shares characteristics with both history and fiction, as Ricoeur defines them, the clear distinction between the two master categories of narrative in his discussion threatens to break down. If a narrative can be at the same time historical and fictional, the divisions between public and private, between truth and imagination, also threaten to collapse. Autobiography thus appears as an unruly supplement to Ricoeur's project, an issue at the margins of *Time and Narrative* that risks problematizing the entire enterprise.

Ricoeur himself does not explicitly consider the status of autobiography relative to the two forms of narrative he analyzes in *Time and Narrative* until the final pages of the work's last volume. Even at earlier points in the argument where it would seem that autobiography should be mentioned, it is not. In a chapter on "the coming together of history and fiction," for example, Ricoeur shows that each of these genres partakes of some of the fea-

tures of the other. As an example of fiction's contribution to historical understanding, he cites the case of the Holocaust. History is limited in this
situation by its commitment to a stance of neutrality, Ricoeur claims. "Here
the biblical command . . . 'Zakhor (remember)' imposes itself. This is
not necessarily an appeal to historiography," he writes. Fiction, because it
can appeal directly to the emotions, becomes necessary to evoke the senti-
ment of horror required for real understanding of the Holocaust's events
(Ricoeur, *Temps et récit*, 3:272, 274). Ricoeur does not cite specific texts that
in his opinion are particularly successful in communicating the emotional
impact of the Holocaust, but it is significant that he has singled out the
modern historical event in whose representation first-person literature has
played the largest role. There is, to be sure, an important body of fiction devoted to the Holocaust, but the works that come to mind most often in this
regard are not novels but the autobiographical memoirs of survivor-authors
such as Elie Wiesel and Primo Levi. In view of the campaign to deny the
reality of the Holocaust, the special truth claims of these first-person accounts have particular importance. They obviously play the role Ricoeur
assigns to fictional narratives in his discussion—that is, the role of communicating the horror that makes us recognize the Holocaust as a unique
event (3:273). But they claim to be *true* narratives, and indeed even truer, so
to speak, than the narratives of history, because their authors actually experienced the events they describe. In this instance, Ricoeur's failure to address the status of autobiography creates a difficulty in his own discussion
and exposes him to the same critiques that have been made of White with
respect to the issue of the Holocaust. An explicit discussion of the role of
autobiography, rather than fiction, in communicating the experience of the
Holocaust would have avoided this danger.

AUTOBIOGRAPHY IN RICOEUR'S THEORY

Ricoeur finally comes to the issue of autobiography in the concluding pages
of *Time and Narrative*, when he recapitulates his argument and tries to define its limits. After repeating his claim that historical and fictional narrative work together to establish a "third time" situated between the time of
the cosmos, completely indifferent to human existence, and the purely subjective time of individual consciousness, Ricoeur argues that the combined
effect of the two forms of narrative is "the *assignment* to an individual or a
community of a specific narrative that one can label their *narrative identity.*"
Only narrative can resolve the paradox of how an individual or group can
be seen as the same even as it changes over time. "Without the aid of nar-

ration, the problem of personal identity is . . . an antimony without resolution" (3:355). This leads to the one explicit, if brief, discussion of autobiographical narrative in *Time and Narrative*. "As the literary analysis of autobiography demonstrates, the story of a life is continually refigured by all the true or imagined stories that a subject tells about himself. This refiguring makes the life itself a fabric of stories," Ricoeur writes. Using psychoanalysis as an example of how individual identity is constituted through the telling and revising of stories, he then compares this process to history: "There one sees, in effect, how the history of a life is made up of a series of corrections to previous stories, in the same way that the history of a people, of a collectivity, of an institution comes out of the series of corrections that each new historian makes to the descriptions and explanations of his predecessors, and, little by little, to the legends that preceded this historiographical work" (3:356).

As Ricoeur notes, however, this process of expressing an identity through a constantly evolving narrative does not lead to a stable result. "It is always possible to tell the story of one's life in several different, even opposing, ways." Autobiography is inherently unstable because it participates in the characteristics of both history and fiction. "The historical component of the narrative about oneself draws it in the direction of a chronicle subject to the same constraints of documentary confirmation as any other historical narrative, whereas its fictional component draws it toward those imagined variations that destabilize narrative identity. . . . Narrative identity thus becomes the name of a problem, at least as much as a solution. Systematic research on autobiography . . . would no doubt confirm this instability at the heart of narrative identity" (3:358).

Ricoeur did not undertake this systematic research in the framework of *Time and Narrative*, but he has pursued some of the issues raised by his concept of narrative identity in subsequent publications, particularly *Oneself as Another*. Surprisingly, in view of the important role played by autobiography in undermining the elaborate framework of the argument laid out in *Time and Narrative*, this later work pays relatively little attention to autobiography as a literary genre. Ricoeur is more concerned here with the problem of identity itself than with the possibilities of narrative. Fundamentally, he wants to explore the problems that arise from claiming that a person retains the same identity over time and in different circumstances. This leads him, like Wilhelm Dilthey, to whom he refers, to eschew discussion of written autobiography in favor of a broader notion of "life story" or "life history," a personal narrative that may be written, oral, or even for-

mulated only in the interior of a person's consciousness (*Oneself as Another,*
141). At times he writes of "autobiographical narrative" as just one possible
form of life story, and he also questions whether we can actually consider a
person as the author of his or her life story, if "life story" is considered as
that person's real life rather than a written narrative of the life: "Does not
the notion of author suffer from equivocalness when we pass from writing
to life?" (160).

To be sure, Ricoeur still refers to the analysis of narrative constructed in
his earlier work, and he reiterates the conclusion reached in *Time and Narrative* that defined autobiography as sharing characteristics of both history
and fiction (114n). But he now brings out what he sees as a distinction that
separates both life stories in general and autobiographical writings in particular from either history or fiction: the fact that they cannot achieve true
narrative unity. One reason for this is that a person can never recount either
the beginning or the end of his or her life. "There is nothing in real life that
serves as a narrative beginning; memory is lost in the hazes of early childhood; my birth and, with greater reason, the act through which I was conceived belong more to the history of others—in this case, to my parents—
than to me. As for my death, it will finally be recounted only in the stories
of those who survive me" (160). Because autobiographers do not know how
their lives will end, they can emplot them in different ways: "Along the
known path of my life, I can trace out a number of itineraries, weave several plots; in short, I can recount several stories" (161). Another difficulty is
that life histories cannot be disentangled from one another: "The life history of each of us is caught up in the histories of others. . . . It is precisely
by reason of this entanglement, as much as by being open-ended on both
sides, that life histories differ from literary ones, whether the latter belong
to historiography or to fiction. Can one then still speak of the narrative
unity of life?" (ibid.).

These distinctions between autobiographies and life stories on the one
hand and the literary forms of history and fiction on the other do not, in
Ricoeur's view, make autobiography an inferior form of narrative, as some
literary critics have insisted. But they do make autobiography different: it
cannot simply be assimilated either to history or to fiction. The "narrative
unity of a life" in a life story "must be seen as an unstable mixture of fabu-
lation and actual experience. It is precisely because of the elusive character
of real life that we need the help of fiction to organize life retrospectively,
after the fact, prepared to take as provisional and open to revision any figure of emplotment borrowed from fiction or from history" (162). And so

"the conclusion of this discussion . . . is that literary narratives and life histories, far from being mutually exclusive, are complementary, despite, or even because of, their contrast. This dialectic reminds us that the narrative is part of life before being exiled from life in writing; it returns to life along the multiple paths of appropriation and at the price of the unavoidable tensions just mentioned" (163). In a separate essay, "Narrative Identity," Ricoeur makes an even more explicit statement on "the epistemological status of autobiography": "It is thus plausible to endorse the following chain of assertions: self-knowledge is an interpretation; self interpretation, in turn, finds in narrative, among other signs and symbols, a privileged mediation; this mediation draws on history as much as it does on fiction, turning the story of a life into a fictional story or a historical fiction, comparable to those biographies of great men in which history and fiction are intertwined."[16] Here the emphasis is not so much on autobiography's unfinished character as on its necessary combination of historical and fictional elements.

A final brief discussion of autobiography appears in the autobiographical sketch Ricoeur contributed to a volume of essays about his work, published in 1995. Although, as we have seen, Ricoeur had come by this date to accord autobiography an important place in his overall theory, his comments about his personal venture into it are relatively conventional, and their apologetic tone suggests that the philosopher found writing about himself a difficult task. He refers to the genre's "pitfalls and drawbacks," principally the fact that it "is selective and, as such, inevitably biased. In addition," he continues, "an autobiography is, in the precise sense, a literary work; in this respect it rests on the sometimes beneficial, sometimes detrimental gap between the retrospective viewpoint of the act of writing . . . and the stream of everyday life." Before beginning his personal narrative, he concludes, "I readily admit that the reconstruction of my intellectual development undertaken here is no more authoritative than one written by a biographer other than myself."[17]

Taken together, the discussions relevant to autobiography in Ricoeur's work thus offer a number of insights into the relations between this genre and its relatives, history and fiction. In contrast to Hayden White, Ricoeur provides a framework that acknowledges the narrative character of history and its relations to fiction without effacing the distinctions between the two genres. The way in which he defines historical narrative not only does justice to historians' sense that their enterprise is unique because of its dependence on documentation; through his discussion of history's relationship to calendar time and the succession of generations, Ricoeur shows that the distinction between history and fiction is not limited to the latter's prerogative of proceeding without regard to factual evidence. When he turns to autobiography, Ricoeur's remarks are less extensive, but he does establish several points. He makes it clear that history and autobiography are in some ways distinct, particularly because the autobiographer is not bound by reliance on publicly accessible documentation in the way the historian is, and because the autobiographer shares the novelist's privilege of exploring the inner experience of time. On the other hand, Ricoeur's approach implies that history and autobiography do share some important features. Both tell narratives that can be fitted into the larger, impersonal framework of calendar time and that therefore can be read as supplementing or revising other similar narratives. Both show how their human characters can be fitted into a succession of generations, which makes their protagonists' experiences unique.

Ricoeur does, however, see autobiography as having some special characteristics of its own, which distinguish it not only from history but also from fiction. In the first place, autobiography is, in his analysis, essentially a hybrid genre: it shares aspects of both history and fiction. It is true that Ricoeur also acknowledges that history and fiction each share some of the other's features, but he nevertheless regards them as having distinctive identities of their own, whereas he is less emphatic about autobiography in this regard. He does not, for example, ask whether either history or fiction necessarily incorporates aspects of autobiography, in the way that autobiography necessarily borrows from these other two genres. The other distinctive characteristic Ricoeur attributes to autobiography is its lack of closure. Autobiographical narratives necessarily lack a real beginning or ending, and they are therefore always subject to revision and reinterpretation. Finally, Ricoeur's prefatory comments to his own autobiographical sketch suggest that the author's unique relationship to this form of narrative generates a tension or anxiety that is not necessarily present in the writing of either history or fiction: the anxiety that comes from the fact that the autobiographical author is caught in the process of defining his or her own narrative identity, without being sure that readers will accept the result.

Ricoeur thus defines autobiography largely in negative terms, emphasizing what it borrows from or what it lacks compared to history and fiction. It is obvious that much of Ricoeur's analysis is derived from Aristotle's distinction between history and tragedy, which he analyzes at length, and depends on the notion that there are only two primary modes of narrative.

It is also clear that despite his openness to many different forms of fiction—
he devotes part of *Oneself as Another* to a discussion of issues about personal
identity raised in modern science fiction—Ricoeur remains wedded to the
conviction that a proper narrative must achieve closure in order to convey
meaning. Postmodernist critiques of the concept of closure in literary texts
go unacknowledged in either *Time and Narrative* or *Oneself as Another.* The
fact that Ricoeur defines autobiography as a genre essentially incapable of
achieving closed or completed form thus appears as a critical judgment,
consigning first-person writing to a lesser status than history or fiction. Finally, it seems clear that autobiography appears at the end of *Time and Narrative* as a disturbing element in the elegant edifice of Ricoeur's overall argument, a leftover piece to be fitted into the structure somehow even
though there is no obvious place for it. Indeed, the issues raised by autobiography are essentially those that drove Ricoeur's subsequent work on narrative identity.

Ricoeur's analysis in *Time and Narrative,* however, does point to the
possibility of according autobiography a larger place in his theory. In the
first place, his way of distinguishing between history and fiction provides a
framework within which one can in fact define the characteristics of autobiography as well, as I have shown. Rather than saying that autobiography
"borrows" these characteristics from history or fiction, as though those two
genres somehow had proprietary rights to them, we can talk of a number of
possible characteristics of narrative that can be combined in various ways,
giving rise to history, autobiography, fiction, and possibly other genres as
well. Ricoeur's approach thus holds out the possibility of a more structured
debate about the relations of these different genres than that generated by
White's work.

Second, however, Ricoeur's work can be read to show that autobiography already occupies a more important part in his thinking than he himself
acknowledges. As we have noted, Ricoeur's entire discussion of the human
perception of time begins with an autobiographical text, indeed with the
text that is generally cited as the foundation of the Western tradition of
first-person writing: Augustine's *Confessions.* Ricoeur treats Augustine's discussion of time as a philosophical essay, which it certainly is, but it is also
part of its author's life story. Augustine launches his discussion with the
personal statement I have already quoted—"What then is time? Provided
that no one asks me, I know"—and he makes it clear that the issue is not
only a philosophical and theological one for him but also an intensely personal one. Ricoeur's reliance on Augustine shows that the insights of auto-

biography are embedded in the foundations of his entire philosophical discussion. Indeed, in an article published separately before the completion of *Time and Narrative,* Ricoeur singles out the *Confessions* as a uniquely powerful model of narrative, "so powerful and enduring that it has generated a whole set of narrative forms down to Rousseau's *Confessions* and Proust's *Le Temps retrouvé.*" Although the inclusion of Proust's novel along with Augustine's and Rousseau's texts reflects a blurring of the boundary between fiction and autobiography, Ricoeur here seems ready to elevate first-person narrative to a central position in his scheme, calling it "this highest form of narrative repetition . . . the equivalent of what Heidegger calls fate (individual fate) or destiny (communal destiny)."[18]

Autobiography also emerges, albeit without acknowledgment, in Ricoeur's discussion of how historical narratives of the past need to be supplemented in order to fully convey the emotional dimension of experience. As we have seen, Ricoeur raises this issue in the context of his discussion of the history of the Holocaust, where he attributes to fiction a function that is in fact largely fulfilled by autobiography or memoir. The controversy over the purported Holocaust memoir of Binjamin Wilkomirski, mentioned in the previous chapter, has underlined how strongly most present-day readers feel about the distinction between testimony written by authors who really experienced the horrors of the "Final Solution" and those who have only imagined it. Ricoeur's singling out of this particular event to illustrate the interdependence of history and fiction in fact points to the way autobiography can be integrated in his discussion.

Most important, however, *Oneself as Another,* Ricoeur's sequel to *Time and Narrative,* clearly reflects his increased awareness of and interest in autobiography's possibilities. The central question of *Oneself as Another*— how can a person both remain the same over the course of a life and yet grow and change?—is clearly a question to which autobiography is at least as relevant, if not more relevant, than either history or fiction. The provisional or unfinished character of life stories becomes in this perspective not a deficiency but a powerful testimony to one of the fundamental characteristics of human experience: the fact that we live our lives without knowing how our stories will look when they are ended. Autobiography, like history and fiction, thus becomes a fundamental tool for the exploration of the human condition, a form of narrative that expresses certain truths that neither of these other genres can communicate as effectively. The fact that life histories are not purely narrative, that they remain embedded in life, can thus be seen as a positive feature rather than a deficit of aesthetic form. *Oneself as Another* can thus be read as an acknowledgment that the elegant bilateral symmetry of *Time and Narrative* is incomplete and needs to be reconfigured with autobiography as a third element.

Ricoeur's approach can be interpreted, then, to provide a framework that acknowledges the common roots of history, fiction, and autobiography while at the same time maintaining a clear sense of their differences. Unlike White, Ricoeur provides criteria by which these three forms of narrative can be distinguished from one another, and he also shows that they serve different, though complementary, purposes. Ricoeur's approach allows us to see that history and autobiography do indeed share some important characteristics that set both of them apart from fiction, namely, the embeddedness of their narratives in the public time of the calendar and in the structured succession of generations. He also helps us to define what separates the two genres: autobiography's ambiguous relationship to documentation, its freedom to explore the inner experience of time in the way that fiction does, and its necessary open-endedness. It thus becomes clear that history and autobiography are indeed distinct but related and that neither can simply subsume the other. Nor is the relationship between them a hierarchical one, in which history as a "scientific" approach to the past relegates autobiography to the subordinate status of source material.

DAVID CARR'S CRITIQUE OF RICOEUR

Ricoeur's analysis of the relations between time, narrative, and identity is rich in insights and potentialities, but it has not been immune to criticism. Hayden White has responded to Ricoeur's critique of his own work by praising *Time and Narrative* as "a considerable advancement over previous discussions of the relations between history and literature based on the supposed opposition of 'factual' to 'fictional' discourse." But White questions whether Ricoeur has really succeeded in freeing history from the grip of fiction, concluding that Ricoeur has in fact demonstrated that the content of history is nothing other than "the vision of human life informing the poetic genre of tragedy" and warning that Ricoeur's argument may lead him ultimately "to collapse the distinction between myth and history, without which the very notion of fiction is difficult to imagine." [19] The phenomenologist philosopher David Carr, on the other hand, has objected that Ricoeur's elaborate construction still leaves narrative embarrassingly divorced from reality. In his view, there is no substantial difference between Ricoeur and White: "In the end for Ricoeur narrative structure is as alien from the 'real world' as it is for the other authors we have been discussing." In his own book *Time, Narrative, and History,* Carr tries to show that "historical and fictional narratives will reveal themselves to be not distortions of, denials of, or escapes from reality, but extensions and configurations of its primary features" (15–16). Whereas autobiography comes into Ricoeur's argument only as an awkward addition, it occupies a central place in Carr's thinking; indeed, he presents it as in some sense the most fundamental form of narrative, the one from which history and fiction are ultimately derived. Paradoxically, however, even though Carr pays more attention to life narratives than does Ricoeur, his argument is less helpful for understanding the relations between autobiography and history than that suggested by *Time and Narrative* and *Oneself as Another.*

Carr agrees with White and Ricoeur on the central importance of narrative and its status as a form of knowledge: "Narrative is our primary (though not our only) way of organizing our experience of time" (4–5). He acknowledges the significance of White's bringing together of issues in the philosophy of history and in narrative theory and of Ricoeur's demonstration of the narrative character even of ostensibly nonnarrative historical approaches such as that of Fernand Braudel (8–9).[20] Carr's fundamental disagreement with White, and with Ricoeur as well, has to do with the question of whether the making of narratives is essentially a matter of imposing form on otherwise incoherent experiences or whether, as Carr contends, experience actually has built into it a narrative structure. Carr distinguishes himself forcefully from White's position that "the notion that sequences of real events possess the formal attributes of the stories we tell about imaginary events could only have its origin in wishes, daydreams, reveries," and as we have seen, he claims that Ricoeur's view is not fundamentally different from White's (12, 15).

To bolster his position that narrative is an extension of, not a separation from, reality, Carr sets himself the threefold task of showing that all human experiences, even the simplest, have built into them a narrative structure, that similar patterns of configuration are found in complex events, and that all events incorporate some element of narration (45–46). Events in our lives and in the real world have beginnings, middles, and ends, departures and returns, moments of suspension and resolution, and "these structures are to be found . . . in the midst of experience and action, not in some higher-level linguistic construction or reconstruction of the experiences and actions involved" (49–50). Furthermore, when we find ourselves involved in action, our ability to respond to the unanticipated and to plan for the future puts us in the equivalent of the narrator's position in a story and thus shows that there is an element of narration in real life. The fact that people often have to explain to themselves what they are doing in order to do it shows, Carr claims, "that such narrative activity, even apart from its social role, has a practical function in life, that is, it is often a constitutive part of action, and not just an embellishment, commentary, or other incidental accompaniment" (60–61). Indeed, this pragmatic function of narration is fundamental, and the aesthetic and cognitive functions of literary and historical narratives—the genres on which Ricoeur focuses—are secondary (71).

Having established to his satisfaction the necessarily narrative nature of all experience, Carr then turns to the issue of life narratives. Like Dilthey, to whom he is heavily indebted, and like Ricoeur in *Oneself as Another,* Carr downplays the distinction between life story as an individual's more or less articulated way of making sense of individual experience and autobiography as a written text. But he insists that "narrative . . . is the organizing principle not only of experiences and actions but of the self who experiences and acts" (73). An autobiographical perspective is thus an inherent aspect of human experience: if we cannot experience our lives as stories, we cannot find a basis for acting in the present and attempting to shape the future (75). To be sure, the sense of that story is never fully clear to us: "We are composing and constantly revising our autobiographies as we go along." But human beings have to see their lives as having some coherence, and indeed, for Carr, "life can be regarded as a constant *effort,* even a struggle, to maintain or restore narrative coherence in the face of an ever-threatening, impending chaos at all levels" (76, 91).

Carr does recognize that telling one's life story to an audience changes the nature of the story, even for its narrator. "Most people have had the experience that they do not quite know what they mean or intend until they try to communicate it to others. . . . Thus telling the story of my action or experience to others can organize or reorganize it for me; telling the story of my life can serve to make a sense of it I have not been aware of before" (112). But he does not pursue this insight by making an analysis of the distinctions between life story and written autobiography. Instead, he turns to an analysis of a second form of past-centered narrative, namely history. Carr applies to history the fundamental phenomenological insight that all our higher-level forms of knowledge are ultimately rooted in ordinary experience. Everyone, including professional historians, has a "non-thematic or pre-thematic awareness of the historical past which functions as background for our present experience." Carr quotes Dilthey's conclusion that "we are historical beings first, before we are observers of history, and only because we are the former do we become the latter" (3–4). History, however, is not simply disguised autobiography: "The historical past . . . is the social, not the individual, past" (100).

Although he is careful not to subordinate individuals to groups and denies that human groups have any kind of objective essence, Carr sees them as genuine entities whose members can speak in terms of "we" just as individuals can speak of themselves as "I." Although groups are made up of individuals, "individuals, in their sense of and use of 'we,' certainly *take* them to exist and . . . their taking them to exist in a certain sense makes it so," he writes (133). Groups can therefore have collective narratives just as individuals have their life stories, and these narratives constitute the groups in the same way that life stories constitute individuals: "*We* act or experience in virtue of a story *we* tell *ourselves* about what we are going through or doing. It can be seen that the roles of agent (*we* act), narrator (*we* tell), and audience (to *ourselves*) turn up again, this time in a plural form" (149). These historical narratives of collective experience, like individual life stories, are constantly being revised, and for the same reasons: "Where such a community exists it is constantly in the process, as an individual is, of composing and re-composing its own autobiography. Like the autobiography of an individual, such a story seeks a unifying structure for a sequence of experiences and actions." Just as individuals make up stories to fend off fears of chaos and death, "the sense of finitude and fragility is part of any community's existence because of the latter's dependence on the attitudes and interests of the individuals that make it up" (163–64).

Just as written autobiographies differ significantly from the stories individuals tell themselves in the course of developing their sense of identity, history, in the sense of the documented narratives told by historians, differs from the stories that collectivities tell about themselves. Whereas Carr says little about autobiography in the strict sense, he does comment briefly on the relationship between scholarly history and the more diffuse phenomenon of collective memory. He is particularly interested in the case of contemporary history, where the scholar writes about events about which his or her community has already constructed a narrative. The historian's narrative will often raise questions about those communal narratives, however, and as a result the historian will frequently be involved in public debates. This does not mean that the historical scholar's narrative is simply one version of the past, on the same level as its rivals. The fact that the historian's purpose in constructing a narrative is cognitive rather than practical—that is, the scholar is ideally interested in understanding the past, rather than using a story about the past to achieve some goal in the present—establishes one distinction; another is that the historian writes about completed events rather than ongoing ones. "By restricting itself to just the past, history indeed avails itself of a special advantage; by cultivating a detached attitude and developing techniques of research it may more greatly satisfy its interest in the truth about the past" (173). The historical narrative will therefore differ from the narratives that constitute collective identity in certain ways, but it constitutes a refinement, a specialized version, of these other narratives, which are in fact the substance of collective life.

Since Carr insists so rigorously on the analogy between individual and collective narratives, it is tempting to try to interpret written autobiography as occupying the same position relative to the individual life story as history does relative to the collective one. It is by no means clear, however, that this move can be made successfully. The historical scholar is not the same person as the politician or the pedagogue who may construct a narrative of a group's experience for what Carr calls practical reasons. Indeed, by virtue of membership in the historical guild, the scholar becomes a member of a social subgroup that has its own rules about what constitutes a narrative of the past, rules that generally conflict with at least some of the premises of the narratives created to sustain group identity. But the autobiographer is necessarily the same person who tells himself or herself the constantly evolving story that constitutes personal identity. The autobiographical author is not telling a story that is definitively concluded, nor can he or she achieve the kind of detachment that Carr posits for the historian. Just as in the case of Ricoeur, Carr's argument raises the possibility that autobiography cannot simply be understood as history on a miniature scale.

For the purposes of our inquiry into the relations between history and autobiography, then, Carr's critique does not refute the differentiation between these two forms of narrative that can be constructed on the basis of Ricoeur's analysis. Even if we accept Carr's contention that reality necessarily has a narrative structure, history and autobiography as forms of writing both retain an important degree of autonomy from this more inchoate level of narrative, as well as a certain degree of distinctiveness from one another. Furthermore, Carr himself qualifies his argument in important ways. He acknowledges, for example, that it is not obvious whether the narrative experience of human existence is in fact truly a universal one or whether it is unique to European culture. In India, for example, where belief in reincarnation is widespread, individuals may have not just one life story to tell but several.[21] Carr sees Ricoeur's argument as an essentially Eurocentric one, and it is true that Ricoeur refers only to historical and fictional texts from the European tradition; for his own part, Carr simply leaves the question of universality unresolved (179–83).

The importance of Carr's approach is its forceful reminder that all the forms of literary narrative do grow out of what we might call a more basic, preliterary experience of storytelling, whether we take this more basic experience to be rooted in reality itself or to be a fundamental aspect of human culture. History and autobiography are related, not only on a literary level but also because of their common origins in the wider human enterprise of making sense of experience by giving it narrative form. Whereas Ricoeur's analysis tends to privilege formal historical, fictional, and autobiographical texts, Carr's approach is more egalitarian, assimilating such works to a larger universe of stories embedded in everyday life. As Carr puts it, for Ricoeur, narrative is fundamentally a form of literature, and "the poetic act seems autonomous and self-moving"; Carr himself wants to see narrative as *our* way of being in and dealing with time," not something exemplified only in works of art and scholarship (184–85).

The question whether the act of composing a narrative actually creates something new or merely expresses meanings already present in experience was at the heart of a dialogue between Ricoeur and Carr published after the completion of *Time and Narrative*. In contrast to Carr, Ricoeur insisted on the dialectical relationship between reality and narrative. "Is not art, in the largest sense, *poiesis*, a function of both revelation and transformation? So that one may say both that *poiesis* reveals structures which would have remained unrecognized without art, *and* that it transforms life, elevating it to another level."[22] Certainly many autobiographers, including historians, have experienced the writing of a life story as such a process of revelation and transformation, rather than simply as a matter of transcribing a preexisting narrative already present in their memory. Although Carr accords autobiographical narrative a larger place in our understanding of the world than does Ricoeur, Ricoeur's insights offer a deeper understanding of the connections between life and narrative.

So far, very few historians who have written their autobiographies have shown any acquaintance with the narrativist theories of thinkers such as White, Ricoeur, and Carr. Instinctively, however, many of them articulate what could be called a Ricoeurian position. When French historian René Rémond prefaces his *ego-histoire* by remarking on "the precariousness of recollection, the unreliability of first-person testimony," and the fact that "everyone has an unconscious tendency to introduce a factitious coherence into the path of his life," or when New Zealander W. H. Oliver writes that "the mind is an active agent; the artefact [*sic*] it composes is woven from a random assemblage of recollections, echoes of recollections, guesses transformed into recollections, imagined happenings imperceptibly made real," are they not echoing Ricoeur's notion of *mimesis* as an active process that adds something to the data, even as it places the life story in the framework of calendar time and the succession of generations?[23] While White and Carr do offer insights that can be fruitfully applied to the understanding of autobiography, particularly as it has been practiced by historians, Ricoeur's approach seems both more suggestive on a theoretical level and closer to the way historian-autobiographers understand their own enterprises.

The critique of Hayden White's and David Carr's arguments and the interpretation or extension of Paul Ricoeur's theory of narrative put forward here are intended to establish two conclusions that are important for the understanding of the relationship between history and autobiography. The first is that, contrary to the contention of White, acknowledging the narrative nature of historical writing does not necessarily mean rejecting the distinction between history and fiction. Ricoeur's analysis of the distinctive properties of historical narrative—its reliance on the calendar, on the notion of the succession of human generations, and on documentary traces—provides a solid basis for distinguishing history from other forms of storytelling. The second point I hope to have established, however, is that Ricoeur's approach can be used to provide a similarly persuasive definition of what distinguishes autobiography from both history and fiction. Autobiography is not, as Carr's argument sometimes suggests, just the writing of history on a smaller scale: it differs from history in some important ways. Historians who venture into the writing of autobiography are not simply plunging into the realm of fiction. Instead, they are engaging in an enterprise whose rules are different from those they follow in their professional work. This second point also has important implications for the literary analysis of autobiography. Just as autobiography cannot be assimilated to history, it cannot simply be treated as a form of novel writing. As the following chapters will show, the autobiographical writings produced by professional historians offer valuable evidence of the genre's distinctive characteristics and the special contributions it can make to the project of making human experience comprehensible that underlies all narrative.

CHAPTER 3   Historians as Autobiographers

The first two chapters of this book have shown why the relationship between history and autobiography is problematic and have used narrative
theory, especially Paul Ricoeur's version of it, to establish a framework for
analyzing that relationship. On the basis of this theoretical analysis, we can
define autobiography as a distinctive form of narrative, related to but not
identical with either history or fiction. Historians who turn to writing about
their own life are neither practicing their profession on a smaller scale nor
writing novels: they are engaging in an enterprise with a distinctive character of its own. In the rest of this book, I will look at the autobiographical
literature that historians have published. The autobiographical production
of historians raises a number of questions. To begin with, why should anyone, other than perhaps historians themselves, be interested in the autobiographies of members of that profession? Second, what special challenges
does autobiographical writing pose for historians? Third, how widespread
has autobiographical writing become among historians? A fourth question
has to do with the motives and circumstances that make some historians
more likely than others to publish personal stories. Finally, I will examine
how historians' autobiographical writing relates to developments in history
itself and how it varies from one national context to another.

THE IMPORTANCE OF HISTORIANS' AUTOBIOGRAPHIES

The autobiographies that have attracted the attention of literary scholars
have tended to be either those that aspire overtly to the character of literature—primarily the work of established novelists, poets, and, nowadays,
literary scholars—or those of authors from "voiceless" groups, whose
breakthrough into first-person narrative can be celebrated as an act of lib-

eration. Historians' memoirs fall into the large area between these two categories, the space of what I have called "ordinary" autobiographies. Few
of them have great literary pretensions, but on the other hand, scholars of
history are by definition experienced authors, whose conquest of the first-
person pronoun is not a cause for astonishment. The phenomenon of historians' autobiography deserves theoretical attention for several reasons,
however. In the first place, the existence and the recent multiplication of
historians' autobiographies demonstrate that autobiographical writing is
not undertaken only for aesthetic reasons, on the one hand, or as a gesture
against oppression, on the other. A full understanding of the phenomenon
of autobiography requires attention to the motives and conditions that produce historians' autobiographies as well as these other forms of personal
narrative. Second, the existence of a large corpus of texts by members of the
historical profession shows that autobiographical writing is not generated
entirely out of personal motives. Historian-autobiographers write as individuals, but they also write as members of a particular disciplinary community. In the introduction to a special journal issue devoted to autobiography,
Philip Dodd has called for an approach to the subject that incorporates
sociological as well as aesthetic criteria. To do this, "the variety of autobiographical traditions and their determinants—of, for example, class, race
and gender—will have to be identified; autobiography will have to be returned to a wider literary and cultural history; the uses of autobiography
will have to be mapped; and contemporary autobiographical practice will
have to be given attention," he comments.[1] The study of autobiographical
traditions and practices among members of a specific professional community provides an opportunity to apply some of Dodd's insights.

A third reason that makes the case of autobiography among historians
of interest grows out of historians' special connection to another of the major forms of narrative through which human beings have tried to understand their experience: history itself. If novelists' autobiographies offer us
unique insights into the relationship between fiction and first-person narrative, historians' autobiographies promise to teach us something about
the connections between autobiography and its other neighbor, historical
writing. Several critics of autobiography have in fact suggested that autobiographical literature written by historians might well have a special role
to play in developing the possibilities of autobiography. Paul John Eakin has
pointed out that in most autobiographies the relationship between individual experience and the larger framework of history is "taken for granted"
and "is in principle not a primary topic of comment." Autobiographers with

a historical consciousness, however, may be uniquely capable of problematizing that relationship and of "redirecting attention to a fact of an equally interesting kind—equally interesting, that is, if we are prepared to ask, along with certain autobiographers turned historians, what it means to be living in history." He takes Henry Adams and Alfred Kazin as examples of autobiographers who consciously reflect on the ways in which historical experience led them to redefine their own view of the relationship between history and individual life, and who thereby create a form of narrative that is "neither history nor personal history but a mixed mode: history as it impinges on the mind of the individual."[2] The humanistic psychologist Mark Freeman similarly turns to a historian's autobiography—that of Jill Ker Conway—in hope of special insights. "Don't some people manage somehow to acquire a consciousness *of* history? Don't they become aware—more aware than others, at any rate—of the ways in which they have been determined, indeed of the very words they have been permitted to speak? Even if we cannot extricate ourselves from history, we can surely aspire to have some consciousness of it," Freeman writes.[3]

The hope that Eakin and Freeman express is that a historically trained autobiographer might be able to connect the story of individual experience highlighted in most autobiographies with the larger flow of collective experience in which it is embedded, and thus overcome autobiography's tendency to attribute to its subjects an excessive degree of personal autonomy. The insight both these authors are formulating resembles Karl Marx's statement that "men make their own history, but they do not make it . . . under circumstances chosen by themselves, but under circumstances directly found, given and transmitted from the past."[4] Every human life is lived in specific historical circumstances, circumstances that not only limit human possibilities but also help shape the personalities of those born into them. Autobiographers do not need advanced degrees in history to be aware of the impact of history on their life, of course. As Karl Joachim Weintraub has argued, modern autobiography arises precisely when a new understanding of individuality is put in the framework of a generalized awareness of the constantly changing nature of the social world, "when the self-understanding and presentation of an individual parallels the emerging historicist mode of understanding human life."[5] When autobiographers with no special interest in history define themselves as products of the era of the Great Depression or as survivors of the Holocaust, they are certainly expressing an awareness that their lives have a particular shape because of those events and that they share those experiences with others of their generation.

Eakin and Freeman suggest, however, that historically trained auto-biographers could achieve something more than this sort of generalized awareness of the importance of historical circumstance that is found to some degree in many autobiographies. Historian-autobiographers should be able to go beyond the simple reporting of the circumstances in which they lived. Their historical training should help them understand and ex-plain how those circumstances came into being: in other words, they should be able to portray circumstances as themselves the result of human actions and not merely as accidental conditions. Both these critics also hold out the hope that historians will be especially adapted to demonstrating, through the examples of their own lives, the complicated process by which the ex-perience of historical events and movements shapes the individual person-ality. Finally, Eakin and Freeman both look to historian-autobiographers in the hope of finding depictions of authors who are particularly attuned to the phenomenon of historical change and who can help readers understand how such sensitivity is developed and what it means to live with an acute consciousness that our social environment is in continual flux.

These are high expectations. They imply that historian-autobiographers should be able to extract certain general lessons about human experience from their professional training and apply these lessons to the analysis of their own life. It is significant that theorists of autobiography have not for-mulated such explicit hopes with regard to the autobiographies written by members of most other academic disciplines. Sociologists, economists, an-thropologists, philosophers, literary scholars—all might potentially have important insights to contribute to the writing of autobiography, but it is only historians who seem to raise such specific expectations on the part of its critics. This is, of course, testimony to the structural similarities between his-tory and autobiography, their common dependence on narrative, and their common concern with the past. On the other hand, Eakin's and Freeman's formulations implicitly suggest that historians' autobiographies might be excused from measuring themselves against some of the standards often ap-plied to other first-person narratives. Perhaps the historian-autobiographer who successfully elucidates the impact of history on individual life need not create an artistic masterpiece in order to be taken seriously—although the examples they discuss, Adams and Kazin in Eakin's case, Conway's memoir of her childhood in Freeman's, are achievements of a high literary order. Furthermore, this implicit devaluation of aesthetic criteria has as its equally implicit corollary a heightened responsibility to historical truth. The critic may excuse a certain liberty with the historical record in the case of autobiographers whose main assets are literary skills or psychological insight, but the judgment of an autobiography by a historian that departs too far from accepted historical facts would probably be harsh. If we are to turn to historians' autobiographies to learn something about the experience of living in history, that history must be authentic.

Theorists of autobiography have thus outlined a particular version of the "autobiographical pact" for historian-autobiographers. In addition to the obligations imposed on any author who wishes to be read as an autobiographer, those who identify themselves in their text as historians should infuse their personal narrative with a perspective derived from their professional training, and they should expect to be held to a higher than usual standard of historical accuracy. In return, they can hope not to be criticized for their inability to write as entertainingly as someone like the literary critic Frank Kermode, whose memoir of his adventures as a junior officer in the British Navy during World War II is far livelier than, for example, the American historian Louis Harlan's account of comparable experiences.[6] Both memoirs reflect the gulf between the highly intelligent young men who unexpectedly found themselves at war and the less educated career officers who found themselves equally unexpectedly promoted to positions of real responsibility. Kermode makes this experience the stuff of black humor, which doubtless captures a very real dimension of the war, but his satirical sketches of "My Mad Captains" are too obviously the product of an author eager to display his storytelling skills to inspire much confidence in their literal fidelity. Harlan's more prosaic account couples his own recollections with general comments about the hierarchical nature of the navy, which "challenged the democratic political credo of American society" and almost inevitably generated friction between college-educated junior officers and their less intellectual superiors.[7] Although Harlan's observation is not based on extensive historical research, it is phrased in such a way that his professional peers would take it seriously, whereas they would probably hesitate to treat Kermode's recollections as reliable historical evidence.

WHEN HISTORIANS BECOME AUTOBIOGRAPHERS

When historians decide to become autobiographers, they are not usually concerned with the issues their project may raise for critical theorists. Instead, they face more down-to-earth challenges. Historians who decide to write about their own life are embarking on a project that is both familiar to them by virtue of their professional experience and yet distinctly different from historical writing. Autobiography and history are both ways of reconstructing past events, usually in the form of a chronological narrative. The similarities between autobiography and history run deeper than this, however. Not only do autobiographers and historians both claim to give factually accurate reconstructions of the past, they also share the double vision that comes from knowing both how things looked at the time and how they look with the benefit of hindsight. Like historians, autobiographers implicitly or explicitly suggest causal connections, underline discrepancies between intentions and results, and point out ironies that are recognizable only in retrospect.

It is precisely because history and autobiography are so closely related that historians who decide to cross the line from one to the other find themselves uneasy about what they are doing. Autobiography may sometimes seem like history in miniature, but any autobiographer obviously has what Dominick LaCapra calls emotionally charged "transferential relations" with his or her own life story, relations that make it impossible to maintain the pretense that an autobiography can achieve scholarly objectivity.[8] As we have seen, historians are very good at recognizing these dangers in other people's autobiographies, and the critical treatment scholars mete out to autobiographical sources ought to be enough to deter any historian from risking such a project. René Rémond, one of the contributors to the volume *Essais d'ego-histoire,* which first piqued my interest in the subject, has eloquently summarized the epistemological reasons that make writing about oneself difficult for most modern historical scholars. The historian's whole training, rather than making the writing of personal history seem natural, raises barriers to it:

> A long tradition has taught [historians] to be on their guard against subjectivity, their own as much as others'. They know from experience the precariousness of recollection, the unreliability of first-person testimony. Their professional training has taught them that everyone has an unconscious tendency to introduce a factitious coherence into the path of his life. They have no reason to believe that they are better armed against these distortions. They have no reason to think that they have any better chance to avoid the tricks of memory that they had learned to spy out in others.[9]

Implicit in Rémond's remarks is the fear that an autobiographical project may destabilize the professional historian's hard-won authority as a reconstructor of the past. If the trained historical scholar is at risk of introducing a "factitious coherence" into his or her personal history, is he or she not at equal risk of having done so in recounting collective history? Alternatively, as the American historian Drew Gilpin Faust suggests, the historian's training may sabotage an autobiographical project. Historians, she writes, "are on the one hand individuals—like all others—struggling to fashion a coherent and stable narrative of our lives that will provide the foundation of a self. Yet we are by education and inclination compelled to be skeptical of such stories."[10] If an autobiography shows a close connection between the scholar's personal passions and his or her academic work, it risks functioning as a subversive "supplement" to its author's historical scholarship, suggesting that some essential element was left out or concealed in the original scholarly project. French historian Annie Kriegel's revelation of her involvement with and subsequent painful break from the French Communist Party, the subject of her later historical scholarship, inevitably raises questions about her ability to describe objectively a phenomenon in which she had a strong personal investment. American historian Joel Williamson's attempt to relate his changing understanding of race and gender issues in southern history to his personal life experience, on the other hand, led some critics to charge that a historian with such a background should not have so obtuse for so long about the significance of an activity like lynching.[11]

The fear of exposing personal involvements that could undermine the authority of their scholarship is not the only obstacle deterring most historians from writing about themselves. They are often acutely conscious that their own stories complicate or run counter to the generalizations they and their colleagues have painstakingly elaborated to make sense of the past. In his memoir of the Holocaust, Saul Friedländer asks, "Can experience as personal, as contradictory as mine rouse an echo here? Isn't the way out for me to attach myself to the necessary order, the inescapable simplification forced upon one by the passage of time and one's vision of history, to adopt the gaze of the historian?"[12] English social historian Carolyn Steedman sees the "usefulness" of her account of her own childhood "in the challenge it may offer to much of our conventional understanding of childhood, working-class childhood, and little-girlhood."[13] The historian who uses his or her own case to question the possibility of generalization about collective experience, however, undermines one of the fundamental bases of the historical discipline. Autobiographies are also a challenge to history because they privilege a temporal framework based on the arbitrary dates of the individual author's life span, ignoring the effort historians put into the project of periodization, the definition of the significant phases of the collective past. The emphasis on personal time in historians' autobiographies some-times seems to subvert the meanings assigned to events in historical narra-tives. The often critical reactions to Paul Fussell's memoir of his combat ex-perience in World War II, *Doing Battle,* with its insistence that the damage done to his body and psyche during the conflict overshadows any broader meaning inherent in the story of the war, demonstrates the tension such clashes of perspective can cause.

In addition to these methodological concerns, historian-autobiographers face the possibility that their personal writings will turn out to embarrass them in the eyes of their peers or of other readers. By revealing how much passion and energy they invested in an academic career that brought them little of the power, wealth, or fame that constitute success in the general culture, historian-autobiographers risk having nonhistorian readers dismiss them for having wasted their life on tempests in teapots. The reviewer who greeted Gabriel Jackson's *Historian's Quest* by asking, "Who cares about the confessional outpourings of an academic historian whose horizon is bounded by grants-in-aid, tenure anxieties, and scholarly articles?"[14] raised a question that doubtless haunts most of those who might contemplate such a project. Even by comparison with colleagues in other academic dis-ciplines, historians often have difficulty explaining why general readers should be interested in their achievements. In the historical profession there is no equivalent to the Nobel Prize, a form of public validation that assures nonspecialists of a scientist's importance even if the content of the prize-winner's work is difficult to communicate. Nor are historians often recog-nized as the founders of intellectual schools or movements, as philosophers, social scientists, and literary scholars sometimes are. Ironically, the fact that history is a relatively accessible and untheoretical discipline makes it harder, rather than easier, to communicate to nonspecialist readers what constitutes outstanding achievement within its ranks.

Even if historian-autobiographers avoid the pitfall of appearing too nar-rowly focused on intradisciplinary matters, they still have to overcome the fear of demonstrating poor judgment about what they include in their stories. Philippe Lejeune, the leading contemporary French critic of auto-biographical literature, has remarked, apropos of intellectual autobiography in general, "I am often confused by the naïveté and the simplicity of mind that takes hold of people who are nevertheless intellectually gifted, and who have acquired a reputation in literary, psychological, or philosophical areas, when they take it into their heads to talk about their own life. Not only does critical sense vanish, and they no longer estimate very well what might interest other people . . . but it especially surprises me that they themselves might be interested in what they are relating."[15] The pages many historian-autobiographers have devoted to their vacation travels demonstrate Lejeune's point. If the historian's recollections are not dismissed as trivial, they are likely to be found awkward. Do we really want to know at what age and under what conditions distinguished scholars had their first sexual experiences, details related in a surprising number of these texts? Authors often see such stories as necessary to demonstrate their determination to admit readers into their personal life, as proof that they really are writing according to the rules of autobiography rather than those of history, and as a way of establishing that they have had the same experiences as ordinary people, but these episodes fit uncomfortably into narratives in which sexuality or bodily experience in general is otherwise not a theme.

Not surprisingly, in view of its importance in their historical work, the issue of documentation often raises special problems for historian-autobiographers. An extreme case is that of Annie Kriegel, whose massive memoir *Ce que j'ai cru comprendre* is studded with professional-looking footnotes, many of them to cartons of the author's personal papers which she categorized in numbered series like those that historians routinely use in official archives. Few historian-autobiographers have wanted to go as far as Kriegel in assimilating their personal narratives to the norms of professional scholarship. Nevertheless, historian-autobiographers do routinely reflect some consciousness of this issue. They are not the only autobiographers to make at least some brief prefatory comments about the documentary sources they may have consulted in reconstructing their personal story, but such remarks are more or less routine in historians' memoirs, whereas they are optional in others'. George Mosse is one of the very few historian-autobiographers who admits explicitly, "I have had to rely almost exclusively upon my memory of the past," and the fact that he emphasizes this situation is itself significant.[16]

More commonly, however, historian-autobiographers make at least some passing reference to evidence from the past. "The memoirist would appear not to need documentary sources, for he relies on the authority of his memory," Holocaust historian Lucy Dawidowicz writes. "Yet memory alone is not dependable. . . . We have all experienced those moments when, as the saying goes, memory deceives us." She mentions rereading letters she had written at the time and continues, "By relying on the discipline of history, I have tried to portray that past truthfully, as it was in life. I have not wanted to retouch it. That was my obligation as one of the last witnesses."[17]

Similarly, the historian of Africa Roland Oliver emphasizes that, except for his recollections of his childhood, "memory has played its part only under the strict control of the hard evidence of contemporary documents surviving in my private papers."[18] Other historian-authors also mention, and sometimes quote from, diaries, journals, and letters, and a few actually conducted research as part of their autobiographical projects. Louis Harlan, for example, sought out former shipmates to compare their memories of naval service in World War II with his own.[19] More than the common run of autobiographers, then, historian-autobiographers recognize an obligation to at least hint at a documentary substructure to their narrative and thereby link their personal enterprise to their disciplinary training.

Another respect in which historian-autobiographers show more self-consciousness than the majority of first-person authors is their concern with the degree to which their stories are representative of group experience. The French historian Alain Besançon titled his memoir *Une génération,* and the Italian Luisa Passerini called hers *Autoritratto di gruppo,* or, literally, "Self-Portrait of a Group." Gaines Post Jr. offers his *Memoirs of a Cold War Son* as a gesture on behalf of what he sees as a misunderstood and neglected age cohort in the United States, those who were too young to serve in World War II or the Korean conflict but too old to have been in Vietnam. "History has schooled us and passed us over," he writes. "We are called 'silent.' It is time we told our stories."[20] These attempts to estimate the representativeness or exceptionality of their personal stories may be difficult to confirm, but historian-autobiographers' concern with the issue is characteristic of their desire to combine aspects of the two genres in their personal writing. More than most other autobiographers, they also strive to fill in the background of their story as carefully as the foreground, to give descriptions of the circumstances they experienced that could serve as history as well as memoir.

Historian-autobiographers' concerns with documentation and the representativity of their experience link their personal writing with their historical work, but most of these authors have been conscious that the project differs in important ways from their other books. Some found the change uncomfortable. Peter Gay claims that writing about himself "proved the least exhilarating assignment I have ever given myself or received from others."[21] Other historian-autobiographers, however, have deliberately emphasized the attraction of a form of writing freed from the normal restrictions of academic prose. "Once I began, I couldn't stop," Carlos Eire reports. "For a scholar it is a marvelous release to be able to write sentence after sentence, and page after page, without stopping for footnotes," Hans Schmitt writes, and Keith Hancock confesses, "I am letting myself ramble and finding it a pleasure, because rambling is an indulgence I have never before permitted myself in writing a book."[22] After writing her own memoir, Kathleen Fitzpatrick encouraged her friend Manning Clark to follow her example, telling him, "You'll never have had so much fun in all your writing life."[23]

For most of these authors, the writing of an autobiography has meant imagining a new kind of audience, more diverse than the community of fellow professionals and students academic historians usually write for, and inventing a new authorial voice. Most historian-autobiographers have followed conventional patterns of chronological narrative, like the English historian Charles Petrie, who wrote, "There would appear to be no valid reason why I should not commence a book that is mainly about myself . . . in any different manner from that which I am in the habit of adopting when I write about others, and that is to say why I should not start at the beginning, and proceed with my narrative, as far as possible, chronologically."[24] But the shift from history to autobiography implies a considerable change in the style of their story. Autobiography requires emphasizing narrative over analysis and concrete detail over generalization. The autobiographer has to exercise talents more often associated with the writing of fiction than with the writing of modern scholarly history, such as the creation of convincing portraits of individuals and the (re)construction of believable dialogue. Brij Lal even writes of inventing a new category of narrative: "I have tried to recall the past creatively, imaginatively, rendering factual, lived experience through the prism of semi-fiction. I call this kind of exercise 'faction' writing. It is the most satisfactory way I know of remembering a past unrecorded in the written texts."[25] In place of the adults who occupy center stage in most works of history, the historian-autobiographer, at least in the early chapters, usually has a child for a protagonist, and the success of the project requires the ability to convey how the world looked from that perspective. The evocation of the terror H. Stuart Hughes felt at age eight when he was taken to visit wax models of medieval prisoners in Mont-Saint-Michel and Peter Kenez's recollection of the overwhelming, uncritical love he felt for the Russian soldiers who liberated his family in Budapest when he was seven are good examples of this.[26]

Ironically, the writing of autobiography is often a challenge for historians because it involves narrating personal experiences that are the common substance of autobiography but that rarely figure in historical accounts.

Many of these authors recount a basically happy childhood, but a substantial number tell stories, sometimes gripping or depressing ones, of parents locked in mortal combat or coexisting in sullen silence. The Australian historian Manning Clark's *The Puzzles of Childhood* is a monumental attempt to understand the tensions between his mother and father that, in his view, shaped his own character: "Why was my mother always so worried, why was my father often so angry?"[27] There are among historian-autobiographers individuals who suffered devastating personal tragedies. Some were victims of great historical disasters, such as the Holocaust or combat during World War II. Others' lives were torn apart by more random events; the Italian philosopher and historian Benedetto Croce, for example, was pulled from the rubble after an earthquake that killed his parents and sister.[28] Edwin O. Reischauer barely recovered from an assassination attempt during his service as American ambassador to Japan, and Inga Clendinnen's memoir was inspired by her near-fatal liver disease. Some historians are weighed down by remorse about earlier life decisions, such as Annie Kriegel's activities in the Communist Party during the Stalin era, leading them to write confessions that evoke the great predecessor of so many life writers, Saint Augustine. When they write about their private lives, historian-autobiographers have had the full gamut of experiences: happy marriages and bitter divorces, rewarding family lives and the devastating loss of beloved spouses or children, painful processes of self-exploration, often in the context of psychotherapy. For many historians, writing about such universal topics without guidelines from their disciplinary training to help them has been one of the major challenges of the venture into autobiography.

MATTERS OF DEFINITION

Despite the discomfort they sometimes feel about this kind of writing and the unfamiliar challenges it poses, historians have created a considerable corpus of autobiographical texts. To be sure, not every comment historians publish about themselves deserves to be called autobiography. Christophe Prochasson has traced the varying ways in which French historians have used the first-person pronoun in their texts, from the time of Michelet to the present, and has shown that they reflect differing ways of defining the contribution that the scholar makes in composing his or her work, but these self-references are usually abstract rather than autobiographical.[29] In the United States, it is increasingly common for scholars to make at least some brief comment on their relationship to the subject of their research. This trend is a significant development in its own right, but these self-reflexive comments are not the same thing as autobiography. Indeed, proponents of this kind of scholarship, with its emphasis on the author's relationship to his or her research subject, have argued that "few autobiographies are truly reflexive" because what they say about the author's self tends to be "merely narcissistic or accidentally revealing."[30] For the purposes of this essay, I define historians' autobiographies as published personal narratives in which the author's own life is the principal subject, by authors who were also, for at least some substantial part of their lives, professional scholars and, in most cases, teachers of history. How many such publications have appeared is difficult to say. My researches have not been exhaustive, and my objective is not to provide a systematic history or catalog but rather to define and analyze the issues that such works raise. I have nevertheless identified close to three hundred books and shorter publications that fall into this category. In deciding whether an author should be considered a historian, I have opted for inclusivity rather than exclusivity; some of the authors discussed here, such as Paul Fussell and Reinhard Bendix, are primarily identified with other academic disciplines, a few, such as Jill Ker Conway, spent more of their academic careers as administrators than as historians, and others, such as Bruce Catton, John Toland, and Jean Lacouture, did their writing outside of the academy. I have nevertheless included them because significant parts of their work have been accepted as historical scholarship and have been widely read by members of that discipline, as well as by general readers interested in history.

Like autobiographers in general, historians who have written about their own life have done so in many different ways. Some of the texts discussed here are full-length autobiographical narratives, telling the stories of their author's life from birth to the time of writing; others focus on some particular episode, whether it be childhood and youth, or a particularly dramatic experience such as participation in World War II. Some historians who write about themselves deal primarily with their personal thoughts and experiences and write what critics and readers are likely to categorize as "autobiography," whereas others write primarily about the external events to which they were witnesses and thus produce what would more often be called "memoirs." In practice, it is hard to see any consistent pattern of difference between personal narratives by historians whose authors have labeled their story "autobiography" and those who avoid the term. *In and Out of the Ivory Tower: The Autobiography of William L. Langer* is a good deal less personal than the Australian historian Inga Clendinnen's *Tiger's Eye,* although the latter is explicitly subtitled *A Memoir*. By virtue of being historians as well as autobiographers, nearly all of these authors find themselves writing about public events as well as private ones, but the main purpose of writing in the first person, for most of them, is to open up a space to talk about themselves and their own experiences.

Although the difference between autobiography and memoir may no longer matter to most critics, it does to a number of historians, who are anxious not to be classified as autobiographers. Peter Gay, for example, claims that "this memoir of enduring a hell in the making necessarily has a melancholy tone that, taken by itself, distorts my personal history." His attitude is similar to that of C. Eric Lincoln, who uses his memories to show how young African Americans in the segregated South learned the boundaries of their condition but emphasizes that he has recorded only "selected experiences" which are "not the *sum* of my life."[31] Gay's and Lincoln's protests express notions that "true" autobiography should embrace the author's whole life, not merely certain aspects of it, and that it should emphasize the author's individual autonomy rather than the weight of historical circumstances in determining the course of his or her life. In France, Pierre Nora has tried to provide historians with a way of writing about themselves without having to consciously engage in autobiography by inventing a new label, *ego-histoire*, a form of first-person narrative that excludes much of the content normally associated with such projects. "No falsely literary autobiography, or unnecessarily intimate confessions, no abstract profession of principles, no attempt at amateur psychoanalysis," he told the contributors to his volume.[32] In a collection of first-person essays by European historians, Luisa Passerini and Alexander Geppert have used Nora's term and followed his lead, arguing that "it is precisely this overlap between autobiography and *ego-histoire* which must be dispelled." In fact, however, they are compelled to admit that "there will always be traces of autobiography in *ego-histoires*," and it is hard to see why most of the articles in their volume, or Nora's, should not be considered autobiographical, provided that one does not define that term too narrowly.[33] Looking back on his earlier initiative in a contribution to the Passerini and Geppert volume, Nora himself wonders whether the idea he proposed is workable: "Between the representation of oneself as a social product and intimate hypersubjectivity, is ego-histoire even possible?"[34]

More important than the distinction between autobiography and memoir is the line that divides both from such nonretrospective and nonnarrative forms of personal writing as letters and diaries. Many historians have left behind documents of this sort, which are invaluable for biographers and for scholars studying the history of historical thinking, such as Peter Novick in his important study of the historical profession in the United States.[35] Historians using sources for research often lump autobiographies together with these other forms of first-person writing, as do some contemporary scholars who have adopted more inclusive terms such as "life writing" or "ego-documents" as a way of knocking down the barriers between "high" and "low" literary genres and challenging a literary canon that has excluded writers from less-favored social and gender categories.[36] When historians do distinguish between autobiographies and other personal documents, they often tend to prefer letters and diaries, on the assumption that they are more reliable evidence of what their authors were thinking at the time of events than are texts written later, and also because they seem more spontaneous and less governed by rules of genre or propriety. Neither assumption is necessarily justified. Jürgen Kuczynski, a historian-memoirist who also wrote a theoretical work on autobiography, argued against privileging the perspective found in letters and diaries over the retrospective view. Hindsight may allow a clearer view of what was really important about past experiences than the author had at the time, and in any event, such documents "are hastily written products of an author who, in comparison to the autobiographer, was a not yet developed or very different person, in any case another person."[37]

Letters and diaries are subject to their own generic rules and never constitute a pure, unstructured account of their authors' thoughts and actions; diaries "can only be relatively autonomous from the culture they inhabit," as the literary scholar Felicity Nussbaum has written.[38] One has only to compare letters written to a parent or spouse with letters that the same author may have written to friends, lovers, professional colleagues, newspapers, or partners in crime to realize that correspondence can reflect elaborate authorial strategies and give just as distorted a record of events as autobiographies compiled years later. Diaries and journals are as subject as autobiographies and memoirs to various forms of self-censorship, even if we set aside as exceptional the bizarre case of former U.S. Senator Robert Packwood, who testified at his trial for sexual harassment that he had deliberately lied in his diary. As historical sources, letters and diaries need to be evaluated just as carefully as autobiographies and memoirs. For my purposes, however, the differences between retrospective narratives—

autobiographies and memoirs—and letters or diaries are fundamental. Only the former involve the parallels with the writing of history—also a retrospective genre—that make the comparison proposed here significant.

Most of the texts I will discuss were published as independent volumes primarily devoted to the experiences of a single author, but I have also considered "coordinated autobiographies," personal narratives composed for publication in collaborative volumes, even though these projects set limits to what their contributors are allowed to write about that are quite different from the boundaries of individual autobiography. Although the essays in such volumes are written in the first person, they often reflect the agendas of the volumes' editors or organizers as much as those of their contributors. The nature of these projects also tends to militate against highly personal revelations or idiosyncratic forms of writing. The attraction of such enterprises, for their contributors, is that they provide a way to finesse the appearance of immodesty that besets the individual autobiography or memoir. These collections are generally justified in disciplinary terms, as contributions to scholarship, and since their contributors write in response to a colleague's invitation, they do not appear to be thrusting their tales on readers. "Coordinated autobiography" has become a significant phenomenon in academic life in general in recent decades, and historians have been among its more active practitioners.[39]

Similar considerations arise when an autobiography is the result of a collaboration between its subject and an interviewer, as is the case with a certain number of the publications considered here, such as the French cultural historian Philippe Ariès's *Un Historien du dimanche*. The interview situation may serve to deter discussion of some issues, such as sexual experience; at the same time, a well-prepared interviewer may prod an author to discuss matters he or she might have preferred to omit. Nevertheless, both "coordinated autobiographies" and "as-told-to" narratives share autobiography's retrospective aspect and its claim to represent personal experience on the basis of memory. To exclude them would be to leave out a significant part of the phenomenon under study here. In particular, these two forms of historians' autobiography have played an important part in establishing the genre's respectability and therefore in making historians more willing to write independent life narratives.

Although I have looked at many forms of published texts, I have deliberately excluded unpublished autobiographies. To historians, who often favor manuscript sources over printed ones in their research, this may seem like a serious omission. It would be hard to obtain access to any significant number of unpublished personal memoirs, however, and more important, the act of publication itself is a critical aspect of the autobiographical act. Authors who publish their autobiography have made a deliberate decision to share at least some aspects of their life with a public, an audience of anonymous readers, rather than just with family members or close friends. In going public, all autobiographers put their life story at risk: what they have published takes on an existence of its own, becomes subject to criticism, and may significantly alter the way others perceive the author. A published autobiography thus represents a very different kind of commitment from an unpublished manuscript. There is, of course, the question of an autobiography published after an author's death, which may or may not have been intended for a wider audience. Edward Gibbon's *Memoirs* is a classic example: the text that we read under that title is an editor's compilation of several incomplete manuscripts, and we cannot be sure how it would have looked if Gibbon had lived to complete it. Oddly enough, however, Gibbon's *Memoirs* is almost the only example of this situation that I have encountered in my research on historians' autobiographies. A few of the other works discussed here, such as George Mosse's *Confronting History,* did not see print until after their author's death, and one living scholar has told me to expect a volume after he passes on, but unlike Gibbon's, these are narratives that have been substantially completed in a form intended for publication during their authors' lifetime.

A HISTORY OF HISTORIANS' AUTOBIOGRAPHICAL WRITING

The examples of Giambattista Vico, whose autobiographical essay, written in 1731, has been hailed as "the first example of the application of the genetic method by an original thinker to his thought,"[40] and of David Hume and Edward Gibbon show that historians' autobiographies are not entirely a contemporary phenomenon. A small number of such texts were written in the nineteenth century, including memoirs of childhood by the French historians Ernest Renan and Ernest Lavisse, and one finds other examples from the first three-quarters of the twentieth century, in addition to the classic work of Henry Adams, which, like Gibbon's *Memoirs,* has always transcended the category of "historians' autobiography." In the 1920s, when their country was the unquestioned leader in historical scholarship, a number of German historians participated in an effort to institutionalize the practice of academic autobiography through a large-scale coordinated project, *Die Wissenschaft der Gegenwart in Selbstdarstellung* (Present-Day Scholarship in Self-Portraits); for the first time, a group of historians wrote about their lives with the avowed purpose of justifying their profession as well as themselves.[41] This set of historians' self-portraits stimulated the publication of a similar collection in Austria after World War II,[42] but other historians' autobiographies that appeared in a number of countries up to 1980 were isolated initiatives.

The corpus of published historians' autobiographies has grown enormously since 1980. This reflects in part the much larger number of people who have been able to make a living as professional historians, thanks to the massive expansion of university education after World War II, but it also reflects changing cultural attitudes toward writing about oneself, both inside and outside the academy. To be sure, only a very small minority of all working historians ever publish accounts of their own lives, but the practice has clearly become more common and more accepted in the past few decades and has even been deliberately encouraged in some parts of the profession. In 1970s and 1980s, several academic journals in the English-speaking world, notably the *Radical History Review* and the *Historian* — the periodical of the American historians' honorary society, Phi Alpha Theta — began to publish autobiographical interviews with prominent historians on a regular basis. A number of historians have also participated in the American Council of Learned Societies' annual lecture series, "A Life of Learning," begun in 1983. The resulting essays were circulated in print and eventually collected in a book.[43] In Australia, a series of autobiographical lectures by historians was founded in 1984, resulting in several subsequent published volumes.[44] Around the same time, Pierre Nora solicited personal essays or *ego-histoires* from a number of his prominent French colleagues, seven of which were eventually published in 1987 as *Essais d'ego-histoire,* the volume that first sparked my own interest in this subject. Nora's French initiative has now been copied on a European level in a volume edited by two scholars at the European University Institute in Florence.[45] In addition, there have been a number of books or journal issues bringing together essays by historians in particular categories: historians who came to England to escape the Nazis in the 1930s, American historians with a special interest in race relations, historians of the Middle East, founding members of the women's history movement in the United States, specialists in the religious history of the American South, historians of the South Pacific, and American historians of Russia.[46]

These interview series and collective volumes not only led a significant number of historians to write — or speak into a tape recorder — about their personal experiences: they were also occasions for theoretical justifications of such enterprises. Already in the 1920s, the editor of the earliest of these collections, Sigfrid Steinberg, saw its contents as a refutation of objectivist claims that historical knowledge existed independently of those who articulated it: "The man cannot be separated from the direction and nature of his work, not to speak of the historical-political coloration of his research results."[47] The notion that historians' autobiographical essays were an effective answer to positivism reappeared in the introduction to the collection of interviews from the *Radical History Review* in 1984; the volume's editors wrote that these texts "affirm . . . the links between personal experience and 'history' that underlie the production of all historical knowledge."[48] The most extensive effort to provide historians' writings about themselves with a theoretical justification has come from Pierre Nora. In his view, having historians examine their personal history was a way to make the profession come to terms with the "shaking of the classic foundations of historical objectivity," which, he claimed, had taught them to "let their work speak for them, to hide their personality behind their erudition . . . to flee from themselves into another era, to express themselves only through others."[49] In the introduction to *Les Lieux de mémoire,* the path-breaking collection of essays on "the history of memory" that he edited in the 1980s and early 1990s, Nora argues that there is a close connection between that project's challenge to the notion of an objectively knowable past and the critique of the traditional definition of the historian's role. "A new personage emerges from the upsurge of history conceived as memory, one ready, unlike his predecessors, to acknowledge the close, intimate, personal liaison he maintains with his subject. Even more, to proclaim it, to meditate on it, to make it, not the obstacle, but the means of his understanding."[50] *Essais d'ego-histoire* was thus the natural complement to *Les Lieux de mémoire,* "sharing the same sort of purpose," as Nora later put it, and *ego-histoire,* according to its promoter, was "a new genre, for a new age of historical consciousness."[51]

It is by no means certain that the majority of historians who have written about their own life, or even the majority of those who have contributed to volumes of historians' autobiographical essays, have accepted the idea that first-person writing by scholars has such wide-ranging theoretical implications. Michael Dintenfass, one of the few historians to have paid attention to the phenomenon, concludes that most recent historian-autobiographers have been reluctant to acknowledge the subjectivity that their own life-writing exercises would seem to imply: "Even for those who have risked the first-person, the self remains a troubling presence."[52] Nevertheless, the existence of these series and collective volumes sends a signal that historians' autobiographical writing is no longer merely the personal initiative of individual scholars and that it can have a serious intellectual point.

Single-author, book-length autobiographical texts by historians have also become more numerous since 1980. Such publications involve a greater commitment on the part of their authors, who normally accept the responsibility for having initiated their project and who are less likely to present it merely as a modest contribution to the understanding of their discipline. The fact that many of the historians who published individual autobiographies after 1980 were major luminaries in the discipline has helped make the practice more respectable: when such notables as A. J. P. Taylor, John King Fairbank, Emmanuel Le Roy Ladurie, Annie Kriegel, Jacob Katz, and Manning Clark have written about their own lives, autobiography can hardly be said to have attracted only fringe members of the profession. These distinguished scholars continued the pattern of the historians' autobiographies that had appeared in the late nineteenth century and the first two-thirds of the twentieth, in which the privilege of publishing the story of one's life was primarily reserved for those who had achieved eminence within the profession and a certain amount of recognition outside its ranks as well. In their structure and content, the memoirs of these elite historians also continued to follow traditional patterns. After introductory sections of varying length on the author's childhood and education, they usually focused on professional achievements, political commitments, and participation in major public events, such as the two world wars.

Although publications of this traditional sort, in which autobiography serves as both a demonstration and a consecration of elite status, still constitute a significant part of the corpus of historians' personal literature, the period since 1980 has seen a great diversification in both the kinds of historians who have written about themselves and in the content of their personal narratives. The opening up of the profession to women, to ethnic minorities, and especially to Jews, who had been virtually excluded from professors' posts in history prior to World War II, has made for a more varied population of authors. Perhaps more significant, however, has been the expansion in the range of what one might call the permissible plots in historians' memoirs. Whereas the dominant pattern in these works, from Gibbon onward, had been the story of the author's success and rise to elite status, the genre now expanded to take in works by self-styled rebels within the historical ranks—H. Stuart Hughes titled his memoir *Gentleman Rebel*—and life narratives by relatively little-known scholars. The impressive collection of historians' autobiographies published in Australia since 1980, for example, was begun by Kathleen Fitzpatrick's *Solid Bluestone Foundations,* the life story of a scholar whose career had been in many ways a study in frustration; she had never been able to find a publisher for her major work.

As the number of historians' autobiographies has grown, more of them have looked not to Gibbon but to the other classic example of a historian's autobiography, *The Education of Henry Adams,* and depicted their authors as bemused spectators of the dramas of their times. Others have pushed back the boundaries of self-revelation, often in radical ways. Manning Clark and Ronald Fraser exposed intimate details of their parents' troubled marriages, and A. J. P. Taylor gave similar details about his own first marriage. Philippe Ariès and several other French historians recounted their participation in quasi-fascist movements, while some of their colleagues flagellated themselves for their commitment to communism. A host of historians from Jewish backgrounds delved into the complexities of their experiences in the Holocaust era. A number of historians have related their experiences of psychotherapy. Robert Hine recounted the saga of a blind scholar, the economist and historian Deirdre (formerly Donald) McCloskey described her sex-change operation, and British classicist and ancient historian Kenneth Dover caused a stir by acknowledging unapologetically that he had helped drive a mentally unbalanced colleague to suicide.[53] In other words, historian's memoirs participated fully in the trends toward diversification of authorship and more extensive self-revelation that characterized first-person writing in general in the last decades of the twentieth century.

One of the most striking elements of this diversification has been the rapidly growing number of historians' autobiographies written by women. Feminist autobiographical criticism has raised questions about women authors' relationship to the traditions of autobiography, and these naturally affect the autobiographical writing of women historians as well as other women life writers. Some theorists have suggested that the linear narrative characteristic of traditional autobiography does not fit the reality of women's lives; others have argued that women are less likely to see themselves as isolated individuals, like the protagonists of most canonical autobiographies, and more likely to stress the involvement of their life with those of others. It is certainly true that women historians have been prominent among historian-autobiographers who have adopted unconventional narrative strategies, as the analyses of the personal narratives of Carolyn Steedman, Luisa Passerini, and Inga Clendinnen in chapter 9 will show. It is also true that the autobiographical narratives of women historians often report a long gap between schooling and the decision to pursue a professional career, so that the curves of their lives do not show the linear progression characteristic of their male colleagues. The memoirs of Susan Groag Bell, Gerda Lerner, Ann Moyal, and Natalie Davis clearly fit in this category, as do many of the contributions to *Voices of Women Historians;* conversely, I have found few accounts by male academics (as opposed to freelance historical authors such as Philippe Ariès and John Toland) that reflect such an indirect path into the discipline.

These gender differences are not absolute, however. There are women historians, even among the first generation of modern female academics, whose life stories adhere to the traditional pattern of education followed closely by professional success—Jill Ker Conway's three-volume saga of her progress from an Australian farm to the presidency of Smith College and Annie Kriegel's epic account of her path from the wartime communist resistance to scholarly and political prominence, for example—and many women have told their stories in conventional autobiographic modes. Nor has literary experimentation been a female monopoly, as the examples of Henry Adams, Hermann Heimpel, Ronald Fraser, and Saul Friedländer show. Although the autobiographies analyzed in this book narrate only the early stages of women's full-fledged entry into the historical profession, they reflect the fact that women now, as of the first decade of the twenty-first century, make up an increasingly important part of the population of historians. The fact that women historians can now write life stories in patterns similar to those of most men might be taken to show that the price of professional success is a willingness to be forced into a mold meant for the other sex, as Bonnie Smith has charged,[54] but it can also be interpreted to mean that women have succeeded in making the structures of the historical profession fit their needs.

QUESTIONS OF MOTIVE

Like most autobiographers, historians who write about their own lives usually feel obligated to give some justification for their project. The motives that historian-autobiographers acknowledge in their texts are no different from those cited by most other life writers. Some speak of a search for self-understanding. Many claim to have started their project at the urging of children or grandchildren; others cite a wish to preserve the memory of their own parents or other relatives. Not surprisingly, given these authors' professional interest in the past, many refer to a desire to record memories of times, places, and ways of life that have now vanished, the "rural past" of the American Midwest in John Hicks's case, a "world of objects and memories that evoked the Old Regime, the Revolution, the emigration, the counter-revolution" in that of the French historian Philippe Ariès, "the experience of growing up in a sugar cane village, poor, vulnerable, and isolated . . . a world that has now almost vanished beyond recognition" for the Indo-Fijian historian Brij Lal.[55] Historians who survived events related to the Holocaust or who were involved in World War II have wanted to contribute their testimony to the historical record. More recently, some historian-autobiographers have begun to present their stories as gestures on behalf of marginalized groups. In short, these authors tend to offer conventional and often rather banal justifications for their projects. They bend over backward to avoid seeming to claim any special status for themselves, any intention of presenting their life story as a model for emulation, or any criticism of the historical discipline's skepticism toward first-person narrative.

Historians of all sorts may reflect on their experiences, but considerations of age, national origin, gender, involvement in certain sorts of historical events, and standing within the profession affect the likelihood that individuals will write about their lives and, even more strongly, the chances that they will be able to get their stories published. Autobiography has traditionally been regarded as a genre of writing especially likely to be undertaken by the elderly, a response to the individual's growing sense of mortality. As the German historian Friedrich Meinecke, who published the first volume of his memoirs at age seventy-nine, wrote, "It is appropriate for an old man to take a look backward and make the development of his character clear to himself from that perspective."[56] The majority of historians' autobiographies certainly fit this pattern. They have often been completed after their author's retirement, and if they have not been published after the author's death, they have in many cases been their last publication. By including in his autobiography the circular letter he had written to friends after suffering a major heart attack, the American historian of China John King Fairbank emphasized the close association between the thought of death and his life-writing project.[57]

When historians follow this pattern of publishing their autobiography late in life, they usually create a certain separation between their professional work and their personal reflections. Historians who publish their memoir twenty or thirty years after the publication of their major historical works have often become removed from the cutting edge of professional debates; in some cases, these memoirists have been almost forgotten in the professional community by the time their recollections appear. Under these circumstances, the publication of a personal memoir is something of a farewell to a historical career, a way of announcing that the author is shifting to another order of concerns. Fairbank dubbed his autobiography a transition "from Chinese studies by Fairbank to Fairbank studies *tout simple*," and A. J. P. Taylor claimed, "This autobiography is evidence first of all that I have run out of historical subjects."[58] In more recent decades, however, it has become more common for historians, and for that matter autobiographers in general, to publish a personal account in midcareer. Saul Friedländer's *When Memory Comes*, Jonathan Scott's *Harry's Absence*, Jill Ker Conway's *The Road from Coorain*, Luisa Passerini's *Autobiography of a Generation*, and Brij Lal's *Mr. Tulsi's Store* were all published well before their authors turned sixty—in Scott's case, even before he had reached forty—and long before they were ready to declare their careers at an end. *Voices of Women Historians*, a collection of short memoirs by American women historians, even includes two contributions from authors who were still in graduate school at the time of writing.[59] In these cases, the relationship between an author's professional scholarship and his or her personal writing becomes quite different than in traditional autobiography.

In some cases, the autobiography serves to announce and justify a change in scholarly perspective. By revealing the traumatic impact of his childhood during the Holocaust, Saul Friedländer made it clear that his scholarship on that topic had powerful personal meaning for him, and indeed he argued that this personal perspective was not a distortion but a way of understanding the past more clearly: "It was only at this time in my life, when I was around thirty, that I realized how much the essential appeared to me through a particular prism that could never be eliminated. But did it have to be eliminated?"[60] After writing the first two volumes of her memoirs, Jill Ker Conway shifted scholarly fields from history to autobiography studies and published a volume on that subject.[61] Explicitly or implicitly, these authors indicate that for them life writing is not a way of saying goodbye to scholarly endeavors but a way of rethinking the meaning of their scholarship.

Age and a sense of being at a turning point in one's career clearly have a strong influence on the propensity of historians to write about their lives, but they are not the only factors. Gender and race have certainly been significant: the overwhelming majority of these texts are by white men, which reflects the traditional pattern of the profession until the last few decades. As we have seen, this pattern is now changing, especially with respect to women authors. Nevertheless, since academic autobiographies tend to get written toward the end of authors' lives, they are unquestionably a "lagging indicator" of changes in the profession, providing a portrait that reflects the characteristics of scholarly life a generation or more before their publication dates. In this respect, the memoir literature produced by historians looks quite different from the general spectrum of autobiographical publications from the last few decades, where—particularly in the United States—women and authors from minority groups have made major breakthroughs. If these groups still remain underrepresented as historian-memoirists, historians of Jewish origin, virtually unrepresented in this literature before 1980, have made a dramatic entry into it since then. The main reason for this has been the powerful cultural pressure to record the experience of the Holocaust; historians whose lives were directly affected by Nazi anti-Semitism make up by far the largest identifiable subgroup among contemporary historian-autobiographers. I have found texts by such authors published in the United States, France, Britain, Germany, the Netherlands, and Israel; they make up the one significant group of writings considered here that cuts across national and language boundaries and the traditions of autobiographical writing they define.

Autobiographies by historians of Jewish origin frequently intersect with another category: writings by historians who changed cultures at some point in their life. The memoirs of Peter Gay, Raul Hilberg, Gerda Lerner, George Mosse, Susan Groag Bell, and many others born in Europe before or during the Hitler era are not only testimonies about Jewish experience but also records of immigrant experiences, and as such they share some characteristics with texts by other, non-Jewish historians who made their careers in new countries, such as the Australian expatriates Keith Hancock and Jill Ker Conway, the Cuban exile Carlos Eire, or the Belgian-born historian of Africa Jan Vansina, who spent most of his career in the United States. Some historians, such as Saul Friedländer, Walter Laqueur, and Brij Lal, defy national categorization: they have lived, studied, and taught in several different countries or commuted between jobs for much of their careers. Authors whose lives have been divided by major experiences such as adaptation to a new culture are often thought to be more likely to reflect on the course of their experiences, and it is certainly true that such historians are overrepresented among the memoirists examined here.

Critics, to be sure, have often refused to accept at face value historian-autobiographers' bland assertions about the motives and circumstances that incited them to write. Many have attacked the general vogue for first-person literature in recent decades as a sign of a pervasive self-absorption in contemporary life, a privileging of the personal and private over the general and the historical.[62] Historian-autobiographers have not escaped such charges. One reviewer of H. Stuart Hughes's *Gentleman Rebel* complained that "this autobiography is all 'auto,' reporting only the memories of an intensely narcissistic author."[63] Other critics have suggested that academic autobiography serves to consecrate the pecking order within the profession. "Are the historians presented in our collection those 'who made it' and are their *ego-histoires* therefore necessarily success stories?" the editors of *European Ego-histoires* ask themselves, admitting that they "invited exclusively eminent members of the historical profession."[64]

It is certainly true that the autobiographical texts discussed here rarely come from authors who found their profession unsatisfying or who repeatedly met obstacles and frustrations in their careers. This is in part, no doubt, because the connections necessary to get an autobiography published during one's own lifetime are usually reserved for those whose writings have been most widely read within the profession or who have occupied positions at prominent institutions. The French *ego-historiens* of the 1980s and 1990s were an extraordinary cohort, many of whom had broken out of the bounds of academia to become public celebrities or journalists as well as scholars; one gets the impression that the publication of so many memoirs by members of this particular group created a certain pressure to join the movement, for fear of letting it appear that one was less important than other colleagues who had done so. On the other hand, the requirement that a historian-memoirist have a broad public reputation ruled out publications by scholars whose careers had been confined to the university world.

In the United States, few historians have achieved the public notoriety of an Emmanuel Le Roy Ladurie or a Georges Duby—Arthur Schlesinger Jr., who held a position in the Kennedy White House, may be the one exception among the historian-autobiographers discussed here, as the front-page review of his memoir in the *New York Times Book Review* shows—but employment at a prestigious academic institution has usually served a similar validating function. From Henry Adams onward, association with the history department at Harvard has been a frequent prelude to published life writing. The memoirs of Harvard faculty members such as Samuel Eliot Morison, William Langer, Arthur Schlesinger Sr. and Jr., Edwin O. Reischauer, John King Fairbank, H. Stuart Hughes, and Richard Pipes can be supplemented by the recollections of scholars who studied there before teaching elsewhere, including Dexter Perkins, Henry May, John Hope

Franklin, Martin Duberman, Jill Ker Conway, Carolyn Bynum, and Mary Beth Norton, to form a narrative about the department that spans more than a century. While no other American university comes close to Harvard in terms of the number of its former faculty who have published the stories of their lives, most other historian-memoirists have also been associated with prestigious institutions, such as Berkeley (John Hicks, Henry May, Reinhard Bendix), Wisconsin (Jan Vansina, George Mosse, Theodore Hamerow, Gerda Lerner, Jurgen Herbst), and Yale (C. Vann Woodward, Peter Gay, Carlos Eire, John Morton Blum). Volumes of shorter autobiographical essays published since 1980 have offset this tendency to some extent, as has the interest in the lives of historians affected by the Holocaust, regardless of where they teach, but the literature of historians' autobiography is clearly biased toward authors close to the top of the disciplinary hierarchy.

Yet even if the pattern of historians' autobiographical publications does function to some extent as a means of "consecration," in sociologist Pierre Bourdieu's sense, accusations of self-promotion and narcissism seem less justified with regard to most historians' life stories than they do with respect to many other contemporary first-person publications. Marketing considerations have played little role in generating such books: there have not yet been any bidding wars among publishers for the rights to a historian's memoir. Vanity is no doubt as common among historians as in any other group, but few of these texts are simply self-satisfied celebrations of their authors' accomplishments. As historians' memoirs have become more self-revelatory, they have also tended to become what the Australian autobiography scholar Rosamund Dalziell calls "shameful autobiographies," highlighting potentially embarrassing aspects of their authors' lives along with their achievements. As Dalziell explains, "the representation of shaming experiences can be a narrative strategy for disarming critics who might seek to cut down to size those who have the audacity to write an autobiography. The autobiographer thus arranges for the narrated self to be perceived by the reader as an 'ordinary person' who shares the common human experiences of fallibility, uncertainty and the fear, or even the recollection, of appearing ridiculous."[65]

While individual historians certainly have their own motives for writing about their lives, the proliferation of such texts is also related to certain collective concerns. Although historians as a group have been less explicit than members of some other academic disciplines about the value of scholars' autobiographies as a recruiting tool or as a way of countering distorted popular images such as that of the "mad scientist," many historian-autobiographers are conscious that their texts represent their profession as well as themselves. While historians-autobiographers may try to avoid appearing boastful about their own achievements, they are, with very few exceptions, strongly positive about the virtues and accomplishments of their discipline and the satisfactions of a career in it. The literature scholar James Sosnoski has suggested that members of academic disciplines model themselves on idealized archetypes of a "Magister Implicatus," even though few professors are able to live up to these models.[66] Whatever they say about their individual author, historians' autobiographies do help propagate such an image. As apologias for history, they reassure other practitioners of the discipline and help maintain history's standing among its rival academic disciplines.

Although more historians are writing about themselves nowadays than ever before, it is much harder to know how widely their stories are being read and in what contexts. These books do find an audience; several historian-autobiographers have assured me that their memoirs have sold more copies than any of their academic monographs. But what kind of reading matter are they? Library of Congress catalogers normally give such works call numbers that place them with books on history, although a few are found in other classifications; Inga Clendinnen's memoir, inspired by a life-threatening illness, is shelved with treatises on liver disease. Scholarly historical journals, on the other hand, often have policies against reviewing such publications, on the grounds that they are not contributions to historical knowledge, even though the same journals will generally review biographies of prominent historians in their sections on historiography. General-interest periodicals are more open to reviewing historians' memoirs, but one suspects that most of these reviews, which tend to be on the bland side, are published more out of a sense of duty to authors who may also have been reviewers than out of enthusiasm for the books themselves. Only a handful of these titles have been issued in paperback by major publishers, and none of them seems to have attracted the attention that the most successful memoirs in other academic disciplines, such as Edward O. Wilson's *Naturalist* or Alice Kaplan's *French Lessons,* have obtained.

Academic authors usually console themselves for the low sales of their publications by hoping that their works are read and cited by their professional peers. References to some historians' memoirs are beginning to appear in scholarly monographs, indicating that other historians are willing to give them at least the same status as firsthand accounts by nonhistorian authors. The critical literature on autobiography presents a mixed picture. A few of these books, particularly those that have taken the greatest liberties with standard autobiographic form, have been warmly received; one scholar has called historian Ronald Fraser's *In Search of a Past* "the most important contemporary English autobiography."[67] Feminist scholars have shown interest in the publications of women historians, whether they are unconventional in form, like Carolyn Steedman's *Landscape for a Good Woman,* or more traditional, as in the case of Jill Ker Conway's *The Road from Coorain.* On the whole, however, this is a body of literature that appears to have been called into existence more by authors' desires to express themselves than by the existence of a clearly defined audience.

CONTEXTS OF HISTORIANS' AUTOBIOGRAPHIES

Historians' autobiographies reflect their authors' individual concerns and their identification with their profession, but they also reflect developments in the writing of history and the distinctive traditions of autobiography in the national cultures to which these authors belong. The past generation has seen a sea change in the practices of the historical discipline itself, one that has involved both a new definition of the proper domain of history and a new judgment about the persuasiveness of arguments based on individual experience versus those derived from generalization. This change can be seen most clearly in the development of social history over recent decades, as it has shifted from an emphasis on statistically measureable manifestations of collective life to various forms of microhistory, the history of everyday life, oral history, and the "history of memory," with which Pierre Nora, the inventor of the term *ego-histoire,* has been closely associated. All of these approaches, with their emphasis on the importance of ordinary individual experience and the historical significance of representations of the past other than those elaborated by professional historians, have provided new justifications for historians who undertake autobiographical projects. It can hardly be an accident that many of the historians identified with the elaboration of these approaches—four of the five principal editors of the well-known French series *A History of Private Life* (Paul Veyne, Georges Duby, Philippe Ariès, and Michelle Perrot), the German historian most identified with *Alltagsgeschichte,* his country's variant of that form of history (Jürgen Kuczynski), the founding editor of the journal *History and Memory* (Saul Friedländer), and such pioneers of oral history as Ronald Fraser, Luisa Passerini, and Lutz Niethammer, are among the historians who have published personal memoirs.[68]

Thirty years ago, social history usually implied the study of anonymous masses, but more recently it has been dominated by case studies, often built around first-person narratives left behind by obscure individuals in the past, such as the eighteenth-century French glass-fitter Jacques Ménétra.[69] Practitioners of microhistory, such as Jonathan Spence, have shown that apparently trivial events, such as the death of an utterly unknown Chinese woman of the seventeenth century,[70] can provide important insights into broad historical processes. Fascinating as such studies of single lives often are, however, they often leave historians frustrated: the evidence is never complete and conclusive enough to answer all our questions about life in the past. Autobiography written by a professionally trained scholar holds out the lure of fully realizing the promise of microhistory. Historians' autobiographies seem to promise us case studies written by experts who know the broader context surrounding their subject's life story and who know all the right questions to ask. In an era in which generalizations about the collective experience of any group have come under suspicion, autobiography sometimes seems to be the only genre with a convincing claim to credibility.

In the light of these developments, historian-autobiographers need not be inhibited any longer by the fear that the canons of their discipline will classify what they lived through as too inconsequential to be worthy of narration. The challenge for historian-autobiographers is now to demonstrate the interconnections between their microhistorical experiences and some theme of broader significance; the possibilities are limited only by the narrator's skill and historical imagination, not by the objective dimensions of the event itself. The death of Jill Ker Conway's father during a drought in remote New South Wales was not of obvious importance except to his family, but his daughter uses it to illustrate the consequences of the importation of European agriculture to a climate unsuited to it.[71] Martin Duberman justifies his narration of his love affairs and his unhappy experiences with a succession of therapists on the grounds that they illustrate how repressive mechanisms against homosexuals operated in the United States of the 1950s and 1960s.[72] The current historiographical climate is thus particularly propitious for autobiographical enterprises.

While the evolution of history writing has favored autobiographical projects among historians from many different countries, historian-autobiographers strongly reflect the national tradition of life writing within which they find themselves. Historians' autobiographies have appeared in many different countries. Even though my research has been limited by my language capabilities, I have read examples from the United States, Britain, France, Germany, Italy, the Netherlands, India, Israel, Australia, New Zealand, Canada, and Fiji, and there have no doubt been similar publications elsewhere.[73] During the first half of the twentieth century, thanks in large part to the influence of the Weimar-era collective project *Die Wissenschaft der Gegenwart in Selbstdarstellung,* Germany was clearly the country that generated the most autobiographical writing by historians. As a result of the impact of the Nazi period, German historians largely abandoned such enterprises; those who had held university posts under Hitler and even those who had been their students found it difficult to write about their own lives. As one recent commentator has put it, the dissonances in the life stories of academics who served or grew up under the Nazis and then became parts of the academic establishment in a democratic West Germany make life writing, which "always assumes the unity of the personality," difficult if not impossible.[74] Hermann Heimpel's *Die halbe Violine,* which was published in 1949, took the author's life story up only to the end of his adolescence in the early 1920s. Heimpel later attempted to write an account of his role in the reestablishment of the historical profession in postwar Germany but completed only fragments of this story; no evidence that he ever tried to recount his life during the Nazi period has been published.[75] The only subsequent book-length autobiographical publications by historians working in Germany are by two scholars of Jewish origin, Jürgen Kuczynski and Helmut Eschwege, who both returned to East Germany after spending the Nazi period in exile. Otherwise, the pre-Hitler tradition of German historians' memoirs has been kept alive only by those who had to leave the country as a result of Hitler.

Many of these German-born scholars spent most of their careers in the United States, where they contributed to making their new homeland the country that produced the largest collection of historians' autobiographies in the last quarter of the twentieth century. This is in part a reflection of the large number of working historians in the country, but it also highlights the role of different national autobiographical cultures in encouraging or discouraging such enterprises. The United States has usually been seen as a culture particularly hospitable to first-person narrative; the American literary tradition is often said to begin with Benjamin Franklin's *Autobiography,* a work that for all its undeniable aesthetic qualities nevertheless offers an accessible model for imitation. Franklin wrote in a simple, straightforward style, and the story he told, of individual success achieved through devotion to the public good, provided an easily imitated and unproblematic structure that other writers could easily adapt. Over the course of the following two centuries, America has democratically embraced many other variants of autobiographical narrative, so that the corpus of historians' autobiographies published here is not only larger than that in any other country but more diverse as well. It includes not only optimistic stories in the vein of Franklin but ironic and pessimistic ones in the spirit of Henry Adams, life stories used as ways of protesting against discrimination and prejudice, immigrant autobiographies in which adaptation to a new culture is a major theme, and radical experiments in the definition of personal identity.

France, another country that produced a large number of first-person texts by historians in the late twentieth century, offers a sharp contrast to the United States. The French autobiographical tradition, according to Michael Sheringham, one of its most acute students, has been a highly self-conscious one; the literary strategies French authors have employed show their "aware-ness of the problems and contradictions which beset [their] undertaking, manifesting the critical insight and self-conscious lucidity which has been a hallmark of French autobiography."[76] Autobiography in France has been so strongly identified with the complex, sophisticated productions of authors like Montaigne, Rousseau, Chateaubriand, Stendhal, André Gide, Simone de Beauvoir, Jean-Paul Sartre, Roland Barthes, and Georges Perec—not to mention the country's most celebrated twentieth-century political mem-oirist, Charles de Gaulle—that historians contemplating such an enterprise face a much more daunting challenge than does the American historian who considers following in the footsteps of Benjamin Franklin. Furthermore, the best-known French autobiographical texts, above all Rousseau's *Confes-sions,* are problematic models for more ordinary mortals. Rousseau took self-exposure to an extent that few people, and even fewer academics, have wanted to emulate; the occasional exceptions, such as the bestselling *La Vie sexuelle de Catherine M.,* only serve to prove the rule.[77] The very prominence of these French high-literary autobiographical texts has helped maintain what leading French students of the genre have labeled an "anti-autobiographic ideology," in which first-person writing is condemned in principle as narcissicistic and self-indulgent, excusable only in the case of a few extraordinary figures.[78]

French historian-autobiographers have reacted to this situation by try-ing to avoid any appearance of literary ambition. Many of the autobio-graphical texts that appeared in France in the 1980s and 1990s took the form of interviews, thereby excusing their authors for expressing themselves in an informal fashion. Whereas American historian-autobiographers in the same period adopted an ever-wider range of narrative approaches, their French colleagues stuck essentially to a single model, the successful career consecrated by public recognition. French texts that deviate from this pattern, particularly the memoirs of Annie Kriegel and Pierre Vidal-Naquet, derive their special energy from their authors' intense grappling with the problems posed by their Jewish origins and, in Kriegel's case, deep involvement with and subsequent rejection of communism. Both are also characterized by an almost defiant rejection of proper French literary form and style. Kriegel herself draws attention to "my endless sentences," one of which runs for more than an entire page.[79] Both she and Vidal-Naquet divide the stories of their adult lives into several disconnected narrative sequences, separating their scholarly, political, and journalistic activities from one another and producing considerable chronological confusion. No reader of these or any of the other recent French historians' memoirs is likely to put them in the same category as the famous texts of the country's literary canon.

Two other countries in which one can speak of national traditions of historians' autobiographical writing are Britain and Australia. The British tradition begins, of course, with a recognized classic, Edward Gibbon's *Memoirs,* which is also generally regarded as the great model for the whole national autobiographical tradition. Gibbon's work was contemporary with Franklin's and Rousseau's autobiographical enterprises, but it gave British autobiography quite a different direction. Like Franklin, Gibbon told a story of individual success through hard work, but his story had a much less democratic flavor. He stressed his family heritage and his status as a gentleman, and the heavy emphasis he put on the issue of literary style in autobiographical writing warned would-be imitators that they would need superior skill as writers. Well into the twentieth century, British historians remained influenced by this elitist model of intellectual autobiography. Like Gibbon, G. M. Trevelyan emphasized his distinguished ancestry—his father was the nephew of the celebrated nineteenth-century historian Thomas Babington Macauley—and, for good measure, the fact that he had grown up in "Shakespeare's Warwickshire."[80] Subsequent British historians have continued to devote considerably more attention than their colleagues elsewhere to establishing precisely the social standing of their parents and grandparents; the title of J. F. C. Harrison's memoir, *Scholarship Boy,* dramatizes the issue. Richard Cobb, a historian-author whose social origins were humble and who may hold the record among historians for having published the largest number of volumes about his own life—four—followed Gibbon on the literary high road. His autobiographical sketches are skillfully polished, reminding readers that before he became a historian he had successfully published several short stories.[81] British historians such as Carolyn Steedman and Ronald Fraser who have wanted to write autobiographies that escape from the Gibbonian mold have been driven to radical and highly self-conscious experiments with narrative form. The American notion that a historian can say something interesting about his or her life in a conventional chronological narrative written in simple, straightforward prose rarely corresponds to the British situation.

Contemporary Australian historians' memoirs stand out because they have had a significant role in establishing a tradition of first-person writing, a relatively recent development in their own culture. Rather than being a small and obscure eddy in the larger pool of autobiographical writing, as in the United States or France, the works of authors such as Keith Hancock, Manning Clark, Kathleen Fitzpatrick, Bernard Smith, and Inga Clendinnen have been regarded as major contributions to the national literature. They are taken seriously by critics and put on the same level as the memoirs of Australian literary and political figures. This is in part due to the relatively small size of the country's intellectual elite, but it also reflects the newness of Australia's sense of cultural identity. The very attempt to write an Australian history that would be something more than a contribution to British imperial history is relatively recent, and many of these historian-autobiographers, particularly Clark, have made major contributions to that enterprise. Their reflections on their own lives are very closely linked to this broader question and thus speak to a wider audience than the parallel texts of their colleagues in most other countries. These works have also had an impact, however, because of their literary quality and their high degree of authorial self-consciousness. In articulating their own stories, Australian historian-autobiographers have developed a distinctive strain of historical life writing.

As we can see, historians' autobiographies, however artlessly they may be presented, are never simple projects. Consciously or unconsciously, they have to respond to the particular expectations imposed on authors who are presumed to have a special sensitivity to the effects of "living in history." To do this, however, historian-autobiographers have to separate themselves from habits ingrained by the practice of their profession. The fact that many historians have done so, particularly in the years since 1980, marks a significant change in the climate of the historical profession. As autobiographical writing has become more common among historians, however, its functions within the profession have become more complicated. The composition of a personal narrative can be both a senior scholar's way of taking leave of a career and a way of reinforcing the same author's standing within the professional hierarchy. As more authors who cast themselves as disciplinary outsiders have embraced autobiography, however, it has also become one way of challenging the profession's structure. Further, even as historian-memoirists position themselves within their disciplinary field, they also have to situate themselves in the particular tradition of life writing within their national culture. The following chapters of this book will explore these many dimensions of historians' autobiographical writing, looking at its distinctive ways of presenting issues that affect historians' professional lives, their engagement with history, and their narratives' relations with other literary traditions.

CHAPTER 4 Two Classic Historians'
Autobiographies: Edward Gibbon
and Henry Adams

TWO SPECIAL CASES

The rapid multiplication of autobiographies by historians since 1980 has made it harder for any one of them to establish itself as a uniquely successful example, assured of a continuing audience that includes both historians and general readers—in other words, as what could be called a classic of the genre. It is not impossible for a contemporary academic's memoir to achieve this status: in 1980 the publisher W. W. Norton admitted biochemist James Watson's memoir about the discovery of the structure of DNA, *The Double Helix,* published in 1968, to its series Norton Critical Editions in the History of Ideas, putting its author in the company of Aquinas, Machiavelli, and Darwin, among others.[1] If one seeks comparable texts in the canon of autobiographical literature by historians, one has to look considerably further back in time, to Edward Gibbon's *Memoirs* (1796) and *The Education of Henry Adams* (1918). Both have had a major influence on the thinking of historians and on the practice of autobiography, and both have continued to inspire new critical readings ever since their publication. Although both works were written in English, their readership has extended to other cultures as well.

Acknowledging the special status of these two books raises the question of their relationship to the rest of the autobiographical literature written by historians. Both Gibbon and Adams are still recognized for the contributions they made to the development of historical writing, and in Gibbon's case especially one might argue that the continuing attention paid to his autobiography reflects his importance for the discipline. Nevertheless, even Gibbon's contribution to historiography has long since been superseded, and few readers turn to his memoir purely because of his stature among historians. There is, of course, the issue of these authors' literary talents. Both have been recognized since their own day as master stylists, peers of the leading writers of their times, a distinction to which few recent historians have pretended. To say that these two works stand out from the rest of the personal writing by historians because of their superior aesthetic qualities is an inadequate answer to the question of their special status, however, and one that raises the obvious questions of how quality is defined and whether artistic success should be the main criterion for judging historians' memoirs.

It might be argued that the continuing interest in Gibbon's and Adams's texts comes not from their importance as historians or from their skill as writers but from their having engaged more fully with the possibilities of autobiography by addressing deeper and more universal issues than the common run of historians' life writing. Did these two authors transcend the limitations of autobiographical writing defined by the writer's profession, and have their works found a wider audience because they do not focus on the limited topics that are commonly associated with historians' life writing? In that case, there would be a serious question of what their autobiographical works share with the rest of this literature. As we will see, however, this is not really the case: the issues Gibbon and Adams raise in their own lives are not that different from those that other historians have treated. I will argue, in fact, that some of the power of these two life stories comes precisely from their engagement with issues that historians, more than other autobiographers, face in recounting their lives. Conversely, reading Gibbon's *Memoirs* and *The Education of Henry Adams* not just as autobiographies but as *historians'* autobiographies offers new insights into these well-known texts.

Gibbon's *Memoirs* and *The Education of Henry Adams* offer two very different examples of how a historian can address the relationship between his or her own life and the wider sphere of history. Gibbon saw a clear connection between his life, his work as a historian, and his autobiographical project. He contended both that studying history had been central to his life and that his sense of history had been nourished and enriched by insights drawn from personal experience. Furthermore, his story portrayed the historian's career in a positive light: it had brought him personal success and allowed him to make a worthy contribution to society. Adams, on the other hand, presented his life as a lesson in disconnection and failure. In his view, his historical works had profited little from his involvement in public affairs, and in any event he did not put them forward as the justification for his decision to recount his own life. That life, as he portrayed it, had brought him little satisfaction and contributed nothing to the wider world. On the other hand, Adams linked the story of his life to history in several ways that Gibbon had not. Adams used his autobiography as an opportunity to write a history of his own times and to put forward a philosophy of history. Despite his conviction that his life exemplified the incoherence of the times in which he lived, the quasi-religious vision of the law of historical change that he articulates at the end of his story was meant to provide an effective conclusion to the narrative of both his individual life and the development of nineteenth-century civilization that makes up the content of his work.

Gibbon might have given his work a more philosophical frame had he lived to put it in finished form. He died leaving the project unfinished, however, and, as one commentator on the text has written, without the intervention of Gibbon's friend Lord Sheffield, who composed a coherent narrative out of the six partial manuscripts he had left behind, "we would not think of Gibbon as having written a great autobiography; rather, we would think of him as a historian who tried to write an autobiography but failed."[2] Although Gibbon did not live to finish his autobiography, he did produce a text that influenced even his most distinguished successor. Adams's *Education,* as we will see, contains many references to the *Memoirs* and can be read in good part as a response to that work. Subsequent historians' memoirs down to the present also frequently mention it. One can thus see Gibbon's *Memoirs* as fulfilling one of the functions by which we recognize a classic: creating a tradition and inspiring and influencing successors over a long period of time. The same can certainly be said of *The Education of Henry Adams.* References to Adams's autobiography occur in the memoirs of many other American historians and even in some texts by historians from other countries; the German communist scholar Jürgen Kuczynski appropriated Adams's title and his third-person style of narration for his own memoir. Even the American Jewish historian Arthur Hertzberg, offended by Adams's anti-Semitism, nevertheless confesses to finding Adams's "pessimism and sense of loss . . . infectiously appealing."[3]

Despite the differences between them, Gibbon's *Memoirs* and *The Education of Henry Adams* do share some important features. Both are intellectual autobiographies, concerned above all with the development of their authors' mind, or, as Adams put it in his title, their education. Both authors had distinguished pedigrees and could have had significant political careers if they had exerted themselves. Like many more recent historians' memoirs, their accounts are in part apologias for existences spent observing, reading, and writing rather than striving to make history in their own right. Both are also highly self-conscious and innovative productions, written with excruciating attention to style. Gibbon was seeking to create a new form of life narrative at a time when the word *autobiography* did not yet exist. Patricia Meyer Spacks, one of the most insightful commentators on Gibbon's *Memoirs,* has written that he recorded "his history as he might set down that of an empire"; she does not add that this was an approach that set his story apart from his models Augustine, Montaigne, and Rousseau, none of whom had portrayed his life as the story of the conscious pursuit of a difficult task.[4] Through devices such as his decision to write about himself in the third person, Adams, for his part, was trying to break out of the confines of the narrative model Gibbon had done so much to establish. For all their importance in the history of autobiography, both texts also share a tendency to draw a veil over their author's private life and feelings. Gibbon dispatched his one emotional attachment to a member of the opposite sex with a famously enigmatic sentence; Adams said nothing at all about the years of his marriage or the devastating impact of his wife's suicide, leaving readers to puzzle over the twenty-year gap in chronology that fractures his account. Finally, both works were only published after their authors' deaths. Adams, it is true, circulated copies of his book to an extensive circle of friends during his lifetime, ostensibly to have the benefit of their criticisms, but he refused permission for its release to the general public until after his demise.

GIBBON'S MEMOIRS: THE HISTORIAN AS HERO

Edward Gibbon's memoir was not the first autobiographical account by a historian—Giambattista Vico had preceded him, and he himself mentioned the personal narratives of David Hume and the French historian Jacques-Auguste de Thou—but it became the first such production to find a substantial audience. This is all the more remarkable in that, as we have seen, Gibbon had not succeeded in putting the work into anything resembling finished form at the time of his death. Sheffield assembled a readable narrative out of Gibbon's multiple drafts, but the surfacing of the original manuscripts in 1894 prompted subsequent editors to propose varying versions; in the most recent, Betty Radice's, some of Gibbon's most famous

lines are relegated to footnotes on the grounds that Sheffield had unjustifi-
ably extracted them from one manuscript fragment in order to insert them
into another.[5] Despite the disputed nature of the text, Gibbon's *Memoirs*
were quickly recognized as a great work of literature. Although Gibbon was
certainly not the first English autobiographer, his work inaugurated a new
era in English-language life writing. In Gibbon's pages, autobiography was
separated from religious confession and made into a purely secular enterprise—indeed, into an instrument for the discrediting of religion. Gibbon's
narrative of how through his own efforts he achieved professional success
and financial rewards made his story emblematic for the individualistic society emerging at the end of the eighteenth century. In contrast to Rousseau,
Gibbon demonstrated that an author could make readers feel as if they were
learning about his inner life even while he maintained a dignified reserve
about his personal feelings. Finally, Gibbon's magnificent prose showed
that autobiography could be high literature, taking its place alongside fiction, poetry, and history itself.

All of these qualities help explain why Gibbon's memoirs have come to
be regarded as a classic in the literature of autobiography, but what connection, if any, do they have with the fact that his story is that of a historian?
Gibbon certainly regarded his profession as the central aspect of his life. It
is true that the statement "From my early youth, I aspired to the character
of an historian," which Sheffield incorporated into the published text, is the
most emphatic of the accounts of the origin of his vocation found in his various drafts, but the story he tells bears out this claim: it is essentially the tale
of how he became the man who wrote *The Decline and Fall of the Roman
Empire* and how he accomplished that task.[6] Unlike many subsequent historians, Gibbon thus makes it clear that he regards the historian's life as an
entirely appropriate subject for narration; he is not in the least apologetic
about having chosen what many of his successors have seen as a limited
theme. What distinguishes Gibbon's memoir from all subsequent historians' autobiographies is the author's confidence in both the importance of
his accomplishments and the interest of his own life story; even critics who
have argued that Gibbon was not as sure of himself as his prose makes
it seem admit that the *Memoirs* cannot be read as "a study of doubt, like
The Education of Henry Adams."[7] Gibbon has no doubt that history is a
vital component of culture and that the *Decline and Fall of the Roman
Empire* represents an achievement of such importance that it justifies him
in putting forward the story of his own life. Gibbon compares himself

not to other historians but to his eminent forerunners in the autobiographical tradition—Pliny, Petrarch, Erasmus, Cellini, Augustine, Montaigne, Rousseau—and asserts, without fear of sounding ridiculous, "That I am the equal or superior of some of these Biographers the efforts of modesty or affectation cannot force me to dissemble."[8] He furthermore assumes that he, like they, will find readers, and for the same reason: "The public is always curious to *know* the men who have left behind them any image of their minds." Indeed, Gibbon speculates that his autobiography may still be read when the history writing that had justified it is forgotten. After all, the memoirs of the earlier authors he has listed are "often the most interesting, and sometimes, the only interesting, parts of their writings." History, he recognizes, is a progressive discipline: a later scholar may build on his accomplishments, as he has built on those of his predecessors. Autobiography, however, is a definitive achievement that no one else can improve on. "I must be conscious that no one is so well qualified as myself to describe the series of my thoughts and actions," Gibbon writes.[9]

Like many subsequent historian-autobiographers, Gibbon opens his memoir with a reflection on the relationship between the writing of history and the writing of autobiography. "In the fifty-second year of my age," he begins, "after the completion of a toilsome and successful work, I now propose to employ some moments of my leisure in reviewing the simple transactions of a private and literary life." Gibbon thus casts the privilege of writing autobiography as an indulgence that he has earned through his public accomplishments. Furthermore, his project, he promises, will truly be carried out for himself alone—"my own amusement is my motive and will be my reward"—and what he is writing "will be secreted from the public eye till the author shall be removed beyond the reach of criticism or ridicule." This emphatic declaration, from one of his early drafts, may not reflect Gibbon's final thoughts on the matter,[10] but his unanticipated death in 1794 settled the issue and put him in the company of most other autobiographers of his time, including Rousseau and Franklin. True, other autobiographers did publish during their own lifetime: the freed slave Gustavus Vassa (Olaudah Equiano) was touring the British Isles promoting his *Interesting Narrative* to great acclaim just when Gibbon was composing his memoirs. But Vassa's publication was explicitly intended to promote a cause—the abolition of slavery—whereas Gibbon wanted his work to appear as a disinterested gesture. Posthumous publication would not only safeguard him against any suspicion of self-promotion; it would also serve as a guarantee of his honesty. Once in the grave, the author could have no further motive to flatter his contemporaries or to withhold potentially discreditable facts about himself.

Gibbon's reference to "criticism or ridicule" reflects his recognition of another difference between his public historical writing and his private life writing. The *Decline and Fall* had necessarily been exposed to criticism; it could not have achieved its purpose if it had not provoked discussion. In the *Memoirs* he recounts his own vigorous polemics on behalf of that work. Clearly, however, he does not relish the prospect of his personal account's being subjected to the same potentially hostile reactions. He sees his memoirs as an extension of himself, and he recognizes that their publication will make both the book and the author fair game for critique. He therefore plans to absent himself from the scene before the book's appearance, leaving it to fend for itself, although he did attempt to ensure that it would get a good reception. He instructed his friend and literary executor Sheffield to keep the project secret: "People must not be prepared to laugh: they must be taken by surprise." [11]

Despite his desire to protect his personal history from the crossfire of criticism that his masterwork had inspired, Gibbon recognizes that his autobiographical project is not unrelated to history. In composing his personal narrative, he draws on lessons he has learned in his historical writing. "As a historian," Karl Weintraub has written, "Gibbon had acquired an expertly honed sensitivity for the dramatic quality of life, and for the fine interplay of an actor and his scene. He understood the rhythms that gave human life an appearance of a whole." [12] Gibbon also understood that, in some respects, his memoir would be judged by the same criterion as his history: "Truth, naked unblushing truth, the first virtue of more serious history, must be the sole recommendation of this personal narrative." Once readers had access to his personal story, Gibbon realized, they would judge the honesty of his historical writing according to that of his memoir and expect him to live up to the same standards in both. In order to produce this conviction of truth, however, the autobiography needed to be written in an appropriate manner, different from that of the *Decline and Fall*. The historian might convey his devotion to truth by a noble style, suitable to the gravity of his subject, and by writing prose whose difficulty might reflect both the complexity of the past and the additional complications introduced by the need to communicate both the truth about that past and the historian's judgments on it, but the autobiographer needed to speak directly and forthrightly. "The style shall be simple and familiar," Gibbon promises, adding that "style is the image of character."[13] While recognizing the connections between these two ways of telling true stories about the past, Gibbon also underlines their differences.

The challenge Gibbon faced was to make the story of a man who did little else beyond writing a history book into a dramatic and interesting one. Although he was confident that his personal story was worth recording, Gibbon recognized that many of the details of his life were not intrinsically of great interest. Unlike Henry Adams, who has been followed in this regard by most contemporary historians, he makes no effort to justify his account of them by presenting it as a contribution to the broader history of his time. He has little interest in recording the social and cultural atmosphere around him, which he takes essentially for granted. He makes no reflection on such differences as he might have noted between the time of his youth and the period in which he was writing, and gives no hint that he expects drastic changes in society in the future. Confident that European civilization is now safe against a repetition of the disasters that had undermined the Roman Empire, he acts as though there were really nothing of historical significance to be seen in the world he lives in.[14] One gleans very little from his pages that illuminates the history of Britain during the Seven Years' War and the American Revolution, no indication that the country was experiencing the early stages of what later historians would label the industrial and consumer revolutions, and not even much that could be used for a social history of the European Enlightenment. Gibbon wrote most of his memoir in Lausanne, close to the French border, during the early stages of the French Revolution, but his only comment on the event was the observation that the aristocratic emigrés from France flooding into Switzerland "are entitled to our pity, they may claim our esteem; but they cannot, in the present state of their mind and fortune, much contribute to our amusement." As a modern critic has put it, Gibbon's comment on the French Revolution seems less like that of a historian than of a grumpy pensioner.[15]

Gibbon's memoir is thus centered on his life, not his times, and above all on his one great accomplishment, the fact that he has written *The Decline and Fall* and has thereby given the world an account of the fall of Rome and the rise of Christianity that is unclouded by religious prejudice and dictated only by reason. The incidents of his personal life have general significance only because they help readers to understand how he came to be the person capable of that achievement. Thus his service as captain in the militia during the Seven Years' War was trivial in itself: his unit never saw action, and he spent his time in meaningless marching about in the English countryside. "The reader may smile," Gibbon allows, at the idea that this experience had any importance, but in fact "the Captain of the Hampshire grenadiers . . . has not been useless to the historian of the Roman Empire" (*Memoirs*, 117). A master of understatement, Gibbon leaves it to his readers to determine exactly what he thinks he had learned, but the potential lessons were many. He had observed the conduct of men under arms, learned something of the relationship between commanders and common soldiers, experienced fatigue at the end of a long day's march, and perhaps intuited something of the irrationality of war, the way great effort can be expended without producing any result. He is similarly laconic about the value of his service in the British Parliament, where he spent eight years as a silent backbencher. He appreciated having had "a near prospect of the characters, views, and passions, of the first men of the age. The eight sessions that I sat in Parliament were a school of civil prudence, the first and most essential virtue of an historian." Again, he omits specifics, but one can presume that he came away with a feeling for the dynamics of assemblies, the play of faction, the effect of oratory (156).

Like all historian-autobiographers, Gibbon needs to account for his vocation. "I *know* by experience that from my early youth, I aspired to the character of an historian," he writes (119). The difficulty is, as many other historian-autobiographers have found, that he cannot give any precise explanation of why he had chosen that particular sphere of intellectual activity over others. He had had a precocious interest in the subject as a child, but he had also read many other forms of literature. Like most historian-autobiographers, he doesn't see his formal schooling as having contributed much to his interest in the subject. "A school is the cavern of fear and sorrow: the mobility of the captive youths is chained to a book and a desk," he pronounces (44). As was common in the eighteenth century, he went to Oxford as a young teenager, but his time there was "the most idle and unprofitable of my whole life" (48). There followed an interlude that was of great importance for the shaping of his character but of less obvious significance in determining his career: his conversion to Catholicism, which led his father to dispatch him to Switzerland for what would now be called deprogramming, and his infatuation with and renunciation of Suzanne Curchod, the future mother of Madame de Staël. The adult Gibbon, the notorious opponent of Christianity, is unapologetic about his youthful religious adventure, which critics tried to use to discredit him. He understands that readers can comprehend the development of his personality only if he and they take his youthful beliefs seriously. In his view, what is significant is not that he had erred, since he has long since renounced Catholicism, but that he had acted out of creditable motives. "I can never blush if my tender mind was entangled in the sophistry that seduced the acute and manly understandings of Chillingworth and Bayle, who afterwards emerged from superstition to scepticism," he writes (62). Like his susceptibility to religion, his abortive love affair also shows that he shares much with the rest of humanity. Gibbon recognizes that "the first consciousness of manhood is a very interesting moment of our lives: but it less properly belongs to the memoirs of an individual, than to the natural history of the species." He conceals his personal feelings behind the famous words "I sighed as a lover; I obeyed as a son" (84).

Gibbon thus returned to England after his four years on the Continent, inoculated against both religious and sexual passion and ready to take up his destiny as a man of letters. He now began seriously contemplating what it would mean to be a historian. In his day, there was no professional community that neophytes entered by a formalized process, but there were role models he could follow. William Robertson and David Hume in particular had recently demonstrated that British authors could succeed in this genre. "The perfect composition, the nervous language, the well-turned periods of Dr. Robertson inflamed me to the ambitious hope, that I might one day tread in his footsteps: the calm philosophy, the careless inimitable beauties of his friend and rival often forced me to close the volume, with a mixed sensation of delight and despair," Gibbon recalls (99). In thus showing himself as a youth measuring how far he had to go to equal the recognized masters of history, he injects an element of tension into his narrative— would he be up to the challenge?—and conveys to readers the magnitude of the quest he was undertaking. Before he could fulfill his ambition and test himself against these established figures, though, he had to find a topic and establish himself in appropriate circumstances. He pursued unsatisfactory ideas for some time, such as a project on the history of the Swiss federation. When he received severe criticism of his efforts at a public reading, however, Gibbon abandoned the whole undertaking and "delivered my imperfect sheets to the flames" (142). Painful to read for any historian, this passage allows Gibbon to demonstrate his devotion to the highest standards of the discipline; like the earlier pages on his youthful religious misadventures, it also humanizes the author, showing that he is capable of blunders and misjudgments.

In the Sheffield version of Gibbon's memoirs, the conception and abandonment of Gibbon's Swiss project come after the description of the visit to

Rome that planted the germ of his great project. Biographical research has shown that the famous description of his moment of inspiration on "the fifteenth of October 1764, in the close of evening, as I sat musing in the Church of the Zoccolanti or Franciscan fryars, while they were singing Vespers in the Temple of Jupiter on the ruins of the Capitol" (136), the most familiar passage from his memoirs and the one most often cited by other historians, is not the whole truth: Gibbon had already been contemplating a Roman topic even before this date. But the scene he constructs brilliantly captures the meaning of what he then set out to do. Readers of the memoirs can see how strongly Gibbon was struck by the spectacle of one civilization's having replaced another, and indeed of having replaced it with antithetical values. At the same time, however, his phrasing implies a comparative evaluation of the two civilizations: the dead world of antiquity still towered over its Christian successor, which remained unable—in Gibbon's view, at least—of constructing anything as grandiose as the ruins it had converted to its own purposes. Finally, Gibbon's passage conveys a sense of the connection between past and present: the ruins of Rome had the power to affect living people, as his example shows. His way of narrating the experience allows the thoughtful reader to grasp in a few lines the significance of the project Gibbon had chosen to undertake. It also demonstrates that a work of history, such as the *Decline and Fall,* can itself be regarded as an entity with a history, one whose beginnings can be located specifically in time and place and whose development can then be followed.

Having thus described in memorable terms the discovery of his great theme, Gibbon turns to an account of how he carried out his project. There was first the matter of establishing a situation in life that would make the writing of a work of history possible. For modern historians, this usually means finding a teaching job, but Gibbon lived in a different age. His father's death gave him an independent income sufficient to live on, but not so large as to deprive him of the spur to achievement. He had also been able to accumulate an adequate library. Gibbon's reflection that "in circumstances more indigent or more wealthy, I should never have accomplished the task, or acquired the fame, of an historian" speaks to the conditions of his own time, but it highlights a truth that still applies today: the long investment of time that historical research requires makes it imperative that the scholar have a dependable source of income and a certain amount of autonomy, whereas the industriousness the profession demands makes it an unlikely vocation for the genuinely rich. As Gibbon puts it, "Few works of merit and importance have been executed either in a garret or a palace." To be sure, many modern academic historians might envy Gibbon's definition of a modest sufficiency: "a convenient well-furnished house, a domestic table, half a dozen chosen servants, my own carriage, and all those decent luxuries whose value is the more sensibly felt the longer they are enjoyed" (153–54). The definition of the "solid comforts" necessary for the successful pursuit of history has changed, but Gibbon's memoir accurately situates it as a form of creative activity that can be carried out only by those who enjoy the right circumstances.

Gibbon then tells his readers how he gradually assembled the necessary materials for his history, put it into writing, saw it through the press, and ensured its success. The problem of making a good story out of the process of historical research bedevils historians' life writing: long days spent sitting in archives and libraries do not have the allure of fieldwork in exotic anthropological locales or of sudden illuminations in the laboratory. Gibbon resolves this difficulty by taking advantage of the autobiographer's liberty in choosing arresting images and flexibility in representing the flow of time. He condenses years of reading and study into one magnificent paragraph, in which the reader follows him as he "plunged into the ocean of the Augustan History . . . , investigated, with my pen almost always in my hand, the original records," made his way "through the darkness of the Middle Ages," learned to direct "the subsidiary rays of medals and inscriptions, of geography and chronology . . . on their proper objects . . . , weighed the causes and effects of the revolution" represented by Christianity, and "privately drew my conclusions from the silence of an unbelieving age" (146–47). The compression of Gibbon's description turns his long efforts into a dramatic adventure while dazzling readers with the range of his erudition; his geographic metaphors—the references to oceans and explorations—put him and his discipline of history on a level with the celebrated enterprises of the intrepid voyagers of the eighteenth century, such as James Cook and the Comte de La Pérouse.

The struggle to find the right form and tone for his book was, Gibbon insists, an arduous one, as difficult and heroic as the research. Once again, Gibbon as autobiographer faces the challenge of drawing readers into the details of a process whose externals seem of little interest, and once again he finds language that casts the work of historical authorship as a genuine creative struggle and a true test of character. "At the outset all was dark and doubtful: even the title of the work, the true era of the Decline and Fall of the Empire, the limits of the introduction, the division of the chapters, and the order of the narrative; and I was often tempted to cast away the labour of seven years." Only by dint of repeated and frustrating experiments did he find "the middle tone between a dull chronicle and a rhetorical declamation." Friends were of little help: "Some will praise from politeness, and some will criticize from vanity. The author himself is the best Judge of his own performance: none has so deeply meditated on the subject, none is so sincerely interested in the event" (156).

Unlike most contemporary academic historians, Gibbon was as involved in the details of the publication of his work as in its research and writing. He was still a virtual unknown in 1775, when the first volume went to press, and the first publisher he approached declined "the perilous adventure." He eventually found a bookseller and printer willing to take on the project, in which he actively cooperated by correcting the proofs. Even though their sales projections were modest, Gibbon claims he had no doubt of the work's success. He was confident of the quality of his work, and he was also certain of his market. "History is the most popular species of writing, since it can adapt itself to the highest or the lowest capacity. I had chosen an illustrious subject; Rome is familiar to the schoolboy and the statesman. . . . I had likewise flattered myself that an age of light and liberty would receive without scandal an enquiry into the *human* causes of the progress and establishment of Christianity." In another expression of the confidence that characterizes his autobiographical narrative, he openly celebrates the book's success: "My book was on every table, and almost on every toilette; the historian was crowned by the taste or fashion of the day; nor was the general voice disturbed by the barking of any *profane* critic." Gibbon "listened to the music of praise," but he was especially gratified by the favorable reception of his peers, Robertson and Hume, even though he claims that "I have never presumed to accept a place in the triumvirate of British historians" (157–58).

With the triumphant success of his first volume, Gibbon reaches the climax of his narrative. "I was now master of my style and subject," he writes: his inner development as scholar and writer was complete, and the acclaim he received from readers and professional colleagues showed that there was no difference between his own estimation of himself and that of the public. Like many future historian-autobiographers, Gibbon underlines his new standing by recounting a foreign trip on which he was feted by important people—in his case, a visit to Paris at the invitation of his youthful *inamorata* Suzanne Curchod, now the wife of Jacques Necker, director general of the French monarchy's finances. Invited to salons, he met the celebrities of French letters as an equal. There was the matter of the "clamorous and bitter" reactions of the English clergy, which eventually drove him to compose a *Vindication,* "expressive of less anger than contempt." In retrospect, Gibbon admits that if he had foreseen the controversy his discussion of Christianity would cause, he "might, perhaps, have softened the two invidious chapters." He had initially been apprehensive about the intensity of the attacks on him, but "my fear was converted to indignation; and every feeling of indignation or curiosity has long since subsided in pure and placid indifference" (159–60). By the time he writes these words, Gibbon has completed his great work, and he can afford to dismiss his critics, even as he acknowledges that he had been unnecessarily provocative.

As Gibbon himself recognizes, his life after the appearance of the first volume of his history is a story of a relative decline, if not a fall. As the successive volumes appeared, he found that "an author who cannot ascend will always appear to sink" (161). He expatriated himself to Lausanne in 1783 to write the rest of the *Decline and Fall,* which was finished in 1787. Better perhaps than any subsequent historian-memoirist, Gibbon sums up the mixed feelings that this achievement inspired: "I will not dissemble the first emotions of my joy on the recovery of my freedom and perhaps the establishment of my fame. But my pride was soon humbled, and a sober melancholy was spread over my mind by the idea that I had taken my everlasting leave of an old and agreeable companion" (180). Like many historical projects, the *Decline and Fall* had gone on too long for its author: the mood of high adventure evoked in his earlier description of the research had long since worn off, and he had had to wait too long for the definitive consecration of his reputation that could come only from its completion. But he also realized that the project had given meaning to his life, and its completion left a void that would never really be filled.

The *Memoirs* themselves became Gibbon's substitute for the now-completed *Decline and Fall.* Gibbon had become so completely identified with his project that the thought of undertaking another major work of history does not seem to have occurred to him. As we have seen, he claims to see in his autobiographical enterprise a challenge as worthy as that of his longer work. He devoted the same thought and concern to its contents and its style as he had to his masterpiece, and as noted earlier, he accurately forecast that it might continue to find readers even after his Roman history had faded from view. He was, of course, still trying to find the appropriate form for his life story when death interrupted him. Commentators such as Patricia Meyer Spacks, W. B. Carnochan, and David Womersley have traced the development of Gibbon's self-portrait as he chose between various ways of presenting his career; he was clearly conscious "that autobiography . . . allows many ways of telling a story," as Spacks has put it.[16] In any event, however, he realized that the satisfactions involved in writing a memoir would be very different from those produced by the writing of a work of history. He would not be around to enjoy its reception or to defend it from potential critics, although he anticipated only too well what they would say: that he had been vain, inconsistent, and, as in his renunciation of Suzanne Curchod, perhaps even cowardly. Writing the *Decline and Fall* had been a way of achieving a balance between Gibbon's needs to satisfy his own inner ambitions and to obtain the public recognition that validated those objectives; writing the *Memoirs* was a more one-sided project, in which Gibbon had to imagine the public response he longed for.

Read from a modern historian's perspective, Gibbon's *Memoirs* seem at once remarkably contemporary and strangely distant. Gibbon's description of the satisfaction that commitment to understanding the past and making it comprehensible to others can give still speaks to his professional colleagues. Although few contemporary historians have been bold enough to take on a topic of the scale of the *Decline and Fall of the Roman Empire,* we still treasure those moments when, like Gibbon sitting on the steps of his Roman church, we suddenly grasp the outlines of a story that presents a worthy challenge. Gibbon's self-dramatizing description of the research process casts historical work the way we like to imagine it: as a heroic endeavor, requiring courage, imagination, persistence, and resourcefulness. Gibbon thus created a representation of the history-writer's life that makes it seem well worth living and that captures some of the profession's enduring characteristics. On the other hand, much in Gibbon's narrative now seems to reflect a bygone era. Gibbon lived at a time before history had become an academic discipline. He made his career as an independent man of letters, and many of the issues that preoccupy almost all his present-day successors—the choice of an institution for academic training, the search for a teaching post, relations with colleagues—played no part in his career. One can hardly imagine Gibbon in a department meeting. He was also never a teacher and so had no contact with an aspect of life as a historian that looms large in most historians' careers, if not always in their personal accounts. Gibbon's life as a historian was divided between the public and the purely personal, the two levels of experience that define the accepted content of memoirs and autobiography respectively; the middle zone of shared professional concerns that absorbs much of the energy of his successors but often seems terribly difficult to write about hardly existed for him.

Gibbon's memoirs are also hard to emulate because the civilization in which he lived differs much from that of today. No contemporary historian is likely to share, or at least admit to sharing, Gibbon's confidence that his historical work had put him in the pantheon of civilization's immortals. Gibbon perceived himself as a creator erecting an edifice that would stand out alone against the sky; today's historians are like architects who have to fit their constructions into an overcrowded city where it seems impossible to find a site not already overshadowed by other buildings. Gibbon's confidence in the uniqueness and importance of his work was linked to his equally unmodern assumption that the civilization of which he was a part was not itself subject to the same processes of historical transformation that he had dissected so skillfully in his treatment of Rome. Brilliant though he was as a historical thinker, he had not fully accepted the notion that all human experience is necessarily time-bound and that both the *Decline and Fall* and his memoirs would come to seem dated from the perspective of later generations. Finally, we are separated from Gibbon's memoir by the very excellence of its style. Gibbon lived before the nineteenth-century attempt to convert history into a science, as opposed to an art. His faith in history as literature and his conviction that the search for an appropriate style was as important a part of both the making of history and the making of autobiography as the search for accurate information clash with modern assumptions about the narration of the past and with modern notions about the impossibility of defining absolute rules for artistic endeavors. With rare exceptions, contemporary historians and historian-autobiographers keep their literary ambitions modest and are anxious not to be compared with novelists or other literary creators, and certainly not with Gibbon himself.

"THE THOUGHT OF POSING FOR A GIBBON NEVER ENTERED HIS MIND": HENRY ADAMS AND GIBBON'S LEGACY

One historian-autobiographer who did not shy away from putting himself in comparison with Edward Gibbon and his *Memoirs* was Henry Adams. Even though he asserts that "the thought of posing for a Gibbon never entered his mind," he was led, according to his own story, "more than once to sit at sunset on the steps of the Church of Santa Maria di Ara Coeli," the place where Gibbon claimed that the idea for *The Decline and Fall of the Roman Empire* had first come to him.[17] The importance accorded to Gibbon's *Memoirs* in Adams's *Education* is not merely a literary device: In a letter written to his older brother during his first visit to Rome, Adams had already credited Gibbon with inspiring his vocation. "I read Gibbon. Striking, very," the twenty-five-year-old Adams reported. "Do you know, after long argument and reflexion I feel much as if perhaps some day I too might come to anchor like that. Our house needs a historian in this generation and I feel strongly tempted by the quiet and sunny prospect, while my ambition for political life dwindles as I get older." A few months later, he assured his brother that he was making efficient use of his time in Europe, "following Gibbon's plan, which you will remember having read in his biography." Almost three decades later, when he finished writing his own great historical work, *The History of the United States during the Administrations of Jefferson and Madison,* Adams once again identified himself with the author of the *Memoirs,* telling his friend John Hay, "In imitation of Gibbon I walked in the garden among the yellow and red autumn flowers, blazing in sunshine, and meditated." Adams's next sentence, however, foreshadows the conflictual relationship his own autobiography would have with his predecessor's. "My meditations were too painful to last," he tells Hay, referring to the memories of his dead wife that the completion of a project in which she had been much involved evoked.[18] *The Education of Henry Adams* would be, among other things, a deconstruction of Gibbon's optimistic life story by a historian who had found that the Gibbonian model did not work for him.

In the *Education,* Adams turns the identification with Gibbon implied by his repeated visits to the famous Roman steps into a way of contesting Gibbon's history and his autobiography. Adams's musings in that consecrated spot led him to conclude that "not an inch had been gained by Gibbon—or all the historians since—towards explaining the Fall" (91). Indeed, the story Gibbon had narrated, the decline and fall of the ancient world's most advanced civilization, strikes Adams as a fundamental stumbling block to the identification of any meaningful pattern in human history: if Rome had been so advanced, how could it have disintegrated, forcing humanity to work painfully for a millenium to regain the ground it had lost? For Adams, this "scandalous failure of civilization at the moment it had achieved complete success" defies explanation (477). "The man who should solve the riddle of the Middle Ages and bring them into the line of evolution from past to present, would be a greater man than Lamarck or Linnaeus; but history had nowhere broken down so pitiably, or avowed itself so hopelessly bankrupt, as there" (301). Furthermore, the epoch Adams had come to identify with most strongly by the time he wrote his *Education* was the very age Gibbon had rejected: the Christian Middle Ages. Adams comments slyly that surely a man as intelligent as Gibbon could not have meant to denigrate the great accomplishments of that period, such as the

Gothic cathedrals, in the way he did: Gibbon must have "felt in fact the respect which every man of his vast study and active mind always feels before objects worthy of it," and the disrespectful remarks he made about the "'stately monuments of superstition'" could not have expressed his real sentiments (386). *The Education of Henry Adams* can thus be read as an argument against Gibbon's confident way of binding life, history, and autobiography together. Adams's own personal account exposes two scandals: the scandal of historians' inability to explain the fall of Rome and the scandal of Gibbon's claim that an individual human life can honestly be presented as a story of positive accomplishment.

Whereas Gibbon had narrated his life as a success story, Henry Adams chooses to present his life as a succession of failures. He presents his education as a story of decline and fall: of how the great-grandson and grandson of American presidents had ended up living a life of insignificance and of how the heroic republic of his forefathers had become the decadent world of the Gilded Age. He does not even claim the compensating success of having achieved from these experiences any special insight into the meaning either of history or of individual destiny. The theme of the *Education,* constantly repeated, is incomprehension: "Education became more perplexing at every phase" (266). The emphasis on failure is, to be sure, something of a pose. If he had never occupied public office, unlike the three generations of Adamses before him, Henry Adams had nevertheless been close to many who had held power and had exercised his share of influence behind the scenes. He had traveled widely and lived a life of material ease. He had known some success as a journalist and as a professor, and above all he had come to be regarded in his own lifetime as "the foremost of our historical writers," as the founding editor of the *American Historical Review* called him.[19] His multivolume *History of the United States of America during the Administrations of Jefferson and Madison,* on which he had labored almost as long as had Gibbon on the *Decline and Fall,* still commands the respect of scholars more than a century after its publication. In writing about himself, however, Adams is not interested in drawing up a carefully documented balance sheet. He chooses instead to use his life story to dramatize a larger theme: the way history, during his lifetime, had increasingly spun out of control, taking with it humankind's pretensions to understand its own nature. He understands that presenting his life as a failure when many readers might have taken it as something of a success has a shock value that serves his purposes.

The Education of Henry Adams is a considerably more complex text than

Gibbon's *Memoirs,* and it has evoked a much more contradictory body of commentary and criticism.[20] Whereas Gibbon sticks fairly closely to the story of his education and his life as a historian, Adams ranges more widely, as befits a man who had tried a number of careers and visited much of the globe. Gibbon makes no pretense of recounting his times along with his life; Adams illustrates the richness of the education from which he has failed to profit by depicting London during the struggle over Britain's possible intervention in the American Civil War, Washington under the Grant administration, and the world at the dawn of the twentieth century, so much so that critics of the *Education* have complained of the "sheer weight of its historical detail."[21] Gibbon says little about the people he encountered during his life; Adams's book is an immense portrait gallery, filled with vivid recollections of his famous family, his friends, and the varied celebrities whose paths he had crossed. The variety of its content is not the only reason for the book's difficulty, however. It is written on multiple levels, combining personal narrative, the portrait of an era, and an argument about the philosophy of history. Above all, *The Education of Henry Adams* is hard to interpret because of the ironic stance from which it is written. By styling himself as a "manikin," an artificial device "on which the toilet of education is to be draped in order to show the fit or misfit of the clothes," and by writing about himself in the third person, as if the narrator had observed Henry Adams's life from some outside vantage point, Adams warns readers that while the book may follow the sequence of its author's life, it will not be held together by the unity of its author's inner self. Adams insists that he is opaque even to himself, a multiplicity or chaos of conflicting personalities.

In addition to the complexities of its content and tone, the reading of *The Education* is made difficult because of what it leaves out. Halfway through Adams's story, the continuity of the narrative is interrupted by the famous gap between chapter 20, which details his experiences as a professor at Harvard in the early 1870s, and chapter 21, "Twenty Years After," which jumps, with no explanation, to the year 1892. The twenty-year gap notoriously swallows up the entire span of Adams's courtship and marriage to Marian "Clover" Hooper, her suicide in 1885, and its devastating effect on him. Adams's autobiography thus omits any mention of the most important person in his adult life and of the tragedy that deepened the dour, pessimistic outlook that characterizes much of the *Education.* For all the abundance of detail about other aspects of Adams's life, most readers sense that it deliberately withholds information that is absolutely critical to an understanding of who he was and to any serious comprehension of his life.

Less often mentioned than the omission of his marriage is the fact that the twenty-year gap in the *Education* also effaces the years of Adams's activity as a scholar of history. Adams's correspondence documents the energy he poured into the research and writing of his *History,* begun during the happy years of his life with Clover and finished in the bleak period after her death, but the only reference to the project in the *Education* reflects a sense of disillusionment. With publication of *History,* Adams writes, he and his friend John Hay, author of a multivolume life of Lincoln, had "written nearly all the American history there was to write. . . . Both were heartily tired of the subject, and America seemed as tired as they" (325). Adams imitates Gibbon in providing a frank assessment of his work's commercial success, but his report is very different from his predecessor's. He "had given ten or a dozen years to Jefferson and Madison, with expenses which, in any mercantile business, could hardly have been reckoned at less than a hundred thousand dollars, on a salary of five thousand a year; and when asked what return he got from this expenditure, rather more extravagant in proportion to his means than a racing-stable, he could see none whatever. . . . As far as Adams knew, he had but three serious readers" (327). Adams's commitment to history becomes just one more example of his isolation from his countrymen: how could he have expected them to pay attention to his work when the country "stood alone in history for its ignorance of the past" (328)?

But it was not his countrymen alone who rejected Adams's history: he himself concludes that all his efforts have served only to demonstrate the worthlessness of historical research. "He had published a dozen volumes of American history for no other purpose than to satisfy himself whether, by the severest process of stating, with the least possible comment, such facts as seemed sure, in such order as seemed rigorously consequent, he could fix for a familiar moment a necessary sequence of human movement," but nothing had come of the effort. He had not convinced other historians: "Where he saw sequence, other men saw something quite different, and no one saw the same unit of measure." In the end, he concluded "that the sequence of men led to nothing and that the sequence of their society could lead no further, while the mere sequence of time was artificial, and the sequence of thought was chaos" (382). History itself, as a method of understanding human experience, was a failure. Although Adams does not expunge his historical work from his narrative as totally as he does the story of his marriage, his dismissive comments about the the discipline and his own accomplishments in it, like his silence about Clover, significantly distort our understanding of his life and especially of his engagement with the project of reconstructing the past.

Adams's negative assessment of his own achievements as a historian betrays his conflicting feelings about his vocation. Like Gibbon, Adams admits that he was attracted to history at an early age, but unlike Gibbon, he is not sure that this has been a good thing. Like most historians, Adams recalls a childhood in which reading was encouraged. His father read aloud to his children, and they discovered on their own novelists like Dickens and Thackeray, both too modern for their parents. "The boy Henry soon became a desultory reader of every book he found readable, but these were commonly eighteenth-century historians because his father's library was full of them. In the want of positive instincts, he drifted into the mental indolence of history," Adams reports. He thus represents his inclination for history as the result of a lack of energy and proper guidance. Like his preference for the simplicities of eighteenth-century poetry over the greater complexities of Wordsworth, it was also a warning sign of his tendency to escape into the past rather than embracing his own century (36).

It is true that Adams does devote an entire chapter, one that some critics have judged to be the very center of the *Education*, to another aspect of his personal engagement with history, his years as a professor at Harvard in the 1870s. Unlike Gibbon, and like most subsequent historian-autobiographers, he had been for at least one important part of his life a teacher as well as a scholar and author. Several modern historian-autobiographers have cited as a source of inspiration the most famous line from this chapter, "A teacher affects eternity; he can never tell where his influence stops," but those who take comfort in that thought rarely remark that it comes from a chapter entitled "Failure" and that that chapter ends the first half of the *Education*, bringing its protagonist to a complete impasse in his existence. Adams does take some pleasure in recalling a few outstanding students, but the general tone of his account is of a piece with the majority of the *Education*. "He was content neither with what he had taught nor with the way he had taught it. The seven years he passed in teaching seemed to him lost." The difficulty was that teaching required him to find some order and meaning in his material, and he had convinced himself that there was none. "In essence incoherent and immoral, history had either to be taught as such—or falsified," Adams concludes. He "wanted to do neither. He had no theory of evolution to teach, and could not make the facts fit one." The company of his fellow professors was no resource for dealing with this intellectual crisis. Adams's memory is that "the lecture-room was futile enough, but the faculty-room was worse. . . . Several score of the best-educated, most agreeable, and personally the most sociable people in America united in Cambridge to make a social desert that would have starved a polar bear." Adams's account, the one unquestioned classic of autobiography by an American professor of history, hardly provides any encouragement for future readers who would follow him in that career (300, 304, 307).

The Education of Henry Adams thus stands at the opposite extreme from Gibbon's *Memoirs* in the way it depicts the historian's life. Adams found satisfaction neither in the writing of history nor in its teaching, and his repetition of the act that in Gibbon's account had generated the inspiration for a great work of history proved futile—indeed, Adams strongly hints that Gibbon's insight was really a delusion. If this negative portrayal of the historian's life were the sum of Adams's message, the *Education* would stand out among historians' autobiographies primarily for the quality of its dyspepsia. Most historians—and most of those who follow other careers as well—have no doubt experienced moments in which years invested in scholarship and teaching suddenly seem futile. Adams's achievement was to invest what most other autobiographers would see as the view from the trough of despond with metaphysical significance. But he also did something else: he seized on the frustrations of his own life as the stuff out of which a different kind of historical revelation could be extracted. What has attracted more recent historians to Adams's text is his success in conveying the complexities of living in the midst of history in the making, and the case he makes for the value of a historian's life story as a kind of measuring stick or test probe for the understanding of his own times. Even as he makes the profession of historian sound utterly demoralizing, Adams paradoxically exalts the power of the historical imagination.

Gibbon, as we have seen, had used his life story to demonstrate that the historian's personal experiences can help broaden his understanding of the past. Like Gibbon in his militia unit and in Parliament, Henry Adams had at times in his life been close enough to great events to have achieved some insight into how history is made. He had, most significantly, served as secretary in the U.S. Embassy in London during the Civil War, when his father, Charles Francis Adams, was the ambassador, charged with keeping the British from intervening in favor of the Confederacy. Later, he had been a privileged observer of politics during the Grant administration and then the special confidant of Theodore Roosevelt's secretary of state, his friend and next-door neighbor John Hay. Whereas Gibbon limited his consideration to the question of how activity in the present could aid the historian in judging the people of the past, Adams uses his experiences as participant-observer to tackle the larger question of what such experience teaches about the ability of those who live in the midst of events to understand what they are seeing. As Paul John Eakin puts it, Adams asks the question "What does it mean to live one's life in history?" As Eakin notes, "Even to ask such a question is to suggest the comparative novelty of the kind of autobiography that seeks to answer it."[22]

Adams's ability to communicate this sense of the interconnection between life and historical circumstances is demonstrated as early as the opening pages of the *Education*. Gibbon had begun his *Memoirs* with some pages about his family's ancestry, but he did not, like Adams, show how this particular ancestry had rendered him "distinctly branded," as Adams does in the celebrated lines in which he compares being born into nineteenth-century America's most famous political dynasty with being "born in Jerusalem under the shadow of the Temple and circumcised in the Synagogue by his uncle the high priest" (3). Through the contrast he draws between the two locations where he spent his childhood, the small town of Quincy and the bustling metropolis of Boston, Adams also underlines the conflict between the austere eighteenth-century spirit of his paternal ancestors, John and John Quincy Adams, and the more forward-looking and commercial nineteenth-century spirit of his mother's Boston family. "From earliest childhood the boy was accustomed to feel that, for him, life was double," Adams writes: as a result of his continuing loyalty to the Enlightenment moralism of the family tradition, he would never be comfortable with the spirit of his own day (9).

For the mature Adams, this is not a contrast between right and wrong. When he describes his first visit to Washington, he recalls how strongly he reacted against the phenomenon of slavery, the antithesis of his family's values, "a horror; a crime; the sum of all wickedness!" (44). But at the same time he was drawn to the more relaxed atmosphere of southern life: "Though Washington belonged to a different world, and the two worlds could not live together, he was not sure that he enjoyed the Boston world the most" (45). Adams's account of his youth thus evokes the contradictory impulses generated in him by the experience of growing up in his particular family and in the special circumstances of pre–Civil War America.

As he entered adulthood, Adams portrays himself not just as the product of conflicting historical forces but also as a would-be participant in the making of history. A young man who, on the occasion of his first visit to the White House, "half thought he owned it, and took for granted that he should some day live in it," could hardly resign himself to a purely private life (46). The most dramatic episode in which Adams was directly involved took place in London during the Civil War, where he served as secretary to his father, the American ambassador. Father and son had a critical task to accomplish: if the British had chosen to support the South, as they seemed inclined to do in the war's early years, the outcome of the conflict could very well have been changed. In the event, the two Adamses helped keep Her Majesty's government from recognizing the Confederacy, but what strikes Adams most in retrospect is how little their success had had to do with any real understanding of the personalities and political forces they were engaged with. The subsequent publication of British politicians' papers and memoirs had shown, he maintains, how little he and the other Americans in London had understood of the motives driving British policy: "They made a picture different from anything he had conceived and rendered worthless his whole painful diplomatic experience" (178). From this experience, Adams concludes that firsthand acquaintance with those who make history is no guarantee of understanding: leading British figures had misled him, and he had been completely unaware of his ignorance. The point is not just that the callow young secretary had been a poor judge of human beings—his more experienced father had done no better—but that all history is made this way. Adams has learned at first hand, and communicates through his autobiography, how different history in the making is from what gets written in history books, and how confusing it is for its participants. His analysis of the disjuncture between the participant's viewpoint and that of the retrospective observer embodies an insight that has struck most subsequent historian-autobiographers and creates one of the strongest links between *The Education of Henry Adams* and less exalted examples of the genre. In particular, Adams's disabused depiction of war and diplomacy is echoed in most of the numerous American historians' memoirs dealing with World War II.

Another crucial contribution that Adams made to the tradition of historically informed autobiography was his demonstration of how the historian could use the story of his own life as a way of defining the characteristics of his age and contrasting them with other periods. As a number of scholars have noted, Adams poses himself as a representative American, incorporating in his own person the conflicting traditions of Quincy and Boston, of North, through his Adams lineage, and South, via the grandmother who had made his father Charles Francis "half Marylander by birth" (19). Like the country at large, he lived through the transformations that changed it from the provincial farming and trading republic of his youth to the great industrial power on the threshold of world domination that he describes in his final chapters. But Adams's ambition went beyond using his story to communicate the historical experience of nineteenth-century America. The inspiration for the *Education* had come to him, Adams claims, as he was completing his study of the development of high medieval culture, a book that can be taken in some ways as an attempt to refute Gibbon's thesis about the baleful effects of Christianity. *Mont-Saint-Michel and Chartres* describes "the point in history when man held the highest idea of himself as a unit in a unified universe." To measure the distance humankind had traveled from the Middle Ages to the present, Adams "proposed to fix a position for himself, which he could label: *The Education of Henry Adams: A Study of Twentieth-Century Multiplicity*" (434–35). Thus Adams's personal narrative would function not just as a microhistorical window into the particular events of his time but as a definition of the very nature of modernity. Born, as he liked to claim, into what was still essentially an eighteenth-century world "when God was a father and nature a mother, and all was for the best in a scientific universe" (458), Adams had lived long enough to witness the advent of "a new world which would not be a unity but a multiple" (457). His personal story would demonstrate this fact just as his study of the medieval world had shown what a unified society looked like.

This is then the historical lesson that *The Education of Henry Adams* teaches, as the narrative follows the process of education that forced its protagonist to realize that the eighteenth-century moral certainties with which he had been brought up, and such nineteenth-century substitutes for them as the belief in progress, could not make sense of the real world of modernity. The institutions of American government, so carefully worked out by the Founding Fathers, had produced the mindless corruption of the Gilded Age: "The progress of evolution from President Washington to President Grant, was alone evidence enough to upset Darwin" (266). The horrific death of his beloved sister Louisa from tetanus, which Adams saw as an unanswerable argument against the notion of a loving God concerned with humanity, and Adams's contemplation of the "chaos of anarchic and purposeless forces" revealed by the jagged peaks of the Alps, which convinced him that there was no underlying order to nature, complete his case against the comforting certainties of nineteenth-century thought (288–89). New scientific discoveries undermined any confidence that humanity was coming closer to understanding the physical world, and psychology was destroying the notion of the unified human personality (397, 433). The personal experiences of Henry Adams, as recounted in *The Education,* thus add up to a comprehensive portrait of the intellectual uncertainty of his age and make clear the enormous gap between a civilization like that which Adams imagined had existed in the age of the cathedrals and that to which he himself belonged.

For most historians, Adams's success in conveying the experience of "living in history" and his use of his personal experiences to embody the characteristics of his historical period are the most convincing aspects of *The Education* and the ones that have most inspired emulation. For Adams himself, however, both his rejection of the satisfactions of the historian's life and his depiction of existence in a world without unity are, above all, stepping stones toward the final move in his narrative, the presentation of his "dynamic theory of history." "Progress," he announced, is not a moral or rational process but rather "the development and economy of Forces." Adams's apocalyptic vision of the accelerating pace of technological development, inspired by his contemplation of the giant electrical dynamos exhibited at the Paris World's Fair of 1900, has as much resonance a hundred years later as it did when he wrote it, although few readers today can accept his conviction that he had discovered the key to a physics or science of history. In these concluding chapters, Adams does after all recast his life as a kind of success rather than a failure: if he had never occupied a position of influence or written anything of value, he has nevertheless in the end succeeded in formulating a comprehensive explanation of the world and of history, and he has overcome the impasse in which Gibbon had foundered, to which he specifically refers in the course of laying out his theory (477). Among other things, the great crescendo of the closing chapters of the *Education* thus concludes the book's long argument with Adams's predecessor as historian-autobiographer by claiming that it is Gibbon who was the true failure, Adams the genuine success.

Gibbon's and Henry Adams's autobiographies thus define two limiting positions between which most contemporary historians' memoirs find their place. Between the two of them, they also cataloged the issues that still preoccupy historians who choose to write about their own life and times. Gibbon, writing before history had become irremediably "multiple" and too complex for any single scholar to master, takes his accomplishment as a historian as sufficient justification for the relation of his own life. His confident assertion of his own monumental status clearly stamps him as a figure from another age. On the other hand, he takes his work as a historian seriously, and in passages that still have powerful resonance for contemporary scholars, he makes a valiant attempt to communicate the process by which he has carried it out. Adams is much more contemporary in his exaggerated assertions of the insignificance of his life and his work, and in his evocation of the difficulties that the participant in history faces in trying to make sense of experience. The influence of Adams's ironic stance can be detected in many other American historians' life stories and even in some of those written by scholars from other countries. In the final analysis, however, *The Education of Henry Adams* stands apart from other historians' memoirs, not only because of the literary quality of its writing but because of the author's claim that his life story illustrates a metahistorical point of universal significance.

Gibbon's *Memoirs* and *The Education of Henry Adams* both contributed to the evolution not just of autobiographical writing by historians but of the autobiographical genre in general. Gibbon, along with his contemporaries Rousseau, Franklin, and Goethe, helped secularize life writing and contributed to its elevation to the level of great literature. As we have seen, the *Memoirs* also contributed to the articulation of an ideology of individualism, in which lives would be valued in terms of their accomplishments. Adams, for his part, showed that autobiography did not need to be confined to the pattern Gibbon had helped establish. *The Education of Henry Adams* is the life story of an antihero, a man who gloried in failure. Adams's innovative use of third-person narration transformed the relationship between author and subject and encouraged other autobiographers to follow in his footsteps by using their life stories as what Adams, in a letter to William James, called "experiments in literary art."[23] Edward Gibbon and Henry Adams demonstrate that the life story of a historian can be a work of literature that speaks to readers other than fellow scholars. At the same time, however, these two classic texts are very definitely historians' autobiographies. They cannot be fully understood without an appreciation of their authors' engagement with the project of understanding and narrating the past. They are thus related to the less well known autobiographical productions of other historians, which explore in their own ways the questions that Gibbon and Adams asked themselves about how individual experience contributes to the making of historical consciousness and how a commitment to history shapes a life. Gibbon's *Memoirs* and *The Education of Henry Adams* will no doubt continue to enjoy a special status, even in an age suspicious of literary canons, but a full recognition of their significance requires a recognition of their links to the wider body of autobiographical literature by historians.

CHAPTER 5

Choosing History: The Issue
of Vocation in Historians'
Autobiographies

AUTOBIOGRAPHY AND THE PROBLEM OF VOCATION: AN EXAMPLE

In Western traditions of autobiography, stories of the discovery or development of a vocation occupy an important place. Recounting how they acquired their professional skills and came to be recognized for their abilities allowed preindustrial artisan-autobiographers such as the Frenchmen Jacques Ménétra and Agricol Perdiguier to convince readers that they were autonomous and productive individuals whose lives deserved recording.[1] The influential model of the *Bildungsroman,* a pattern followed by many autobiographers, stresses the finding of a vocation as the central event in an individual's life. Finding and mastering the occupation that most suits one's talents and character is, in this model, a great drama in which the protagonist's personality takes its mature form. These stories may give the process more coherence than it had at the time and may underplay elements that did not contribute to the eventual outcome. Even if these stories are partly mythologized, however, they are still significant: they reflect powerful cultural models of how the self is shaped.

Autobiographical stories about the development of a vocation also demonstrate autobiography's special ability to explore questions about the nature of the human will and the extent of its power in shaping lives, a feature of the genre Richard Freadman has emphasized in his *Threads of Life.* The question of how a young person makes the choice to follow a highly specialized career such as history—a career that is not dependent on the possession of a specific talent, such as musical or mathematical ability, and one that is hardly ever explicitly urged upon children by their parents or com-munity—is an opportunity to explore issues such as the relative weight of social circumstances, family background, individual desire, and chance in shaping human lives. Because becoming a historian is always at least in part a matter of choice, the "insider's view" on the subject is irreplaceable: auto-biographical evidence is the only kind we can have on the issue. The light historians' autobiographies shed on these questions is relevant not only to members of their profession but to the broader issue of how much auton-omy anyone has to shape a life in our complex, modern societies.

To be sure, the notion that all life stories can or should be structured around the choice of a vocation cannot be accepted uncritically. The mod-ern generalized, secularized model of vocation is a relatively recent devel-opment, although university teachers represent one of the classic profes-sions where this model can be traced back to Middle Ages. Today, when young people are told that they should anticipate changing careers several times over the course of their life, the idea of a life story structured around the discovery of a vocation may be turning into an anachronism. Even dur-ing the period covered in the autobiographies discussed here, the ability to make an orderly progression from childhood enthusiasm to adult career was a relatively rare privilege, as both women's historians and scholars of work-ing-class life have pointed out. As we will see, the overwhelming majority of historians' autobiographies are stories about children whose families gave them the luxury of an extended period of development while teaching them to anticipate that they would and should eventually find a well-defined ca-reer that would give meaning to their life. These are largely stories of grow-ing up in middle-class circumstances and in societies whose basic structures seemed solidly established. Even those historians who grew up in poverty usually remember a childhood shaped by a cohesive family and supportive school environments, and even the numerous European historians from Jewish backgrounds whose lives were violently disrupted by Nazism man-aged to fit themselves back into this pattern.

Because he was so thoroughly imbued with the model of the *Bildungsro-man*, the first volume of the memoirs of German historian Friedrich Mei-necke (1862–1954), published in 1941, offers a useful point of departure for considering how modern professional historians have dealt with the issue of vocation, just as Meinecke's second volume will later serve as a good focus for discussing what historians write about their professional career. Al-though the rarefied intellectual history he practiced is now out of favor, Mei-necke was for much of the twentieth century a scholar whose work opened new methodological perspectives and exemplified the highest standards of the profession. In his own memoirs, Felix Gilbert, one of those students who carried Meinecke's influence to the New World, recalls how "Meinecke had shaken up German historical scholarship by emphasizing the relations among intellectual movements, political thought, and political action." He was "a great teacher" whose lectures "were beautifully organized" and whose seminars "provided a rigorous training in historical methodology."[2] Like Gibbon and Adams, Meinecke wrote about his personal life and about the great public events of his time in his autobiography, but the core of his narrative dealt with the experiences that compose the modern academic career: the choice of a discipline, advanced study, the search for a job, the shaping of major scholarly works, relations with professional colleagues, the internal life of academic institutions, interactions with students, the workings of professional journals and academies. The challenge he faced was to show how the details of this rather specialized world could be interwoven with themes that could interest readers other than his professional peers, such as the development of a distinctive individual personality.

Meinecke's autobiography is useful for understanding the problems contemporary historians face in writing about their vocation because, unlike Gibbon and Adams, he entered the profession when its structures were taking the forms they still, to a remarkable extent, retain. His teachers included men like Johann Droysen, who had been one of the pioneers in the "scientific revolution" in history in the first half of the nineteenth century, when professional history became defined by its emphasis on the discovery and interpretation of primary sources and when the seminar course became the obligatory *rite de passage* for entry into the field.[3] By the time Meinecke published his memoirs in the 1940s, seminar training and archival research had become familiar routines, but when he was a student they were still new and exciting. Goethe's influence on Meinecke also inclined him to treat questions of vocation seriously in his memoirs. Meinecke, who recalled regularly reading aloud to his wife from Goethe's *Dichtung und Wahrheit* during the early years of their marriage, had written that that work was "the climax of [Goethe's] historical thought and writing."[4] Goethe is associated with the idea of the individual life as a *Bildungsroman,* a story in which the discovery and mastery of a vocation is the central drama. More than the models offered by Gibbon or Henry Adams, the *Bildungsroman* provides a justification for taking such issues seriously in the account of an individual's life.

Meinecke presents the development of his interest in history as the result of a complicated interaction between milieu and personality. His childhood had exposed him to both continuity and change. He had been born in 1862 in a small provincial town, where his father held the position of postmaster, inherited from his own father. Meinecke's father was still a member of a guild, and local landmarks included the ruins of the medieval castle of Albrecht the Bear, forefather of the Prussian Hohenzollern dynasty. "One lived in the past and the natural outgrowths of the past," Meinecke recalls (*Erlebtes*, 29). When he was nine years old, however, his father was transferred to the new German capital of Berlin. "This contrast between my childhood in Salzwedel . . . and the environment in the large city of Berlin influenced my whole attitude toward life and gave it a romantic cast," Meinecke writes; he would not come to adulthood taking the values of Salzwedel for granted, but he would retain a certain nostalgia for the organic community into which he had been born (44). Berlin, still in some ways an overgrown provincial town when the Meineckes arrived, grew into a metropolis during his school years; in contrast to the unchanging milieu of his childhood, Meinecke now experienced the constant flux and instability of the modern world.

Meinecke sees his vocation as having roots in his family and school experiences as well as in his exposure to the great transformation represented by the unification of Germany. Like many historians, he came from a family with some tradition of intellectual interests: several of his maternal ancestors had been pastors. He remembers learning to read at an early age, and he did well in school. As a young boy, he loved exotic stories about American Indians; later he became enthusiastic about poetry and the works of Schiller, Goethe, and Shakespeare. His early schooling contributed less to his sense of vocation. His teachers in his *Gymnasium* years were not particularly inspiring, and he graduated without any clear sense of his future direction. In his teens he had dreamed of becoming a novelist, but by the time he finished the Gymnasium, he had come to understand that he was better suited for one of the academic disciplines. His strongly religious parents hoped he would enter the ministry; aiming for an academic post was an acceptable compromise that enabled him to pursue intellectual interests without having to subscribe to their orthodoxy. He was still torn between several possible disciplines, including philosophy and philology, which in his day included the study of myth and national character. But he eventually decided in favor of history, which "fitted with the essential character and needs of my nature." His choice was both a positive and a negative one. He rejected philosophy and philology because "I lacked the determination needed to work one's way forward through abstract thought processes," but also because "the world of history seemed closer to real life to me, richer and more colorful than the world that the philologians of the time offered" (101).

His choice of vocation settled, Meinecke recounts the various stages leading up to a professional historian's career. More than most historian-autobiographers, Meinecke conveys a sense of how the years of apprenticeship were inseparably connected to the professional life that followed them. His student years, for example, were a time when he was encountering the perspectives of a variety of teachers but also the moment when he first encountered the peers of his own age with whom he would collaborate and compete for the rest of his active career. Unlike Gibbon and Adams, Meinecke sees himself as part of a cohort and understands that his intellectual development as a historian had been linked with the formation of durable relationships with his contemporaries, "friends, who at the same time were seeking the same way in life as I was and also were so far ahead of me as thinkers and men, that I had to look up to them and thereby develop out of my immaturity" (149). Even as he describes these intense friendships, however, retrospection allows Meinecke to intimate that some of them would be shattered by professional rivalries and political disagreements. "None of us anticipated the many intersections of our lives and researches, . . . the depth of the oppositions that would develop among us, and the passions they would generate" (105).

During his years of university study at Berlin and Bonn, Meinecke was exposed to a number of different professors' approaches to history. In retrospect, he thought one of the most important lessons of this period of his life was learning to distinguish between teachers like the popular Karl Lamprecht, a lively and dramatic lecturer but, in Meinecke's mature view, a superficial thinker, and others who showed him a way into the deeper aspects of historical scholarship. Looking back, he is also acutely conscious of how much of his time and energy had gone into nonacademic activities, particularly his membership in a nationalist fraternity; he regrets having left Bonn, where the historical training was of higher quality, to return to Berlin, where his student group was located. Certainly he had not yet developed a historical outlook of his own. Instead he had absorbed "the positivistic mood of the time, which sought as much as possible to give the human sciences [*Geisteswissenschaften*] a precise and empirically assured character." But he was far from having completed his intellectual development when he received his doctoral degree in 1886. He remembers himself as "a mole, searching in the dark for his path" (119–20).

THE HISTORY-MINDED CHILD

In spite of his reputation as a remote and elitist figure from the past, Meinecke's description of the relationship between his childhood experiences and the formation of his vocation has a good deal in common with the narratives of many more recent historians, women as well as men. Meinecke's sense that his interest in history owed a great deal to the experience of having been born into a world that was on the verge of disappearing is common in these memoirs. It is not surprising to find this perception in the writings of scholars born in the nineteenth and early twentieth century who wrote memoirs two generations later, such as Arthur Schlesinger Sr.'s recollections of small-town life in Ohio in the 1890s and Philippe Ariès's reminiscences about visits to relatives who kept alive the atmosphere of the French Old Regime in the 1920s, but it occurs even in John Brewer's more recent account of growing up in Liverpool in the 1950s. "It may seem as if I overemphasize Victorianism," Brewer writes, "but I was surrounded by it. I lived in a decayed Victorian city, I went to a school founded by (among others) the Gladstone family."[5] Clearly some such perception helps make retrospective sense of many historical vocations.

Meinecke's depiction of the relationship between his family experience and his future vocation also resonates with that found in many other historians' memoirs. The Meinecke family's circumstances were relatively modest but sufficient to support a child who showed bookish inclinations. The fact that several of his mother's relatives had been pastors meant that there was a precedent in the family for a career requiring academic training: Meinecke did not have to struggle to convince his parents to support him through the Gymnasium and the university. Very few historian-memoirists, even those from poor backgrounds, recall childhoods in families that were truly indifferent to intellectual and cultural interests. French social historian Pierre Goubert is a rare example: his father had had only four years of schooling, and the idea that Pierre might continue his education after finishing elementary school was an unfamiliar one. "'Going on in school' after age twelve was something that never happened in my family or in my milieu, where parents thought that a twelve-year-old youngster should 'earn his bread,'" Goubert writes; it took the intervention of his elementary school principal, who convinced his mother that her son might become a schoolteacher with a regular income and a pension, to overcome their resistance.[6]

More typical of future historian-autobiographers from poor families was the experience of William Langer. Born in Boston in 1898, he was the son of poor German immigrants, and his father died when he was still in infancy. He had to start working at part-time jobs from the time he was nine and could not afford to buy a hot lunch at school during his high school years. Nevertheless, his mother, unlike Goubert's parents, was determined to see him get an education. Although the family couldn't afford books, he was able to use the local public library, and when his elementary-school teacher recommended him for the prestigious Boston Latin School, his mother supported the idea. Later she stood up to friends and relatives who thought that letting her son attend Harvard when he was old enough to work was "preposterous."[7] In Langer's case, as in that of Monroe Billington, another future historian born into a poor American family, parents made sacrifices to keep their son in school because he seemed headed for a career in the ministry, a profession with deep meaning even for the uneducated.[8] Where parents' resources were inadequate, state-subsidized scholarships for aspiring schoolteachers sometimes filled in, as in the cases of the Australian Bernard Smith, the New Zealander Keith Sinclair, and the Indo-Fijian Brij Lal.[9]

The number of future historian-autobiographers who grew up in circumstances of real wealth is even smaller than the number who had to overcome poverty. There are a few: George Mosse's father was a millionaire publisher and press baron in pre-Hitler Berlin, Felix Gilbert's family, bankers, were also part of the German moneyed and cultural elite, and Samuel Eliot Morison grew up in a Boston Brahmin family and was grateful that he never had to consider whether to "do anything but what his tastes and talents impelled him to do, no matter how unremunerative."[10] In France, Emmanuel Le Roy Ladurie's father was a wealthy landowner of aristocratic descent. The pattern one finds most often in these stories, however, confirms Edward Gibbon's observation that few historians are born either in garrets or in palaces. Lawyers, engineers, independent businessmen of various degrees of success, clergymen, schoolteachers, civil servants, doctors, and a few university professors: the range of paternal occupations is remarkably consistent.[11] Children born into such middle-class households were usually brought up in urban environments; unlike the future sociobiologist Edward O. Wilson, for whom "Nature was my companion of choice,"[12] they were unlikely to spend much unsupervised time out of doors, except perhaps during summer vacations. They could expect to continue their schooling well beyond the elementary level, had easy access to reading material and, one intuits, suitable surroundings in which to devour it, and enjoyed such privileges as the opportunity to travel, often including trips abroad. They also had in their own families role models of fathers (and a few mothers) with professional careers, and they understood early on that this was the type of future they were to seek. As they look back, they often see these conditions as strongly related to their future choice of vocation.

The most important thing most of these historians indicate they inherited from their family background was an early impetus to take an interest in culture, and especially reading. John King Fairbank was born in a small town in South Dakota, far from the centers of American cultural life, but his parents' "interest in the culture that raw mid-America was avidly acquiring from Europe directed me outward and eastward." When he seemed to have exhausted the resources of the local schools, his parents sent him to a New England academy.[13] In England, Gareth Stedman Jones's schoolteacher parents "lived in a world of books."[14] Jurgen Herbst's father encouraged his child to wander through the stacks of the great research library in their home town of Wolfenbüttel.[15] On her remote Australian homestead, Jill Ker Conway was home-schooled and "introduced to study as a leisure activity, a gift beyond price."[16] Her fellow Australians Keith Hancock and Manning Clark both grew up in clerical households where books were common, as did the American John Hicks and the German Jew Helmut Eschwege, whose father was a Talmud teacher. Most future historians who escaped the Holocaust came from more assimilated Jewish families than Eschwege's, but their recollections almost invariably evoke parents with intellectual interests and a concern for education.

Accounts of growing up in bookish households are not limited to white male historians. Most African American historians who have written about their upbringing, such as John Hope Franklin, Darline Clark Hine, and David Levering Lewis, also came from educated backgrounds. Franklin's mother was a schoolteacher, his father a lawyer, and he "grew up believing that in the evenings one either read or wrote."[17] The Indian historian and diplomat K. M. Panikkar sounds a similar note: many of his relatives were schoolteachers, and as soon as his family noticed his interest in reading, he was taught English, and eventually he was encouraged to go to Oxford.[18] Women historians also usually write about parents who supported their intellectual interests, even in periods when it was not yet customary for women to aim at academic careers. One finds remarks to this effect in the essays that Karen Offen, Frances Richardson Keller, Margaret Strobel, and Barbara Winslow contributed to the collective volume *Voices of Women Historians*, for example, and the French scholar Annie Kriegel, born in 1926, says her mother insisted that she should have the same education and plans for the future as her brothers.[19]

Future historian-memoirists were not just exposed to books: they usually developed a precocious love for them. The Czech-born Susan Groag Bell is one of several who use the word *voracious* to describe their childhood reading habits.[20] Arthur Schlesinger Jr. devotes an entire chapter in his memoir to his childhood reading, because he sees this early absorption in books as itself a characteristic of a world that has now been lost. "Now that television has replaced the book in the life of the young," he writes, "mine may have been the last generation to grow up in the high noon of the print culture. Perhaps it may be of historical interest to recall the profound excitement, the abiding fulfillment, books provided in those ancient and no doubt unimaginable days." There is no reason to doubt these recollections of a childhood love of reading, but it is also clear that these depictions of children happily absorbed in books serve not only to explain but also to justify later careers built around reading and writing by demonstrating the impact that books can have on their readers.

To a remarkable extent, historian-autobiographers remember enjoying similar kinds of books in their youth. Like several other historian-autobiographers, Schlesinger retained powerful memories of the fairy tales he listened to and thinks that this literature influenced the way he would later look at history: "The classical tales tell children what they unconsciously know—that human nature is not innately good, that conflict is real, that life is harsh before it is happy."[21] More memoirists discuss the books they enjoyed once they could read for themselves. These memories often refer to adventure narratives set in distant times and places, like the tales of American Indian life Meinecke had read in his youth. For those who grew up in the German-speaking world in the first part of the twentieth century, the Wild West adventure stories of Karl May were unavoidable: Herbert Strauss claims to have read at least sixty volumes of them.[22] "I lived with Jules Verne," French historian Alain Besançon has written, and historians as diverse as French Catholic businessman's son François Bluche, Harvard professor's child Arthur Schlesinger Jr., Orthodox Hungarian Jew Jacob Katz, and assimilated French Jew Pierre Vidal-Naquet mention a childhood love for that author and his world of what Bluche calls "triumphant bourgeois, Yankee artillery-men, unemotional engineers."[23]

In the English-speaking world, a number of future historians grew up on the now-forgotten historical novels of G. H. Henty. In his memoir

Schlesinger, a Henty fan, compiles a list of other scholars and public figures who had shared his passion. Schlesinger also enjoyed H. Rider Haggard, Robert Louis Stevenson, and Alexandre Dumas.[24] Howard Pyle's version of the King Arthur legend is remembered by H. Stuart Hughes; Howard Zinn and Charles Roland mention *Tarzan*.[25] Those who were children in the 1920s were often also exposed to another type of adventure story: books about the Great War. Raoul Girardet, a future military historian, had many relatives who had been in the French army and grew up on tales of that heroic struggle. "This immense collective legend was, without any doubt, a living reality for me, and so intensely inscribed in the deepest parts of my memory that I find it impossible to separate those images from my very earliest memories," he writes.[26] Canadian-born historian Henry Ferns remembers how moved he was, long after he reached adulthood, to meet one of the Canadian pilots whose exploits he had read about in his youth.[27]

Like Meinecke, many historian-autobiographers also recall a precocious introduction to literary classics, sometimes at their parents' behest, sometimes on their own. For those from religious households, the great introduction to high literature was often the Bible, which French historian Michelle Perrot calls "my foundational book."[28] Jill Ker Conway discovered Shakespeare and poetry in her teenage years; Philippe Ariès read Shakespeare and French poets Baudelaire and Verlaine; Brij Lal's teachers in colonial Fiji introduced him to Shakespeare, Tennyson, and Matthew Arnold.[29] Like Henry Adams, Alain Besançon in France, Gareth Stedman Jones in England, and Howard Zinn in the United States all recall the impact Charles Dickens had on them. "Today, reading pallid, cramped novels about 'relationships,' I recall Dickens's unashamed rousing of feeling, his uproariously funny characters, his epic settings—cities of hunger and degradation, countries in revolution, the stakes being life and death not just for one family but for thousands," Zinn writes, giving a sense of why this author looms so large in the memories of many historians.[30] For a good number of future historians, the books of the great authors also had great personal meaning, as the way in which they began to understand the problems of life. Manning Clark's father "coaxed me into reading books," Clark recalls, "holding out the hope that there I might find comfort, there I might find answers to some of the puzzles of childhood. Books, like life, were schools for those seeking wisdom and understanding."[31] Barbara Kanner, daughter of immigrants who had come to the United States, found in serious reading "a secret set of mentors. . . . More importantly, these authors also showed that there were more truthful, more satisfying ways of telling stories than my relatives knew existed, methods that could turn narration into a valuable tool for preserving past truth."[32]

Whether they read adventure stories or classics, these future historian-autobiographers clearly embraced their parents' concerns with culture and learning. Through reading, however, they also began to display their own autonomy, choosing books they enjoyed and, in many cases, accepting without demur the label "bookworm." Reading was a pleasurable escape for many of them, but the preference most recall for adventure stories, novels, and plays reflects an interest in stories about "real" people and their problems—in other words, the stuff of history rather than pure fantasy. Few of these memoirists mention reading historical works per se, other than volumes devoted to the Great War. The titles mentioned also have a certain masculine bias. None of these authors mention, for example, Laura Ingalls Wilder and the Little House series, often cited by American women historians of my generation as an inspiration for their interest in history; my wife, who grew up in Germany, recalls that Annemarie Selinko's *Désirée*, the story of a young woman who nearly married Napoleon, had a big influence on her eventual pursuit of the subject.

Historian-autobiographers do also mention other youthful interests. Lawrence Stone and Peter Gay were stamp collectors, as I was. Walter Laqueur ran in track meets, and Stone claims poor coaching blighted what might have been a promising cricket career.[33] Still, the impression one gets from the overwhelming majority of these memoirs is of young people who opted for the world of books and stories at an early age and who enjoyed lively narratives set in exotic times and places. Like the theoretical analyses of Hayden White, Paul Ricoeur, and David Carr, these autobiographical stories underline how deeply narrative and history are intertwined.

Another childhood experience many future historians recall as significant for them was travel. These memoirists grew up before the age of cheap and quick mass tourism, but most of them belonged to the minority of families for whom travel was considered a normal and necessary part of life, so that they had early opportunities to see parts of the world that they recall as different not only in space but also in time. Although Eric Hobsbawm's central European Jewish family was relatively impoverished, he recalls that "boys from families such as mine expected to go to Paris sooner or later," so that when he finally saw the city at the age of fifteen, "I was excited, but not surprised."[34] For many of the future French historians, summer visits to grandparents or other relatives brought home the contrast between urban and rural life, between the present- and future-oriented milieu in which they lived and one oriented to the past.[35] For a number of future American historians, a childhood trip abroad served as a strong stimulus to an interest in history. For Henry May, a year spent visiting England and France "was the single most formative experience in my childhood." In it lay "the beginnings of a feeling for the past, a sense of its continuous presence and endless fascination."[36] The Australian-born Jill Ker Conway's childhood trip to Ceylon confronted her with a non-Western civilization and a different scale of time: "Seeing these remains was an unexpected culture shock which meant that Europe could never again seem 'old.'"[37] These trips obviously reflected the relatively privileged status of many future historians' families; they also conveyed the importance these parents attributed to having their children acquire cultural capital, as opposed to power or material possessions.

Family background, reading, and travel may have predisposed these youths toward their future vocation, but even among young people with a strong interest in historical narratives, only a few actually grow up to make the writing and teaching of history their life's work. Furthermore, this is not a choice that can be made at an early age. By its nature, history is not a field open to child prodigies: the abilities it requires take time to manifest themselves, and unlike musical talent or a genius for numbers, they are relatively nonspecific and can presage many different careers. Some historian-autobiographers do claim, like Edward Gibbon, that they were sure of their vocation early on, but these cases are exceptional. Arnold Toynbee, whose mother wrote historical works, is the only one of these memoirists who claims that his vocation was essentially determined by parental example.[38] The British G. M. Trevelyan, whose family tree included the great nineteenth-century historian Macaulay, writes, "I never remember desiring to be anything else. . . . I never had dreams of being a general, or a statesman or an engine-driver, like other aspiring children."[39] Felix Gilbert claims that the first book he ever read entirely on his own was a history book and that immediately after reading it, he told his mother that he too was going to become a historian, although in fact he considered several other careers before committing himself.[40]

Among the historian-autobiographers who write of having known their vocation since childhood, a few have seen a deep existential reason for that choice. One of the most emphatic is H. Stuart Hughes, who claims to remember not only the moment when he realized he wanted to become a historian but why. When he was eight, Hughes's parents took him on a tour of

Europe. He was both attracted by the differentness of life in another country and traumatized by some of the things he saw, such as wax models of prisoners in the medieval dungeons of Mont-Saint-Michel. "I recreated in my imagination," he claims, "the dreadful scenes that had shaken me to my depths. . . . And so this early I had discovered my vocation: I was to be a historian of Europe. To pursue the study of history, I had already glimpsed, was the only way to sort out the confused and contradictory residue of my travels." [41] Like Hughes, the French historian Pierre Chaunu sees a fascination and fear of death, rooted in childhood experiences and especially the loss of his mother when he was nine months old, as decisive for him. He had three early ambitions: to be a soldier, a doctor, a historian. Looking back, he sees a common element in all three: "It is death that I will drive back. Either by keeping the exteriorized menace at a distance, or in wresting from death the buried memory of those who had . . . marked the space and time of my childhood, or by driving back death itself like Pasteur and his followers, who the secular republican school worshipped." [42]

Hughes and Chaunu are unusual, however, in their insistence that they became historians out of some life-defining need. So are memoirists who recount a sort of illumination or conversion experience to historical sensibility during their adolescence. One of these is the German scholar Hermann Heimpel. Heimpel's father, an engineer, had no particular interest in history, but on a visit to his father's small hometown when he was about eleven, Heimpel was struck for the first time by the difference between its old buildings and traditional lifeways and life in the up-to-date metropolis of Munich where he lived. An uncle showed him how the buildings in Lindau reflected the centuries in which they had been constructed. Later the same relative showed him old family documents that allowed him to reconstruct for himself how his ancestors had lived. Reading them, Heimpel "experienced for the first time the magic of old papers, the old-Frankish stamp, the red, decayed seal. He tasted these old times, that were somehow his own, his own despite their difference, the present in the past, the familiar in what was alien, history, time, time the reconciler." In one document he saw that his grandfather's university diploma had been signed by a famous historical figure he had learned about in school: he could connect his family's history to that of his country. Immersed in these family materials, Heimpel sensed "that history is different from what is in the history books," and he fell under its spell. Throughout the rest of his career, the same feeling of wonder would reoccur, reminding him "that man only lives in full consciousness when he recognizes himself as living in time." As a result of this quasi-religious experience in his childhood, "time had come to him, this our human time."[43] Heimpel's account provides a memorable reconstruction of how a young person acquires a sense of time's importance, even if it probably also reflects a later encounter with the ideas about historicity of his sometime colleague at the University of Freiburg Martin Heidegger, one of whose students Heimpel married.[44]

While Heimpel's autobiography is particularly vivid, the experience it recounts is not entirely unique. As a child, the French historian Philippe Ariès recalls, he saw a close connection between the existence of God and the existence of the past. He became obsessed with the project of compiling for himself a complete chronology of the past, without any gaps. "You wouldn't have to push me very far to get me to recognize in my communion with the past my earliest religious experience."[45] Bruce Catton was also propelled into history by a moment of existential revelation, when he learned in school about the Mound Builder Indians who had once lived in his native Michigan: "Looking into the misty past for men who were no longer there could give one a different perspective on the present. Perhaps what we ourselves were doing would leave no more traces than those men had left. . . . This was chilling but it was also exciting."[46] Less philosophically, the English historian J. F. C. Harrison, like Heimpel, writes of being initiated into historical research in his early teens by his grandparents' stories and old papers. "Although at first I had some difficulty in deciphering the legal script on the parchment indentures, I was now squarely launched into the stuff of history. Like Molière's character who discovered that he had been speaking prose without knowing it, I was soon engaged in historical research."[47]

Most historians, however, recall a more gradual development of interest in history, shaped by a complicated pattern of circumstances and choices rather than by a deep psychological need or a moment of illumination. Like Meinecke, most tend to attribute less importance to their schooling than to family milieu and reading in shaping their vocation. Many have memories, good or bad, of their elementary-school years, but none record anything specific about the history instruction they may have received at that level. Most remember being good students, although a few emphasize that they were just the opposite as children. The most common topos about experiences in secondary school is the inspiring teacher: the instructor who both made the subject come alive and revealed to the student that history could be a career, as well as explaining the steps necessary to achieve such a goal. The British historian of France Richard Cobb mentions the arrival of a dynamic history teacher at his school as "the first of a number of happy accidents that . . . have altered for the better the languid, rather sluggish course of my life."[48] Raoul Girardet evokes a lycée professor who showed him that "it could, after all, be a respectable thing for an adult to teach history and, to be sure, to consecrate his life to it."[49] Lawrence Stone recalls Robert Birley, whose "endless fund of enthusiasm for whatever topic happened to be uppermost in his mind" made him "dazzlingly successful as a history teacher." Birley helped Stone win a scholarship to study history at Oxford and also arranged for him to spend six months studying in Paris before the start of his university courses.[50] One gets the impression from many of these passages that it was less the content of the instruction than the teacher's personality that affected the students. Sheila Rowbotham remembers the "sardonic voice" and "bantering humour" of the history teacher who stood out from the other instructors at her dreary boarding school.[51] In Heimpel's case, the teacher who interested him the most in history was not even his history instructor but a Latin teacher so affected by the drama of World War I that he spent his class time telling students about its origins rather than teaching his own subject.[52] These examples all come from memoirs by historians educated in Europe; American historian-memoirists hardly ever mention specific high-school history teachers. This difference probably reflects the differences between British grammar schools, French lycées, and German Gymnasia, where students might have the same teacher for several years, and the larger, more impersonal, and less selective American high schools.

Australian historian-autobiographers comment more than those from other countries on the impact of the history lessons they learned in school, because of the discrepancy between the country they lived in and the curriculum they were taught. "We might have been in Sussex for all the attention we paid to Australian poetry and prose," Jill Ker Conway writes. In history and geography, she says, "we learned about Roman Britain and memorized a wonderful jumble of Angles, Saxons, Picts, and Boadicea."[53] In Manning Clark's memory, "it was an education designed for a governing class in that country which ruled over a large portion of the world, the Empire on which the sun never set—but Australia had neither a governing class nor an Empire. It was an education for an aristocracy: Australia was a democracy."[54] Certainly such an education produced a very different relationship to the past from that absorbed by future historians who grew up in the United States, England, France, or pre-Hitler Germany, where the stories in schoolbooks produced a sense of identification with the environment that students were already familiar with, and told students that great historical events had occurred in the places where they lived. Some young Australians found the emphasis on English history positive, giving them a wider perspective on the world. Bernard Smith felt what he learned about Australian history was limiting, "explorers forever dying of thirst in the bush or being speared by Aborigines." Writing of his boyhood self in the third person, he continues, "But the study of European history gave him a sense of his place in the scheme of things; it was like standing between two mirrors, a mirror of the future and a mirror of the past, and seeing himself stretching away in both directions; a sense of tradition."[55] Only autobiographical retrospect reveals the peculiarity of growing up on one side of the world while being taught to identify with the history of a country on the other.

Although experiences in secondary school were often important in starting to convert a childhood interest into a sense of vocation, historian-autobiographers usually see other aspects of their adolescence as more important to them. In the first place, secondary school did not require them to commit themselves: only when they arrived at the university would they have to choose a definite course of study. Second, many of them portray themselves as being much more involved with other aspects of their life during their teenage years. The discovery of sexuality, conflicts with parents, involvement with sports or youth movements—all these experiences remain more vivid in these authors' memories than whatever went on in their classrooms. A large number of them write about adolescent years that coincided either with World War I or with the political and ideological dramas of the 1930s and 1940s. Frequently they remember world events, rather than classroom instruction, as what motivated them to think about history. The history Leon Litwack was given in school "contradicted much of what I sensed, learned, and experienced outside the classroom," he recalls. It "was someone else's history, not my history, not the lives of my parents, friends, and neighbors."[56] The accounts of secondary-school experiences in memoirs of authors of European Jewish origin who had to flee Nazism reflect the surprising fact that most were able to finish their schooling even after Hitler came to power. They were hardly likely to remember their classroom history lessons as a source of intellectual inspiration, however, and those who emigrated often had to wait years before they could resume their education. In Berlin on the eve of Hitler's takeover, Hobsbawm remembers learning "absolutely nothing" from his Gymnasium history teacher but being decisively affected by the dramatic events taking place in the streets outside.[57]

As in Meinecke's account, the years of university study strike most historian-autobiographers as the moment when they decided both that history
was what interested them most and that they wanted to prepare for a career
teaching and writing it. A few future historians, such as Philippe Ariès,
George Mosse, and Gerhard Masur, had to overcome parental opposition
to such an impractical choice. Michelle Perrot's parents were unhappy, not
because she wanted a professional career but because they thought she
should choose a more promising field. As she recalls, "History in those days
[the 1940s] was not a particularly attractive discipline; it didn't have the
public image it has now."[58] In Fiji, on the other side of the planet, Brij Lal
had to overcome the opposition of his parents and his entire village, for
whom teaching of any kind was a low-prestige occupation; they could not
understand why a bright young man would not want to study medicine or
law.[59] Gershom Scholem, who claims he developed his passionate interest
in Jewish history during his early adolescence as a form of revolt against the
assimilationist outlook of his German-Jewish family, and Mark Naison, author of a memoir about how he decided to study African American history
despite the opposition of his lower-middle-class Jewish parents, are perhaps
the only historian-autobiographers to portray their choice of vocation as a
form of generational revolt.[60] Usually these authors write as though their
parents accepted the choice of academia and as though the final choice of
which discipline to pursue was essentially left up to them.

MOMENTS OF CHOICE AND MEMORIES OF MENTORS

It was at the university level that most of these memoirists encountered true
mentors and role models, often prominent scholars who can be described
more easily in their narratives than secondary-school teachers because their
names will mean something to historian-readers. Although a minority of
these memoirists describe themselves as certain from the start that they
wanted to study history when they reached the university, many more echo
Friedrich Meinecke in recalling a process of choice, if not a real sense of
conflict. Many considered professional careers, such as law, which parents
often saw as a more practical course for bright children interested in public
affairs. Several chose history over the ministry, which William Langer,
Monroe Billington, Shepard Clough, and a number of the contributors to
the volume *Autobiographical Reflections on Southern Religious History* came to
feel required a degree of personal commitment they were not sure they
could sustain.[61] Gareth Stedman Jones was one of several future historians
who considered a career in journalism. He finally decided that "my inabil-

ity to let go of a question until I had finally exhausted its meaning to my satisfaction, did not accord happily with a professional observance of deadlines and ensuring a reasonable income."[62] Others turned to history when they realized they lacked the talent or drive for artistic careers, like Carl Schorske, who had hoped to be a singer, Australian Bernard Smith, who could not find a public for his avant-garde paintings, and Henry May and Manning Clark, who had both contemplated becoming poets or novelists.[63]

Those who were already set on becoming professors or scholars often still had to choose between various disciplines, as Meinecke had, and their reasons for embracing history were often similar to his. Karen Offen switched from a science major to history, having decided that it "seemed to be the queen of the sciences, inviting, encompassing, infinite . . . and potentially useful."[64] Her attraction to what she perceived as history's breadth and inclusiveness is echoed in many scholars' accounts. For Pierre Vidal-Naquet, "doing history was . . . the best way of involving myself in everything that inspired me, history itself, of course, above all that of my own times, . . . philosophy and literature."[65] The Australian Kathleen Fitzpatrick found history "to be, from the first, broader and more humane than English, not hostile or defensive in its attitude to other forms of knowledge but seeking, as far as possible, to embrace them." Compared to literature, her other interest, "its whole posture was more liberal in that it allowed for differences of interest and opinion, and it seemed, in a way, more sure of itself, less prone to demand adherence to the orthodoxy of the moment and cheerfully resigned to the likelihood of having to retreat from positions that were no longer tenable."[66]

Half a world away from Fitzpatrick's Australia and several event-filled decades later, Annie Kriegel chose history over literature and philosophy because "it treated concrete events, it was on a human scale, made by and for men, and it confirmed the fact that, in spite of constraints and necessities, they had some freedom of action and enterprise."[67] In Greece in the early 1960s, Antonis Liakos chose history over philosophy because "history seemed to offer a less unstable ground for understanding than philosophy did," whereas the American Carolyn Bynum, whose parents were both Ph.D.s, decided that history "provided a way of defeating my mother's extraordinary philosophical mind" because "historical context gave me a weapon against metaphysics."[68] In the 1930s, Henry May gravitated toward history both because it seemed relevant to such contemporary questions as "wars, changing societies, and revolutions" and because of a "fascination with the past because it was the past, because it was different, because it had or seemed to have a structure or a story."[69] A number of historians who were heavily involved in political movements saw the discipline as a natural extension of their activism. Australian Marilyn Lake switched from literature in the 1960s because "history allowed for the play of youthful idealism and suggested the possibilities, indeed probability, of social transformation. History allowed for vicarious political victories as we mocked the conservatives and poured scorn on the reactionaries."[70]

Summing up the remarks made by the contributors to *Essais d'ego-histoire,* Pierre Nora detects a sense that the choice of history over other disciplines represented a certain inhibition or lack of confidence. "Several openly admit that they didn't consider themselves capable of reaching the heights of philosophy or worthy of associating with the great works of literature," he claims. He sees their choice as "an act of intellectual and social modesty, imbued with a spirit of seriousness, a humble submission to the facts of reality and to solitary work in archives and libraries."[71] The passages I have cited from historians' memoirs suggest that most of them put their choice in a more positive light. These authors recall being attracted to history because of its inclusiveness and variety, its relative insulation from ideological dogmatism, and above all because of what they saw as its connection to the reality of human experience—all features as well of the autobiographical mode in which they later made these reflections. The contemporary theorist Katherine Kearns has stigmatized this way of characterizing history as a form of anti-intellectual professional ideology, a way of rejecting "those who fail to fit the terms and thus prove themselves . . . as *too* intellectual to care about material specifics historically displayed (philosophers, theoreticians, psychoanalysts)."[72] Although they do not share Kearns's negative evaluation of history, many historians do clearly see the separation between history and other forms of intellectual endeavor in similar terms: history struck them as the academic discipline most connected to reality and least dependent on abstract theory. As several of these comments indicate, the storytelling aspect of history was another attraction, no doubt related to many future historians' childhood love of lively narratives. Whether made for negative or positive reasons, however, the decision to study history is portrayed in these memoirs as a defining choice, involving not just the selection of an occupation but also the adoption of an attitude toward the world. In committing themselves to history rather than some other subject, these autobiographers see themselves as exercising their autonomy and making conscious decisions about what kind of person they would be.

For many historian-memoirists, the attractions of history were embodied in specific university teachers. In recollections of undergraduate years, the emphasis is usually on teachers who inspired enthusiasm for the subject and for academic life. For Kathleen Fitzpatrick at Melbourne, the decisive moment in her life was a course with Ernest Scott, a great lecturer who had the gift of making "the people of the past" he spoke about become "real in a way in which the named persons in text-books never had been."[73] At the University of Manitoba, a teacher named H. N. Fieldhouse had a similar effect on Henry Ferns: "In a few minutes he made me feel that the university was worthwhile, a place to which I wanted to return."[74] Both Fitzpatrick and Ferns subsequently came to feel that the teachers who had initially moved them so much were basically rather shallow thinkers. "When eventually I began to see through him I realized he was a great actor," Ferns wrote, and Fitzpatrick's hero Scott came to strike her as "informed and intelligent but not profound."[75] Writing their memoirs allowed both these authors to acknowledge how much they owed to these teachers but at the same time to dramatize the poignant insight that acquiring a vocation often means growing beyond the level of the instructors who kindled it.

Relations with professors encountered in graduate school call forth the most complex comments in these stories of *Bildung*. At this level, future historians were now looking not only for inspiration but also for professional training; they were also in a position to understand their teachers' personalities better than they had at the undergraduate level. Henry May distinguishes between the brilliant but erratic Perry Miller, "capable of tormenting a student from the podium and then treating him as a comrade," who stimulated his intellect but intimidated him too much to be a true mentor, and the less scintillating but more supportive Arthur Schlesinger Sr., whose "great gift was for gently guiding each student to a topic that fit his interests and abilities and then leaving him alone."[76] Unlike undergraduate study, graduate training often included painful experiences as the authors learned the rules of history as an academic discipline. At Hebrew University, one professor reduced Evyatar Friesel's early papers to shreds. "It would be a long time until I dared again to affirm, in historical matters, anything about anything. But at least I recognized what had happened to me, and I was grateful to [him] for his rigorous treatment of my work. . . . This was the first step in a very beneficial process of academic development," Friesel writes.[77]

Few future historians escaped having at least one such traumatic experience. Encountering the Sorbonne's traditionalist training in positivist research methods, Philippe Ariès endured ordeal by boredom, "which had to be surmounted, but this boredom was like a rite of initiation and diminished as one's knowledge became more substantial, the connection of facts more familiar. It was a form of asceticism through which the historian, a man of austerity, learned to put aside the passions of his own times."[78] Advanced training was a shock to H. Stuart Hughes as well. His "vocation as a historian had declared itself early. But how could a child of eight know the quota of dreary labor the historical profession entailed? Not until I reached graduate school did this particular fact of life hit me in the face."[79] In such stories we recognize familiar themes from the world of the *Bildungsroman:* the struggle to acquire skills that seemed easy from the outside and the need to prove oneself worthy in the eyes of established members of the group one seeks to enter. While the task in question, usually the writing of a seminar paper, may not have much significance in the eyes of the world, casting it as a challenge of the protagonist's endurance and ability to learn makes a story that can be meaningful even to nonhistorian readers. A few historian-memoirists mention the high emotional price that graduate school required. Peter Carroll, who later left academia altogether, remarks that the demands of his program in the mid-1960s meant that "we blithely permitted the real history of the times to pass us by" and that "it also absorbed any sense of a private life"; like Nikki Keddie, who became a leading American specialist on the Middle East, he implies that the strain of such concentration started to break up his marriage.[80]

Because of the highly centralized nature of the French educational system, the memoirs published by French historians between 1980 and 2000 often relate common experiences and therefore make the patterns in historical training clearer than the more diversified narratives from other countries. In France, students aiming for an academic career almost all aspired to enter the prestigious Ecole normale supérieure. Admission was a virtual guarantee of future success; Pierre Vidal-Naquet, who failed the entrance exam three times, felt as if the sincerity of his vocation was being questioned.[81] Those who did get in were inevitably thrown together with other students who would become lifelong peers and rivals, especially since many of those who were there in the post–World War II years also joined the same student cell of the French Communist Party. Members of the school's Party group included a veritable pantheon of future leading historians: Maurice Agulhon, François Furet, Emmanuel Le Roy Ladurie, Annie Kriegel, Alain Besançon, Denis Richet, and Claude Mazauric, as well as many others.[82] Those who decided to earn a higher degree wound up working with the same thesis directors at the Sorbonne, so that their accounts of their relationships with their mentors provide comparative portraits of a few individuals.

The consistent comments in these memoirs about one of these figures, the social and economic historian Ernest Labrousse, suggest the qualities that make a successful doctoral director. Unlike the inspirational teachers many future historian-autobiographers had encountered in their undergraduate days, Labrousse was not a powerful and charismatic personality but rather one whose character was "veiled by a sort of discretion close to sexual modesty," as Pierre Goubert has written. Only years later did Goubert learn of his director's youthful career as a Socialist Party activist and journalist, a career that he had renounced but that seems to have made him understanding of his politically committed students in the 1940s and 1950s. Although Labrousse still had strong political views of his own, Goubert and other students remarked on his "openness, his acuity of intellect, his sudden intuitions, and the accuracy of his replies."[83] He let students propose their own research topics but did not hesitate to criticize their choices. Having just read Simone de Beauvoir's *The Second Sex* in 1949, Michelle Perrot wanted to work on the history of feminism. "This proposition brought a smile to his face," Perrot recalls. "'You want a very trendy topic.'" Instead, he urged her to study patterns of strike activity in the late nineteenth century. Perrot followed his advice, thereby perhaps retarding the development of French women's history by several decades.[84] When Annie Kriegel informed Labrousse that, having quit the Communist Party, she now planned to research its origins, she encountered a similar reaction: "'Delicate, *Madame,* delicate.' He would have much preferred to have me propose a more distant epoch and an issue less subject to polemics. But, recognizing that it would be this topic and no other, he agreed, perhaps thinking that if I became discouraged, he would have a chance to make suggestions." More stubborn and self-assured than Perrot, Kriegel forged ahead. Labrousse insisted that she approach her subject as rigorously as any other historical topic, even making her spend an additional year revising when new sources surfaced after she had had the thesis printed. In retrospect, Kriegel was grateful for his rigor: his insistence kept her work from immediately being dismissed as outdated because of failure to address these materials.[85] As these vignettes show, the secret to Labrousse's success was his respect for his students' individuality: having given them the benefit of his advice about their topics, he supported them even if they chose to ignore it, and tolerated their political engagements, all the while insisting that they adhere to the highest possible professional standards.

The French *ego-historiens* and their contemporaries are the only group of historian-autobiographers whose choice of vocation was strongly associated with a particular historiographic movement: the so-called *école des Annales,* the distinctive French historical current of social, economic and cultural history identified with the journal *Les Annales* created in 1929 by Marc Bloch and Lucien Febvre. By the time scholars such as Pierre Goubert, Emmanuel Le Roy Ladurie, and Jacques Le Goff came to write their memoirs, the fame of the *Annales* school, at least in France, had spread well beyond the walls of the academy, and the question of these authors' relationship to it formed an important part of their self-presentation. The *Annales* itself is the only scholarly journal whose bound volumes inspired youthful historical vocations. Reading it "made me what I am," medievalist Georges Duby wrote; Annie Kriegel was fortunate in discovering a set shelved outside her room at the women's branch of the Ecole normale supérieure.[86] Identifying oneself with the *Annales* approach of "total history" was a way of revolting against the concentration on politics and foreign affairs in traditional history and of feeling that one had joined the discipline's avant-garde. The *Annales* school offered the advantage of being sufficiently cognizant of the weight of social and economic factors in history to seem respectable even in the eyes of young scholars tempted by Marxism, without requiring them to adopt a set of dogmas that often contradicted their research findings.

One issue about which surprisingly little gets said in historians' memoirs is the question of how they chose the specific field to which they would devote themselves. In a well-known essay published in 1969, the English historian of France Richard Cobb posited that his own choice of topic had reflected an unconscious need for the "acquisition of a second nationality, of a second identity." He thought his case was not unique: any historian's specialty "will always be dictated to some extent by his own sense of involvement and by a certain feeling of identification with the period and with the country to which he devotes his research."[87] As a fifteen-year-old schoolboy in England, C. P. FitzGerald developed a passion for Chinese history because he quickly realized it was "a vast world of fascinating history of which I knew nothing whatever: it did not enter into the school curriculum at all (a strong point in its favor)."[88] As exemplified in Cobb's and FitzGerald's decisions to immerse themselves in the histories of countries to which they initially had no personal connection, the logic of such choices is not always obvious, and it is sometimes only through an elaborate process of free association that it can be established. Not all historian-autobiographers have wanted to concede that their choice of subject matter has such deep roots. Mitchell Snay, an American historian from a Jewish background who chose to study the religious history of the South, "was dimly aware at the time of wanting to write about something far removed from my personal concerns. I . . . wanted a strong demarcation between my personal past and my present life as a historian." But he argues that this desire for a sort of second identity was not the only determining factor. "My dissertation was conceived at a specific point in historiographic time and reflects those current trends in historical writing. The personal influence of my advisor was decisive. Finally, several key books served as inspirations and models."[89] Historian-autobiographers are thus divided on the question of how much their choice of subject matter truly reflects something about their inner self.

ALTERNATIVE PATHS

The fact that many historians' autobiographies written two or even three generations after Friedrich Meinecke still follow the basic pattern of his story about how his interest in history developed into a vocation is testimony to the relative stability of middle-class life patterns and of educational structures throughout the Western world, at least up through the 1960s. (It is still too early to tell whether scholars whose childhoods were lived in the age of television and the Internet will have different stories to recount.) Nevertheless, several groups of historians born in the first half of the twentieth century reached the point of writing autobiographies by different routes, particularly those whose lives were altered by the Holocaust, women, and those who lived exclusively by writing history rather than holding academic positions. Significantly, none of these groups report family backgrounds very different from those of any other historian-autobiographers. In terms of their origins, the French, German, and Austrian children of Jewish descent born between 1900 and 1935 who were to become professional historians after 1945 form one of the most thoroughly middle-class groups in this study: their fathers were almost invariably either independent businessmen or members of the educated professions. Women historian-autobiographers' family origins are somewhat more diverse—Jill Ker Conway's father was a sheep rancher in Australia, and American Joan Hoff and Australian Patricia Grimshaw came from working-class backgrounds—but the predominant story is also one of middle-class upbringings with easy access to books and schooling. This was the case for a future popular historian of the Civil War, Bruce Catton, whose father was a smalltown schoolmaster; another freelance historian, John Toland, had a more bohemian family background, but his parents still encouraged his love of school and reading, and he managed to get himself into Phillips Exeter Academy despite their lack of financial support.[90]

Where the narratives of these groups diverge from the Meinecke pattern is in the transition from secondary schooling to professional career. For members of these groups, there was usually no chance to follow the well-laid-out path from childhood reading and the encounter with an inspiring secondary-school teacher to university training. For the historians of European Jewish origin, the reason was Hitler. Although a surprising number managed to finish their Gymnasium studies as late as 1939 or even later, they then had to go into exile. Gerda Lerner, imprisoned and then released just in time to take her Austrian graduation exams after the Anschluss, writes that "my promising academic career, that wonderful utopian goal toward which all my energy and hopes had gone during those weeks in jail, vanished in the storm that swept over Europe and over our lives. I would not get back to it for over twenty years."[91] Some of the Jewish refugees who reached England found that it was the policy of the welfare agencies supporting them to insist that they prepare themselves for manual trades, lest the British population think that Jews were being given greater privileges than the rest of the population. Those who settled in Britain, the United States, or Palestine had to accustom themselves to a new language. The males usually wound up in their new country's armed forces, sometimes after a period of detention as enemy aliens.

No matter how passionately interested in history they may have been before they were uprooted, the chances of these exiles' making a career teaching and studying the subject must have seemed quite remote to most of them for many years. Certainly none of them could have foreseen that the anti-Semitism that had prevented Jews from obtaining posts at most American universities would disappear as quickly as it did after 1945. In the late 1930s and early 1940s, as George Mosse recalls, "history and English were subjects reserved for so-called Anglo-Saxons." In the course of his career, he would be the first Jew to teach history at two major American state universities.[92] Some of these scholars did resume their education as rapidly as possible after whatever disruptions emigration and war had imposed on them, but others did so only after long detours. Evyatar Friesel, whose family had gone from Germany to Brazil in 1939, dropped out of high school and worked for a time as a journalist there before deciding to join a kibbutz in Israel in 1953. Only after he had become disillusioned with collective life and agricultural work did he reconnect with his youthful interest in history.[93] Walter Grab, who had emigrated directly from Austria to prewar Palestine, worked in his family's leather-goods firm for twenty years and did not start university studies until 1958.[94]

The several dozen historians from such backgrounds who went on to make an academic career and then wrote about their life are, of course, an unrepresentative group. It is impossible to know how many young refugees had similar aspirations but were unable to realize them or accustomed themselves to a different kinds of career and lost interest in scholarship. It is nevertheless remarkable that so many of them eventually made it through college and graduate school and into the ranks of the professoriat. Many found that their background made academia easier to assimilate into than other aspects of their new homeland. As the German-born Helmut Koenigsberger writes, "My upbringing in a liberal-minded professional family was certainly important; but it would not have been very different in a similar family in England."[95] In some cases, their experiences had given these young refugees an intense and very focused determination to understand the historical causes of Nazism and the Holocaust. Raul Hilberg, whose family had been driven out of Vienna, remembered watching Hitler's troops entering the city in 1938 and thinking, "Some day I will write about what I see here."[96] Others were less explicitly driven by hatred of the Nazis but still strongly determined. Georg Iggers arrived in the United States in 1938 at the age of twelve, uprooted from his German homeland and his mother tongue; his father, who had been an independent businessman in Hamburg, was lucky to get a poorly paid job in Richmond, Virginia. Nevertheless, Iggers writes in his autobiography, "on the whole, my life turned out as I had imagined it in my youth: I wanted to be a scholar and a teacher, and I managed to do that."[97] The impression one gets from reading these narratives is that the cultural *habitus* acquired in their authors' early years was so powerful that not even the cataclysm of exile and war could disrupt it.

The life stories of the women scholars who were part of this group — Annie Kriegel, Gerda Lerner, Susan Groag Bell, Nechama Tec — show how difficult it is to distinguish what in their lives was the result of their experience of being classified as Jews and what resulted from their sex. All came from middle-class households. Tec was still a small child during the war, but the other three were well along in their secondary schooling;

Lerner, as we have seen, managed to graduate from Gymnasium even after having been thrown in jail in an effort to intimidate her parents into emigrating. Whether any of them would have aimed at a professional academic career if the war had not intervened is impossible to know. Kriegel did enroll in the women's Ecole normale supérieure after her experience in the Communist resistance movement, but for some time after the war her real commitment was to her work as a party militant, which carried her to a post on the central committee of the Paris region; in the United States, Lerner was also active in Communist-dominated groups and had various nonacademic jobs. Bell had become interested in history almost accidentally during the postwar years she spent in Britain, when she was a live-in companion for Barbara Hammond, a celebrated scholar, but "at the time, it did not in my wildest dreams occur to me that I might ever study, let alone be a historian myself." In a pattern familiar from many studies of women's lives in modern America, she followed her first husband to various places in the United States for ten years and did not even decide to complete an undergraduate degree until 1960, when she was in her midthirties.[98]

As we have seen, a number of male Jewish exiles tell similar stories of long delays before they put themselves on the historical career track. But these Jewish women's accounts are also similar to those of many women whose lives were unaffected by Nazism. Scholarship in women's studies has made the story of how qualified women were discouraged from pursuing academic careers during the years from 1945 to 1970 all too familiar. Collective volumes of autobiographical essays by women historians published in the United States and Australia include a number of testimonies by women who were drawn to history but who interrupted their studies for some years, either because the thought of pursuing a professional career seemed unrealistic or because they subordinated themselves to the needs of husbands and children. Many needed the assurance of an experience like the one Australian Jill Julius Matthews recalls when she describes the impact of the first college class she had with a woman instructor in 1966: "Somewhere in the labyrinth of my mind was the sound of a door opening, an unconscious recognition that there was more that a girl with a degree could do than become a teacher or a librarian."[99] Natalie Zemon Davis, a future president of the American Historical Association, represents a more complicated case. She grew up in the 1930s in comfortable middle-class surroundings, including plenty of books. She went to a good private school and later to Smith College, where she recalls having inspirational women professors, and from an early stage she was sure she wanted to study history.

Even her women professors assumed, however, that a married woman could not have a professional career.[100] Davis's husband, himself an academic, was supportive and believed in "equality of careers," but the two of them nevertheless took it for granted that she would go where his jobs were, and the peripeties of life with a husband blacklisted for his refusal to testify during the McCarthy period meant that she could not seek a teaching job until the 1960s.[101]

Davis's story highlights the vocational dilemma that confronted many future women historian-autobiographers. As in the case of most of their male colleagues, their families and teachers supported their interest in study up to the end of their undergraduate years; it was only when they began to think seriously about pursuing a professional career that their experiences diverged from the general pattern we have seen in these accounts. Jill Ker Conway's success in her studies had given her an "inner feeling that I had found something I could do well. . . . Now I had a purpose in life." But when she was turned down for a position in the Australian diplomatic service on gender grounds, "it came home to me that my sex rendered my merits invisible." In the long run, she came to see this as a valuable experience: "I needed to be made to think about what it meant that I was a woman, instead of acting unreflectively as though I were a man, bound to live out the script of a man's life."[102] But to achieve her ambition of becoming a historian, she needed to break out of the bonds of family, by moving away from her demanding mother, and the restrictions of her own society, by going to graduate school in the United States. Even at Harvard in the 1960s, she would still run up against the hard fact that the institution that allowed her to develop her talents would not consider women for the junior positions routinely given to its most promising young male Ph.D.s.[103]

This does not mean, however, that the autobiographical narratives produced up to now by women historians are entirely filled with denunciations of sexism. In her *Autobiography of a Generation,* the Italian historian Luisa Passerini has commented on the fact that her entire generation of Italian student radicals identified more strongly with their fathers, who often had a past that had included involvement in the resistance to fascism, than with their mothers.[104] Fathers who encouraged their daughters' intellectual interests appear more often than mothers in the autobiographical narratives of women historians, and a number of these stories also feature supportive husbands or lovers. The women historians' memoirs that have appeared up to now are almost entirely by scholars trained at a time when there were few senior women historians to serve as mentors, but most found enough sup-

portive male teachers to offset the unpleasant experiences they also encountered. Conway is outspoken about the extra burdens women graduate
students faced at Harvard in her day "by the mere fact of being female.
There was no way to expiate the invitation refused, however gracefully, or
the sexual innuendo deliberately misunderstood. A woman's work had to be
just that much better, more theoretically daring, more brilliantly researched
to shame naysayers with ulterior motives." Yet it was a male professor, Donald Fleming, whose interest in women writers gave her the opportunity to
see that they could be serious subjects for historical study: "It dawned on me
that I could study the lives of other women *and* be taken seriously. It was a
shock. A wonderful shock, but a startling jolt to a mind conditioned to the
male point of view."[105] Autobiography thus provides a more ambivalent
portrait of the process by which women obtained historical training than
one might imagine.

The life stories of nonacademic historians are a useful reminder that not
all history is produced within the confines of universities with their well-
worn routines. John Toland, who eventually won a Pulitzer Prize for his account of the beginning of America's war with Japan, is an extreme case but
an instructive one. Although he recounts his childhood love of reading and
his schooling in terms very similar to those used by many future professors,
his youthful ambition was to become a playwright or novelist, and he leav-
ened his college experiences during the Depression with summers spent rid-
ing freight trains, "staying in everything from flophouses to haystacks. . . .
This was life in the raw, and I loved it." A stint in the army helping to organize stage shows for soldiers led him into a marriage with a dancer and
jobs on the fringes of show business. Only at the age of forty-two did he finally abandon his dreams of writing fiction and accept a freelance contract
for a historical project, whose success led him into a new career, defined not
by a succession of university positions but by a series of book projects.[106]
Rather than a *Bildungsroman,* Toland's story is a picaresque chronicle in
which his emergence as a historian is presented as something of an accident.

Historians' autobiographical memoirs thus suggest a number of conclusions about the stories that scholars tell when they try to account for their
choice of vocation. Unlike the popular stereotype of young people who
grow up to become artists or poets, the protagonists in these narratives
rarely depict themselves as having been gripped by an irresistible need for
self-expression that required rebellion against their upbringing and education. Nor, with a few significant exceptions, do they tend to put forth deep
psychological explanations for their turn to history. The stories they tell put

more stress on cultural and sociological factors than on unconscious motives fully understood only in later life. For most of these authors, becoming a historian meant incorporating some of their parents' and teachers' values into their own lives. They usually remember childhoods lived out in reasonably comfortable material circumstances, with parents who tolerated or even encouraged bookish inclinations and who were able to guarantee that their children would be able to pursue their schooling through the university level. On the whole, these are stories of destinies firmly if unobtrusively shaped by family and culture, stories that fit with historians' inclinations to see individuals as being largely products of their backgrounds rather than with the emphasis on individuality that is often associated with autobiography.

Within this framework, however, these authors still see room for significant exercises of agency in their lives. Bookish children from middle-class families can become many other things besides professors, and as we have seen, parents rarely suggested the specific career of historian to these authors. Nor did any of them become a historian simply by accident. The inspirational teacher who appears so often in these narratives plays an important role but not a decisive one: becoming a historian requires a conscious and sustained commitment, one continued long after contact with any one teacher has been lost and sometimes kept up even when the future historian has progressed to the point of finding the formerly inspirational teacher a shallow charlatan. Despite their sensitivity to the influence of family, educational institutions, and social structure, historian-autobiographers thus portray themselves as much more than passive products of a process of social reproduction. Through their personal examples, they demonstrate that vocational choice, seen from the inside, remains an important existential moment and an opportunity for the exercise of the will, even for those who live in a modern middle-class milieu with a solid and predictable structure.

Nonacademic readers may find the distinctions between professing history, literature, and philosophy hard to fathom, but historian-autobiographers see their choices of one academic discipline over another as important acts of self-definition. In opting for history, they tend to see themselves as having made a choice to engage with reality, as opposed to abstract thought or imagination: history, as they depict it, is the academic discipline with the closest connection to authentic human experience in all its fullness. The paradox involved in this way of describing the choice of a historical vocation is that the reality historians devote themselves to is a mediated one, accessed not through interaction with other living human beings but through the study of documents and traces. By stressing the role of reading, and especially the reading of adventure stories, in their childhoods, these historian-autobiographers portray themselves as having been devotees of imagined realities, worlds into which they could escape from less interesting surroundings. Some youthful readers of Karl May and Jules Verne no doubt grew up to become anthropologists or journalists, seeking out real-life situations reminiscent of the adventure tales they loved when they were children. Those who became historians, however, were attracted by the possibility of telling stories about people they could not really meet or observe. But the stories historians choose to tell are nevertheless presented as *true* stories, not as products of their authors' imagination. What historians' personal narratives of their early lives seek to show us is how certain people come to dedicate their lives to the enterprise of giving actual human experience the shape and coherence of fiction. In writing their autobiography, these historians reaffirm this choice, telling realistic stories of that inaccessible personage they know better than any others: their younger self. In this way, their autobiographical enterprises demonstrate the curiously ambivalent nature of the "reality" that historians deal in, and the difficulty of separating it sharply from autobiography.

CHAPTER 6   Speaking of Careers: Historians
            on Their Professional Lives

Historians' autobiographies often say relatively little about their author's professional career. In many cases, readers learn that the author is a historian only from remarks in the book's preface or on its cover. This pattern is paradoxical: if the story of the acquisition of a vocation is worth telling, one would imagine that the story of the narrator's experiences in his or her chosen occupation would be equally meaningful. Social psychologists have often recognized, as Everett C. Hughes wrote in a classic article, that "a man's work is one of the more important parts of his social identity, of his self, indeed, of his fate, in the one life he has to live."[1] More recently, Al Gini has expanded on Hughes's insight, arguing that "for most of us the primary source of ego boundaries is our work. In work we come both to know ourselves and to orient ourselves to the external world. Work establishes a 'coherent web of expectations' of the rhythm, direction, and definition of our lives, which allows us to feel contained within precise outlines."[2] The part-time history instructor who produced a lively weblog about the challenges of her situation in 2001–4 titled "The Invisible Adjunct" underlined the connection between job and identity when she explained her concealment of her name as an expression of "the condition of anonymity and invisibility that characterizes adjunct teaching." In a professional sense at least, without a real job, she was not "capable of asserting an independent and fully visible individuality."[3] Since work is so crucial to identity, self, and the shape of life, it would seem to be the natural stuff of autobiography for those fortunate enough to have regular jobs. And yet in historians' accounts of their lives this is often not the case.

There are several reasons why many historians have difficulties finding an effective strategy for narrating the story of their adult career. One is a certain sense of modesty or even shame about the status of a life spent thinking and writing; this is related to the notion that academics' lives, like many other forms of modern work, are inherently lacking in drama. Even historians tend to see writing and teaching history as less significant than "making history" as a political or military leader, than writing novels and philosophical treatises, or than simply participating fully in "ordinary life." Another obstacle arises from the fact that these stories are necessarily representations of their authors' profession as well as of their individual lives. Part of the price of being a member of any professional community is an obligation to maintain the group's image in the eyes of outsiders. As Erving Goffman has pointed out in *The Presentation of Self in Everyday Life,* this requires passing over in silence certain aspects of professional life, notably conflicts between the group's stated ideals and the actual behavior required of members who want to succeed within the group. Members of a group, for example, are likely to maintain "that it was not necessary for them to suffer any indignities, insults, and humiliations, or make any tacitly understood 'deals,' in order to acquire the role" of a professional.[4] In an autobiography, however, such silence means omitting much of what actually shaped an individual's life and gave it drama. Women's narratives sometimes challenge this tendency to conceal the more unsightly aspects of professional life by exposing practices that betray institutionalized gender bias. Yet since most women historians who reach the point of writing a memoir did have a successful career, they too have acquired a stake in maintaining the image of the profession. In addition, women who write after having obtained a suitable academic position do not wish to present themselves as ungrateful complainers or open themselves up to charges that they received favorable treatment because of their sex.

In the face of these obstacles to writing extensively about their career, historian-autobiographers often simply omit the topic and emphasize either the experiences they had which seem more universal, such as childhood, or else those that involved participation in public events generally recognized as "historic," such as wars and political movements. The silence about professional life characteristic of many historians' memoirs is part of a larger phenomenon that affects academic autobiography in general. The years of childhood and education are years when characters are being formed and existential decisions taken. Furthermore, in describing the early period of their life, academic autobiographers need not be inhibited by fear of their professional colleagues' reactions, as they have to be when writing about their accomplishments in academic life. Reviewing a volume of personal essays by members of his discipline, American sociologist Charles Tilly complains that when "forced to confront their own lives, sociology's practitioners . . . tidy them up, mute their passions, avoid vivisection of their motives, portray themselves as bemused players in a game they do not run, treat their own careers as a series of breaks, lucky or otherwise." The authors, he found, tended to downplay conflict in their lives and to avoid critical comments about other members of the profession.[5]

Reactions to academic autobiographies that break this mold, such as James Watson's account of the discovery of the structure of DNA, show how sensitive scholars are to such transgressions. Reviewers commented that Watson's *The Double Helix* was "fascinating reading . . . but for some of its participants it's also a bit embarrassing." The book's "bleak recitation of bickering and personal ambition" threatened to discredit the scientific enterprise it purported to describe. The editor of a volume of autobiographical essays by other scientists, Joshua Lederberg, explicitly presented his colleagues' stories as an answer to Watson's book, which had made readers expect "narratives of chase, competition, and interpersonal stress rather than accounts of imagination gratified and cooperation achieved."[6] As these comments demonstrate, an academic memoir that says too much about its author's personal striving for success or suggests that academic accomplishment results from anything except diligent effort and luck is likely to raise peers' hackles. Environmental historian Stephen Pyne's account of how he won a prestigious MacArthur fellowship—"it fell out of the sky: the gods really are crazy"—is a model of acceptable public response to good fortune.[7] Traditionally, men and women who devote their lives to any of the academic disciplines are assumed to have made a commitment to a project—the pursuit and dissemination of understanding and knowledge—that goes beyond their private interests and indeed requires a certain renunciation of those interests. An autobiography that portrays its author as having behaved in ways inconsistent with that commitment obviously raises problems. This is especially true in history, a discipline whose progress is hard to represent as a succession of spectacular breakthroughs and discoveries to which a single individual could lay claim. The frequently repeated characterization of historians' work as "contributing a brick to the edifice of knowledge" reflects a conception of historical scholarship as a collective process, with little scope for flamboyant individuality.

If historians are cautious about stressing their scholarly accomplishments, they are even more reticent in discussing their work as teachers. Evaluating one's own pedagogical achievements immediately suggests vanity and gives an author the appearance of substituting himself or herself for the voiceless subalterns who sat in the lecture hall. "Academic autobiography, it seems to me, should steer well clear of the classroom," the historian of Africa Roland Oliver has written, "even if it creates the misleading impression that dons spend little time doing what they are mainly paid to do."[8] The often critical comments historian-autobiographers make about their own teachers, even those they found inspirational in their youth, are doubtless a warning to them not to overestimate their own impact.

The energy historians put into committee work and academic administration also vanishes with little trace from most personal accounts. Historian-autobiographers occasionally acknowledge the passions these activities can stir, but they are acutely conscious that interesting outsiders in these matters without losing their sympathies is almost impossible. Medieval historian Norman Cantor's chronicle of his unhappy trek through administrative positions at several American universities between the late 1960s and the early 1980s provides plenty of clues as to why the author's evaluation of his own accomplishments differed so much from those of the people he worked with. The accusatory tone of Cantor's writing and his dismissive treatment of those who crossed him makes it all too clear how he earned the nickname "Stormin' Norman."[9]

The fact that historians' autobiographies tend to be written by successful scholars who liked their jobs is another reason for their lack of drama and tension. Stories of smooth progress from first appointments at provincial institutions to final arrival at Oxford, Harvard, or the École des hautes études make up the majority of these narratives. The conventions that govern the genre inhibit much delving into the mechanisms by which such upward mobility is helped along; academic novels, whose characters, as we all know, bear no resemblance to actual persons, whether living or dead, can be much more revealing about such matters. The paths by which historians' memoirs are produced also effectively screen out memoirs by Ph.D.s who never found good jobs or never wrote significant books, even though, in the hands of a writer of real insight, whether and how one can maintain a commitment to history under such conditions might be interesting and important questions.[10] Narratives like that of Stephen Pyne, who found it difficult to combine his interest in the history of fire with a conventional academic career and who left a position at a major research university for one at a less prestigious institution, are rare.[11] So are memoirs by authors who left history for some other occupation. We may eventually hear from former Speaker of the House of Representatives Newt Gingrich, who started his career as a college history professor, but his life story is unlikely to be cataloged as a historian's autobiography. The second and third volumes of Jill Ker Conway's memoirs tell the story of her move from teaching and scholarship to academic administration, ending with her years as president of Smith College, but hers is the only such text I have encountered in my research.

In addition to a sense that modesty is incumbent upon professional academics and that some aspects of professional life need to be shielded from public scrutiny, historian-autobiographers are often inhibited from discussing their work by what they see as its repetitive and unstorylike character. Those who deal at some length with their professional career are grappling with a problem that extends beyond the realm of academic autobiography: how can one make a story out of a career spent sitting at a desk, performing repetitive actions that result in an intangible product, a contribution to the "information economy"? Unlike sports stars, history professors do not establish themselves through an agonistic struggle with their peers, nor do they, like politicians, progress toward higher offices with greater responsibilities. Nor can historians evoke sympathy by casting their work life as a struggle to maintain a sense of selfhood in the face of tasks that are "degrading, debilitating and dehumanizing," as many other workers do. A widely cited study found that professors at American urban universities were more satisfied with their jobs than were members of any other occupational group, and critics of academia have had an uphill task getting their colleagues to recognize what they do as "work."[12] Fritz Ringer and Howard Zinn, colleagues at Boston University during the stormy years of authoritarian president John Silber's reign, are the only historians who have written at any length about experiences as faculty labor-union militants.[13] As the Harvard historian Richard Pipes has written, "The rewards of a full professorship at a major university . . . are unique": lifelong job security, a light workload, and virtually complete autonomy. Although Pipes adds that "scholarship is lonely work" and that "scholars are psychologically less secure than most people" because of their dependence on the judgment of their peers, he recognizes that these complaints are not likely to evoke much sympathy.[14] Presenting their work lives as character-testing ordeals would also contradict the sense of the *Bildungsroman* with which most historians begin their memoirs, in which the profession appears in a positive light. Only a few historian-autobiographers, particularly those from a working-class background who have had difficulty adjusting to the academic milieu, have used their memoirs to express a sense of disillusionment with their occupation.[15]

Once they obtain an academic position, most historians settle into a routine of scholarship and teaching in which little of external interest seems to happen. It was recognition of this fact that led Arnold Toynbee, a historian-autobiographer who deliberately made his life outside the academy, to give up his Oxford donship: "The gravest [disadvantage of being a don] was one that is intrinsic to the educator's job at all levels. The rhythm of educational work is, and seems bound to be, cyclic. Each year the conveyor-belt brings to a teacher, for him to educate, a new annual batch of pupils of the same age as the batches that have passed and the batches that are still to come; and the teacher has to give each successive batch the same instruction." Such a life, in Toynbee's view, was neither worth living nor worth narrating: "If life has no direction, nothing happens in it; but when nothing happens in life, time does not stand still; time flows on, but flows imperceptibly. One finds that it has gone before one knows where one is."[16] If we accept Toynbee's picture of the historian's life as accurate, such a career would offer few opportunities for the exercise of the will that gives meaning to the stories of vocational choice examined in the last chapter. Toynbee was an exception among historians because of the scope of his ambitions—his *Study of History* spans the entire history of civilization—but his assessment of academic historical life is not unique. The British historian Eric Hobsbawm, whose career, unlike Toynbee's, was spent in university positions, has written that "academics spend most of their working time on the routines of teaching, research, meetings and examining. These are unadventurous and lacking in unpredictability by the standards of more high-profile living." Indeed, Hobsbawm worries that a group of historians may be "even less distinguishable from an assembly of insurance company executives than collections of other university teachers," suggesting that this problem is particularly acute for members of his discipline.[17]

How much of professional life gets left out of most historians' memoirs becomes clear from the rare narratives that, for one reason or another, ignore the guidelines that normally deter such autobiographers from publishing things that convention has classified as embarrassing. Three striking examples are the autobiography of the well-known British historian A. J. P. Taylor and those of two American historians, Monroe Billington and Peter J. Carroll. Taylor's book reflects a deliberate adoption of a strategy of provocation: he claims that his publisher made him remove seventy-six potentially libelous passages from the text.[18] Billington's, which seems to have been self-published, is probably as candid as it is because he felt sufficiently isolated from the mainstream of the profession not to worry about what other historians would say about his remarks, whereas Carroll's is the story of a man who left academia in midcareer.

Taylor claims that his early upbringing made him a person destined to ignore rules, including those of his profession. He maintains that his parents gave him no moral guidance whatever. "I had to work everything out for myself without knowing what principles to work from," he asserts. "Lacking any loyalty to the family, I went on to be without loyalty to any creed or class or nation. I was a nihilist for good or bad. I see now that this is what annoys others in my writings. They complain that I am controversial, deliberately provocative or wrong-headed. I do not mean to be. It is simply that I do not share the principles or prejudices of others."[19] Taylor's account suggests that this story of his upbringing is not always literally true—his parents, for example, became passionate supporters of the Bolshevik Revolution after 1917 and communicated this enthusiasm to their son—but it serves as a justification for violating the normal canons of academic autobiographical restraint.

Applied to the story of Taylor's professional career, this means that he feels free to express many sentiments his more conventional colleagues would keep to themselves. Having been turned down for a fellowship in 1924, he feels driven to point out that "I have become a much more distinguished historian than . . . the boys who got scholarships at Balliol when I got none"; for good measure, he adds that he succeeded as a journalist, whereas his Oxford history tutor failed. He boasts about the money he made during the 1950s, when he became a popular television personality, rates a set of public lectures he delivered in 1956 as being "in delivery, as in contents . . . my most triumphal achievement," and relishes the opportunity to explain exactly why he decided to cut off relations with his longtime friend Lewis Namier, another celebrated historian, after Namier arranged for Taylor be offered a Regius professorship at Oxford, but on terms that Taylor thought beneath his dignity.[20]

Together with Taylor's unusual frankness about other aspects of his private life, notably the intimate details of two of his three marriages and his unabashed defense of the highly controversial positions he took in many of his books, his depiction of life in academia gives the impression of an author out to reveal truths that his colleagues are too cautious to admit. Taylor's brashness makes his memoir more interesting to read than many other historians' life stories, but precisely because Taylor takes such pains to emphasize his maverick status, the credibility of his portrayal of professional life becomes suspect. He comes across as someone who often deliberately set out to irritate and provoke others and whose self-proclaimed indifference to their reactions was only feigned. It is also clear that the provocative tone of his account is in part a strategy to vindicate the equally provocative nature of many of his historical writings. Most other historians have not accepted Taylor's general claim that history is essentially a series of accidents, nor his specific assertion that Hitler was no more responsible than other European leaders for the outbreak of World War II. By writing a more candid memoir than most of his colleagues, Taylor tries to establish himself as someone willing to tell painful truths even at his own expense, a self-portrait meant to reinforce the credibility of his professional work. Sometimes, however, the candor of his personal account has the opposite effect. A historian who writes that a visit to Lenin's tomb at age nineteen convinced him that the Soviet leader "was a really good man, an opinion I have not changed," conveys the impression of a scholar who jumped to conclusions without much attention to evidence.[21] One would hardly want to pretend that other historians never experience the feelings of envy, competitiveness, and self-satisfaction that Taylor emphasizes, but one ends the book with a sense that he protests too much about their role in professional life.

Unlike Taylor, Monroe Billington, a historian of the American West, made a professional career far from the spotlights of fame, earning his Ph.D. at the University of Kentucky in the 1950s and teaching at the University of South Dakota, the University of Toledo, and New Mexico State University. While he, like Taylor, has a few scores to settle with old colleagues, much of his book is taken up with tedious accounts of the courses he taught and the academic politics of his departments. The most striking passages in Billington's book, however, are those in which he consciously raises issues that undoubtedly also concerned most of his better-known peers but that a sense of propriety or caution keeps them from writing about. It is common to find other American historians mentioning the salary they received during their first year of teaching, as a way of stressing how poor they were when they started out, but Billington is the only one who reveals what he earned all through his career. "I have not made various comments about my salaries throughout my working years to impress my readers," he writes. "Indeed, I mentioned my earliest salary figures to reveal how little the amounts were. Since the income of a salaried professor is generally less than the income of comparably educated and experienced people in the business world,

I have not mentioned the later figures in any spirit of braggadocio. Rather I have talked about salary simply because it has been a part of my life."[22]

Anyone who has been a professor knows that salaries are indeed an almost universally shared concern among academics. Billington's honesty about the matter exposes one of the taboos that usually limits academic autobiography. He is also far more open than most such authors in revealing how emotional academic politics can become. At one point, his colleagues at New Mexico State ousted him from his post as department chair. Writing more than twenty years after the experience, Billington still had not digested it: "Try as I might, I could not heal the wounds that I believed were unjustly inflicted upon me. The seven years of my chairmanship were followed by despondency, despair, and depression," and the ordeal led to the breakup of his marriage.[23] By showing how deep such scars can be, Billington again exposes one of the limits of more conventional academic autobiographies. The code of academic professionalism requires its adherents to pretend to regard something like election to a chairship as a matter of indifference or even a burden. To admit that it really mattered in one's life, and that being voted out of office was a devastating experience, puts an author outside the pale, even though honesty would compel many academics to admit that they know what Billington is talking about.

While Billington stayed in academia despite painful experiences, Peter J. Carroll wrote his memoir to explain why he had given up university life altogether. His memoir, although published only in 1990, reflects the critique of academia that flourished in the 1960s, especially its demand that scholars cultivate "the separation of feelings from judgment" and treat "expressions of the self" as "human errors best kept under control." As a graduate student, Carroll kept himself insulated from the political and cultural dramas of the 1960s, but they hit him with full force when he started teaching and realized the implications of black and Native American perspectives for the positive narrative of American history that had framed his understanding of the subject. In an attempt to understand both himself and his subject matter better, Carroll was attracted to the new subdiscipline of psychohistory, but he was frustrated by his colleagues' hostility to its insights. He recalls feeling increasingly trapped, despite the security of a tenured position at a major university: "My career extended to the horizons of time, forever unchanging, forever the same." Eventually, he drew the logical conclusion from his unhappiness and gave up his position to become a freelance author, a decision that paralleled his rejection of an unsatisfying marriage in favor of a partnership without legal sanction. The credo he proclaims at the end of his story, to the effect that "we are all exceptions to the rule. It is what makes us human," provides an ideological frame for his personal dissatisfaction with academia as well as for his engagement with autobiography.[24]

In writing about their careers, most historian-autobiographers have been unwilling to go as far as Taylor, Billington, and Carroll in violating the tacit conventions of academic life. Few have been willing to acknowledge, for example, the part that personal feuds and struggles against powerful older figures in the profession often play in academic careers. Some sense of this does emerge from the largely concordant references in recent French historians' memoirs to Fernand Braudel, the acknowledged head of the *Annales* school in the 1950s and 1960s. Braudel, who ruled over the institution now known as the École des hautes études en sciences sociales and the journal Marc Bloch and Lucien Febvre had founded, controlled a vast amount of academic patronage. The many portrayals of Braudel in these memoirs add up to a collective indictment of an oppressive and manipulative mentor whose undeniable intellectual ability did not offset his unpleasant characteristics. He was quick to take a dislike to certain people, remaining hostile to them throughout their careers, and he had very firm notions of what research topics were suitable. The medievalist Jacques Le Goff owed much of his career to Braudel and in his memoir calls him "a writer of exceptional ability who had a formative and creative influence on history and historians," but Braudel's behavior eventually convinced him that "this man, who we had admired as a historian and an administrator, and, we thought, as a man, reveal[ed] in private an outlook that we could not respect."[25] Uninterested in Holocaust survivor Léon Poliakov's research on the origins of hatred of the Jews, Braudel told him, "As long as you occupy yourself with anti-Semitism, you won't get anywhere with me."[26] When Pierre Goubert, realizing that "a close and lasting collaboration (a vassal relationship?) was unthinkable," turned down Braudel's invitation to become his assistant in favor of a teaching post at a provincial university, Braudel denounced him at a public meeting of the École faculty.[27]

The French historian-autobiographers who recount unpleasant experiences with Braudel nevertheless went on to have successful careers. Very few historian-autobiographers tell of careers shaped by real crises or debacles. Lawrence Stone, later one of the most distinguished historians of early modern English society, is one of the few whose discomfiture was so public that he could not pass it over altogether. He saw his career nearly shipwrecked when a better-known scholar, Hugh Trevor-Roper, demonstrated the inadequacies of one of his first scholarly publications in what Stone, in an autobiographical essay, called "an article of vituperative denunciation which connoisseurs of intellectual terrorism still cherish to this day." Stone comments, "What I learnt from this episode—learnt the hard way—is that before plunging into a public archive, it is first essential to discover just why and how the records were kept, and what they signified to the clerks who made the entries."[28] In other words, he treats the episode purely as an intellectual learning experience. How he felt about it at the time, how he found the strength to put his academic career back on track, whether he ever spoke to Trevor-Roper again—these issues are not addressed. There is more emotion in H. Stuart Hughes's account of the departmental donnybrook he lived through at Harvard when his second wife, also a historian, was turned down for promotion there, leading the couple to move to another university. "What was the point, I wondered, of enjoying so much prestige at Harvard when I was powerless in the case I cared about most?" Hughes asks, but when he invites readers to agree with him that he should have been allowed to participate in the deliberations about the matter, he probably loses the sympathies of most of them.[29] This example underlines the risks facing historian-autobiographers who are too open in revealing the conflicts that can arise between personal and professional values. Nonacademic historians, whose careers depend much more directly than those of their university colleagues on the reception of their books, are more likely to let the emotions generated by professional setbacks break through in their memoirs. In their "dual autobiography," Will and Ariel Durant devote an entire chapter, titled "Indicted," to the aftermath of a particularly savage critique of their volume *The Age of Louis XIV* in the *New York Times*. "My poor William took a long time to recover from that murderous review and its many echoes," Ariel writes; the book's healthy sales, however, salved his wounds.[30]

One reason recent historians' memoirs tend to emphasize success rather than obstacles is that many of them reflect the experiences of scholars who entered the profession during the period of academic expansion that followed World War II. That American universities grew enormously in this period is well known, but similar growth occurred in the rest of the Western world. Between the early 1950s and 1967, the number of history teaching jobs in France more than doubled.[31] When New Zealander Keith Sinclair started teaching in the 1950s, universities there were poorly funded, but "the situation was to change rapidly." By the time he became head of the department ten years later, it was "the beginning of an academic boom," allowing him to tell a story of striking accomplishments.[32] It is not just an effect of age casting a glow on earlier periods of life that makes these authors look back on the early stages of their career so positively: their memories reflect a certain reality.

Unsurprisingly, since the majority of these memoirs are written by historians of unusual ability, most of these authors had little difficulty finding a first job, although most had initial positions at institutions less prestigious than those where they later ended up. Although many express nostalgia about their early jobs, hardly any of these authors resisted the lure of positions at major research institutions when they had the opportunity. George Mosse writes in glowing terms about the "broadness of experience" he enjoyed during his years teaching at the University of Iowa in the early 1950s, but he seems to have regarded the reasons for his move to the larger and more prestigious University of Wisconsin as self-evident.[33] Annie Kriegel had her first French university post in Reims before moving to the Paris-area campus of Nanterre. "In twenty years, I never found the same pleasure in teaching at Nanterre that I had at Reims," she writes, but it is clear that she never considered the possibility of turning down such an opportunity.[34]

One finds little in these memoirs about the maneuvering required to obtain prestigious positions; most of these authors give the impression that opportunities magically appeared before them, with no special effort on their part. Historian of Jewish social life Jacob Katz, who turned to research at an advanced age and had a particularly difficult time making his way into the university system, is one of the few to give some hint of the struggle that can be involved in making a scholarly career. For him, the decision to give up a stable high-school teaching position for an untenured and poorly paid university lectureship, "without promise of tenure or a family pension, appears in retrospect as almost irresponsible recklessness."[35] Gabriel Jackson, tarred with the communist label during the McCarthy period, is the only memoirist who admits to having misled the head of a hiring committee (my father, as it happens) to obtain his first tenured position, after a long succession of temporary jobs, but he tells this story as an example of the effects of political harassment on academic careers, not as a comment on the normal reality of university career making.[36] For the most part, historians who have written about their professional experiences have accentuated the positive. They have thereby set themselves the challenge of telling an interesting story in the absence of the emotionally charged elements that provide the spark in most personal narratives.

FRIEDRICH MEINECKE: AN EXEMPLARY CAREER STORY

Because he self-consciously undertook to make his professional experiences into a meaningful story while remaining respectful of the discipline's collective self-image, Friedrich Meinecke's memoirs provide a useful starting point for discussing how historian-autobiographers can make meaningful narratives out of their careers without flouting the proprieties of academia. The first volume of Meinecke's memoirs has the familiar form of a *Bildungsroman* and ends literally at a high point, with his wife scaling one of the mountain paths he loved to hike in order to bring him the letter offering him his first academic appointment. "The stages of the climb upward, the first struggles with the world one finds oneself in, are much more interesting than the times in which a person, now integrated into that world, does his duty within it and satisfies the demands of the day," Meinecke writes at the beginning of his second volume.[37] Indeed, much of the interest of the second volume of his memoirs comes from his account of his involvement in debates over the conduct of the war that began in 1914, an activity not directly connected with his professional work. Nevertheless, Meinecke titles this volume *Straßburg, Freiburg, Berlin,* highlighting the importance of the three academic appointments he had held and, by implication, the importance of his work as a scholar, teacher, and academic politician. The tone in which Meinecke tells this story is carefully chosen to prevent it from striking readers as trivial. He does not exaggerate his problems or achievements, but neither does he minimize them or treat them in an ironic or offhanded way. He leaves no doubt that professional accomplishment and recognition mattered to him. Describing his reaction when he was offered a professorship at Berlin, the most prestigious of German universities, Meinecke writes, "I had now received more than enough external honors, to an extent that I could never have dreamed of. I freely confess that I was not capable of the virtuous and exemplary indifference with which Jakob Burckhardt treated such things."[38] This honesty is perhaps a violation of the code of academic professionalism, but admitting what academic success had meant to him allows readers to identify with him as a person and not merely as a practitioner of an esoteric craft.

The first volume of Meinecke's memoirs concludes by recounting two critical moments in his career. The first is internal: the development of his mature historical outlook, in which he moved beyond the "positivist spirit of the time, which sought to give the human sciences as precise and empirically grounded character as possible," which had characterized his student days, and articulated his own approach, one that would seek the "meaning of political events" through an analysis of their protagonists' thought. He had thus reached the point at which he was ready to make an original contribution to the writing of history.[39] But this was also the period when Meinecke became the associate editor of the most important German historical journal, the *Historische Zeitschrift*, and then its editor-in-chief. He is well aware of the importance this appointment had had in his career. When the previous editor, Heinrich von Sybel, made him his assistant in 1893, at the age of thirty-two, Meinecke became "all at once, within the guild of German historians, a man with whom one corresponded when one wanted to publish something in the discipline's principal organ, and someone who could provide much joy and inflict much sorrow through the choice of reviewers for new books." When Sybel died two years later, Meinecke—who still did not hold a university professorship—maneuvered skillfully to ward off the claims of a much better known scholar, Karl Lamprecht, whose approach to history Meinecke and other conservatives opposed.[40] The story demonstrates both Meinecke's sensitivity to the political stakes within academia and his ability to play the game successfully. The conjunction of these two episodes in Meinecke's narrative shows his awareness that intellectual ability is only one part of what making a career as an academic requires.

The years Meinecke spent in his first two jobs, at Strasbourg and later at Freiburg, were a time of continuing personal growth for him. He had to confront Wilhelmine Germany's version of multiculturalism, as he accommodated himself for the first time to universities with Catholic faculty and where he also had colleagues of Jewish origin. As a result of friendships with Catholic colleagues, "the overly strong fear of the Catholic world that I had grown up with . . . fell away almost without my noticing it."[41] Meinecke had been a "determined anti-Semite" during his student years, but he claims that his experiences as editor of the *Historische Zeitschrift* forced him to rethink his attitude. He found himself obliged to rely on Jewish specialists for reviews in certain areas and found some of them to be not only well-qualified academically but engaging personally. "Cases of this sort," he writes, "made me generally more tolerant. I was and remain—down to the present— sensitive to all the lesser and greater weaknesses and faults inherent in Jews, but from then on I lived by the rule of evaluating each case separately."[42] Meinecke's phrasing—written in the midst of the Holocaust but published after its end—testifies to the limits of his ability to overcome the prejudices of his culture, but also to the degree to which he had in fact grown away from his original conservative beliefs as a result of his professional activities.

In retrospect, the deepening conflicts within German society and the increasing danger of war overshadowed the more personal concerns that shaped Meinecke's life at the time, but he understands that these private matters had their importance. Above all, he stresses those moments when something altered the regular routine that characterizes most established academic careers. "Job offers and travel are the main things that give the life of German professors some movement and manage to keep it from going stale," he notes.[43] Even after nearly forty years, he was still angry about the circumstances in which he had felt compelled to leave his first job, in Strasbourg, for a position at the university in Freiburg. "It is tiresome to speak of things that should be left in one's professional and personal papers. But they once determined the course of my life, and in addition they are characteristic of the way the bureaucracy in the Reichsland [Alsace-Lorraine] conducted itself then," he explains.[44]

Relations with professional colleagues also occupy an important place in Meinecke's narrative, much more so than in Gibbon's and Adams's. Meinecke seeks to understand the attractions that led to friendships, even among those who held divergent historical views, and he is also alert to the tensions that underlay even his closest professional bonds, such as his long friendship with Otto Hintze, the other leading scholar of his generation. In a letter written while he was at work on his memoirs, he worries that he might have expressed "too much resentment, too much anger over the stupidities of my personal opponents from the past."[45] Meinecke brings his students into his narrative by showing that his interaction with successive generations of them was one of the most important ways he remembers experiencing the changing atmosphere of the world around him. Shortly after the year 1900, for example, he began to recognize that his students were bringing to class a "new idealism . . . an increased passion for spiritual and intellectual matters. . . . They enthused about Stefan Georg and Rilke, who I could only appreciate to a limited extent."[46] Mention of promising students killed in the war allows him to put a human face on the tragic losses it had caused. "I can hardly speak of the blooming circle of students I had before the First World War, without . . . thinking of the dark fate that so many of them met," he writes.[47]

In his memoirs Meinecke says relatively little about the scholarly books that were the basis of his career. None of them reached a general audience in the way that Gibbon's *Decline and Fall* had. He is nevertheless concerned to show how his research had been linked to the progressive development of his life. As a student, he had been interested in more distant periods of German history; it was one of his professors who first assigned him a project on the early nineteenth century, the era that would become his specialty. The same professor's request that he review an important publication on the history of nineteenth-century Prussian conservatism proved decisive. It gave Meinecke the opportunity to work out for the first time what he came to regard as his personal method of analysis: "My own nature drove me to the sometimes perilous way of working from the ideas—seen not as abstract formulas, but as forces working within souls—to the real events, and seeing ideas, embodied and developed by individual personalities, as the stuff of historical life." At the same time, he became conscious that this set of problems had great personal meaning for him. In the book he was reviewing from a critical perspective, "it was the world of my parents' home and the friends of my father, whose higher regions suddenly appeared before my eyes."[48]

Because of a severe stuttering problem, Meinecke had long doubted that he could obtain a teaching post, but after the completion of his first major book, a biography of one of the leading figures in the Prussian reform movement of the Napoleonic period, he became impatient with the limitations of the work as an archivist-scholar that he had been doing. Using the talent for metaphors that was one of his strengths, both as a historian and as an autobiographer, he communicates the issue in terms even nonhistorians can understand. The historian bound to a single archive, even one as rich as the Prussian state depository, "is a mariner bound to a single stream," he writes, "whereas the university teacher can dare to sail along different coasts and eventually, perhaps, on the high seas." Although it would take him thirty years to complete them, the ideas for the three major books that would define his career all came to him soon after he landed his first teaching post, when he was having to explore for the first time the broad themes of modern European history in order to construct his courses. This experience convinced him of the importance of teaching for scholarship.[49] These three projects were all connected to Meinecke's personal experience as someone who had made the transition from the old world of Prussia to the new world of post-Bismarck Germany. Running through them was the conviction that that new world was not, as many people claimed, the negation of the past but that it incorporated many vital elements of the earlier period. Pursuing this insight allowed Meinecke to turn from archival documents to the writings of the great German thinkers of the classical period. This was an exhilarating experience, but he fretted about reactions to his work, which challenged the pieties of German conservatives, German nationalists, and German progressives. As he waited for the publication of his first major book, *Cosmopolitanism and the National State,* anxiety made him seriously ill. It took positive reactions from respected colleagues to restore his morale.[50] Without going into the details of his scholarship, Meinecke thus succeeds in conveying its main themes, their relationship to his personal life, and the importance these projects had for him.

Unlike Henry Adams, Meinecke presents his life as a model for a historian's career, one that proceeded logically from childhood enthusiasms through professional training to mature accomplishment, and in which the historical consciousness attained in adulthood allowed the articulation of apprehensions dimly grasped earlier. There is little place in Meinecke's vision for the scholar whose life had not developed in this organic pattern: for someone who had had to struggle to gain access to education, for example, or whose life was disrupted by external events. From the perspective of contemporary autobiographical scholarship, it is easy to dismiss Meinecke's autobiography as an example of what now seem like untenable assumptions about the the universality of certain kinds of life experiences. It is true that Meinecke ends his memoir, whose second volume he completed at the start of 1944, by recounting the calamitous end of World War I and forecasting an even more disastrous outcome for its successor. He was well aware that his professional career had coincided with a period of national stability that had now vanished beyond recovery. Even as he anticipated the end of the world he had known, however, Meinecke did not question the presuppositions on which the academic life of his time had been built. He took for granted the hierarchical structure of university life, the relationship between the state and the academy, and the support that his wife had provided by running their household so that he could get on with his work.

As Patricia Grimshaw, an Australian historian, has written, stories of progressive and seemingly natural career development such as Meinecke's reflect a particular and often gendered perspective: "The notion of agency implied in 'making history' actually seems to be more suited to male historians who have begun their careers expecting life-long employment and have hoped for a life-long scholarly engagement."[51] Nevertheless, the ways Meinecke addresses the experience of being a professional scholar are useful in delineating the issues that arise in such a project, even when written by someone whose career took a very different path. Meinecke himself was aware of the limitations of taking a professional career as the center of a personal narrative. "One has trouble capturing things, if one starts, as has been done here, to divide the content of one's experiences into different categories and puts professional experiences forward as the essence of the whole," he muses. "In that way, one gains a fixed middle point, but on the periphery of the life-circle there is much that is diverse and colorful, that was also important to us, sometimes more important than what we experienced in our careers, and that came together with that experience to form that amazing whole, sometimes self-evident, sometimes seemingly full of secrets, that we call our life."[52] Even for Meinecke, the story of his professional career was not the whole story of his life, and taking the stages of that career as the framework for his narrative gave his story a unity that he recognized as in some ways artificial. On the other hand, however, Meinecke rejected the notion that a professional life is too insignificant to justify retelling. Above all, for Meinecke, his career had been the arena in which he had discovered who he really was and what he cared about. His story is essentially an account of self-discovery, not a celebration of accomplishment.

ADVENTURES IN THE HISTORY TRADE

Like Meinecke, other historian-autobiographers have tried, with varying degrees of success, to communicate to readers the significance of their professional work and to demonstrate that historians' careers can, in fact, be made the subject of narrative. Some authors have taken up the challenge of explaining the process of historical research and writing itself. Others have recounted the evolution of their views on central historical problems, and a few have made a story out of the development of their particular historical subfield. Historians whose careers have not flowed as smoothly as Meinecke's have shown how they overcame the obstacles in their paths. Finally, in narratives of the campus upheavals of the 1960s, historian-memoirists of two generations have confronted the question of whether the structures of university life that Meinecke took for granted deserved to be defended.

Ever since the Rankean revolution of the nineteenth century, working in archives has been the defining feature of academic historical research, just as participant observation distinguishes anthropology and laboratory experimentation the natural sciences. Making a good story out of long days spent leafing through old documents and filling in notecards is a challenge. The contributors to *Adventures in Russian Historical Research*, a collaborative volume by American scholars, were emboldened to write about their research experiences because the frustrations most of them experienced during the Cold War period and the changes that occurred after 1991 illustrate the larger historical changes that took place in the former Soviet Union.[53] Even researchers who have had to work in archives only under "normal" conditions can sometimes draw readers into their experiences, however, by communicating the way such work makes one feel "magically connected" to the past, as Drew Gilpin Faust has written.[54]

The French medievalist Georges Duby insists on the physical aspect of the process, the actual contact with these artifacts of the past. Presented with a bundle of medieval documents, he recalls, "I untied it and slipped my hand between sheets of parchment. Taking one of them, I unfolded it, and already I felt a peculiar pleasure. . . . Along with the palpable delight goes the sense of entering a secret preserve. When the sheets are opened up and flattened out, they seem to fill the silence of the archives with the fragrance of long-vanished lives. One can almost feel the presence of the man who, eight hundred years earlier, took up his goose quill, dipped it in ink, and began to form his letters."[55] Another French social historian, Arlette Farge, has written an essay on archival work, *Le goût de l'archive,* which is cast in the third person but has a strong autobiographical flavor. She recounts the confusion of the first-time user trying to orient herself in a new archive, the little rituals of longtime researchers competing with each other for the best seats, and the solidarity established among those who can understand each others' remarks to the effect that "Y 10139 is in much better shape than X(2B) 1354."[56] Working on a contemporary topic, Annie Kriegel had to hunt down her own sources, an accomplishment she considered vital to her success: "Gathering one's own data, even if it takes a lot of time and effort, allows one to observe *in situ* exceptions, incongruities, ambiguities that require reframing the subject and the initial hypotheses."[57]

For Farge, even the process of taking notes by hand in the archive is essential to achieving a comprehension of the documents: "The taste of the archive is acquired through this artisanal gesture, slow and inefficient. . . . As if the hand, in reproducing in its way the shape of the syllables and words of the past, in preserving the syntax of a past century, introduces itself into time more boldly than through paraphrases, in which the mind [of the historian] is already sorting out what seems important to it."[58] Reading over those notes, Duby writes, "is a captivating game whose charms are similar to those of exploration, detective work, and fortune-telling." Gradually, in the course of reading and rereading this material, "mechanisms far more delicate than those of the most marvelous computer come into play—including those of that inevitable and indispensable magician, the imagination."[59] It is here that the act of historical creation takes place, as the historian elaborates the sense and meaning of the documentation from the past and turns it into a narrative that will figuratively bring the dead to life.

These stories of work in the archives communicate both the specificity and emotional attraction of historical research and the quality of imagination it requires: they put historical research on the same plane with more prestigious endeavors such as scientific experimentation and creative writing. In order to transmit this sense of the experience of archival research, of course, these writers have, like Edward Gibbon, availed themselves of the autobiographer's privileges of telescoping many different experiences into a single moment of narrative and of employing literary imagery. A literal recapitulation of weeks or months in the archives would kill any narrative.

Readers of a novelist's autobiography may be interested in details of the writing process that produced the works by which the author entered their lives, but historians know better than to assume that their books are so meaningful to their readers that the circumstances under which they were written will be of much interest. More often, historian-memoirists will look back at the trajectory of their major projects and try to elucidate its logic—or, in A. J. P. Taylor's case, try to demonstrate that it had no logic at all, thereby vindicating his larger claim that "most things in history happen by accident."[60] Four historians who made particular efforts to shape the story of their successive projects into a meaningful narrative were C. Vann Woodward, a leading scholar of the American South, the French medievalist Georges Duby, the British historian of Africa Roland Oliver, and the Holocaust scholar Raul Hilberg.

The story of C. Vann Woodward is that of a man born and bred in the American South, who turned to history as a young man in order to make sense of the tensions between his loyalty to his region and his critical view of many aspects of its culture. "How could I reconcile being a Southerner with so many impulses then considered anti-Southern?" he asked himself.[61] Writing a book about the late nineteenth-century populist Tom Watson, a figure who embodied what he saw as the contradictory mixture of admirable and deplorable aspects of the region, was the answer. The project had the unintended side effect of launching Woodward on a professional career that was interrupted but not significantly redirected by service in World War II. His next book, *Origins of the New South*, was broader in scope. Woodward had deliberately set out to challenge the prevailing orthodoxy in the field, which emphasized the elements of continuity in southern society more than the rupture associated with the notion of a "New

South" in the late nineteenth century. In retrospect, Woodward thinks the favorable reception of his book was due less to his scholarly skill than to its appearance just at a time when southern society was beginning to experience the radical discontinuities of the civil rights era; he clearly displays an acute sensitivity to the historical circumstances surrounding his own career (*Thinking Back*, 67–68).

This is even more obvious in the case of his next book, *The Strange Career of Jim Crow*, his investigation of the origins of legal segregation, which was published just after the Supreme Court's historic 1954 decision in *Brown v. Board of Education*. In explaining how he, a white son of the South, came to write a book that was seen as delegitimizing the region's racial institutions, Woodward was driven to include an autobiographical parenthesis retracing the encounters with blacks and the experiences outside the region that had formed his perspective on race issues (85–88). As for the book itself, its impact was quite different from what he had anticipated. Unexpectedly for a southern white, he found himself being quoted by Martin Luther King, and in the 1960s "what had originated as a modest communication to a Southern academic audience had swelled into a mass paperback publication for a national and quite mixed audience of vast numbers" (92–93). Fellow scholars, on the other hand, were more critical of the book, accusing Woodward of being "too personally committed to a point of view" and of shaping his picture of the past to fit the needs of the present (94). Woodward's next book, *The Burden of Southern History*, struck him as something of a reversal of *Strange Career*. Instead of undermining one of the central myths of southern identity, *The Burden of Southern History* used lessons from the experience of his region to critique what he saw as the dangerous illusion of innocence embedded in mainstream America's view of itself.

Woodward's purpose in making a retrospective review of his scholarly work is neither to insist on the importance of his accomplishments—the fact that he had been invited to deliver the series of lectures that resulted in the book was sufficient testimony to his professional status—nor to argue with his critics. He concedes from the outset that some of his work has become outdated or unfashionable, but his purpose is not to update it. Instead, he wants to make his ideas comprehensible by explaining the context in which he had articulated them. Like other autobiographers, Woodward recognizes that he cannot escape the record of his earlier views: "One may defend, deplore, or revise them, but disown them—never" (4). *Thinking Back* provides an eloquent demonstration of how a historian can situate the professional aspect of his life in the larger panorama of the history of his times.

The persuasiveness of Woodward's book comes partly from the obvious relationship between his topics of research and the great public dramas of American life in the 1950s and 1960s, and partly from the tone of his writing. Unlike A. J. P. Taylor, for example, he does not insist on comparing his successes with those of other scholars, and he treats his critics respectfully even when he rejects their views. Woodward also portrays himself as a professional who values his peers' informed judgment over that of the general public. Commenting on the way *The Strange Career of Jim Crow* came to be cited in civil rights–era debates, he writes, "I was appalled by the reckless disregard for context with which the quotations were frequently used. The carefully noted exception, the guarded qualification, the unstated assumption, the cautionary warning was often overlooked or brushed aside" (93). He thus puts himself on the side of academic values as against worldly success, even in a good cause. Even as he identifies himself with the professional scholarly tradition, however, he takes pains to stress the larger cultural significance of his discipline. He had not only been a thoroughly professional scholar, but he had devoted his whole life to the study of a relatively limited topic, the history of his native region. But he associates himself with the example of the southern novelists of his generation—the generation of William Faulkner—and "the proof so magnificently presented in their work that the provincial subject matter we shared was no trap of obscurity but an embarrassment of riches, a treasure of neglected opportunities" (144). Woodward's narrative is thus a justification not only of his own work but of scholarly history in general, which he places on the same level with the greatest accomplishments of modern fiction.

Georges Duby's *History Continues* lacks the moral scope of Woodward's self-assessment, a fact that seems to have embarrassed the historian who wrote the foreword to the American translation; he comments that "it recognizes no clear failures, false starts, or troubling anxieties, but presents the embellished coherence of a successful career. Nor is it a work of long and profound meditation."[62] As we have seen, Duby is successful in giving a sense of why the procedures of historical scholarship can come to have deep personal meaning for those practicing them. When he turns to describing his own professional career, he tries, like Woodward, to situate it in the context of larger cultural and political developments. In his case, this means explaining the unique conjuncture of circumstances that allowed fortunate members of his professional generation in France to become not just established professors but public celebrities. Whereas A. J. P. Taylor credits his comparable success in Britain to luck and to his own abilities, Duby sees larger factors at work. He completed his thesis around 1960, just in time to take advantage of the wave of interest in France's rural past stimulated by a growing consciousness that the country's traditional agrarian sector was disappearing. Encouragement for Duby's work came from professional peers, from publishers who recruited him for various projects, and even from the French government, in the form of a proposal from agriculture minister Edgar Faure for the publication of a collectively written *Histoire de la France rurale.* Duby helped edit this work, which became one of the classics of French social history.[63] In retrospect, he sees himself as having been influenced by powerful currents of thought that he no longer entirely embraces, such as the Marxist writings of Louis Althusser and the structuralist anthropology of Claude Lévi-Strauss, and he recounts the steps by which he gradually moved away from these frameworks to a more subjective approach (*History Continues,* 61–63, 82).

After 1970, Duby became one of several professional French historians who became famous far beyond the academy, writing best-selling books and appearing regularly on radio and television. Duby does not seize on this recognition to make claims about his own importance, although his account certainly implies this; he uses it instead as an opportunity to demonstrate through his personal experiences the changed status of the French historical profession in general. "A century after history withdrew from the marketplace and took refuge behind the opacities of erudition, it now showed renewed interest in the literary business and the possibility of reaching a wide audience," he writes, adding that "emerging from our dens proved beneficial, not just for ourselves but for historical knowledge" (89–90). It is true that when he became involved in television production, he felt "more disoriented than I did among publishers and literary critics, who, like my fellow scholars, are men of the book, of the written word" (113). Even the literary marketplace was not entirely benign, since it meant that "the books we write . . . have become products of mass consumption, commodities trumpeted to the public by means of advertising" (107). Although his own story is one of satisfying achievements, Duby is gloomier about the prospects for the historical profession as a whole, complaining that "the academic environment" has "gone sour" and that "intellectual debate is, quite frankly, far less vigorous than it was thirty or forty years ago" (128, 131). He does not ask himself whether his own cohort's pursuit of extra-academic success had anything to do with these developments, and indeed such self-examination would have looked hypocritical in an account of so much recognition and prosperity. As a personal record of the experience of a group of historians who achieved a status almost unique in the modern history of their profession, *History Continues* is not without interest, but it lacks the pathos of Woodward's account of a career devoted to questioning the cherished myths of a society to which he remained deeply attached.

Another example of a historian's autobiography in which professional career and accomplishments are recounted at length for reasons other than simple self-celebration is Roland Oliver's *In the Realms of Gold: Pioneering in African History*. Oliver considers his story worth telling because it is also the story (from his particular point of view) of the emergence of precolonial African history as a recognized branch of historical scholarship, and thus of a significant change in the relationship between European and African cultures. After World War II, the British government recognized that its African colonies would eventually follow India on the path to independence and, in Oliver's version, made a benevolent decision to promote understanding of their histories, both in Britain itself and in Africa. Oliver, attracted to British imperial history by the accident of having been born in India, was funded to travel extensively in Africa to figure out what could in fact be learned about the precolonial past, and he developed methods for extracting a picture of past eras from the oral traditions preserved in African societies.

The story of Oliver's travels in East Africa with his wife and a bulky tape recorder during the early 1950s are more colorful than most historians' accounts of days in the archives, and his mention of the eighteen-month separation from their baby daughter that he and his wife endured in the name of his research indicates what a great personal investment both of them made in his project, but *In the Realms of Gold* is not primarily a travelogue. Oliver's real theme is the struggle to get the very idea of African history taken seriously at a time when "would-be historians of Africa had . . . to face the open incredulity of nearly everyone they met about whether their whole endeavor could possibly be worth while" (*In the Realms of Gold*, 138). Hence the story of the first academic conference devoted to the subject in 1953 occupies an important position in his narrative. When the London *Times* published a major article on the meeting, it was a real victory: "To read all this in such a public place was indeed to feel that my subject was at last on the map" (146). Similarly, his appointment to a readership and later a chair of African history at the University of London, the establishment of the International Congress of Africanists in 1962 and the African Studies Association in Britain in 1963, and his appointment as coeditor of the *Cambridge History of Africa* a few years later are all presented not as milestones in a personal career but as indices of his field's gradual rise to academic respectability, despite the hostility of established historians in other fields. Hugh Trevor-Roper, for example, claimed in the early 1960s that "there is only the history of the Europeans in Africa. The rest is darkness" (quoted 284). By establishing a graduate program in his field in London, Oliver felt that he was contributing to the intellectual emancipation of Africa: students recruited from that continent would receive training that would allow them to establish traditions of scholarship in their own countries.

Like Woodward and Duby, Oliver tells his own story partly to make a larger point about changes in the world around him. When he began his work in the early 1950s, the atmosphere was optimistic: he thought the British colonial regime could work with indigenous elites to prepare a smooth path toward eventual independence. He also believed that European-style universities could take root in African societies and that they would eventually be staffed by faculty from the region. Events moved faster than he had expected, however. By the late 1950s, he had come to realize that "all of tropical Africa had reached the end of an era" and that independence was about to be achieved, but he and other Western observers were still generally hopeful about the continent's future. "No one at that time had remotely got the measure of Africa's demographic problem," he claims, and no one anticipated the rapid descent of many of the newly independent African countries into dictatorship and abject poverty (225–26).

By the time of a failed international conference in Senegal in 1968, it had become clear that the future of African history lay neither in Britain nor in Africa itself but in the United States—a major disappointment for Oliver, both on personal grounds and because of his investment in the dream of turning the subject over to African scholars (318). Oliver's account is thus a bittersweet mixture of achievements and frustrations: African history did become accepted as a serious academic field, but the hope that this intellectual success would contribute to a general transformation of sub-Saharan Africa into a prosperous and progressive part of the community of nations was not realized during Oliver's scholarly career. Oliver's version of his role in the development of African history is contested—some African-born historians see his autobiography as a sort of neocolonialist enterprise, in which the benevolent author presents their continent with the key to its own past—but he has at least sought to give it a meaning going beyond his own personal story.

The examples of Woodward, Duby, and Oliver show that some historians' professional careers can be presented as stories of real significance, even when most details of the authors' emotional engagement with their professional milieu are omitted. Clearly this is easiest for historian-autobiographers who see a central theme in their work and who also see that theme as having a direct relationship to major issues that affected both the profession as a whole and the world outside it. Holocaust historian Raul Hilberg's personal narrative serves as a warning, however, that opening up a major new field of scholarship does not necessarily assure personal success. In the early 1950s, when Hilberg decided to make the destruction of the European Jews the subject of his dissertation, he "knew . . . I was separating myself from the mainstream of academic research to tread in territory that had been avoided by the academic world and the public alike" (*Politics of Memory*, 66). Hilberg claims that lingering anti-Semitism as well as the "peculiar subject of my doctoral dissertation" kept him from landing a proper job for many years (94). He faced even greater frustration in the effort to get his massive manuscript published. A series of presses turned him down, and Jewish institutions devoted to the study of the Holocaust would not help him because of his controversial conclusion that Jewish victims had not done enough to try to save themselves (106–17).

In 1961, the University of Chicago Press finally published the first edition of *The Destruction of the European Jews*, which has become the central pillar of Holocaust scholarship, but this was not the end of Hilberg's struggles. The chapter in his autobiography that covers the fate of his book is entitled "The Thirty-Year War." The lack of interest in his subject persisted for some time, and when changing circumstances led to greater attention to the Holocaust, other authors who had done much less firsthand research than Hilberg garnered the success that he thought should have come to him. Plans for a German translation fell through, Jewish audiences continued to react angrily to Hilberg's emphasis on the victims' passivity, and he recognized that he would not be hired by any prestigious university. By the late 1960s, Hilberg felt that his entire life was falling apart. He withdrew for a time from active scholarship and threw himself into university administration. The publication of an expanded American edition of his book in the mid-1980s and then of a German version finally brought him widespread recognition but also forced him to confront the paradox that his work was most accepted in the country whose citizens had forced him and his family to flee (123, 142–46, 164, 167, 175). The prickly personality that emerges from the pages of *The Politics of Memory* undoubtedly accounts for some of its author's difficulties, but by no means all of them. Whereas the narratives of Woodward, Duby, and Oliver implicitly suggest that historians who dedicate their lives to meaningful themes will receive appropriate recognition and be able to look back with satisfaction, Hilberg's story demonstrates that such an outcome is not guaranteed, even for a scholar whose importance has come to be universally acknowledged.

Stories about lives dedicated to a single master theme enable historian-autobiographers to shape coherent personal narratives, as long as they are willing to depict their professional activities as the center of their life. The memoirs of many scholars at least as distinguished as Woodward, Duby, Oliver, and Hilberg—those of Pierre Vidal-Naquet and Eric Hobsbawm come to mind—do not produce this effect, even though these authors devote some serious attention to their professional work. In Vidal-Naquet's and Hobsbawm's cases, however, it is clear that the authors never wanted to be defined only or primarily as historians, and the stories of their political engagement and their general reflections on the eras they lived through drown out what they have to say about doing history. This does not necessarily make their books inferior as memoirs—for many readers who have no special concern with the profession of history, they may be more, rather than less, interesting—but it does help explain the paradox of the many historians' life stories that insist on the satisfaction they derived from their career while giving readers little sense of that career's actual content.

THE CHALLENGE OF THE 1960S

For historians who lived through them, the campus movements of the 1960s were the one point in their life when they had to decide whether the traditional values that had shaped their scholarly career were worth defending or whether they needed to invest themselves in trying to change the nature of academia. Regardless of their position on the issues of the times, for a number of these author what Henry May calls the "learning and self-searching" forced on them in the 1960s had a clear connection with their later decision to write a personal memoir, even if the events of those years wind up occupying only a minor part of it.[64] May's comment, reflecting his experience as a faculty member who had to deal with the campus movements at Berkeley in the 1960s, is a relatively tolerant one for a member of the professional generation who was at midcareer in that period. Many others remember the period in highly negative terms. For Annie Kriegel, the French student protests of May 1968 were "an aggression, as brutal as a bolt of lightning, that annihilated [the university]."[65] Student demonstrations at his Colum-

bia campus made "my last years of teaching the bitterest of my life," Shepard Clough writes, and Harvard professor Richard Pipes never forgave colleagues who "were prepared to give up all that made our university great in
order to pacify the mob."[66] Many older historian-autobiographers were by
then in positions of campus authority, which gave them, as the Israeli historian Jacob Katz puts it, "the opportunity to experience at first hand the
weight of responsibility and leadership so familiar in abstract terms," but
also the responsibility of defending institutions to which they had committed much of their life.[67] Even those whose subject areas benefited from the
radical atmosphere were not necessarily sympathetic to it. Interest in the
non-European world increased the number of students in Roland Oliver's
African history courses, but he found it difficult to teach in an atmosphere
of "euphoria that caused its adherents to feel that all initiative and all decision making should henceforward belong to persons aged eighteen to
twenty-one," he writes. "Like many others of my generation I look back on
the five years of student estrangement as an unhappy period, when I wondered if I had taken up the wrong profession."[68]

Even historians of Oliver's generation who still defined themselves as
leftists or progressives when they came to write their memoirs usually remember the 1960s in negative terms. "We, or at least congenitally pessimistic middle-aged reds such as myself, already bearing the scars of half a
lifetime of disappointment, could not share the almost cosmic optimism of
the young," Eric Hobsbawm says.[69] A lifelong jazz fan, he was out of place
in the era of rock music. Having run for the United States Senate as a left-
wing alternative to Ted Kennedy in 1962 and having been an early opponent
of the Vietnam War, H. Stuart Hughes was surprised to find himself "out-
flanked" by radical students who rejected his attempt to distinguish between his role as citizen and his role as professor. They "wanted the university, *as an institution,* to take a stand against the war," Hughes notes,
which contradicted his conviction that academia represented values of its
own that should not be subordinated to politics.[70] George Mosse, also active in the antiwar movement, sympathized with students' demands to be
treated as adults and helped abolish "the old policy of *in loco parentis*" on the
Wisconsin campus, but he disapproved of some student protest tactics and
found himself trying to get them to think more critically about the consequences of their actions.[71] At UC–San Diego, Gabriel Jackson, whose own
career had nearly been scuttled by the anticommunist hysteria of the 1950s,
found himself at odds in the 1960s with student protestors "inebriated . . .
by Friedrich Nietzsche's scornful, violent rhetoric calling for the destruction

of existing bourgeois values and the 'transvaluation of values' by an elite that had not been corrupted by the prevalent hypocrisy and cowardice." Like most of his generation, he saw himself as having made a choice for academic values over immediate political goals. "The war would be over in a few years, but the university would be there for generations."[72] At New Mexico State, Monroe Billington, who considered himself sympathetic to civil rights, was nevertheless relieved when a black student who objected to being called a Negro dropped his class: "I was glad he did not return if he was expecting to use the class as a platform for the expression of his anger or for disrupting a learning environment."[73]

A few historian-memoirists whose careers were already established did participate in pedagogical experiments inspired by the 1960s atmosphere, but in hindsight they recognize that these efforts achieved little. Maurice Agulhon hoped that the 1968 movement might modify the authoritarian structure of French university life; he was disappointed when radical student leaders rejected the possibilities for reform embodied in the law passed by the French government after the demonstrations.[74] Georg Iggers, who had been active in civil rights movements in the American South and later in opposition to the Vietnam War, describes the idealistic attempt to find an alternative to conventional academic structures at the University of Buffalo in the late 1960s and his participation in a faculty sit-in to protest the unleashing of police against student demonstrators, but he seems to have accepted the return to normal routines at his campus after 1970 with little objection.[75]

Two historians who recount personal engagements in efforts to change the nature of university education were Carl Schorske and Martin Duberman. Schorske, who played a central role in faculty responses to student protests at Berkeley from 1964 to 1969, writes, "I went through the same rhythm of anguish, illusion, hope and disabusement that is so often the lot of participants in intense social crises." As part of an effort to "reconcile . . . faculty authority and educational renewal," he tried to restructure his courses at Berkeley to give students a more active role in their own education: he set up "satellite seminars" with student-defined topics in conjunction with his lectures, seeking to create "a healthy dialectic between the interpretive scheme of my lectures and the ideas and existential concerns of the students reflected in each seminar's special theme." The rising violence on the Berkeley campus soon drove him away, however. (When I was an undergraduate student in one of his courses, I happened to visit his office on a day when a demonstrator had thrown a large rock through his window.) Looking back, he says that he "went to Princeton in order to save if possible my scholarly work."[76] Martin Duberman, meanwhile, fled from that same Princeton department after the painful failure of an experimental course that he team-taught with a psychotherapist. "Our aim was to create a promising hybrid," Duberman recalls: "traditional academic exhange in an intimate setting that put a premium on openness and honesty rather than on the usual classroom staples of fear, concealment, and game playing." Instead the class fell apart, with the therapist telling students that Duberman "had been manipulative, had indirectly exerted control over the choice of topics and the course of discussion even while theoretically rejecting authoritarianism in the classroom."[77] Duberman blames his colleague for bad faith, but his own account suggests that the effort to combine discussion of history with a deciphering in "real time" of classroom psychodynamics was inherently problematic.

More positive assessments of the impact of the 1960s occur in the memoirs of historians who were just beginning their careers or were still students at that point, and particularly in the recollections of women. Fritz Ringer, who was an assistant professor at Indiana University during a student strike there in 1969, sympathized with student demands, though not with the confrontational tactics they used. "Above all," he writes, "I remember the 'strike' at Indiana as an exemplary experiment in education. The undergraduates I taught in those days were avidly interested in the ideas and social issues we discussed. They cared about the debates they had with each other and with me."[78] For the Italian Luisa Passerini, 1968 was the year that formed the identity of her entire generation, "a worldwide phenomenon that is not yet completed and is thus difficult to grasp." The student movement's rejection of older models of academic professionalism in favor of commitments to "the everyday, to subjectivity, less separated from life," was the start of the process that ultimately led, several decades later, to the writing of her autobiography.[79]

The autobiographical essays in the American collection *Voices of Women Historians* and the Australian volume *Feminist Histories* contain numerous testimonies to the liberating effect of the 1960s and early 1970s on women. The ferment of the period both opened new career possibilities for women and made possible the study of women's history as a subject. "Those early days were exhilarating!" Renate Bridenthal recalls.[80] Sheila Rowbotham's memoir of the 1960s, *Promise of a Dream,* stresses the sense of possibility that pervaded the period for those who hoped to combine activism and history. In France, the future historian of the Lacanian psychoanalytic movement, Elisabeth Roudinesco, had a totally different memory of the pedagogical experiments inspired by May 1968 from that of older memoirists who had been professors in those years. At the new campus of Vincennes, from 1969 to 1974, "no professor repeated for the hundredth time a textbook that had gone through a hundred editions and each of them instead gave the impression of creating a future book as they spoke, with the desire of submitting each line to the judgment of the audience."[81]

Although the movements of the 1960s, with their questioning of established academic structures, were essential in opening the historical profession to women, those women who went on to become historians do not always have an unequivocally positive recollection of the period. Passerini came to see first the oppressive elements of the male-dominated leftist groups she had been involved with in the 1960s and then the confining nature of the women's groups she joined in the early 1970s. By 1975–76, she had decided that a commitment to activism was incompatible with her interests in history.[82] Roudinesco's emergence as a historian also required a rejection of the Lacanian cult she had originally found so liberating. Dissatisfied by a movement that she saw becoming "a caricature of a Bolshevik party . . . I was not far from the idea that in this crisis, in which theory proved ineffective, the recourse to history could have a saving grace for a whole generation."[83] Even the historians' memoirs most imbued with "the spirit of 1968" thus ultimately affirm the value of the professional academic history that the students of the time were often protesting against.

The ways in which women historians' memories of the 1960s differ from men's testify to the difficulty women have had in fitting themselves into the standard plot of careers designed for men. As yet, few of these texts come from the post-1960s generation of women who could plan for a career in the same way as men. As the previous chapter has shown, the connection between female historian-autobiographers' interests as teenagers and their eventual emergence as historians is often much less direct than is seen in their male counterparts. For many women, it was the upheaval caused by the radical movements of the 1960s and the early stages of the women's liberation movement that convinced them both of the importance of history and of the possibility of women's achieving full status in the academy. None of the male historian-autobiographers who have published stories of their lives had the experiences that Sheila Rowbotham, Lynn Weiner, and Sandi Cooper recount of struggling on the margins of the profession as a poorly paid adjunct or untenured lecturer for many years. Only the tremendous expansion of universities in the 1960s and the period's cultural turmoil finally enabled many of these women to secure a regular position. By the end of that decade, the women's movement was taking shape, and as Cooper writes, "everything was changing from the world of my childhood, schooling, and early professional expectations."[84] Even women whose curricula vitae might make it appear that they had no difficulty obtaining jobs at prestigious institutions sometimes recall facing real ordeals. In 1969 Carolyn Bynum, a future president of the American Historical Association, became one of the first women hired as an assistant professor at Harvard; yet her memories are anything but triumphal. "The tremendous weight of discrimination against women came down on me like a ton of bricks—the isolation, the difficulties, the opposition, and, yes, even the hatred." Cochairing the university's Committee on the Status of Women "left me quite politically exposed," she recalls. "I received hate mail, even threats, and at one point had to seek police protection. . . . A male junior faculty member suggested that I was trying to get tenure by troublemaking."[85] It is not surprising that many women historians have particularly warm memories of the creation of the first networks of women scholars in the years around 1970. Male historians' autobiographies often refer to important friendships, as we have seen in the case of Friedrich Meinecke, but even in the case of authors from groups that had been discriminated against, they tell stories of individual career success. None of them convey the sense of having found in their colleagues the "wide and comforting safety net of likeminded spirits" that Susan Groag Bell evokes.[86]

Historian-autobiographers' reflections on their professional careers thus demonstrate that some elements of a life spent in academia can be effectively incorporated in a personal narrative. As Meinecke was already aware, such an enterprise has its perils. Few autobiographers want to give the impression that professional activity really absorbed all their thought and passion. In a culture that cherishes the notion of a "true self" prior to the modifications imposed by interaction with society, to portray oneself as entirely absorbed by one's occupation is almost a denial of one's humanity. The very act of publishing an autobiography is a way of asserting the author's existence as something more than a member of a particular profession. At the same time, however, an autobiography covering the adult life of a person identified as a historian that fails to give some sense of what significance that career had for the author is bound to seem incomplete. Accepting the challenge of incorporating the experience of professionalism into a personal narrative does, however, impose some restrictions. The autobiographer whose book too flagrantly contradicts the profession's strictures against overt ambition or explicit concern with money risks a certain ostracism. Nevertheless, as Meinecke's narrative shows, a historical career ineluctably entails some desire for status, power, and financial rewards. The difficulty of writing about these matters without seeming to trivialize oneself is one of the limitations of historians' autobiography, and indeed of academic autobiography in general.

The most successful narratives of professional lives in history are those that use their authors' personal experiences to help nonspecialist readers see how historical work is linked to larger issues. These may involve showing how the specialized routines of archival research can extend and channel the creative powers of the human imagination, or how a historian's personal career was related to larger political or social transformations. In many of the narratives examined here, accounts of the events of the 1960s are occasions for authors to reveal how deeply the special values of academia had become embedded in their lives or, conversely, to show how challenges to established academic structures made new kinds of careers possible. Through the personalized medium of autobiography, historians thus assert that academic careers are not merely vehicles for personal aggrandizement within a limited arena.

The success of some historians' efforts to draw readers into the details of their working life demonstrates that there are ways of turning contemporary professional careers into meaningful narratives. The enterprise remains a perilous one, however. To tell at least some of the truth about a life in academe without appearing smug about one's accomplishments, bitter about one's frustrations, jealous of the rewards reaped by others, or disloyal to one's discipline, and at the same time to make the story stimulating, is not easy. Despite the generally acknowledged importance of work in most people's lives, only a few careers can easily be recounted along plot lines that our culture recognizes as inherently interesting. Historian-autobiographers, who often turn to personal narrative because they want to transcend the boundaries of their professional life, thus find it difficult to draw general readers into the details of the experiences that shaped the career that was so important to them. For this reason, most historians' memoirs continue to be judged largely for their skill in narrating their authors' personal life, and especially their childhood, or for what they say about their author's engagement with public historical events of their own time, the topic to which we will now turn.

CHAPTER 7   Historians' Autobiographies
and Historical Experience

As the two preceding chapters have shown, what historians' autobiographical writings tell us about the shaping of private lives and about the experience of history as a profession is often important and sometimes unexpected. Probably, however, most readers turn to historians' autobiographical
writings in hope of finding insights into the interaction between individual
lives and the public events that are history's customary domain. Historians
who personally experienced the two world wars, the Great Depression,
and the rise of mass political movements ranging from Communism and
Nazism to the campaign for civil rights in the United States might be
expected to have something significant to say about how their lives were
affected by such unquestionably "historical" events. Almost all the authors considered here have written about the intersection between their life
and the large-scale historical events of their times; many of them devote
more of their text to their experiences of war or politics than to their childhood or their professional career. By addressing these topics, historian-
autobiographers help show how autobiographical writing can make contributions to the understanding of human experience that are different from
those offered by either history or fiction.

Modern historian-memoirists' involvement in public historical events
has taken many forms. Some historians, such as those subject to Nazi persecution, whose memoirs will be discussed in the next chapter, have led
lives shaped in dramatic ways by large-scale events, while others lived
through the tumults of their times without being personally affected by
them. Some historians were involved for at least part of their lives as sub-

ordinate actors on the stage of history—as low-ranking soldiers or sailors in wartime or as rank-and-file supporters of political and social movements. And a few had privileged opportunities to witness the making of major decisions or even exercised some direct influence on the outcome of historical events. Although the Indian historian K. M. Panikkar calls the publication of his classic work on *Asia and Western Dominance* a "landmark in my life," the pages he devotes to his history writing are brief interludes in a memoir focused primarily on his role in politics and diplomacy.[1] Edwin O. Reischauer served as U.S. ambassador to Japan in the 1960s, the second volume of his Harvard colleague Arthur Schlesinger Jr.'s memoirs—not yet published as I write—will presumably describe his role in the Kennedy administration during the same period, and Richard Pipes was the Reagan administration's adviser on policy toward the Soviet Union in the early 1980s. In France, Annie Kriegel held a significant position in the Communist Party during the early 1950s. In Fiji in the 1990s, Brij Lal was a member of the Constitution Review Commission that attempted to restore democracy after a period of authoritarian rule. Lal, New Zealand historian Keith Sinclair, and American scholar H. Stuart Hughes campaigned, albeit unsuccessfully, for seats in their national legislatures. In one way or another, many historian-autobiographers have been as historically important as many of the individuals historians write about.

The intensity with which historians remember these experiences in the realm of history varies as much as the nature of the experiences themselves. For many, immersion in history was part of growing up, a phase they left behind once they found their true vocation. At the other extreme, however, there are a number of historian-activists for whom public engagement formed the core of their life and for whom being a historian was simply one way among others of pursuing that engagement. This category includes the dedicated German communist Jürgen Kuczynski and the American political activist Howard Zinn, but also such scholars as Alfred Grosser in France and Edwin Reischauer in the United States, two historians whose lives were largely defined by efforts to improve relations between the country where they lived and the country in which they were born—Germany in Grosser's case, Japan in the missionary son Reischauer's. Historians also differ widely on the question of how significant historical events were in their lives. Some scholars see public events as having essentially defined the shape of their existence; others see themselves as following their private trajectory in spite of what was going on around them. Finally, historian-memoirists also take widely differing views of how much impact their experience of history had on the history they taught and wrote. Some use their first-person narrative to show how events of their times influenced the way they understood the life of the past; others see little connection between their own experiences and those of the people they studied. Historians' memoirs, rather than offering a single answer to the question of what it means to live in history, thus give a variety of perspectives on the issue, reflecting the variety of ways in which historians engage with the events of their times.

The late twentieth-century historiography to which the historian-autobiographers discussed here contributed is often marked by a determined turn away from the military and political matters that had traditionally dominated historical narrative and that would have undoubtedly constituted most of the history taught in schools and universities prior to the 1970s. Scholars such as Jürgen Kuczynski, Emmanuel Le Roy Ladurie, Natalie Zemon Davis, and Gerda Lerner are associated with approaches to history emphasizing the study of ordinary people's everyday lives, the impact of economic conditions, analysis of cultural patterns, and relations between the sexes. The autobiographical writing that they and their contemporaries have produced often touches on such issues, but when they try to communicate what defined the uniqueness of the times they lived in, they frequently highlight the wars and political movements that are downplayed in their scholarship. In historians' hands, autobiography, though frequently seen as a venue for the exploration of private experience, proves difficult to disassociate from the most public of public affairs.

To some extent, one might attribute this to the magnitude of the events twentieth-century historians lived through. The two world wars, the era of totalitarianism, the Holocaust, the invention of the atomic bomb, the Cold War, and the civil rights era in the United States were indeed significant events by the standards of any epoch. Historically minded individuals who lived through them may well have felt that they were affected by events of an intensity that earlier generations did not know. It is difficult to decide whether the years from 1914 to 1970 were truly a unique period in human experience or whether each generation finds reasons to think that the concatenation of events it witnesses has greater impact on human consciousness than any that went before. As we have seen, Edward Gibbon's memoirs suggest that he did not consider the history of his own day particularly interesting. The Seven Years' War enters his narrative because it channeled him into military service, but he did not claim that it had changed his life or the society in which he lived, and we have noted his dismissive comment about the French Revolution, which other evidence shows affected him more than his memoirs acknowledge. *The Education of Henry Adams,* however, like many twentieth-century historians' memoirs, reflects a sense of a life shaped by cataclysmic historical events. In his life story Adams was responding to the democratization of American politics, the Civil War, the drastic change in the European balance of power resulting from the unification of Germany, the imperial conflicts of the years around 1900, and the dramatic changes in technology that, to him, foreshadowed even more apocalyptic transformations. His example warns us against any facile assumption that the mid-twentieth century was a period whose wars and political events were inherently more traumatic for contemporaries than those of any previous era.

HISTORIANS AT WAR

There is nevertheless no denying that historians born in the first decades of the twentieth century belonged to generations harshly affected by events of great magnitude. The two world wars defined an entire era. Wars are, of course, a classic theme of historical narrative, fiction, and memoir literature, and historian-autobiographers who discuss their own experience of them face the challenge of saying something meaningful about a subject already represented in powerful and often conflicting ways by other authors. In the hands of both historians and novelists, war stories have been occasions for portrayals of human purposefulness and heroism on the one hand and the shattering effects of trauma on the other. Most historian-autobiographers, however, have told war stories that differ from those found in classics such as Robert Graves's *Goodbye to All That* and Erich Maria Remarque's *All Quiet on the Western Front.* Unlike the two great war leaders whose memoirs of World War II are also classics of historical literature, Winston Churchill and Charles de Gaulle, these future historians did not experience a sense of mastering events, but they also do not portray themselves as victims whose sense of self was shaken by war's violence. In their professional writing, historians emphasize climaxes and moments of significance; in recounting their own recollections of warfare, however, many of them have found themselves writing about years spent in activities of no real importance. As historians, they are able to justify these unheroic and undramatic narratives as contributions to a fuller understanding of the past, whereas "ordinary" war memoirists might feel inhibited about putting such seemingly unimportant details on paper. Historian-autobiographers are thus in a position to depict aspects of wartime history that other forms of war narrative rarely include.

Although World War I inspired a huge amount of testimonial writing—as well as perhaps the first significant literary study of this phenomenon, Jean Norton Cru's *Du témoignage,* published in 1929—relatively few historian-autobiographers were directly involved in the fighting. It is also important to note that the majority of historians' memoirs that discuss World War I were composed after the start of its sequel and interpret the first war's significance in light of that event. Bruce Catton, claiming that he realized as a boy in 1916 that the war in Europe marked the beginning of a new phase of history, adds, "It took another war a generation later to make things clear. We see now, face to face, what was seen then only through a darkened glass."[2] Arnold Toynbee, whose health problems kept him from fighting, emphasizes the unexpectedness of the ordeal of 1914 compared to what happened in 1939: "Our psychological unpreparedness made the violence of the shock, when it came, proportionately great."[3]

Out of six American historians who have written memoirs and who were of military age during World War I, three—John Hicks, Roy Nicholls, and Arthur Schlesinger Sr.—never served at all; one, Dexter Perkins, spent a few months in France with the U.S. Army's Historical Section; another, Albert Guérard, was never actually assigned to a unit; and only one, William Langer, fought at the front. "The reader will perceive that this is no heroic story of military service," Perkins remarks of his pages on the period.[4] Langer wrote a brief history of his unit's engagements, but his autobiography says little about the subject. He had enlisted "because I felt that I could not afford not to play a role, however modest, in so stupendous an historical event," but he does not remember the experience in the traumatic terms in which history books and postwar fiction describe it.[5] Among European scholars, even fewer went on to write about their personal experience of combat. The British historian G. M. Trevelyan served in a medical unit on the Italian front for three years. Although he lived through the catastrophic defeat of Caporetto, which inspired Ernest Hemingway's *A Farewell to Arms,* Trevelyan's autobiographical recollections of the war are detached and unemotional. He is conscious of having had "a much 'better time' during the war than nine people out of ten. The break in my work had been all to the good, because it had given me a touch of practical life and affairs and a glimpse of history in the making. I had been too bookish an historian."[6] Given the magnitude of the suffering the war caused, Trevelyan's emphasis on the benefits he derived from it, which is similar in tone to Gibbon's famous passage about his own noncombatant experiences in the Seven Years' War, seems almost fatuous.

Rather than recounting combat experiences, the majority of references to World War I in historians' memoirs deal either with the view from the home front or with insights into the making of wartime policy. Two of the most intense recreations of the experience of the war are those of the German historians Hermann Heimpel and Friedrich Meinecke, both written in the 1940s and shaped by an acute awareness of how Germany's second defeat was inscribed in the catastrophe of the earlier war. Heimpel's memoir traces his development from a schoolboy writing patriotic war poems in 1914 to a troubled adolescent trying to reconcile school lessons about the *Iliad* with the reality of lengthening casualty lists, hunger, and mounting political divisions in wartime Germany by 1917. He and other teenagers were drafted to perform agricultural labor and were outraged when the landowners refused to pay them. Worst of all, there was the realization, dawning earlier for the young than for their parents, that "we are indeed the Germans, we are on the right side, but we can nevertheless lose the war." For him and his schoolmates, this was a shattering insight that cast all their beliefs into confusion.[7] The implication in Heimpel's memoir, which he started writing between bombing raids in Germany at the beginning of 1945, is that this destruction of values in the first war had made the rise of Hitler possible.[8]

Heimpel's war memories are those of an outsider, someone who did not yet have the historical training that might have provided special insight into the reasons for the outcome of the war, and someone with no way of influencing it. Friedrich Meinecke, a generation older than Heimpel, had been in a different situation. Meinecke participated intensely in the conflict, as an enthusiastic patriot and as a participant and observer of the politics that shaped the country's policies. Writing his memoirs in the midst of World War II, Meinecke tried both to explain what had made the first war different from its successor and to understand how history had taken the disastrous turn that, he implied, had led to Hitler. For Meinecke, as for so many Germans, the earlier conflict had been a justified war of national defense and the patriotic unity in the first days of August 1914 an unforgettable experience. The Social Democratic Party's decision to abandon its prewar pacifism marked the overcoming of the deepest division in the national community. "With it was completed what had been, for two decades, my concern, my desire and my hope," Meinecke wrote in 1944. "Even today (1944), in old age and after all the bitter experiences of three decades and new deviations, divisions, and, finally, forcible assaults on our national life, I still identify myself with the feelings that moved me . . . in that moment."[9] He had expressed his patriotism at the time by writing a book that tried to capture the rapturous mood, *The German Revival of 1914,* and contributing to a volume in which leading German academics refuted the accusations made against their country in the outside world (*Straßburg,* 197, 199–200).

Since his death, there has been continuing controversy about how aggressively annexationist Meinecke was during the war. In his memoir, Meinecke portrays himself as a voice of reason in the war-aims debate that went on behind the scenes during the conflict, although he had not supported the July 1917 Reichstag resolution urging the German government to seek a compromise peace. A diary entry from October 1918, included in the memoir, shows him still confident that Germany did not need to rush into peace negotiations and still hopeful that Alsace-Lorraine could be retained (251, 266). In domestic politics as well, his evolution was significant compared to that of his milieu but still very limited. It took him most of the war to convince himself that the elitist Prussian three-class voting system had to be abandoned in order to preserve the lower classes' loyalty to the country, and he indignantly rejected his friend Otto Hintze's conversion to pacifist and democratic ideas (220–21, 226, 269).

Although Meinecke's memoir thus indicates that he, like most German academics, remained convinced of the justice of his country's cause throughout the war, he also claims to have learned important lessons that changed his thinking. The most important of these resulted from his friendship with Richard von Kühlmann, a leading German diplomat who became foreign minister during the later, more desperate stages of the war. When Kühlmann invited Meinecke to spend several weeks with him in the neutral Netherlands in 1915, it "was my first contact with an active diplomat, or with anyone closely involved in decision-making." Meinecke recalls being struck by the contrast between the outlooks of "the scholar, who had spent long years thinking on a theoretical level about the secrets of power politics, and the practitioner." He was also shaken by Kühlmann's argument that the war had been a mistake from the point of view of securing Germany's place in the world. "Everything about this war was more problematic . . . than I had realized during the patriotic enthusiasm of the August days. Could I still see it as an unavoidable, impersonal destiny? Could not other men and other decisions have given things a completely different course?" (205–6). As Meinecke reconstructs matters in his memoir, this contact with someone actually involved in the making of high policy changed his understanding both of politics and of history.

The difficulty for Meinecke, as he sees it in retrospect, is that he and the friends who came to share his views were unable to influence events. He put his energies into a movement to oppose the nationalistic *Vaterlandspartei*, an organization supported by many of his more conservative colleagues, but his smaller group lacked the "agitatorial power of persuasion" of their rivals and made little impact on public opinion (235). His group dreamed of limited reforms implemented from above. Even in retrospect, Meinecke wonders if his group's concessions to "the ever more extensive democratization of modern constitutions" had not been "too hasty and short-sighted," considering that democratization had opened the door to Hitler (244). But the violent forces of the time had overwhelmed him and his friends. In a diary excerpt from September 1918, he had written, "These times leave natures such as mine only the choice between being pushed aside or being turned into one of the many tiny gears in the gigantic war machine. The destiny of the individual life is fearful, today and for the future." In 1807, as Meinecke had shown in his historical writings, a group of elitist thinkers and politicians had been able to rescue Prussia and pave the way for a German future, but in his own time, "ideas and forces, will and wisdom have separated themselves" (264). Meinecke, who thought he understood the historical lessons of the Prussian reform movement so well, was unable to emulate the heroes he had written about.

For Meinecke, as for the youthful Heimpel, the war was thus a deeply disturbing experience. Both their autobiographies reflect the shock of discovering that the assumptions on which they had built their lives were unfounded. The teenaged Heimpel could blame this on his parents' generation and embrace new values—values that would lead him, for a time, to acceptance of the Third Reich—but for Meinecke this was more difficult. His autobiography breaks off with the revolutionary troubles in Germany immediately after the armistice and so does not describe his efforts, as one of the so-called *Vernunftrepublikaner* or "republicans of reason," to support the Weimar Republic without fully embracing its democratic presuppositions. Nor does it explain how he continued his academic career, which indeed reached its peak in the 1920s. Implicitly, however, the autobiography foreshadows the feeling of helplessness he would experience when the Nazis took power in 1933. Writing his memoirs was the only way he could express, if only in muted form, his sense of how the irrational forces of history had destroyed not only the carefully crafted life and career he had built up for himself before 1914 but also those aspects of German national life he most valued. Even though he never saw a shot fired in anger, Meinecke, more than any other historian-memoirist of the World War I era, conveys the tragic sense of a civilization tearing itself apart and of individuals realizing their helplessness in the face of events.

Stories like Meinecke's and Heimpel's were already history to the generation of scholars whose published memoirs appeared after 1980. These authors were born during or shortly after World War I and experienced its sequel as adolescents or young adults. Regardless of what kind of history they subsequently wrote, when they looked back at their lives, these scholars recognized how the Great War of 1914–18 shaped both their life and their sense of what history is. As a child, Jacques Le Goff recalls, "I lived in a world where . . . the memory of the war obsessed everyone," and Raoul Girardet speaks for all his French contemporaries when he describes "the time of my childhood" as the era "when the monuments to the fallen were still new." [10] In the United States, Henry May also grew up on stories about the war. "To children the Great War and all wars seemed part of the past—terrible but romantic. Sometimes we wondered whether anything as exciting would ever happen again." [11] Australian historian Russel Ward strives to convey "what it felt like to grow up in the shadow of that bloodbath fought on the other side of the planet." [12] From childhood on, these memoirists had been aware that the war separated their lives from a dimly understood era before 1914 when everything had been different. For this generation, a sense of the possibility of sudden and radical historical change was almost unavoidable; so was a recognition that they would have to reconstruct the past to truly to understand themselves and their own time.

By the early 1930s, many future historians had become obsessed with the prospect of another catastrophe. As Eric Hobsbawm remembers, "Throughout the decade the black cloud of the coming world war dominated our horizons." [13] For many of these memoirists, this fear was translated into a youthful commitment to ensuring that there would be no repetition of the disaster that had poisoned the lives of their parents' generation. May's memoir describes the "peace strike" he participated in as a Berkeley undergraduate in 1936–37, and Carl Schorske remembers opposing a Harvard professor who argued for American involvement in the coming conflict.[14] However naive the pacifism of the 1930s may appear in retrospect, it did represent a precocious awareness of the way war can impinge on individual lives. The rising political tension of the later 1930s moved many of these memoirists from pacifism or indifference to ideological commitment, usually on the left. George Mosse, by then living in England, remembers that the Spanish Civil War "aroused our passions and engaged our emotions, determining our political attitudes for a long time to come."[15] R. G. Collingwood, an older scholar, used his autobiography, published just before the start of World War II, as a vehicle for announcing his conversion to ideological commitment: events such as the Munich agreement, he says, "impinged upon myself and broke up my pose of a detached professional thinker."[16] World War II thus fell upon young people who had anticipated and dreaded it and in many cases had devoted themselves to trying to ward it off. Even as students, they had understood that the crisis facing them had historical roots, however simplistic their analysis of them, but they had also learned that history could seem to escape from human control.

Given what they saw at stake in the conflicts that led to World War II, one might expect historians' memories of their own involvement in it to convey a sense of meaningful participation in a great cause. With very few exceptions, historian-autobiographers who write about the war accept the pervasive collective reading of it as a necessary evil, despite its staggering human cost. The relative absence of moral disquiet about the war is highlighted by many of these authors' reflections on their reactions to the dropping of the atomic bomb in 1945. When he wrote his memoir, Arthur Schlesinger Jr. was surprised to find letters showing that he had initially been upset by the event; he remembered only a feeling of relief that the war would soon be over. From the historian's vantage point, however, he considers Truman's decision fully justified. Edwin Reischauer had grown up in a missionary family in Japan but says that the war raised no moral issues for him: "The Japanese war machine had to be stopped for the sake of world peace and in the long run for the Japanese themselves." He was initially dismayed by the bombing of Hiroshima; his work in decoding Japanese transmissions made him think that the enemy was on the point of surrendering. Like Schlesinger, however, he was convinced by later historical research that the bombing was necessary. Howard Zinn is critical in retrospect of the use of the bomb, but he does not condemn himself for having been primarily pleased in 1945 that he would not have to serve in a possible invasion of Japan.[17] Historian-memoirists thus see no great moral issues either in the deployment of the weapon or in their personal reactions to its use, and historical research actually led several of them to view the Hiroshima bombing more favorably than they had at the time.

Although historian-memoirists consider the war justified, few of them see themselves as having made any significant contribution to its outcome, and many of their memoirs reflect a sense of bemusement that they could have been involved in something of such importance and yet have spent years of their own lives in essentially trivial activities. It is true that this collection of historians' memoirs includes very few accounts of battlefield experiences. Paul Fussell's *Doing Battle* and William Manchester's *Goodbye, Darkness* are the only texts that highlight personal traumas of an intensity comparable to that which many historians imagine as having characterized front-line combat. Most of these authors' contemporaries, whether American, British, French, or from Australia and New Zealand, instead tell stories that emphasize the discrepancy between the scope of the conflict and their own experiences. African Americans and Jewish exiles from central Europe, two categories of future historians who might have been expected to embrace a war against racist Nazi Germany, had difficulties when they tried to do so. On Pearl Harbor Day C. Eric Lincoln tried to enlist, but a recruiter told him, "We ain't taking no niggers in the Navy today." John Hope Franklin was turned down by the Navy and the War Department's historical office; his experiences "raised in my mind the most profound questions about the sincerity of my country in rejecting bigotry and tyranny abroad."[18] German-born refugees such as Hans Schmitt also initially found themselves barred from volunteering, although he was later drafted and, because of his language background, assigned to intelligence operations concerning Germany. Schmitt recalls being perplexed when a black army officer he befriended on a wartime train trip asked him not to insist on challenging segregated seating arrangements; he could not understand how the country could be fighting racism in Europe while tolerating it at home.[19]

The stories told by white male historians who did serve in the American or British and Commonwealth military during World War II fall into three categories. Many found themselves far from the front lines, occupied with often-meaningless activities that had little apparent bearing on the war's outcome. Their historical training put some in situations where they could supposedly contribute to the making of policy, but the reality usually turned out to be much different. And a few did have searing experiences of combat that deeply influenced their view of history afterward. Historians whose experiences later struck them above all as evidence of the amount of wasted energy expended in wartime are the most numerous. For example, A. J. P. Taylor writes, "For most of the time I remained an observer, continuing my teaching at Oxford on a more laborious level. However what I did otherwise was funny though of no conceivable importance and, I think, did no harm." He gave public lectures on current events and was eventually recruited into the Political Warfare Executive, where he claims to have "received an enormous salary" for doing very little.[20] Eric Hobsbawm, called up for service in England in February 1940 but kept out of any meaningful position because of his foreign origin and his left-wing views, recalls that "I had neither a 'good war' nor a 'bad war,' but an empty war. . . . Reluctantly I got used to the idea that I would have no part in Hitler's downfall."[21] In the United States, Henry May volunteered for service and was selected to learn the Japanese language. He was not actually sent to the Pacific until mid-1944 and saw very little actual fighting, although he considers himself to have learned a great deal from his military experience.[22]

Louis Harlan was in the U.S. Navy, and his ship was part of the flotilla supporting the D-Day landings in Normandy, but in retrospect he doesn't think his worm's-eye view of combat gave him much insight into what was happening. When he returned home on leave, he realized that "our engrossment in our own little corner of the global war, and our very limited engagement with the enemy, had left me woefully ignorant of the strategy and geopolitics of the war. The folks back home actually had a clearer view than we on the scene."[23] New Zealander Keith Sinclair was called up just before Pearl Harbor. After two years spent in New Zealand itself, during which he learned that "for most men the worst aspect of being in the armed forces is boredom," he volunteered to be sent overseas. When he returned home, he was "a very different person from the seaman who sailed in 1944." But the experiences that had changed him were not those of combat: "I had seen much of the world; I had passed in tough and competitive training courses. Much of what I had learnt—Morse code, semaphore, gunnery, chemical warfare—was of no future use to me. But more important, I had met and mixed with all sorts of people, and learnt to get on with them, whether rough-necks or British diplomats. I had been to numerous London plays and concerts."[24] Sinclair's sense that the most important result of his wartime service was exposure to people from different backgrounds is shared by the American Gabriel Jackson, who spent four years in the American military, first as an aircraft mechanic and later as a photography interpreter and cartographer. For Jackson, who had just graduated from Harvard, working "with men who were belligerently proud to have quit school at the minimum legal age and who never looked into a book" was an educational experience.[25]

The cumulative picture that emerges from the many historians' memoirs that fall into this pattern is above all a reminder of how much of wartime military life consisted of noncombat activities that rarely make it into historical accounts. A subtext in many of these stories, rarely commented on explicitly by their authors, is that bright, educated young men were often deliberately selected for positions likely to keep them out of front-line service. As a graduate student at Harvard in the early 1960s, the Australian Jill Ker Conway "couldn't believe my ears when I heard my Harvard graduate student colleagues telling me with real pride that they'd been smart and found an intelligence job during the Korean War, and that my faculty instructors had served almost to a man in the OSS during the 1939–1945 war. I could see . . . that it was another form of American efficiency for the state to preserve the lives of its educated elites, but it didn't square with my old British ideas about civic duty or the codes of honor I'd previously taken for granted." [26] In fact, however, the war stories told by British historians diverge little from the American pattern.

The OSS participants Conway mentions may have been sheltered from physical danger, but their memoirs and those of scholars who occupied similar positions during the war are among the more interesting testimonies about the experience. Like Henry Adams during the Civil War and Friedrich Meinecke in World War I, these historians and those who served in comparable jobs elsewhere in the government and military were able to witness the process by which major policy decisions were made; they were also directly confronted with the question whether historians could make any special difference under such conditions. Harvard historian William Langer played a central role in creating the OSS's Research and Analysis section, which he headed from September 1942 until 1946, and he recruited many of his own graduate students for this unit. Langer's memoirs make it clear that, having devoted much of his career to studying the causes of World War I, he saw the OSS as a unique opportunity to offer government leaders the benefit of historically informed analysis that could help them avoid the mistakes of their predecessors. Furthermore, as a historian, he understood the special privilege the situation offered him. With State Department encouragement, for example, he was able to set to work during the war on a subject of burning interest, the relations between Vichy France and the United States. "It is not often that a historian has a chance to work with such recent materials," Langer comments in his autobiography.[27]

Chosen in June 1941 to direct the compiling of the official history of the British war effort, Keith Hancock was similarly attracted by the idea of seeing history from the inside while at the same time being able to infuse policy making with historical insight. He understood that writing history as a paid government official imposed certain constraints: he had to observe the Official Secrets Act and the principle of "the impersonality of the civil service," which meant that he could not single out individuals for praise or blame and his team's work was reviewed by the government departments it covered before publication. But he felt the positive potentialities of the project outweighed its limitations.[28]

Langer and Hancock, both old enough to remember World War I, both look back on their engagment in its sequel in a basically positive light, but most of the younger historians who later wrote autobiographies remembered their experiences differently. What they did was usually intellectually stimulating—the OSS was "a second graduate school," as Carl Schorske puts it—and valuable for their future understanding of history.[29] But it was also intensely frustrating, as they realized that the military and the higher levels of the U.S. government were not really prepared to take their views seriously. H. Stuart Hughes, who titled the wartime chapter of his memoir "War as Education" in homage to Henry Adams, claims to have been more accurate in forecasting the course of the war than were U.S. policy makers. He correctly predicted that the French would scuttle their own navy in 1942 rather than let it fall into German hands, and he disagreed with the U.S. military's assessment that the Russians would lose the war on the eastern front. "With Roosevelt hopelessly bungling American policy toward France," Hughes felt compelled to make the strongest possible arguments in favor of support for de Gaulle. Despite these repeated demonstrations of the contribution a bright young scholar could make, he found his policy recommendations regularly ignored. In addition, by the end of the war, he felt inferior to the men who had actually seen combat. "Theirs had been a real war. Mine had possibly not been a war at all. It had been more like a *Bildungsroman*—an extended education that had ended in weariness and dread."[30]

Hughes's sentiments were hardly unique among OSS veterans. On the basis of his experience in China in the 1930s, John King Fairbank was recruited to the OSS's Coordinator of Information office. As part of a large collective effort, he found it difficult to see what he was accomplishing: "Granted the stakes were sometimes higher" than in academic work, but "one's own achievement seldom seemed so." He wrote memos warning that in its one-sided concentration on the military aspects of the war in China, the United States was losing its chance to influence liberal intellectuals and build a base of civilian support. By the end of the war, he had become convinced that a revolution of some kind and the overthrow of the Chiang Kai-Shek regime that the United States was supporting were inevitable, but he also realized that he had no chance of helping to change American actions. "Our China policy was on the skids but the American public didn't yet realize it."[31] Like Hughes, he concluded that his wartime efforts had been of little use to anyone.

Excluded from active military service because of poor eyesight, Arthur Schlesinger Jr. worked for the Office of War Information in Washington and later for the OSS. Although he worked with highly intelligent people and kept himself busy, he doesn't think any of this work had much impact: "There was an air of unreality about it all." He wanted to be sent overseas, closer to the action, but a false report charging that he had communist sympathies stood in the way. His bureaucratic struggle to clear his name "left me with an unnerving feeling of impotence." When he finally reached London, he was upset to discover that even OSS analysts there had little influence. Summing up his memories of the war as a whole, Schlesinger writes, "It was, I suppose, a Good War. But like all wars, ours was accompanied by atrocity and sadism, by stupidities and lies, pomposity and chickenshit."[32] Shepard Clough worked for the State Department and had similar experiences. "Not only was I of the opinion that our section was very badly directed," he writes, "but I was dismayed, to put it mildly, when my expertise was used for ends of which I disapproved."[33] Ironically, the only historian-memoirist who took part in U.S. intelligence activities during the war and later regarded his activities as genuinely worthwhile was Jürgen Kuczynski, the exiled German Communist, who worked for the Strategic Bombing Survey in 1944–45. This allowed him to transmit valuable information to the Soviets.[34]

The sense of disillusionment conveyed in the memoirs of future historians who worked for the U.S. government during the war was fully shared by Henry Ferns, who was on Canadian prime minister Mackenzie King's staff from 1940 to 1943 and then in that country's Department of External Affairs: "At first I was mesmerized by the thought that I was at the centre of the political world in Canada and at least on the edge of world politics at a decisive historical crisis. I had encountered unparalleled good luck which had located me not just in a grandstand seat but right in the arena. Maybe I was only a ball-boy, but what a game!" Gradually, he came to realize that the memoranda he compiled were making no real difference; his efforts "were an almost total waste: of my time, the taxpayers' money, office space, stenographic services, everything. . . . I contributed nothing to the war against the Nazis and the Fascists. The one public cause which commanded my greatest concern was the one in which I had the least share. Why this should have been so remains something I do not completely understand."[35]

The future historian-memoirists who had tried to use their professional skills to serve the Allied war effort had discovered that historical insight was not enough to allow an individual to make a dent on the shaping of actual history. Most acknowledge that their wartime activities were valuable in terms of their own education, but many were frustrated by the result of their efforts. H. Stuart Hughes dismissed the entire OSS venture as a "futile waste."[36] They returned to academia after the war with a sense of relief. "There was no doubt in my mind that I had more to offer as a scholar and teacher than as a government bureaucrat restricted by my superiors and government policy," Reischauer writes.[37] In many cases, the postwar anti-communist backlash added to their sense of the absurdity of their wartime efforts. Although none of this group had a real sympathy with communism that lasted beyond the war years, most had urged support for democratic leftist groups in the countries they studied, which was enough to land them in hot water later on. Fairbank was called to testify before a Senate committee, and Hughes was forced out of the directorship of Harvard's Russian Research Center; Reischauer got off more easily, merely being dropped from his post as a State Department consultant.[38] In retrospect, Fairbank and Hughes both recognize that they were overly optimistic about the possibility of cooperation between democratic and Communist movements in China and Europe after the war, but the politicians who harassed them understood even less about the world than they did. The lesson for these scholars was that there was no possibility for critically minded historians to contribute to the making of American government policy after the war.

The sense of disillusionment in the memoirs of the historians who were actually called on to exercise their professional skills during the war is not as strong as the bitter and angry reflections of Paul Fussell, the scholar who has been most outspoken about the toll the war took on his body and soul. Fussell, a twenty-year-old second lieutenant in the infantry, was severely wounded in an encounter with the Germans in March 1945. "How a young person so innocent was damaged in this way and what happened as a result is the subject of this book," he writes in the introduction to his memoir, which covers much of his life but is entitled simply *Doing Battle*. Whereas other historian-memoirists tend to portray their army training as tedious and sometimes comic, Fussell views the process as inherently malevolent. "I had undergone nineteen months of verbal abuse and humiliation, exhaustion, anxiety, muscle pain, and boredom. In barracks I had listened to hours of the nastiest raised-voice slander of 'kikes' and 'niggers.'" Neither he nor his fellow soldiers had any sense of what they were fighting for. "We took it for granted that we were engaged, somehow, in opposing totalitarianism, both German and Japanese, and we were willing to do that, but what it was all about interested us hardly at all." His first day on the battlefield dissipated his illusions about human life: "Suddenly I knew that I was not and would never be in a world that was reasonable or just." He and the other men did their duty, but not out of courage or conviction. "We were maintaining our self-respect, protecting our manly image from the contempt of our fellows."[39]

Doing Battle, published at a time when the United States was awash in celebrations of the heroism of the "greatest generation," was meant as a contrarian text. Fussell associates his memoir with the antiwar writings of survivors of World War I, such as Wilfred Owen and Robert Graves, which had been key texts in his most widely read scholarly work, *The Great War and Modern Memory.* The purpose of that book, he writes in *Doing Battle,* had been to make readers "weep as they sensed the despair of people like themselves, torn and obliterated for a cause beyond their understanding."[40] The unrestrained anger that pervades *Doing Battle* sets it apart from other memoirs by historians who saw actual combat, such as my former colleague Charles Roland, whose unit was in the thick of the Battle of the Bulge. Roland vividly remembers the horrors of combat; he describes soldiers who "broke under the stress" and others who deliberatedly wounded themselves to escape the front lines. But the main thrust of Roland's account is to show how "the character and patriotism of the soldiers," all of them quite ordinary people like himself, "proved to be sufficient" to win a war whose necessity seemed obvious to him.[41] Not surprisingly, Fussell's book was criticized for his apparent indifference to the stakes in the war. Fussell is not the only historian-memoirist to acknowledge, however, that combat duty unleashed violent emotions in him. William Manchester, who unlike Fussell does not question the justification for the war, nevertheless makes it clear that he was thoroughly traumatized by his experiences, to the point where he could not write about them for more than thirty years. When he was finally able to do so, he found that "some of my actions in the early 1940s make no sense to me now."[42] Joel Colton, who describes himself as a "mild-mannered bespectacled professor," admits that for many years after the war he carried in his wallet a "grisly" photograph of a suspected Gestapo informer who committed suicide in his custody after VE Day as "an uneasy token of my personal revenge over the Third Reich."[43] Even if *Doing Battle* represents a minority voice, it is a reminder that there were future historians whose wartime experiences were genuinely traumatic and that that sense of trauma could stimulate powerful scholarship.

Anglo-American historians' recollections of the war years are stories of participation in a collective effort that had a definite effect on history, even if their authors have negative feelings about their own role. Their French contemporaries have very different stories to tell. Published in the 1980s and early 1990s, these accounts form part of a larger debate on the nature of the *années noires,* the black years of the Occupation, that followed the breakdown of the national myth of a France united in resistance propagated in the Gaullist era. The first of these French historians' memoirs to be published, that of Philippe Ariès, revealed that this much-loved public figure was an unapologetic former member of the quasi-fascist Action française who had started a lengthy civil-service career under the Vichy regime. The generally favorable reception of his memoir, which came out in 1980, marked a stage in the rehabilitation of the French Right, after many years in which the country's intellectual life had been dominated by leftists.

Future French historians such as Ariès, Raoul Girardet, Pierre Goubert, and René Rémond were in the army during the defeat of 1940, but none remembered it with the burning anger and frustration that characterizes that first-person philippic by a historian from an older generation, Marc Bloch's *Strange Defeat.* In some cases, their personal experiences were totally at odds with the obvious collective meaning of what was happening. Rémond, a young officer candidate, recalls enjoying the taste of adult responsibility his post provided, despite the circumstances; he left the army in 1941 "with a certain amount of regret."[44] The future French historians who lived through the war as civilians often continued their studies almost without disruption. Pierre Chaunu recounts his annoyance at being chased out of the Bibliothèque nationale in August 1944 by librarians trying to safeguard the books during the liberation of Paris.[45] Alfred Grosser, a German-born Jew who faced the threat of having his French citizenship revoked, managed to pass the exam for a teaching certificate in June 1943. "In the middle of the war? In defeated France? Under the Vichy regime which had enacted the *statut des juifs?* Looking back, it still astonishes me," he writes.[46]

The stories of two French historians who were active in the French Resistance, Raoul Girardet and Annie Kriegel, break with the pattern of most of their colleagues' recollections. Both of them stand outside the mainstream of Resistance stories, however, and the lessons they draw from their experiences do not fit comfortably with standard representations of the period. Prior to the war, Girardet had been a friend of Ariès and a militant in the Action française movement, sharing its exaggerated nationalism. The defeat of 1940 deprived him of his sense of membership in a nation with a glorious tradition: "I found myself stripped of the core of what had been, until then, mine." Unlike most of the older members of the movement, however, he did not let his dislike of the fallen Third Republic persuade him to accept Vichy. As to why he chose to stay in France rather than escaping to North Africa and joining the Free French forces, he writes that "the story-like character of my double life satisfied a certain taste for the unexpected and the fantastic that I would not have found in uniform." His activities had serious consequences—he was arrested in early 1944 and spent several months in prison, narrowly escaping deportation to Buchenwald—but the lesson about history he claims to have learned is to distrust "a certain logical and rationalized conception of History" and to give full weight to "the unforeseen, to luck, to the accidental." In recounting this period of his life in his memoir, he wanted to revise standard conceptions of the Resistance. In his view, "disorganization, carelessness, vanity, and ambition had their place there, alongside courage, selflessness, and sacrifice."[47] Girardet's unheroic story of his wartime activities served as an occasion to challenge both popular representations of the Resistance experience and tendencies in the historiography of the subject; it was also an opportunity to rehabilitate the right-wing movements he had been active in before and after the war by showing that at least one of their members had opposed collaboration.

Kriegel's account of her Resistance activities is in some ways more conventional than Girardet's. She joined a Communist youth group in 1942, and she takes the activities she engaged in seriously. She is sure that the mimeographed tracts she helped distribute in her *lycée* were important, regardless of their political content, because they "bore witness to the existence of a movement," and her recital of the ways her group obtained the materials to produce them is therefore a meaningful contribution to history. Where Kriegel departs from the boundaries of standard French accounts of the Resistance, at least those written prior to the 1990s, is in her emphasis on the role that her Jewishness played in her situation. Although she had been born in France, the Communist group she joined was part of the JC-MOI, the party's underground organization for immigrant workers. Although the general theme of Kriegel's memoir was to insist on her Frenchness, her pages on the war are a forthright assertion of the fact that for French Jews like herself, "what counted, what corresponded to our lived experience . . . was that everything followed from the central fact that we were Jews." On the other hand, however, she refuses to use her memoir to heap blame on the Vichy government or the general French population for not doing more to aid the Jews.[48]

With a few exceptions, historians' personal accounts of the two world wars thus tend to contrast the relative insignificance of their own experiences to the scale of the events that went on around them. Although many of these authors credit the war with broadening their sense of human experience, usually by bringing them together with people from other social backgrounds, few see the war as a genuinely transformative experience in their life. Those who were already studying or teaching history before one or the other of the wars interrupted their life returned to their career afterward. Only a handful credit war experience for inspiring their vocation as a historian, and even they often do so in roundabout ways. Louis Harlan remarks that "with unconscious irony I cast the die in favor of history under many illusions about my wartime experience as historic. I knew very little about history as a scholarly discipline or about the nature of scholarly research into the whys and wherefores of human experience. I tended to think of history instead as epical narrative or as a grand panorama painted on a broad canvas," or in other words as something very different from the impression he gives in his own narrative of wartime service.[49] Paul Fussell plunged back into the college studies war service had interrupted, not to make sense of his wartime experience but because colleges and universities struck him as the social institutions "the most dramatically opposite to the army"; for many years he devoted himself to studying eighteenth-century English literature, and it was only the Vietnam War era that turned his attention to war memoirs as a scholarly topic.[50]

William Palmer, who made extensive use of many of the autobiographical narratives discussed here in his study of what he calls "the World War II generation" of American and British historians, is convinced that "many of them . . . developed further insights about their discipline from the crucible of military service," but what these insights were is not easy to define.[51] In these narratives, the real history of the war is almost always being made somewhere else, not where the authors happen to find themselves. These first-person narratives also rarely cross paths with other genres of war memoirs. They are not like the stories told by political or military leaders, who were in positions to make decisions and direct events, and, with a few notable exceptions such as Fussell's, Manchester's, and Roland's accounts, they are also not stories of testing under fire. At the same time, however, historian-autobiographers rarely make their accounts of war into absurd tragedy or black comedy, the modes in which so much twentieth-century war fiction has been written. The contrast between their own petty or frustrating experiences, on the one hand, and the immensity of the stakes at issue, on the other, seems to make it difficult for many of these historians to find clear meaning in what happened to them. Nevertheless, most of these memoir authors are convinced that their war experiences were important for their individual development and their comprehension of history. One senses that what most of them learned, however, is that history seen close up rarely resembles the history in history books.

HISTORIANS AS ACTIVISTS: COMMITMENT IN RETROSPECT

Just as they grapple with the historical problem of the individual confronted with events on the scale of the world wars, so historian-memoirists bring their special perspective to the question of the causes and consequences of ideological commitment. Whether it is Emmanuel Le Roy Ladurie describing his involvement with the French Communist Party or Mark Naison explaining his engagement with African American studies, this issue dominates many of these texts. Historians' autobiographical writing about experiences of ideological commitment is quite different from their writings about involvement in armed conflict. In writing about their war experiences, historian-autobiographers are talking about events that were beyond their control and in which they found themselves engaged involuntarily. When they discuss their experiences of partisan engagement, however, they are describing commitments they entered into through deliberate choice. Stories of such commitments consequently raise issues about personal responsibility in ways that accounts of war experiences typically do not.

Political and social movements are, like war, common topics of historical inquiry, but seen in autobiographical retrospect, the experience of activist engagement often appears differently from the way it does in historical accounts. Historians are interested in the origins and development of such movements, their internal debates and divisions, and their successes and failures. Autobiographers writing about movements they participated in may deal with some of these topics, but they are usually most interested in the intersection of the movements they joined with the trajectory of their own life, and the aspects of engagement they describe often turn out to be far removed from what historical scholarship has come to define as important. Furthermore, autobiographers' recollections about their experiences of commitment are often most intense when they have come to judge those experiences quite differently from the way they did at the time, or when the collective judgment of history has made those experiences seem problematic. Such situations drive autobiographers to write confessions explaining how they came to believe and do things they now regret or apologias defending past positions that even they may now find objectionable. Historians may denounce or defend movements they study, but their relationship to their subjects is usually quite different: the issue of their personal responsibility for the past they are describing does not arise.

The movement with which the largest number of twentieth-century historians were strongly engaged and which has inspired the most passionate autobiographical accounts was communism. Especially during the dramatic period that spanned the Great Depression, the struggle against Nazism, and the early stages of the Cold War, joining the Communist Party seemed to offer many of these scholars a way both of explaining history and of helping to move it in a desirable direction. As they lived through World War II and the postwar period, these historians' affiliation with communism, whether brief or durable, often had a great impact on their lives. By the time most of them came to write their memoirs, however, both the attraction of the communist movement and the ways involvement in it affected their subsequent life had become difficult to explain to younger readers. Most of these authors realized, however, that any account of their lives had to deal with these issues, which have preoccupied so many twentieth-century memoirists throughout the Western world, to the point where failure to address them on the part of those who were at any time sympathetic to the party would be seen as a major violation of the autobiographical pact of honesty. For those who write as ex-communists, describing the communist phase of their life requires explaining, to themselves and to their readers, how they could have made what they now see as a terrible mistake. In doing this, however, most of them are at pains to avoid portraying themselves as simply stupid or incapable of thinking for themselves, admissions that would cast doubt on their competence as historians. For the minority of historian-autobiographers who retained communist sympathies down to the era when the Soviet system finally collapsed, there is a different challenge: explaining why they persisted in their loyalties when history itself seemed to have condemned the movement.

The list of sometime communists among historian-autobiographers is a long and cosmopolitan one: it includes the French scholars Emmanuel Le Roy Ladurie, Alain Besançon, Annie Kriegel, Maurice Agulhon, Elisabeth Roudinesco, and Gérard Noiriel; the Englishmen Eric Hobsbawm and E. P. Thompson; the Canadian Henry Ferns; the Australians Bernard

Smith and Russel Ward; the Germans Jürgen Kuczynski and Helmut Eschwege; the Israeli Walter Grab; and such American historians as David Montgomery, Staughton Lynd, Gerda Lerner, and John Toland. In writing about their experiences with communism, historian-autobiographers face challenges that are both historical and personal. By the time they wrote their memoirs, most of these scholars had become ex-communists. Honesty required them to admit that the movement had meant a great deal to them at one point in their lives, but they had to explain—to readers and, in many cases, to themselves—how they could have been attracted to something that later came to seem so repulsive. Those like Eric Hobsbawm and Jürgen Kuczynski, who remained loyal to communist ideals long after the great disillusionment of the 1950s, faced a different but equally difficult problem: how to explain why they had maintained their faith in a world increasingly antagonistic to communism and how they had coped with the collapse of the Soviet Union.

Joining the communist movement meant more than simply embracing a set of political ideas. It was, as most of these historians recall, a total commitment, requiring a total personal engagement. As E. P. Thompson puts it, "One had this extraordinary formative moment in which it was possible to be deeply committed even to the point of life itself in support of a particular political struggle that was at the same time a popular struggle."[52] For bright young people who saw the world going terribly wrong in the 1930s, the communists seemed to offer the best hope of rescue. Henry Ferns, who joined the party in 1936, writes that "the very worth of Bolshevism lay in the fact that the Bolsheviks were men of strong will, courage, and determination in the service of what they and we conceived to be ordained by history." In addition to promising a strategy for fighting evil and injustice, the communist movement offered many of those who joined it an escape from the confining structures of their previous life. Ferns remembered that the party provided "an alternative where school and sex and family background were matters of little or no concern. . . . It broke down barriers and liberated young people from shyness and inhibitions with which many felt they had lived too long."[53]

Among the historians who have written most strikingly about the passage from communist militancy to ex-communist disillusionment are the French scholars who were in the party during the late 1940s and early 1950s. Looking back, French ex-communist historians such as Alain Besançon, Maurice Agulhon, Emmanuel Le Roy Ladurie, and Annie Kriegel are unsparing both with themselves and with their former movement, even though the worst outrages they were personally involved with concerned the treatment of fellow French party members suspected of ideological deviations, not participation in Stalinist crimes. "At some level, one realizes that we played a part in the worst the century produced, in a vast enterprise of evil," Besançon writes.[54] The ways in which these memorists explain their attraction to communism tend to be complex and to suggest both the overdetermination of such decisions and the element of uncertainty that remains in any such attempt to plumb one's past actions. None of these authors were sociologically predestined to support a movement for proletarian revolution: all came from bourgeois origins. There were public reasons for their adherence—the prestige the party gained from its role in the wartime resistance, the sense that communism was history's winning side—and private ones. For Le Roy Ladurie, joining the party was a way of rebelling against his father, who had been a minister under Philippe Pétain, and of asserting his individual identiy; for Agulhon, party activity compensated for a certain emotional immaturity. "I broke the records for discipline, devotion and obsessive scrupulosity, sacrificing my private life," Agulhon muses, "less from a spirit of true sacrifice than out of a deep incapacity to take on a private life."[55]

Only the Jewish Annie Kriegel, who entered the party during the Occupation as a way of fighting back against Nazism, finds her decision essentially unproblematic, seeing it as both "unavoidable and, at the time, honorable." It was Vichy's persecution of the Jews that drove her to join the communists and thus to have to pay "the exorbitant price . . . of a debt that can never be repaid, for this decision that was, at the time, as ineluctable as it was honorable." Ineluctable because the rival Gaullist resistance movement was "essentially military and overwhelmingly masculine," with no use for sixteen-year-old girls, but also because only in the communist movement could a French Jew, "after having lost one's name, one's lodging, one's neighborhood, school, trade, home, recover a sense of belonging."[56] This passage is an excellent demonstration of Kriegel's ability to use her sense of history to put her own life in historical context: unlike Agulhon, Le Roy Ladurie, and Besançon, she does not reduce her communist commitment to a matter of adolescent immaturity but shows how it came to seem the only appropriate response to the historical situation she found herself in.

Kriegel's treatment of her communist commitment is more complex than that of most other scholars because her engagement with the movement was more extensive. She had been not merely a party member but one of its leaders: for several years she sat on the central committee of the Seine

Federation, with special responsibilities for matters involving intellectuals and students. When she became a historian, Kriegel's communist past was never a secret. Her academic contemporaries remembered her activities all too well, and Kriegel comments that her students enjoyed discovering "traces of my old excesses" while doing their own research.[57] Furthermore, her academic research was devoted almost entirely to the history of the communist movement, although she rigorously avoided any mention of her connection with her topic in her scholarly publications. As we have seen, her dissertation director, Ernest Labrousse, had tried to steer her away from the subject, but Kriegel had ignored his warnings. Nevertheless, her massive thesis, *Aux origines du communisme français*, whose publication in 1964 established her as the leading expert on the party's past, owed a great deal of its success to its appearance of scrupulous conformity to the model of objective, scientific scholarship.

Kriegel's memoir certainly makes the connection between her research topic and her own life clear, but the result is not to discredit her scholarship. Her detailed account of how she did the research for her book shows that only someone with her extensive inside knowledge could have tracked down the sources she used, many of them provided by elderly ex-militants. It is also clear from her memoir that the process of historical research provided her a bridge out of the party. The separation from the organization that had dominated her life for more than a decade was a painful one. As she wrote, "One does not discard . . . a whole bundle of beliefs and attitudes that impregnate all the aspects of one's personal life with a flick of the wrist."[58] She was ousted from her party post at the end of December 1953, but it took her some time to completely break with the movement. Researching its past was a way of remaining connected to the communist milieu while gradually coming to see it in a different light. Her growing consciousness of the discrepancies between the party's official version of its past and the evidence her research turned up reinforced her movement away from its dogma. In this respect, Kriegel's account echoes those of several other former communist historians. Le Roy Ladurie, for example, writes of his shock when he realized that a disgraced former party leader had been removed from a historical photograph in a party publication: "Formed by university training, he knew what such tampering implied."[59] These scholars' attachment to historical professionalism gave them a solid ground from which to challenge communist ideology.

By the time she came to write her memoir, Kriegel had turned against leftism in all its forms; it is thus somewhat surprising that her portrayal of the French Communist Party of the early 1950s is a relatively positive one. Unlike many intellectuals who passed through the Party during this period, she had real contact with the rank-and-file membership and came to understand how the movement enabled the French working class to acquire "the dignity of a collective agent." She speaks with respect of the worker militants she met, of the working-class communist women who "tried to face up to the unglorified but strenuous demands of a life divided among family, work, and militancy," and even of French party leader Maurice Thorez's wife Jeannette Veermersch, one of the great defenders of Stalinist orthodoxy.[60] Her memoir is not an occasion for settling her scores with the party, which she had done in other ways; it is rather an occasion for reexamining her own life and the place the party had had in it.

As an abjuration of error, Kriegel's massive and detailed memoir is in the great tradition of first-person confessional literature, but it is a confession infused with historical insight. As a historian, Kriegel understands that it was not personal weakness alone that drove her to join the party and to remain in it for over a decade. Furthermore, her memoir reflects certain continuities in her life that connected her communist phase to her later career. It is clear that the feisty, outspoken author of *Ce que j'ai cru comprendre* is the same person whom her one-time party colleague Besançon remembered "holding off several policemen with menacing swings of her book-bag" at a demonstration.[61] Despite her rejection of the party and all its works, the tone of her recollections reflects a certain pride in her accomplishments as an organizer and leader. As she moved away from communism, Kriegel did not simply retreat into academic professionalism. She became a regular contributor to a number of French journals and newspapers and a leading figure in the French Jewish community. The extraordinary length of her eight-hundred-page memoir is in itself testimony to the energy and determination that were the basis of her personality. Although she came to reject her commitment to communism, Kriegel clearly remained throughout her life an activist, determined not just to describe the past but to change the future.

This lifelong commitment to activism links Kriegel's autobiography in curious ways to those of two prominent historians who kept their loyalty to communism even after the collapse of the Soviet system. Like Kriegel, Eric Hobsbawm and Jürgen Kuczynski came from Jewish backgrounds. Hobsbawm, the younger of the two, grew up in Austria, but family circumstances resulted in his arriving in Berlin in 1931, just prior to Hitler's takeover. In his view, there was no real alternative for him but to embrace the one militant movement willing to stand up to the Nazis: "The months in Berlin made me a lifelong communist, or at least a man whose life would lose its nature and its significance without the political project to which he committed himself as a schoolboy, even though that project has demonstrably failed, and, as I now know, was bound to fail," he writes in his memoir, published in 2002. In a chapter titled "Being Communist," Hobsbawm admits that the collapse of the Soviet regimes, "leaving behind a landscape of material and moral ruin," shows "that failure was built into this enterprise from the start." He retains his admiration for the accomplishments of "those inspired by this conviction," however; "if I did not leave the Party in 1956, it was not least because the movement bred such men and women."[62]

For Hobsbawm, the party provided a model of engaged activism that emphasized dedication, efficiency, and a willingness to endure a certain amount of boredom—qualities also required of successful academics. Marxist theory also had a powerful attraction: "What made Marxism so irresistible was its comprehensiveness. 'Dialectical materialism' provided, if not a 'theory of everything,' then at least a 'framework of everything,' . . . providing a guide to the nature of all interactions in a world in constant flux" (*Interesting Times*, 132–33, 97). Hobsbawm recognizes that Marxism proved deficient as a guide to historical understanding as well as political practice: "national or other collective or historical identities were far more important than we then supposed," and communism's utopian ideals have lost much of their attraction in the face of "the range of goods, services, prospects and personal options which are today available to the majority of men and women in the incredibly wealthy and technologically advanced countries of the West" (138, 136). He also recognizes that it was in some ways easier to retain loyalty to communist ideals in England, where the movement remained a powerless minority, than in the countries where the party actually held power. Communists in Eastern Europe "did not have the advantage, which maintained our morale, of enemies who could be fought with conviction and a clear conscience: capitalism, imperialism, nuclear annihilation" (143).

In spite of these various critiques of the movement, however, Hobsbawm still retains his basically positive assessment of communism, and he has no sympathy for "the repentant sinners" among his contemporaries (151, xii). Aside from Hobsbawm's questionable assertion that communists had a virtual monopoly on devotion to freedom and justice, the difficulty with his autobiographic posture is its refusal of the opportunities of hindsight. Hobsbawm is capable of applying a certain amount of historical perspective to the phenomenon of communism, but he seems wedded to a strangely unhistorical notion of his own personality. Loyalty to the ideological commitment he made as a teenager, when he knew much less about history and could not foresee many of the events that would follow during his lifetime, is central to his conception of himself. Hobsbawm's case shows that a person can make very real contributions to historical knowledge without being able to translate those insights into understanding of himself.

The German social and economic historian Jürgen Kuczynski's memoirs reflect an even more complicated relationship between personal experience, communist commitment, and autobiographical acts. The two volumes of Kuczynski's memoirs were written under radically different circumstances. The first, covering the author's life from his birth to the end of World War II, was completed in 1971, when the German Democratic Republic seemed solidly established. By 1992, when Kuczynski published his second volume, covering his life from 1945 to 1989, the East German state had disappeared, and Kuczynski was under attack for his earlier loyalty to it. The problem Kuczynski faced in writing the story of his early life for a communist audience in 1971 was that his background and education hardly fit the proper proletarian mold. He came from a prominent German Jewish family; in his own memoir, Hobsbawm, a friend of Kuczynski, mentions that one of Kuczynski's ancestors had made a fortune developing the fashionable Grunewaldviertel of Berlin.[63] Kuczynski himself preferred to recall a great-grandfather from whom he had inherited a copy of the first edition of the *Communist Manifesto*.[64] His father was an economist with left-wing sympathies. Kuczynski himself, however, was not immediately converted to the leftist faith. After realizing in the early 1920s that his Jewish origins precluded an academic career in Germany, he left, not for the Workers' Paradise in the east but for the heartland of capitalism across the Atlantic. From 1926 to 1929, he was in the United States, associated with the Brookings Institute, then a hotbed of future New Dealers, and the American Federation of Labor. East German readers must have been surprised by Kuczynski's fond memories of his years in "the only country in history to have had two great victorious bourgeois revolutions," his description of the War of Independence and the Civil War (*Memoiren*, 120).

Kuczynski made up for this by recounting how he finally joined the German Communist Party in 1930 and was impressed by his first visit to the Soviet Union. He was quickly recruited into the German party's leadership, but Hitler's seizure of power in 1933 forced the party and Kuczynski underground; he fled to England in 1936. Like Hobsbawm, he sees his confrontation with Nazism as decisive in giving his political ideas permanent form: "Since then I have hardly changed, either for the worse or for the better" (270). Writing about this period in 1971, he demonstrates his faithfulness to the party by admitting that he had at first been reluctant to oppose the British declaration of war on Hitler, as party policy required in 1939, but that he had quickly come to understand his error. His expertise on the German economy led in 1944 to his being recruited to work for the U.S. Strategic Bombing Survey, an engagement that he justifies to his 1971 East German readers by pointing out that it paved the way for his quick return after the war; when he did reach Berlin in 1945, he caused a stir by visiting the Communist Party's reopened office in his American officer's uniform (360– 62, 376–77, 399–402, 416). The first volume of Kuczynski's memoirs thus emphasizes the rather roundabout process by which a bourgeois intellectual came to join the proletarian movement. For its East German readers, Kuczynski's life story was no doubt a welcome relief from stereotyped accounts of the lives of party militants from proletarian backgrounds.

By the time Kuczynski came to write the second volume of his memoirs, describing his life in East Germany after 1945, he had very different issues to deal with. Rather than telling a story of how a member of the bourgeoisie had come to qualify as a party stalwart, he now wanted to show that he had been, as the title of this volume puts it, "a loyal dissident" who had stood up for the true ideals of communism against a bureaucracy that had denatured them. This task was difficult, because his narrative shows both that he remained consistently obedient to communist orthodoxy and that he he accepted with little protest a heavy dose of humiliation from the East German party leadership. He had initially expected to be named finance minister of a Soviet-backed German government but quickly found himself shunted into lesser jobs and realized that he was fated to remain a "politically engaged scholar," studying history rather than making it. He recounts but does not reflect on experiences that clearly indicate how distant postwar reality was from his ideals. Charged with promoting German-Soviet friendship, he quickly learned that few people on either side were eager to put aside the hatreds generated by the war; in 1948, as anti-Semitism resurfaced in the Soviet Union, he was ousted from his post anyhow.[65] He claims that Nikita Khrushchev's 1956 speech "gave him wings" and made him voice his criticisms of Stalinist orthodoxy, but he was quickly brought to heel. Threatened with denunciation as a "revisionist," he saved his academic position by promising not to publish any commentaries on current affairs.

Although he maintains that he had been in serious danger in 1957 and

1958, Kuczynski describes the period of ideological rigidity from 1959 to 1970 as a good one for him. His memoir makes no mention of the building of the Berlin Wall in 1961 but does record that in 1969 he was awarded the Order of Karl Marx (*'Linientreue Disident,'* 101, 115, 130, 193). Party leader Erich Honecker, who replaced the old-style boss Walter Ulbricht in 1970, kept Kuczynski on tenterhooks about the future of his academic enterprises. Much of the later part of Kuczynski's memoir is taken up with accounts of his efforts to stay in favor with Honecker, whom he served as an anonymous speechwriter. Despite his close ties to the country's leaders, Kuczynski did acquire a reputation as a dissident during the 1980s, particularly after the publication of an essay, *Dialog mit meinem Urenkel* (Dialogue with My Great-Grandchild), in which he contrasted what he saw as the true teachings of Marxism-Leninism with the practices of the regime. Writing after the fall of the Wall, Kuczynski boasts that he had come to be called "'the people's spiritual leader' . . . what a gift for fate to bestow on me in my ninth decade of life!" To the very end, however, what Kuczynski hoped would come out of the increasing dissatisfaction with the regime was a return to the real principles of Leninism (391, 388). The sudden absorption of the former East Germany into its capitalist rival state in 1990 and the triumph of the "one-hundred-eighty-degree neck-swivelers" was a distinct disappointment for him (7).

The situation created by the fall of the Wall left Kuczynski exposed to critics who questioned his self-representation as an outsider in a regime that had regularly bestowed honors on him and asked why he had never concluded that there was something fundamentally wrong with the system (10–11, 15). Replying to these attacks in the opening pages of *'Ein Linientreue Disident,'* Kuczynski reasserts his fundamental faith in socialism. At the same time, however, he argues that he has a duty to leave behind a record of how he had seen events as they happened, rather than critiquing his earlier views with the benefit of hindsight (12, 15). This represents a departure from the standpoint of his first volume of memoirs, in which he had judged his entire early life according to the standard of his later communist beliefs.

Kuczynski's memoirs provide a sobering example of how difficult autobiographical writing can be for those who clung to a rigid ideological commitment through radically changing circumstances. The second volume of his memoirs shows that the reputation he gained in the 1980s as a dissident was based in good part on a misunderstanding: he never abandoned his fundamental commitment to Leninism. The personality that emerges from his autobiographical writings is not an attractive one: a man of undoubted intelligence, he was unwilling to jeopardize his relatively privileged position within a system whose failings he knew only too well. Furthermore, as shown by Kuczynski's silence about such matters as the construction of the Berlin Wall and the pervasiveness of police spying in East Germany, his critique of the regime was focused primarily on its more venial sins. At the same time, however, there is no doubt that Kuczynski achieved his aim of leaving behind an important historical document. Precisely because of his refusal to question his ideological commitment, his memoirs are a fascinating window into the world of those who made the communist system the historical force it was for so many decades. They are also a unique case study of the ways in which the unexpected course of history can complicate the writing of an autobiography.

The memoirs of Annie Kriegel, Eric Hobsbawm, and Jürgen Kuczynski all reflect European experiences of communism. In the United States the communist movement never achieved the political importance it did in France or Germany, and even its influence on intellectual life was largely confined to the 1930s. Most American historian-memoirists who belonged to the party did so only briefly, in their youth, like John Toland, whose fascination with the experiences of the homeless during his college days led him to join in 1940. He could never digest the obligatory ideology, however, and lost his interest in the movement in the course of the war.[66] Gerda Lerner, an Austrian Jewish refugee who arrived in the United States in 1939, became involved with communist-front organizations during the war, when friendship with the Soviet Union was encouraged. She did join the party, but her main commitment was to the Congress of American Women. She claims in her memoir that experience with the party's indifference to women's issues helped move her away from communist orthodoxy. The main effect of her communist experience, however, as she portrays it in her memoir, was to expose her and her husband to McCarthyite harassment. "Had cold-war hysteria not taken such extreme forms we would have left the party years earlier than we did," she claims.[67]

While European historians' accounts of partisan engagement usually reflect experiences with highly structured movements such as the communists or, in the cases of several French historians, the right-wing Action française movement, the forms of personal political engagement that most American historians remember more typically involved less formal groupings, particularly the civil rights movements of the 1950s and 1960s. American historians have certainly had strong interests in political causes; indeed, the large number of self-proclaimed radicals among American historian-memoirists means that the politically committed are, if anything, overrepresented in this literature. Furthermore, the political activities of American historian-autobiographers were often quite important: they include John Hope Franklin's and C. Vann Woodward's participation in preparing the NAACP Legal Defense Fund's briefs for the 1954 *Brown v. Board of Education* school-desegregation case, James Silver's and Howard Zinn's roles in the southern civil rights movements of the 1960s, and Martin Duberman's role in gay activism in the 1970s and 1980s. Engagements of this sort did not require the same total personal and ideological commitment as those recounted by their European contemporaries, however, nor do they stimulate the same degree of autobiographical reconsideration. In general, the narratives of engagement in American historians' memoirs are stories of participation in movements whose principles have now triumphed and of the personal overcoming of unexamined prejudices. Even when they once held views that they later came to regard as wrong, as in the case of the historians who were pacifists in the 1930s but eventually supported American entry into World War II, these writers do not see their ideas as a problem requiring analysis or moral judgment of their earlier selves.

Ironically, one reason for this difference in tone between European and American historians' memoirs is that American historian-autobiographers more frequently suffered for their political commitments. Any sense of guilt they may have harbored for sins of political misjudgment is overshadowed by what they see as the unjustified treatment they endured. At a time when a number of their French contemporaries were participating actively in a communist party without suffering any career repercussions—"perhaps even the contrary," according to Alain Besançon[68]—numerous American historians were facing groundless accusations. Natalie Zemon Davis's passport was confiscated because of her husband's association with the Communist Party. In the 1960s, long after the fall of Senator Joseph McCarthy, political activism still carried risks. Howard Zinn was fired from his job at Spelman College because of his civil rights activities, and state legislators drove James Silver out of Mississippi. In the same period, French historians François Bluche and Raoul Girardet report being arrested on suspicion of involvement in assassination plots against de Gaulle without any consequences to their careers.

When American historian-autobiographers grapple with the problem of evil in their lives, they usually write about pervasive social attitudes they may have shared, particularly anti-Semitism and prejudice toward blacks, rather than about explicit political choices they made. Anti-Semitism often seems to stand out in the recollections of historians who grew up in the pre–World War II era as the strongest instance of moral evil that they had to confront on a personal level. In part, this is because prejudice against Jews pervaded academic life during their student years to such an extent that even John Hope Franklin writes that "the most traumatic social experience I had [at Harvard] was not racist but anti-semitic," and in part because, as H. Stuart Hughes writes, the situation of blacks seemed to be "a fact of nature, regrettable to be sure, . . . but doubtless unalterable in my lifetime."[69] Unlike joining or leaving the Communist Party, sharing or shedding the prejudices of one's era was not an individual decision or the result of a dramatic conversion. For the American historian-memoirists who highlight the issue, the reference to anti-Semitism serves to show the evolution of American attitudes in general and to underline the difference between past and present, rather than to reveal something special about their own character.

Racial issues engaged many American historian-autobiographers whose lives spanned the 1950s and 1960s, particularly those from the South or those who found themselves teaching there. As a teenager, Dan T. Carter responded positively to his South Carolina school principal's exhortations to oppose the 1954 Supreme Court decision: "Like most whites, I thrilled to the mobilization of white resistance." But it took relatively little to change his mind. When he saw whites beating up peaceful civil-rights demonstrators in 1960, "I realized that the racial moorings of a lifetime had been severed," and he soon joined the civil rights movement.[70] Wayne Flynt tells a similar story: "At first my fierce pride in southern history and southernness kept me from completely rejecting the South's racial culture. But by my senior year in college, 1960–61, when the Freedom Riders came through my hometown and their bus was firebombed by local thugs, I was furious."[71] The narrators in these conversion stories typically see their segregationist attitudes as reflections of their upbringing. Melton McLaurin, whose *Separate Pasts: Growing Up White in the Segregated South* is a powerful personal account of how white children absorbed the rules of segregation and learned to impose them on blacks, shows that the youth of that time could hardly have done otherwise. It is with their awakening to the evil of racial prejudice that they become moral agents, and the values they then embraced are the ones they still see as correct. Unlike the repentant sinners in classic conversion narratives, therefore, they do not need to search their soul to understand how they could have been so mistaken in their previous life.

The drama in American historians' accounts of their involvement with racial issues comes from the intensity of the opposition they sometimes faced, not from struggles within their own breast. James Silver, whose *Mississippi: The Closed Society* caused an uproar in that state in the early 1960s, tells the story of a very gradual development toward the realization that he had to use his abilities as a historian to oppose segregation. Born in New York and educated in North Carolina, he had not grown up with ingrained attitudes about race, but even after he joined the University of Mississippi faculty in 1936, "comprehension of the plight of blacks in the South came to me slowly." Silver explains how witnessing the effects of racial bias during his military service in the Pacific and visiting professorships in Scotland and at Harvard after the war broadened his thinking, but conditions in Mississippi made measures such as school desegregation seem utopian even after the 1954 Supreme Court ruling. He participated in private meetings at William Faulkner's home that aimed to "forestall the violence that was soon to become the hallmark of Mississippi," but it took the atmosphere of terror that developed in the state after James Meredith successfully sued to end the university's exclusion of blacks to drive Silver to take a public stand, which led to his being more or less driven out of Mississippi. Looking back at the course of his life, Silver saw the moment when he decided to voice his opposition to segregation and violence publicly as a kind of conversion experience. "Until some moment in the Meredith affair I had been running through life scared, desiring above all to be accepted. . . . After a decade of troublesome decisions I arrived as if by the wave of a magical wand at the point where there was no doubt as to my course." This is a dramatic conclusion but not exactly an Augustinian one: as he tells it, Silver's heart had been in the right place all along, and he had merely needed to develop the courage to act openly in accordance with its promptings. Silver is critical of the more radical turn taken by writers of black history after 1965, calling some of it "historical nonsense," but his memoir, published in 1984, is not a rethinking of his own earlier positions.[72]

Silver's memoir is representative of the personal accounts of American historians whose views were largely set before the development of the radical movements of the 1960s. Mark Naison represents a younger generation whose engagements were shaped by that decade. *White Boy* was written to explain why Naison, from a New York Jewish family, persisted in making a career in the field of African American studies at a time when the position of white scholars of the subject had become increasingly contested. Naison's commitment to the field was both personal and ideological. Growing up in

New York, he had been attracted to black popular culture as a way of distancing himself from the "insular, homogeneous" milieu of his parents. Reading James Baldwin's *Another Country* in 1963 convinced him of the moral imperative behind the movement for black liberation. "Wanting the grandeur of this modern crusade to spill over into my own life, I became a civil rights partisan, determined to raise the awareness of my peers about the nation's legacy of racial inequality." As a student at Columbia, he was shaped by his involvement in the radical SDS movement and by a passionate love affair with a young black woman. He participated in the building seizures at Columbia in 1968 but faced a crisis when his girlfriend joined an all-black group that insisted on conducting its own protest, separate from the other radical students.[73]

In autobiographical hindsight, Naison is strongly critical of the violent tendencies that developed within the essentially white SDS group after 1968, but his condemnation of leftist radicalism lacks the zealous tone of David Horowitz's *Radical Son,* the memoir of another white radical and coauthor of books about the Kennedy and Ford families who was strongly engaged on behalf of black causes in the 1960s but later came to feel a need to repent for those commitments.[74] After participation in one SDS action landed him in jail, Naison decided things had gone too far. Rather than emphasizing his condemnation of the group's tactics, however, he stresses his own wish for "a normal life . . . and a career I was committed to. It was time for me to face the limits of my political commitments and advance the causes I espoused in ways that seemed more practical and safe." Even after his relationship with his black lover had fallen apart, he remained dedicated to teaching and researching in the field of African American studies. The second half of his book recounts the challenges he faced, both from African Americans who questioned his role and from white colleagues and administrators who saw such programs as unfortunate concessions that should be phased out. Naison's story is thus a tale of steadfastness on behalf of "the only utopian ideal that had ever moved me . . . the vision of an interracial community invoked by Martin Luther King and the civil rights movement."[75]

Naison's account, which stresses the essential continuity of his commitment to racial justice, has much in common with *Why Weren't We Told? A Personal Search for the Truth about Our History,* a memoir by Australian historian Henry Reynolds, a leading figure in the struggle for recognition of Aboriginal rights. These stories contrast with the retrospective narratives of some European scholars of his generation, such as Luisa Passerini and Elisabeth Roudinesco. In the 1960s, Passerini belonged to the Situationist group, whose provocative and often highly theatrical operations aimed at subverting established leftist movements as well as ruling institutions. In the early 1970s, parts of the Italian radical movement turned to violent tactics. For Passerini, however, the notion that there was a "good" student movement in the 1960s that turned "bad" later is "a method of self-defense, . . . a typical tactic for saving one's identity," that fails to acknowledge that "the connections between the movement of '68 and terrorism are one of the most difficult historical problems of recent decades."[76] She also participated in the early stages of the Italian feminist movement in the 1970s, but there too she finds much to criticize, including her own unthinking acceptance of a leading position in the group, which separated her from ordinary women. Whereas involvement in historical research and teaching was Naison's way of continuing the commitment originally expressed in his activism and his personal life, for Passerini a turn to scholarly professionalism was a way of escaping from the contradictions she had encountered in her radical phase.[77] Elisabeth Roudinesco's story has many parallels with Passerini's. She, too, was intoxicated by the radicalism of the 1960s. As the energies liberated by the movement of May 1968 dissipated, she threw herself into the Communist Party and the radical psychological school led by Jacques Lacan. By the end of the 1970s, however, she had come to feel that both these movements were stagnating and turning oppressive: "The school became a party, the cause was a synonym for a religion." Like Passerini, and like Le Roy Ladurie and Kriegel a generation earlier, she saw a turn to historical research as a way of consecrating the break with her earlier beliefs.[78]

Historians' retrospective accounts of their experiences of political and ideological engagement, whether written by members of the generation that lived the mid-twentieth-century era of combat against fascism and racism or by younger historians whose adult lives began in the 1960s, thus reflect important differences between Europe and the United States. European scholars have most often retold their activist experiences in the mode of tragedy: their efforts to promote good causes led them unwittingly to embrace movements that they and the world around them would later see as evil. Historian-autobiographers like Eric Hobsbawm and Jürgen Kuczynski, who have refused to see their actions in this light, have found such interpretations imposed on their memoirs by their critics. For many of these European authors, a commitment to history became a form of redemption, a way of gaining a perspective on their ideological commitments that allowed them to disentangle themselves from error and, eventually, to understand how they had gotten into such situations. On the other side of the Atlantic, narratives of commitment have usually had a different shape. American historians who worked for civil rights, against the Vietnam war, or for rights for women see themselves as having contributed to causes that they still identify with; history textbooks and conventional wisdom now generally celebrate those movements. For many of these scholars, a career in history was not a repudiation of engagement but a way of continuing it under different circumstances.

Whether they write in a confessional mode or see their past commitments as still justified, historian-memoirists do acknowledge that partisan engagements, like participation in war, taught them historical lessons that could not be learned from books and documents. Historian-autobiographers' accounts thus argue against the ideal of a guild of cloistered historical analysts, recruited at a tender age and sheltered behind the walls of universities. Historians need experience of participation in history, and people with historical training have special contributions to make to the process by which collective history is shaped. At the same time, however, personal accounts often emphasize how uncertain the connection between commitment and outcome can be. Historians' memoirs of political engagement are often stories of unintended consequences, and as we have seen in many war memoirs, they are sometimes frustrating stories of an inability to make any contribution to history at all. In considering the limits of their abilities to understand and influence the outcome of the historical events they were involved with, historian-autobiographers shed new light on the extent of individual autonomy and responsibility, a classic issue in the domain of autobiography. These personal accounts also often underline the tendency of personal engagement to come into conflict with commitment to historical accuracy and truth. Although historians learn from being active in the world, most of them have also concluded that to make the study of history one's primary identity requires judging one's accomplishments by standards other than their visible impact on public affairs. More poignantly than most other autobiographical texts, historians' memoirs bring home this perhaps unwelcome historical conclusion.

CHAPTER 8

Holocaust Memories,
Historians' Memoirs

Among historians' memoirs that deal with historical experience, the group
of publications by scholars of Jewish origins whose lives were directly affected by the Holocaust occupies a special place. No other historical event
has inspired so many personal accounts, and no other group of contemporary historians has shown such a propensity to record their personal experiences.[1] The fact that historians from this particular group have been so
prone to writing about their own lives suggests that the general issues raised
by the confrontation of history and autobiography are especially intense
with respect to the this event. These historians' published recollections are
just part of a much larger body of survivor testimonies, but they have become a significant part of the literature of first-person recollections from
the Holocaust era. Historians whose lives were altered by the Holocaust,
however, are not simply echoing the themes of the better-known survivor
accounts. Their stories are often at odds both with the dominant tendencies in the larger body of survivor literature and with major assumptions
about modern Jewish history. These memoirs thus raise important questions about representations of the Holocaust and about the construction of
twentieth-century Jewish identity.

As we have seen in earlier chapters, first-person testimonial literature
has come to play a larger role in defining historical memory of the Holocaust than it has with respect to any other event. In the field of the Holocaust, secondhand scholarship is often seen as necessarily lacking the power
of conviction found in direct testimonies. Survivors' memoirs have sometimes been accorded an almost sacred status: Elie Wiesel, the archetypal

survivor-witness, has been quoted as saying, "I want eventually to establish a principle that every manuscript [survivor's memoir] should be published."[2] David Patterson, author of a study of Holocaust memoir literature, argues that even the reading of such works has a sacred function: the reader "must become not an interpreter of texts but a mender of the world, a part of the recovery that this memory demands."[3] Whether historians have a right to give priority to their scholarly reconstruction of this particularly painful episode of the past, as opposed to the accounts of it given by its victims, is consequently an especially charged question.

Although historians are understandably reluctant to get drawn into arguments about what happened at Auschwitz with survivors who have a number tattooed on their arm, their usual concerns about the reliability of autobiographal testimony exist here, too, as we have seen earlier in the discussion of French Holocaust historian Annette Wievorka's critique of memoir literature. Wievorka is unusually candid about the critical attitude Holocaust historians often take toward memoir sources, but she is by no means unique. Raul Hilberg, the dean of American Holocaust scholars, has also distanced himself from reliance on such retrospective accounts. Hilberg has pointed out that, by definition, all survivors of the Holocaust were exceptional cases, and historians relying on their testimony get a biased picture because they "did not interview the dead."[4] In Hilberg's view, which is also the standard wisdom of history manuals, the historian should seek as much as possible to work from sources generated at the time of the event and written without any eye toward telling a story. Hilberg has described the excitement of constructing history from such documents, each one "an artifact . . . the original paper that once upon a time was handled by a bureaucrat." In their seeming objectivity, such artifacts appear far removed from memoir sources, and since they do not tell their own stories, documents leave the creative work of interpretation to the historian, the importance of whose role is thus underlined. When historians write up their research as comprehensible narratives, Hilberg comments, "the words that are thus written take the place of the past; these words, rather than the events themselves, will be remembered. Were this transformation not a necessity, one could call it presumptuous, but it is unavoidable."[5] Like Wievorka, Hilberg posits that the historian's methods produce a representation of past events that is in some sense truer and more accurate than that of those who were actually there.

Is there a paradox in the fact that Raul Hilberg makes these criticisms of autobiographical accounts of the Holocaust in the pages of his own autobiography, and that he makes his impassioned defense of the procedures of scientific scholarship in history in the context of explaining the intense personal meaning this research had for an Austrian-born Jew who had had to flee to the United States and who found little interest in the Holocaust there, even among historians? Aren't historians who turn to the necessarily subjective genre of autobiography in fact acknowledging, as Walter Laqueur does, "that those who were not witnesses, however thorough their research and innovative their explanations, are missing one whole dimension"?[6] The fact that so many historians whose lives were affected by the Nazi era have chosen to venture onto the subjective ground of autobiography demonstrates the genre's powerful pull and the special compulsion to testify that historians, like all others affected by these events, have come to feel.

The autobiographical narratives examined in this chapter form a corpus defined by two features. First, all of these authors' lives were directly and personally affected by the Nazi persecution of the Jews in that they were forced to flee their prewar homes and, in most cases, that they lost close family members during the Holocaust. Second, all also subsequently published significant works of historical scholarship, although a few held academic appointments in other disciplines (Reinhard Bendix, Raul Hilberg, Jürgen Kuczynski, Dan Segre, Nechama Tec) or had careers largely outside of academia (Reuben Ainsztein, Jacques Presser). About a quarter of these memoirists can be categorized as scholars whose main publications have dealt with the Holocaust and directly related issues. Half or more never addressed this subject outside of their memoirs, and the others wrote one or more historical works on themes related to the rise of Hitler or the Holocaust while being primarily concerned with other topics.[7] With the exceptions of Friedländer and Tec, these authors followed the classic pattern of autobiographers and published their memoir late in their career, often after retirement, and indeed a good number of these authors have now died.[8]

Aside from Saul Friedländer's *When Memory Comes*, none of these autobiographical texts has yet generated much critical discussion in its own right. Most have been reviewed with respect, in view of the painful experiences they recount, but Mitchell Hart's comments, in a critique of three of the books discussed here, that the authors "are far better historians than they are autobiographers" and that they are "uncomfortable with revealing too much of their inner lives, whether emotional or mental," probably reflects a wider reaction to many of them.[9] Although the intersection of their personal lives with the rise of Nazism is what usually justifies the writing of these memoirs, the gravity of the events looming in the background of their stories seems to inhibit many of these authors, making the details of their experiences seem insignificant but at the same time preventing them from flavoring their stories with the humor or irony that is a redeeming feature of many autobiographies. When they are read as a group, however— admittedly a procedure that their authors did not foresee—they tell us some significant and interesting things, both about their authors and about larger issues. What they communicate is, first of all, a keen sense of how baffling the upsurge of Nazi anti-Semitism was to Jews from acculturated backgrounds in western and central Europe. Second, these texts illuminate the role that a commitment to the professional study of history played in the lives of people who had experienced how uncertain other forms of identity could be. In particular, as we will see, commitment to historical scholarship often took precedence over identification with Jewishness, even after the Holocaust. Finally, these texts demonstrate the transformative nature of the autobiographical act itself. For many of these authors, writing a memoir has been not only an opportunity to reflect on the process by which they developed their mature self but a moment of redefinition, putting earlier senses of self into question.

The historians who have written memoirs in this category are in no sense a representative sample of Jews whose lives were affected by Hitler. Nine-tenths of them are male. In contrast to the death-camp survivor memoirs, among whom German Jews are relatively rare, these texts are heavily skewed toward authors of German, Austrian, and French origin; East European Jews, who made up the overwhelming majority of Holocaust victims, are severely underrepresented. This tilt obviously reflects the well-known facts that German Jews had better chances to escape from Hitler, since Nazi policy until 1940 was to encourage Jewish emigration, and that Jews in France had relatively good chances of survival. The predominance of Jews from western and central Europe among these authors has a number of consequences. One is that these memoirists turn out to come from economically successful and highly assimilated families; unlike Jews from eastern Europe, neither they nor their parents had any reason to question the notion that history was working in their favor prior to 1933. Second, most of these historian-memoirists experienced the Nazi persecution of the Jews as a process that developed over several years, allowing the possibility for various reactions, rather than as a sudden thunderclap leaving only the most desperate of choices, as was often the case for Jews in eastern Europe. Finally, as children, these authors shared the language and culture of their neighbors. This meant that, to some extent, they were in a position to understand their persecutors, but at the same time, it also meant that persecution threatened their sense of identity in particularly painful ways. In contrast, survivors from places like Poland had always felt alienated from their surroundings. All of these characteristics help explain why these historian-authors would be more inclined than most Holocaust survivors to try to understand their experiences from a historical perspective.

The fact that historians with these origins make up by far the largest group of contemporary historical scholars to have written their memoirs demonstrates the degree to which they have been, in spite of themselves, affected by the larger cultural currents working to define Holocaust memory. At a time when efforts are being made to record the testimony of every living Holocaust survivor, it would be surprising if professional historians who lived through these events should remain silent. It is important to stress, however, that these historians do not consider themselves Holocaust survivors in the sense of Elie Wiesel, Primo Levi, or Gerda Weissman Klein. I have not yet found a historian's memoir whose author had the misfortune to pass through the German camps; the majority had either emigrated from Europe before the war or else managed to evade capture by hiding.[10] Remembering his relatives' sense of abandonment when he obtained an emigration visa from Germany in 1938, Reinhard Bendix asks himself, "How can the person who can still escape, relate to one who is fatally trapped? To me the question was unanswerable in 1938, and it still is."[11] Even Saul Friedländer, who lost both his parents and who survived the war hidden under a false identity, writes, "I had lived on the edges of the catastrophe; a distance—impassable, perhaps—separated me from those who had been directly caught up in the tide of events, and despite all my efforts, I remained, in my own eyes, not so much a victim as—a spectator."[12] What they endured was often terrifying enough—Walter Grab describes being yanked off the street in Vienna by Nazi toughs, forced into a cellar room smeared with stinking feces, and ordered to lick the walls clean, and Gerda Lerner was held in a Nazi prison for several weeks as a hostage for her missing father[13]—but they still experienced only the outer circles of hell. As David Weiss Halivni, a survivor of Auschwitz and several other camps, has written in his own memoir, "Those who survived the camps themselves . . . survived on totally different terms from those who went to a foreign consulate in '38 to struggle for a visa."[14]

These texts may thus seem marginal to the larger body of Holocaust memoirs. Nevertheless, it is clear that the majority of these historian-memoirists would not have undertaken their projects if their lives had not been disrupted by the Holocaust, and they are certainly aware that readers who pick up their books are also likely to have read *Night* or *Survival in Auschwitz* and to put these less traumatic memoirs in that context.[15] Some of them express unease about being identified with this literature. Peter Kenez asks himself "why people are so proud of having been persecuted. . . . Why do I, like others, cling to my own story of misery?"[16] But when Peter Gay asserts that "even the most fortunate Jew who lived under Hitler has never completely shaken off the experience," he establishes a continuum between his own testimony and that of survivors who had more extreme experiences.[17] The idiosyncrasy of their stories, compared to the standard narrative found in historical accounts, does make some of these authors nervous. Friedländer, as we have seen, wondered whether he would not do better to "attach myself to the necessary order, the inescapable simplification forced upon one by the passage of time and one's vision of history, to adopt the gaze of the historian."[18] But others see this as the special contribution of their memoir. Paradoxically, however, the historian-memoirists also insist on their individuality vis-à-vis the collective portrait that has emerged from the survivor literature. By structuring their memoirs in ways that are distinctively different from those of most camp survivors, and above all by historicizing their own experiences, these historian-memoirists raise questions not about the veracity of survivors' accounts but about the interpretation of the Holocaust experience that is implicitly proposed in much survivor literature and, above all, about the nature of collective Jewish memory.

We can see how the perspective that comes from historical training affects the way in which these authors reconstruct their experience by comparing the ways they structure their memoirs with the narrative structures common to the best-known Holocaust survivor memoirs. Three contrasts stand out: the extended historical time frame of the historians' memoirs, as opposed to the dramatically foreshortened time span in the most widely read survivor memoirs; the emphasis put on the distance between narrator and protagonist in the historians' memoirs, as opposed to the tendency toward identification of the two in survivor memoirs; and the treatment of Jewish identity in the two groups of writings. The Holocaust survivor memoirs that have been most widely read usually make little effort at putting their authors' pre-Holocaust life in any kind of historical perspective. For the purposes of an Elie Wiesel, a Ka-Tzetnik 135633, or a Primo Levi, this background is on the one hand essentially irrelevant—all that matters in their story is that they were defined as a Jew by the Germans—and, on the other hand, not something they claim any special ability to explain. The dramatic impact of their testimony comes from the terrifying suddenness with which they found themselves thrust into the death-world of the camps and from the complete disjuncture between what Ka-Tzetnik calls "Planet Auschwitz" and the rest of human experience. Any narrative energy expended to depict themselves as persons who had a history and an identity prior to the Holocaust experience would necessarily detract from this impact. For the same reasons, many survivor memoirs say nothing about their author's life after the Holocaust. The fact that these texts exist at all implicitly testifies to their authors' survival and their determination to bear witness, but their texts express the conviction that the details of their postwar lives belong to a completely different order of reality from what they experienced during the war.

Survivors' memoirs thus reflect a sense that the Holocaust cannot really be understood as a historical event, or even an autobiographical one. Auschwitz comes out of nowhere and leads nowhere, and the months or years spent there do not connect up with the before and after of the survivor's life. The survivor's memoir thus challenges one of the fundamental presuppositions of the historical enterprise: the conviction that all past human experience can, at least in principle, be fitted together in a unifying temporal framework. Some of these memoirs inadvertently reflect the fact that Auschwitz itself had a history—that conditions in the camp varied over the course of its existence and that the particularly hellish circumstances recorded in Wiesel's *Night* correspond, for example, to the Germans' frantic efforts to exterminate the large Hungarian Jewish community in a very short time—but recording the history of their lethal environment is not the purpose of these texts. The survivors' memoirs implicitly assert that history, as a form of understanding, will never succeed in integrating what happened in Auschwitz into any kind of comprehensible narrative. At the same time, by cutting the author's experiences before and after Auschwitz out of the picture, the classical Holocaust survivor narrative denies the possibility of a real autobiography. The camp survivor's personal experience in Auschwitz is completely unrelated to who the memoirist was before the war, and in a metaphorical but very powerful sense the survivor-memoirist died in Auschwitz, so that his or her life afterward is equally disconnected from the occurrences related in the memoir. The contrast between Wiesel's unforgettable self-portrait in *Night* and the diffuse and often tedious record of his career in his more recently published *Memoirs* testifies to the difficulty that even a writer of real genius has encountered in trying to reframe his life story as a continuous narrative.

Related to the survivor memoir's deliberate rejection of historical continuity and historical context is its minimization of the distance between narrator and protagonist. The Holocaust memoir aims to produce an effect of immediacy, as though we were seeing events directly through the author's eyes as he or she experiences them. Thus the Israeli survivor-author Ka-Tzetnik puts his recollections of "Prayer in Auschwitz" in the present tense, describing how "the skeletons hurtle forward, leaping from the planks upon which they had lain inert but a moment ago. Hungry flames spurt from their eyes, faster. Faster—Soon the noon soup will be dished out!"[19] His narrative technique pulls readers into the camp experience, but it hides from them the process of memory by which he has reconstructed the story and its retrospective character. Passages in which the author exercises the autobiographer's privilege of reflecting on the difference between the experience of events at the time and how they appear in retrospect are rare. The effect is a powerful concentration of the reader's attention; the possibility of achieving any critical distance from the narrator is minimized.

The final aspect of these two bodies of memoirs that I want to emphasize has to do with their differing treatments of their protagonists' Jewish identity. In survivor memoirs, Jewish identity appears as a matter of fate, and the protagonist's own attitude toward it, although it may vary widely, is ultimately irrelevant. Wiesel was a deeply religious adolescent, Levi a complete agnostic, but both were Jews as far as the Germans were concerned, and that became the overriding determinant of their fates. It is this that makes it possible for critics such as David Patterson, in his commentary on survivor literature, *Sun Turned to Darkness,* to interpret all survivor memoirs as acts of Jewish religious renewal, even when their authors explicitly disavow any religious convictions.[20] Furthermore, because survivor memoirs—Ruth Klüger's *Still Alive* is a notable exception—are frequently silent about their author's post-Holocaust life, readers are usually left with little or no clue as to their author's relationship to their Jewish identity after the Holocaust, and it is clear that many readers have filled in this blank by assuming that the author strongly self-identified as Jewish. As we will see, historians' memoirs suggest that this is a more difficult issue than a reading of survivor testimonies as building blocks of Jewish memory allows.

In contrast to the familiar survivor memoirs, historians' personal narratives normally have a long historical prologue, and even if they do not follow their author's life down to the time when the memoir was written, they do make it clear that that story went on beyond 1945. They also do not show the tendency to minimize the distance between narrator and protagonist that we have seen is common in other Holocaust memoirs; instead, they emphasize it, and in particular they remind us that all these authors became professional historians after the war. When they look back on their earlier experiences, they do so through the prism of this professional training, which they did not have at the time, and they thus necessarily see things differently from the way they did then. Finally, the question of identity is much discussed in these texts, and the authors' comments on it are evidence of a strong desire not to let their life be entirely defined by what happened to them during the Holocaust years. In this respect, their decision to write an autobiography functions as one more way of complicating the issue of how they see themselves and how readers are likely to define them.

As we have seen, most of these memoirists came from a specific kind of background: their parents, and often their grandparents, had acculturated themselves strongly to the society around them, adopting its language and mores. These accounts typically begin with a more or less extended family narrative, usually a story of worldly success: tales of Jewish peddlers or ghetto dwellers of the early nineteenth century whose children and grand-children prospered and, in many cases, moved into the ranks of the educated professions. The point to these stories is, of course, to answer the historical question of why the European Jews of the 1930s did not recognize the peril threatening them; the answer suggested in these books is that their experiences gave them confidence that outbreaks of anti-Semitism would be at most temporary setbacks in a longer story of progress. Furthermore, these authors' parents had usually identified themselves so strongly with their homeland that the thought of leaving was difficult to contemplate. Almost all of the German- and Austrian-born memoirists recall families steeped in German culture, as comfortable in their environment as the Kriegels and Vidal-Naquets were in their French milieu or the Segres in their Italian one. Of all these authors, only the Lithuanian Reuben Ainzstein grew up speaking Yiddish. Even the Pole Nechama Tec and the Hungarian Peter Kenez both underline the fact that their families lived in primarily non-Jewish neighborhoods. Only Kenez recalls his father's life as having been significantly affected by anti-Semitism, which had prevented him from achieving his ambition of studying medicine in prewar Hungary. Although a few of the German-Jewish memoirists, such as George Mosse and Felix Gilbert, whose families were socially prominent and who therefore felt particularly exposed, saw the handwriting on the wall and left the country immediately in 1933, most remained until a good deal later, often until after the Kristall-nacht pogrom finally made it clear that Jews had no future in the country.

These memoirists thus see themselves and their families as products of the social changes that had transformed European society over the previous century. They also historicize the question of their families' Jewish identity. Very few of these authors grew up in a strongly religious household. Three of the thirteen contributors to a volume of essays by historians who settled in Britain were actually raised as Christians from birth, as were Felix Gilbert (a descendant of Moses Mendelssohn), Gerhard Masur, and Susan Groag Bell, whose Czech Jewish parents had both converted and never discussed the matter with her.[21] Hans Schmitt's father, himself of mixed Protestant and Catholic heritage, had broken completely with religion, and his mother did not tell him of her Jewish roots until he starting coming home from school and repeating the anti-Semitic phrases he learned from other boys.[22] Saul Friedländer writes, "In our family, if memory serves me correctly, Judaism as a religion had completely disappeared," and Gerda Lerner's family regularly put up a Christmas tree.[23]

The high degree of assimilation in these families did not always imply a complete absence of Jewish identity, but it was certainly an attenuated and sometimes conflicted identity that left the future authors uncertain of how to define themselves and unprepared for the discrimination imposed by the Nazis. Gerhard Masur, the only one of these authors old enough to have held a university position in Germany in 1933, was so far removed from his Jewish ancestry that he was able to keep his job until 1935 because he could prove that he had served in an anti-Semitic nationalist *Freikorps* in 1919–20.[24] Though his parents were both of Jewish ancestry, Pierre Vidal-Naquet was not even circumcised. Bendix went through a secular bar mitzvah cer-emony, without learning any Hebrew, but his parents taught him and his sister to avoid what they considered "Jewish mannerisms.'"[25] Kriegel writes that her parents taught her "that we were different, but without the substance of this difference being made explicit."[26] Friedländer claims he did not realize that his family was Jewish until he started elementary school at age six and found himself being taken out of his regular classroom for Jewish religious instruction, and Tec remarks on the contradictory nature of her father's instructions that she assimilate to the surrounding Polish soci-ety but that she not deny her Jewish heritage. Only a handful of these authors came from families that consciously resisted assimilation. Georg Iggers, who was just entering school when Hitler came to power, took refuge in Zionism and Orthodoxy. Helmut Eschwege came from a family of Orthodox Jewish schoolteachers, and Herbert Strauss's Catholic mother, who had converted to Judaism to marry his father, took her new faith more seriously than her husband did.[27] Jacob Katz was educated in a yeshiva, although he pursued secular readings on his own. Protected by his Hungarian passport and a clear sense of purpose, he actually remained in Germany for several years after 1933 to finish his studies. With these exceptions, however, these future historians' families did not embrace any version of Jewish identity, whether religious, ethnic, or Zionist, that would have made sense of the anti-Semitism they were to encounter.

This historicization of their families' situations is brought out especially strongly in the contrasts these authors recall between how they reacted to the discovery that their Jewish origins now entirely defined their fate and how their parents responded. The differences they recall demonstrate how strongly these responses were colored by different positions in the stream of Jewish history. The parents, who usually had some childhood experience of religious practice to draw on, often began to reaffirm their identity as Jews. Schmitt's mother made a brief attempt to learn Hebrew.[28] Bendix's father, who had officially withdrawn from the Berlin Jewish community in 1918, discovered a sense of solidarity among the Jewish prisoners in the concentration camp where he spent two years in the mid-1930s. He began attending religious services after reaching Palestine in 1938, although he remained fundamentally skeptical about religious faith.[29] Vidal-Naquet's father opposed the formation of an umbrella organization for Jews in France because it meant accepting an identity separate from that of other French citizens, but he spent time reconstructing the family tree and told his son the story of the Dreyfus Affair. In France in December 1941, the Friedländer family celebrated Hanukkah for the first time in the future historian's life. Meditating on the experience, Friedländer concludes, "When crises occur, one searches the depths of one's memory to discover some vestige of the past, not the past of the individual, faltering and ephemeral, but rather that of the community, which, though left behind, nonetheless represents that which is permanent and lasting."[30]

The future historian-autobiographers had no such memory of Jewish identity to fall back on. Not all speak of enduring an identity crisis— Walter Laqueur writes, "I was what I was and it did not seem a life-or-death matter to belong to a group"[31]—but all realized that their sense of self was now under assault from outside. Hans Schmitt found the experience baffling: "I was still a German, albeit a troubled one."[32] "For the first time in my life, I had to give serious thought to my Jewish origin, because what had been lurid sensationalism a short while ago had suddenly become government policy," Reinhard Bendix recalls.[33] He tried out various alternatives to his parents' liberal Jewish identity, including Marxism and Zionism, before emigrating and trying to separate himself from all ethnic and ideological ties. Dan Segre was devastated when his gentile Italian girlfriend, who had shared his opposition to Fascism, cut off relations with him to avoid violating the racial laws Mussolini imposed in 1938.[34] Friedländer's parents tried to ensure his safety by placing him in a French Catholic boarding school. Hastily baptized and renamed Paul-Henri Ferland, he was entirely cut off from his former life. Nechama Tec was eventually housed with a gentile family, although she remained in contact with her parents and sister. She was taught to pass herself off as Polish and recalls "an odd confusion of emotions—fear because I was losing touch with my real self, but a kind of pleasure, too, because it was so easy to give up and become my newer, safe self."[35]

In France, as we saw in the previous chapter, Annie Kriegel actively chose a new identity by becoming involved with a Communist resistance group. The Communist movement offered an active way of resisting the Nazis, and it held out the attraction of a future society in which the consciousness of ethnic difference that had imposed itself so catastrophically under Hitler would be abolished. While Kriegel traded her parents' Jewish and middle-class identity for a Communist commitment, Léon Poliakov, also from an assimilated background, found himself working for a good part of the war with a group of Orthodox Jews. He was not converted himself, but he was deeply impressed by their "vitality" and "astonishing faith."[36] Whereas history seemed determined to impose one particular identity—Jew—on these young people, their recollections are thus of multiple possibilities and experiments. Furthermore, whereas their parents reacted to the crisis by accepting the notion that their efforts at assimilation had been unrealistic, many of these children responded by even more determined efforts to show that their identity was not entirely subsumed in their Jewish origins.

In contrast to most authors of survivor memoirs, then, these historian-memoirists identify themselves as products of history, and indeed of a highly specific history—one that set them apart from the majority of Holocaust victims. They also connect their stories with the history of the post-Holocaust world. Because their authors are identified, at least in the prefaces to their books, as professional historians, it is always clear that they had a career after the war period, and indeed a career that involved a critical effort to understand the past. Most of these books follow their authors' lives at least through their return home or their settlement in a new country and the completion of their education, and often much further than that. In many cases, their youthful experiences in Nazi Europe serve only as a short prologue to the longer story of their adult life. Kriegel's sprawling autobiography devotes far more energy and passion to her involvement with the French Communist Party after 1945 than to her wartime experiences. Evyatar Friesel reduces his account of his childhood to a "German overture" in a story that is mostly about his subsequent life in Brazil and Israel. In contrast to the best-known survivor memoirs, where the author's post-Holocaust life is left as a blank, these are usually narratives in which we see the protagonist overcome, with greater or lesser difficulty, the hurdles placed in his or her path by Nazism and, frequently, emigration and go on to achieve considerable success in life.

Like the anchoring of these stories in the pre-Hitler era, their prolongation past the crises of the Holocaust years serves to emphasize the interaction between the authors and the history of their time. This form of narrative also serves to emphasize the distance between the autobiographical author and the protagonist of his or her story. If the survivor memoir derives its impact from its ability to make us feel that we are directly immersed in events, the historian's memoir takes a more roundabout route, in which the author seeks to win our trust by showing his or her ability to use historical perspective to explain a personal past. Professional involvement with historical study is not incidental to these stories: it is often presented as the way the author succeeded in restoring purpose and meaning to a disrupted life, and "historian" or "scholar" is often the identity these authors embrace most wholeheartedly. After five tense years of coping with adult responsibilities in the hostile environment of Nazi Germany, Reinhard Bendix "came to the University of Chicago with a pent-up desire for academic work as a liberating experience." He eagerly embraced the notion of scientific objectivity: "I had seen enough extreme partisanship to last me for a while."[37] Often the commitment to history followed a period of engagement in such partisanship and served as a path out of it. George Mosse campaigned actively for anti-Fascist causes during the 1930s but allowed himself to become increasingly absorbed by academic life after the war; he went from rallying support for the Spanish Republicans to urging the abolition of the football team at the University of Iowa. Saul Friedländer's postwar ideological commitment was to Zionism, but for him, too, academia served as a refuge from an excessively encompassing historical reality: that of Israel in the 1950s, a society so consumed by its own practical needs that it had no time for the intellectual life he sought.[38] It is clear that for many of these authors the study of history came to represent a way of countering the lies that had shaped their lives in such traumatic ways. For George Mosse, "history . . . took the place of religion, with the advantage that history is open-ended and not exclusive."[39] History's liberalism and willingness to submit its own conclusions to critical examination made it an attractive alternative to the all-encompassing political ideologies of the mid-twentieth century but also to the embrace of an all-consuming Jewish or Zionist identity.

The choice of history also opened possibilities for direct engagement with issues related to the events that had shaped these authors' lives, but not all of them chose this course. During the war, Pierre Vidal-Naquet's father had specifically impressed upon him the role that historians could play in opposing tyranny and oppression. The elder Vidal-Naquet recounted to his son the struggle to prove Dreyfus's innocence, and Vidal-Naquet writes, "I remain marked by this story which proved that truth could be discovered — and that historians have a role to play here." The father also read the boy Chateaubriand's famous encomium of Tacitus, in which the great romantic author celebrates the Roman historian's exposure of the crimes of the emperors.[40] But Vidal-Naquet learned that history could equally well serve as a form of escape from twentieth-century concerns. To complete his graduate studies, he wrote two long papers, one on Plato, the other on Jean Jaurès, the French socialist and supporter of Dreyfus. "This tension between a philosopher who went back into the cave after contemplating the idea of the Good and the orator . . . who tried to rescue men from the cave makes a good allegory of the contradictions that have defined and always will define my historian's life."[41]

Vidal-Naquet's sense of the two possibilities opened up by historical scholarship—engagement with the events of one's own time and escape into unrelated epochs—characterizes the reactions of this group of memoirists as a whole. Only a minority of them have devoted the bulk of their scholarly work to the Holocaust. Many are quite conscious of having used their academic career as a way of distancing themselves from that event. Evyatar Friesel notes that the Holocaust was "a theme I had been avoiding for years," and Peter Gay avers, "I have deliberately refused to dwell on the mass murder of Europe's Jews," adding, "We all have our defenses to help us get through life, and these happen to be mine."[42] Richard Pipes "deliberately shied away from reading about or viewing films and photographs" dealing with the Holocaust and decided that since other scholars had written enough on the subject, he could teach the lesson of how "evil ideas lead to evil consequences" by dealing with communism rather than Nazism.[43] The cases of those memoirists who did become specialists in Holocaust studies show the importance that commitment to historical perspective had in allowing them to achieve what they thought was a necessary distance from the subject. In the early 1950s, Raul Hilberg was considering studying the treatment of war crimes in international law when "I woke up. It was the evidence that I wanted. My subject would be the destruction of the European Jews." He would approach the subject, however, not by expanding on his personal experience but by tracing how it appeared from the perpetrators' side. "The perpetrator had the overview. He alone was the key. It was through his eyes that I had to view the happening, from its genesis to its culmination." Above all, he would look for objective evidence, for documents.[44] He would cling to that choice and, indeed, define his entire academic career around it.

Léon Poliakov wanted to discover "the secret of the executioners . . . the circumstances in which the leaders of the Third Reich had decided to kill me, along with millions of other human beings whose special characteristic was to have been born in one bed rather than another." Like Hilberg, he nevertheless understood that he had to adopt the persona of the impersonal historian to make his work effective: "My sensibility had become professional, so that I treated Auschwitz and the SS killers without any apparent emotion; think of a doctor's or a priest's impassive reaction to suffering and death."[45] George Mosse was one of those who originally pursued topics far removed from the Holocaust—his first books were on Reformation England—but who later shifted to research on the roots of Nazism; he saw this "attempt to make sense out of the history of my own century" as "also a means of understanding my own past."[46] Only Saul Friedländer suggests that the connection between his own experiences and the way he worked as a historian altered his notion of how history should be done. As he worked on his early projects—a study of U.S.-German relations in 1939–41 and a collection of documents on the Vatican's role during the war—Friedländer came to realize and to accept that his own experiences necessarily influenced his way of understanding his findings. "It was only at this time in my life, when I was around thirty, that I realized how much the essential appeared to me through a particular prism that could never be eliminated. But did it have to be eliminated?"[47]

Whether or not they chose to do historical research on the Holocaust era, historical training gave these authors a sense of perspective on their personal experiences that is reflected in the tone and structure of their memoirs. The concern with background and context that characterizes most of these books, and that often weakens them as autobiographies, reflects the tendencies of the historical discipline. It is probably no accident that the two of these memoirs that deliberately depart the most from conventional linear historical narrative—Saul Friedländer's *When Memory Comes* and Dan Segre's *Memoirs of a Fortunate Jew*—are among the most effective of these works. By adopting a more "literary" approach, these authors have freed themselves to speak in a more individual voice. Even these texts, however, are quite different from the classic Holocaust survivor narrative. Their authors' professional historical training—explicitly referred to in Friedländer's case, implicitly demonstrated by the structure of the narrative in Segre's, with its lengthy discussion of the history of modern Italian Jewry as reflected in the story of his family—creates a distance between narrator and protagonist that is absent from the writings of someone like Elie Wiesel. The recognition that history provides at least the possibility of an alternative narrative of the Holocaust era means that the historian-memoirist's first-person narrative is relativized; what it gains in perspective it loses in dramatic force.

The identification with the historical discipline that defines these texts also has a bearing on another of their characteristics: their dramatization of their authors' often difficult relationship with their Jewish origins in the postwar era. With varying degrees of explicitness, almost all of them express deeply conflicted attitudes toward the Jewish identity the Holocaust period forced on them. In the way they discuss their relationship to Jewishness, their feelings about Israel, and their connection to their European homeland, all make clear that the process of self-definition has been a continuing one, not something fixed once and for all by the events of 1933–1945. Few of these memoirists were prepared to accept the apparent lesson that their Jewish origins were the determining fact of their life, even though their stories are framed by the arbitrary way in which Nazi anti-Semitism affected them. Hans Schmitt, although he would be considered Jewish under halachic law, is the most emphatic: "I was not a Jew and had no intention of becoming one."[48] Of the authors who mention their marriages, a good number took non-Jewish spouses. Reinhard Bendix, one of them, comments, "Hitler's Nürnberg laws provoked a certain defiance in me,"[49] thus casting his break with the Jewish tradition as at the same time a protest against the Nazi attempt to force Jewish identity on him. Pierre Vidal-Naquet, both of whose parents died in Auschwitz, agreed to a Catholic marriage because "the religious question didn't matter to me."[50] Georg Iggers, devotedly Orthodox as a child, found himself estranged from the Jewish communities he encountered in the United States. He and his wife, also a European Jewish immigrant, belonged to a Unitarian church in the 1950s; in their joint autobiography, his wife comments that her husband "always hoped to find a Jewish community where he would feel comfortable and for which he could engage himself. He has never succeeded."[51] So long as he remained in Hungary, Peter Kenez recognized that he could not shed his Jewish identity. But his intention was to stop identifying himself as Jewish as soon as he reached the West, and he made no objection to helping the uncle who welcomed him when he reached the United States perpetuate the masquerade he had adopted in passing himself off—even to his wife—as a Presbyterian.[52]

Conflicted attitudes about Jewish identity or a sense of not belonging wholly to any group is a common theme in these memoirs. Reinhard Bendix indeed makes this issue the center of his self-analysis. He found himself torn between many identities, unable to affirm any of them wholeheartedly and particularly conscious of his inability to find personal meaning in the Jewish tradition. In his teenage years in Germany, "Nazi coercion seemed to me the worst possible reason for turning religious." Because he was able to emigrate before the war, he was excluded from "the mass extermination that followed and the spiritual crisis that went with it." He was therefore able to retain his faith in liberal individualism and universalism, which he saw his mixed marriage as affirming.[53] Forced to live in an adopted language, he felt that he had "lost one country without gaining another." He found a welcoming home in the American university system while "keeping my distance from its full impact and attempting to develop an intellectual perspective of my own." Indeed, Bendix came to believe that isolation and marginality were in some senses inherent to modern academic life, a result of the degree of "specialized competence" the modern world requires.[54] The concept of "partial group membership" that Bendix develops in his memoir expresses the sense that he never had an organic, all-embracing identity.[55] Despite what he considered as his successful integration into American society, George Mosse "continued to consider myself a European and a permanent outsider." Jewish religious beliefs played no part in his postwar life; his only departure from religious agnosticism was a brief flirtation with Christian socialism.[56]

Of all these memoirs, Saul Friedländer's *When Memory Comes* reflects most powerfully the uncertainties of self-definition that beset many of these historians. *When Memory Comes* is not just a memoir of Friedländer's Holocaust experience; above all, it is a recollection of the intense difficulty he had afterward in coming to terms with what had happened to him. Left in a boarding school run by traditionalist French Catholics during the war, the orphaned Friedländer came to identify with his new milieu, to the point of dreaming of becoming a priest. "Though conscious of my origins, I nevertheless felt at ease within a community of those who had nothing but scorn for Jews."[57] Even when he was made the ward of a Russian Jewish family in Paris in 1946, he was slow to embrace a Jewish identity. He recalls participating in the family's seder in 1946 but refusing to eat meat because the holiday fell on Good Friday. Two years later, Friedländer did abruptly quit school to join the fight for Israel's independence. His very arrival in the country dramatized the difficulty of taking on a new "Israeli" identity, however: the ship he sailed on was the *Altalena,* a vessel chartered by the rightwing Irgun movement and later sunk off the beach of Tel Aviv on orders of David Ben-Gurion, who feared that its cargo of weapons would be used to challenge the authority of his newly installed left-wing government. Settled in Israel, Friedländer felt alienated and longed for the more sophisticated intellectual culture of France. In his memoir he writes, "I was destined, therefore, to wander among several worlds, knowing them, understanding them . . . but nonetheless incapable of feeling an identification without any reticence, incapable of seeing, understanding, and belonging in a single, immediate, total movement."[58]

Friedländer's articulation of his sense of fractured identity is more extreme than that of the other memoirists in this group, and his effectiveness in conveying a "dispersed sense of self" has made his work a touchstone for literary critics of contemporary autobiography.[59] Almost all of these texts, however, give some indication of a divided attitude about Jewish identity. Authors who mention their relationship with Israel, including the four (Friesel, Grab, Katz, and Segre) who settled there permanently, express divided feelings about the Jewish state. George Mosse, who divorced himself almost entirely from Jewish concerns in his American life, was nevertheless powerfully drawn to the self-confident Israeli "New Jews" he discovered when he began to visit regularly in the 1960s. He admits that they "represented a normalization, an assimilation to general middle-class ideals and stereotypes which otherwise I professed to dislike. But I could not help myself; faced with this Zionist ideal my reason and historical knowledge were overcome."[60] Georg Iggers was unable to make such an adjustment. "The land struck us as very foreign and much more Oriental than we had imagined," he writes, and he was put off by the "chauvinism of many people."[61] Annie Kriegel's profession of support for Israel in her memoirs is offset by a condemnation of other aspects of the Jewish mentality, especially the utopian longings that, in her view, had led all too many Jews to communism. She calls for the Jewish world to undertake a "cleanup project . . . on itself in order to contribute to the healing of the world as a whole" by eliminating this tendency. The Israeli achievement she hails most positively in her autobiography is not the creation of a Jewish society but the rupture with socialist economic policies following the right-wing Likud Party's election victory of 1977.[62] Helmut Eschwege, on the other hand, was so aggrieved by the mistreatment he received as a member of the Communist Party in wartime Palestine that he returned to Germany in 1946. Only as he became disillusioned with the East German regime did he become more sympathetic to Israel.[63]

Surprisingly, the element of their identity that these authors often seem least conflicted about is their link with their native country. Left-wing convictions led Jürgen Kuczynski and Helmut Eschwege to resettle in East Germany immediately after the war. Their cases were exceptional, but experiences in postwar Germany played a large role in motivating the authors born there to write their memoirs: Evyatar Friesel and Walter Laqueur both indicate that they began their autobiographical project as a result of visits to their native country, and Gay's title, *My German Question,* highlights the issue. All assert—some with a certain sense of surprise—that they found themselves feeling in some sense at home there. Friesel opens his book with the line "Heidelberg was an easy city to live in," and E. P. Hennock, whose father was murdered in Riga in 1941, comments that he "greatly enjoyed" his first visit to postwar Germany.[64] As he became a recognized commentator on European affairs in the 1950s, Laqueur decided that he understood Germany better than England or France: "The fact that I was born in that country and spent some of my formative years there apparently counts as much as learning and observation in later life."[65] Gay is also explicit about the clear movement in his life toward "reconciliation" after the war and the extent to which he eventually "integrated Germany into my self-perception."[66] George Mosse ends his memoir by explaining how his family got back its extensive real-estate holdings in Germany after the fall of the Wall. What made him most uncomfortable there by the end of his life was the fact that he could too easily be identified with his German origins: "I wanted to be measured solely by my own accomplishments. . . . I am still not comfortable when in Berlin I am presented to audiences as the grandson of Rudolf Mosse."[67]

The fact that these authors all made their private peace with Germany—and most quite a bit more than that, since a number of them took major parts in efforts to promote reconciliation between Germans and the rest of the world[68]—does not, of course, mean that they want to minimize or efface the crimes of the Nazi era. With the exception of Raul Hilberg, they are unanimous, however, in asserting that Hitler's policies did not represent the whole truth about German attitudes toward Jews. All are at pains to avoid simplistic portrayals of the Germans, even in the Nazi period. Laqueur writes, "I knew from my own experience that if it had been up to most individual Germans, there would not have been a Gestapo, or military attacks in every direction, or the mass killings of Jews and others."[69] Werner Mosse says he has "tried to counteract the widespread tendency to view all earlier German-Jewish history under the aspect of the Holocaust— the Jewish variant of the 'Whig interpretation' of history."[70] All question Gershom Scholem's famous assertion that there had never been a real synthesis of German and Jewish culture; George Mosse underlines the contradiction between Scholem's argument and "the German lifestyle and German culture of the Scholems," whom he knew in Jerusalem.[71]

Hilberg represents a special case. His memoir offers little sense of any identification with his Austrian background, but he claims that the reception of his book in Germany compensated him for the misunderstanding and rejection he has faced in the United States and Israel.[72] For most of his fellow autobiographers, however, the reconnection with Germany reflected above all a recognition that, whatever Hitler had done to them, their early life had left an indelible imprint that any honest account of their experience could not deny. Paradoxically, most find it easier to keep a distance from their Jewish identity than from the land of their birth, no matter how badly the latter treated them.

The generally positive assessment of pre-Nazi German culture in these memoirs means that they are of limited use in answering one question that one might have expected them to shed light on: the conditions that made what they see as a basically tolerant community susceptible to violent anti-Semitism. George Mosse recalls witnessing the "enthusiasm and élan of the crowd" at a Nazi rally, and experiencing anti-Semitism personally at the boarding school he attended, but he does not probe very deeply into the sources of the phenomenon, which at the time did not keep him from developing a strong sense of German nationalism.[73] None of these memoirs offers insights into the rise of Nazism comparable to those in a first-person account by the non-Jewish German Sebastien Haffner, *Defying Hitler,* a brilliant demonstration of the way personal experience can be used as a starting point for wider historical generalization.[74] Nor do any of these memoirs reflect the tortured process of individual self-questioning recounted in Jurgen Herbst's *Requiem for a German Past,* the first-person account of an "Aryan" German of the same generation as most of these Jewish historian-authors, who eventually left his country to pursue a career as a historian in the United States. Herbst, who had been a Nazi youth leader as a teenager, had initially tried to convince himself that the traditions of German Idealism in literature and Prussian military honor, both incorporated in the personality of his father, a schoolmaster and army officer, had remained unstained despite Hitler. By the late 1940s, however, he had concluded that the existence of positive elements in German culture "will never and can never excuse or make me forget or even overcome the vileness and unspeakable evil that surrounded that past."[75] His judgment is considerably harsher than that of any of the Jewish historian-memoirists.

This process of reconciliation and reclaiming of youthful identities that characterizes the memoirs of German-Jewish historians can also be noted in the case of most of the memoirists who were not of German origin. Although French collaboration with the German campaign against the Jews has been a major subject in the country's public life for the past several decades, the French historian-memoirists make little mention of the subject. Only the Russian-born Léon Poliakov makes explicit reference to the impact of anti-Jewish attitudes on his career in France after the war. Pierre Vidal-Naquet, who has been a leading spokesman against French negationists, emphatically identifies himself as "a Jewish Frenchman, rather than a French Jew or a Jew in France,"[76] and Alfred Grosser titles his book *Une vie de français* (A French Life). Susan Groag Bell tried to return to Czechoslovakia after the war and was surprised to find that she was not accepted there—more, however, because she had been part of the country's German-speaking minority than because of her family's Jewish origins.[77] In the case of those from eastern Europe, one has to look outside the text of their memoirs to find clues to their attitudes about their birthplace. In the years after the publication of her memoir, Nechama Tec wrote a carefully balanced book about Polish gentiles' behavior toward Jews during the war;

its tone certainly suggests a desire to bridge gaps with her country of origin. Peter Kenez has directed an American university study-abroad program in Budapest since the fall of communism.

The treatment of postwar identity in these accounts thus reveals something that Holocaust survivor memoirs, with their silence about their authors' postwar lives, usually obscure: those who suffered under Nazism were often determined not to let the experience define their identity permanently. A conventional "master narrative" about post-Holocaust Jewish history would have us believe that that experience, coupled with the creation of Israel, strengthened Jewish identity; these memoirs, unrepresentative though they are of the larger Jewish world, at least raise questions about these assumptions and draw our attention to the fact that most survivor narratives in fact tell us little or nothing about how their authors subsequently thought about themselves. Hans Schmitt is admittedly a special case among these memoirists, one of the few who did not have two Jewish parents, but his repeated protests that he was never a Jew are simply an extreme version of a point made by many of these authors. All, in one way or another, want to assert that even the extreme historical events they lived through at such a personal level did not rob them of their personal autonomy, an autonomy they exercised by refusing to accept the notion that Jewish origins essentially determined their identity. To the extent that they recognize an unchangeable, externally shaped aspect of their personal identity, it is more often that furnished by their mother tongue and their early childhood experiences than one rooted in their ancestors' religion. Paradoxically, these memoirs, so strongly linked to Jewish fate, often portray their authors as more German or French than Jewish.

Becoming historical scholars enabled these men and women to free themselves from the weight of their personal histories. Through their choice of subject matter, they could either engage themselves with or separate themselves from their own past. But the decision to publish a personal memoir meant a significant change for many of these authors. Trained in history, they could hardly ignore the impact of an event as large as the Holocaust in their own life. The effect of these publications, however, has been to reconnect their authors to the larger story of Jewish fate from which many of them had worked hard to distance themselves. All, even Hans Schmitt and Gerhard Masur, explicitly acknowledge their Jewish ancestry, and all accept the challenge of explaining what that fact had meant in their life. All have had to realize that their memoir would be shelved with books on Jewish or Holocaust history and read, as they have been in this analysis, in the context of the broader literature of Jewish Holocaust memory.[78] In many cases, writing an autobiography clearly meant not just recalling their life but reevaluating what that life had meant and putting into question some of the fundamental decisions they had made.

How should one interpret these historians' decisions to expose their lives to this kind of rereading? The fact that many of these authors emphasize their ambivalent attitudes toward their Jewishness certainly militates against any reading of these texts as confessions of an inauthentic relationship to their origins. Annie Kriegel indignantly rejects the notion that her reconnection with Judaism as an adult was in any sense an act of *t'shuva* or repentance.[79] Nevertheless, the act of autobiography is at some level a reenactment of the return to Jewish origins that many of these authors describe their parents as having attempted in the Nazi era. It is a way of giving the Jewish element in their life some personal meaning after all and of recognizing that the life being described would have been completely different in its absence. In many cases, this autobiographical act appears to be the author's first public reconnection with this aspect of his or her background for a long time. The publication of an autobiography thus proves to be a transformational act in its own right, and one that concedes that the author may not have had as much freedom to define a relationship to the Jewish past as he or she had long wanted to believe.

In evoking their personal Jewish past, however, most of these authors are returning in memory not to a vibrant self-consciously Jewish milieu but to a situation in which Jews were voluntarily exchanging their sense of separateness for a sense of belonging to the larger community within which they lived. The garden of Eden from which these survivor-memoirists were expelled was not the shtetl or the secular Yiddish culture of Theodore Hamerow's Polish actor parents, but the bourgeois liberal world that seemed momentarily to have triumphed in Europe after World War I. The strong sense of attachment many of these authors express to the country where they settled after their escape from Nazi Europe—usually the United States, Great Britain, or France—is generally associated with gratitude for having found a place where the promise of assimilation was actually kept and where they could decide for themselves whether they wished to be identified as a Jew. Even Gerda Lerner, who suffered considerably from American intolerance during the McCarthy period, asserts that obtaining U. S. citizenship in 1943 was "like being reborn" and insists that her adopted country's constitution remains "the best model for democratic governance yet devised by human beings."[80] In short, this body of autobiographical literature challenges the notion that the experience of Nazism led those who experienced it to question the premises of Jewish assimilation.

Even as their autobiographical acts acknowledge that their lives were framed by historical events, however, these authors also affirm the importance of the individual perspective in understanding the past. Their stories frequently run counter to standard generalizations about Jewish experience under the Nazis. At a time when it is fashionable to write off assimilation and acculturation as fundamentally misguided developments in Jewish life, these memoirs recall the lived experience that made such behavior seem reasonable to their parents and even to many of these authors. Peter Gay complains about critics who disparage German Jews for their efforts at assimilation. "What makes these hostile questions all the more infuriating is that they barely conceal a knowing and derisive undertone: Whatever happened to you served you right."[81] These memoirs also demonstrate the fault lines that ran through every Jewish group, even individual families. Gerda Lerner, who had been able to obtain a visa and enter the United States in 1939, was baffled by her mother's refusal to leave southern France even as danger mounted in 1941. Only decades afterward was she able to understand why her mother, who had found there a love and an opportunity to develop her artistic talents that she had never enjoyed in her native Vienna, "chose to pay for her art with her life" despite the toll her behavior took on her daughter and her husband.[82] In contrast to the main body of Holocaust survivor literature, these less dramatic personal narratives also demonstrate the importance of linking pre- and postwar events to those of wartime for understanding how survivors experienced what happened to them. They thus offer a model of Holocaust-era memory quite different from that found in the more widely read survivor memoirs.

What, finally, are the implications of these historians' memoirs for their authors' status as historians? These texts, which are usually sober and understated, hardly seem to justify the kinds of fears about the undermining of reasoned analysis of the past that Annette Wievorka expresses about survivor memoirs. None of these historians shows any conscious intent of destabilizing the authority of the historical discipline; indeed, by stressing their commitment to historical scholarship, these authors, like historian-memoirists in general, tend rather to reinforce that authority. Nevertheless, they know that autobiography is not simply history. When Peter Gay writes that his life is "the kind of story that is usually lost amid the clamor of historical events,"[83] he reminds us how much of past experience exists as a kind of penumbra to history, a zone of the past where historical narrative does not shine its beams. The writing of history is necessarily selective; it cannot englobe the entire record of the past. Autobiography has the potential to illuminate parts of that penumbra and even to persuade historians that the spotlights of their discipline need to be redirected.[84] These historians' memoirs, for example, suggest that historians need to reexamine the question of whether the Holocaust experience necessarily strengthened survivors' sense of Jewish identity and convinced those who lived through it that assimilation was an impossible life strategy. Autobiography, even historians' autobiography, is thus not merely source material for history; it is an alternative way of narrating the past, capable of teaching historians some important lessons.

These memoirs constitute, then, if not a conscious critique of history, at least an implicit questioning of its limits. Gay's comment reminds us that he, like every historian, has a private story to tell that has special meaning for its author. Like all these historians, he imports his historical training into his memoir, carefully putting his own memories into their historical context, but at the same time he embraces the individualism of autobiography and the opportunity it provides to write about matters—his stamp collection, the soccer team he cheered for—that tell us something about him but little about history. The authors of these memoirs want to be read and recognized as more than scholars, on the one hand, and as exemplifications of the patterns of Holocaust-era history, on the other. Careful as they are to respect the authority of history, in its double sense as an academic discipline and as a record of collective experience, these historian-memoirists nevertheless want to go beyond its limits. In addition to constituting a return to the authors' Jewish origins, these memoirs constitute a setting aside of the authors' scholarly identity and an insistence on what they share with the rest of humanity. Like all historians' autobiographies, they are graphic reminders of how powerfully even professional scholars can find themselves drawn to this alternative form of narrative about the past. Even if the texts discussed here are not fated to enter the canon of great autobiographies, they are important evidence of history's need to recognize the legitimacy of autobiography's alternative vision of the past.

CHAPTER 9   Historians and the Reshaping
of Personal Narrative

As we have seen, historians' autobiographies can contribute to the understanding of the historical profession and of some aspects of historical experience. The example of Gibbon reminds us that historian-autobiographers
have been part of the tradition of modern autobiography since its incep-
tion, and the growing number of historians' autobiographies in the last decades of the twentieth century paralleled the expansion of the genre as a
whole. The expansion of personal narrative during this period was more
than just a quantitative phenomenon, however: it was also marked by
important innovations in the nature of autobiographical literature. The
question whether historians, writing as autobiographers, have contributed
to this expansion of the possibilities of autobiography is an important one.
If historian-autobiographers had merely continued working within the
familiar patterns of traditional autobiography, one could legitimately ask
whether their experiments in combining history and personal narrative had
offered anything original to the latter genre. In fact, however, a number of
historians have articulated significant and distinctive approaches to the
problems of autobiography. These achievements, whose importance has often been recognized by literature scholars, have demonstrated that the enterprise of writing about a historian's life can have important implications
for the very definition of autobiography.

The issue of innovation in autobiographical form has been an important
one in recent criticism. If the only possibility of development in autobiography were to lie in variations in its content, rather than experimentation

with form, the genre would risk degeneration into stale formulas, and it could hardly claim the same status as other forms of literature, such as the novel, that have demonstrated a capacity for change and renewal. This danger is highlighted by the longstanding tendency to assume that autobiography reached its mature, canonical form with the great examples written in the decades just before and after 1800: Franklin's *Autobiography*, Rousseau's *Confessions*, Gibbon's *Memoirs*, Goethe's *Dichtung und Wahrheit*. All of these were essentially chronological narratives, beginning with the author's birth or perhaps some account of his ancestry and following his life through the stages of childhood, youth, entry into active life, and, in most cases, mature accomplishments. All were written in the first person. This distinguished them from history and from novels narrated in the third person; it also reflected the assumption that human beings are autonomous selves, capable of imposing order and coherence on their experiences.

The standard pattern of autobiographical narrative exemplified in this canon served many purposes. Its rootedness in the apparently natural pattern of human life made it easy for readers to identify with such works' protagonists. They too—or at least the male readers among them—could arrange their memories in a similar design. The use of the first person also produced an effect of familiarity. It related autobiographical discourse to everyday speech, making it an extension of how ordinary people might talk about themselves or write in such nonliterary forms as letters or journals. By contrast, the third-person narration in both works of history and literature was a device that separated them from most readers' personal experience: few people, other than professional writers, have much occasion to speak or write at length in such a style. The apparent naturalness of autobiography made it an egalitarian form of writing, easier for nonprofessional authors to emulate successfully than either history or fiction, but it also threatened to make autobiography a rather static genre: if Rousseau and his contemporaries had virtually exhausted the potentialities of personal narrative, their successors could only rework familiar formulas, with little hope of achieving anything startlingly original.[1]

The recent blossoming of critical interest in autobiography has been motivated in part by the creative innovations of contemporary life writing. In a polemic in favor of what he calls "the new model autobiographer," published in 1977, John Sturrock praises authors who have abandoned the conventions of classic autobiography, particularly its chronological form. "If the object of autobiography is to take possession of our past in as original and coherent a way as possible, then chronology works against that object by extending the past merely conventionally and claiming itself to be the source of life's meanings," he writes.[2] In a study of the French tradition of literary autobiography, Michael Sheringham points to the importance of the radical experiments with autobiographical form carried out in the 1970s by Roland Barthes and Georges Perec. Barthes, whose *Roland Barthes par Roland Barthes* presented its author's reflections on his life as a series of fragments arranged in alphabetical order by theme, and Perec, who intertwined a frankly fictional narrative with his recollections of his childhood as a Jew in hiding in Vichy France in his *W, ou le souvenir d'enfance,* both abandoned the first-person narrator and the chronological framework of traditional autobiography. Both blurred the boundaries between autobiography and other genres, such as the essay and the novel. Their purpose in making these experiments was to find ways of writing about personal experience that did not presuppose the existence of a unitary, reflexive self. As Sheringham concludes, they "helped to rescue autobiography from the paraliterary doldrums to which the genre had been consigned by some aspects of contemporary theory, and to rehabilitate it as an endeavour worthy of serious intellectual consideration."[3]

Although the examples of unconventional autobiography Sheringham cites are by male authors, they exhibit features that some critics have seen as characteristic of feminist autobiographical texts. Liz Stanley has identified feminist autobiography with texts that "self-consciously and self-confidently mix genres and conventions. Within them fact and fiction, fantasy and reality, biography and autobiography, self and others, individuals and networks, not only co-exist but intermingle in ways that encourage, not merely permit, active readership." Such texts "challenge the boundaries of conventional autobiographical form, indeed play with some of its conventions such as the 'autobiographical pact' of truth-telling, a narrative that moves uni-directionally from birth/beginning to maturity/resolution/end, and the insistence on a unitary self."[4] The fact that such characteristics can be found not only in autobiographical texts by women but in the works of male authors suggests that the attraction of autobiographical experimentation is not merely a matter of gender: not all men find their experience reflected in the patterns of traditional autobiography, either.

One might assume, however, that few historian-autobiographers would be attracted to such antinomian efforts to redefine the nature of autobiography. The historical profession has shown remarkable resistance to efforts to introduce similar innovations in its own practice. Self-conscious efforts at blurring the boundaries between history and fiction by the inclusion of imagined dialogue and other devices, such as Simon Schama's *Dead Certainties,* have generated brief flurries of comment but have inspired few imitators.[5] If Thucydides were to come back to life, he would find a great extension in the range of historians' interests, but he would still find the form and style of most historical writing familiar. To the extent that they are influenced by their professional experience when they write about their own life, historians would seem unlikely to challenge the standard conventions of autobiography, particularly its predilection for chronological narrative. The shift to writing in the first person is, of course, not habitual for most historians, but it serves neatly to keep autobiography separated from history and makes it clear that the historian-autobiographer is conscious of the difference between the two. As we have seen, historian-autobiographers are often at pains to show that they also know how to keep fiction from creeping into their personal narratives: their frequent references to the documentation supporting their life-writing enterprise identify them with the realm of truth.

It is certainly true that the overwhelming majority of historian-autobiographers can be counted among the practitioners of standard forms of autobiography. Some seem to have deviated from customary patterns without intending to, because of an inability to find a satisfactory form for their stories. The rather uncoordinated narratives of two recent French Jewish memoirists, Annie Kriegel and Pierre Vidal-Naquet, give this impression. In both, the story of the author's life is told in unconnected segments dealing with different aspects of their career, a procedure that creates a fractured chronology and suggests a certain difficulty in reconciling different aspects of the author's personality. A few historian-autobiographers, however, have set out deliberately to test the boundaries of autobiographical form, with the conscious intent of showing that such experiments offer new perspectives on the experience of history as well as the representation of the self.

The great forerunner of such experimentation among historians was Henry Adams, whose device of self-narration in the third person challenged the notion of the coherent, autonomous ego, capable of defining itself by telling a life story. Adams's experiment has directly inspired some contemporary historian-autobiographers. His most unexpected emulator is undoubtedly the East German Marxist historian Jürgen Kuczynski. The subtitle of the first volume of his memoirs, "The Education of J. K. as Communist and Scholar," evokes *The Education of Henry Adams* even while distancing itself from its "bourgeois" forerunner. In his writing, Kuczynski alternates passages written in the third and the first person, with the unidentified third-person narrator referring to the subject of the work as "J. K." and commenting on the author's success (or lack of it) in living up to communist ideals. Formulas such as "Let us let J. K. speak for himself," employed to mark shifts from third- to first-person narration, have the effect of making it seem as though someone else is speaking in the third-person sections. This method, which leaves the reader uncertain whether the text is a biography incorporating first-person documents or a genuine autobiography, was no accident. Kuczynski subsequently explained that he adopted this strategy, thinking that he was creating "a style all my own," to dramatize his sense that in writing his memoir he was seeing himself as though he were another person. "It was less a fact than a wish for objectivity. I wanted to observe myself as another, whom I could treat with distance. . . . I [wrote] as 'I' only when there was something important that I wanted to say in a personal way, or when I was quoting from letters."[6] In effect, Kuczynski tried to find a stylistic mechanism that would reconcile the writing of a subjective autobiography with a commitment to the objective truth of communist doctrine, so that he could, for example, explain the views he held in the years before he joined the party while underlining his own "naiveté and ignorance of the class struggle" at the time.[7]

However awkward Kuczynski's procedure may seem, and however remote the problems of a communist intellectual seeking to be honest about his past while affirming his wholehearted commitment to that ideology now appear, his example shows that historian-autobiographers are not precluded from making important stylistic experiments with the genre. Since the late 1970s, a number of historians have written about their own lives in ways that have expanded and revised the commonly accepted definitions of autobiography. These experiments have not been efforts to escape from history: most have had the deliberate aim of producing autobiographical texts that would throw new light not only on personal experiences but also on aspects of collective experience. Historians' autobiographies and memoirs that stand out in this regard include Carolyn Steedman's *Landscape for a Good Woman*, Ronald Fraser's *In Search of a Past*, Luisa Passerini's *Autoritratto di Gruppo* (*Autobiography of a Generation*), Saul Friedländer's *When Memory Comes*, Inga Clendinnen's *Tiger's Eye*, Martin Duberman's *Cures*, and Deirdre McCloskey's *Crossing*.

As befits experimental efforts, these texts differ significantly from one another. The British historians Fraser and Steedman and the Italian Passerini have all tried to blend the writing of their own life with that of others, but in very different ways. Fraser, a noted proponent of oral history, uses interviews, primarily with adults who had been servants in his family's house during his childhood, to reconstruct a picture of his milieu that contrasts strongly with his own recollections and to create an understanding of his parents that he could not have arrived at on his own. Steedman uses her background in social and women's history to construct a double life narrative, that of her mother as well as her own. Whereas these two authors are concerned primarily with bringing together the perspectives of different generations, Passerini puts her experiences in the context of those of her contemporaries, the generation of students in the 1960s. All three of these texts raise important questions about conventional autobiography's tendency to isolate its author's story from those of others, and unlike most historians' memoirs, all have attracted significant attention from critics. Laura Marcus calls Fraser's and Steedman's "two of the most innovative British autobiographies of the past decade," pathbreaking because of the way they show "the interrelation between theory and experience, the interplay of different voices, and the representation of the past as a complex and elusive terrain."[8] Joan Scott praises Passerini's work for finding a way around "the narcissistic aspect of the 'confessional' literature so much in vogue these days among literary critics in the United States."[9]

Whereas Fraser, Steedman, and Passerini all looked for ways that individual memoir and the reconstruction of others' experiences could mutually illuminate each other, the works of Friedländer, Clendinnen, Duberman, and McCloskey follow the more common pattern of autobiography in being centered on their authors' personal life story. All relate forms of extreme experience that raise significant questions about personal identity. Friedländer, who survived the Holocaust era in France by being hidden in a Catholic school and taking on a new name and identity, struggles to make sense of what he sees as an irremediably fractured life narrative and to understand how it affects his professional work as a specialist on that time period. Like the other experimental texts discussed here, Friedländer's has attracted considerable commentary. Paul John Eakin devotes a section to *When Memory Comes* in *Fictions in Autobiography,* and proponents of the history-of-memory movement among historians have seen the work as a manifesto for their cause, "a model for a new kind of historical narrative that can incorporate elements usually reserved for the domain of fiction," as Sidra DeKoven Ezrahi has written.[10] Clendinnen's memoir takes as its point of departure a different kind of life-threatening experience, a near-fatal illness. The hallucinations from which the author suffered during her treatment provided her a personal demonstration of the fluid boundary between memory and fiction, and her text deliberately mixes the two, expressing her conviction that identity is a fragile thing and that we must distrust "the 'I,' with its absurd pretensions to agency." [11]

Duberman and McCloskey have both pushed the limits of a fairly common theme in American autobiography, the coming to consciousness of a member of an oppressed minority, homosexuals in Duberman's case, transsexuals or gender crossers in McCloskey's. Both books, however, are more than indictments of the discrimination inflicted on those who transgress social norms. By insisting on the author's identity as an academic professional, each of these memoirs forces readers to recognize that such experiences can be inflicted not merely on socially marginal deviants but on individuals who are recognized members of the academic community. Each also invokes the author's historical expertise, contextualizing personal experiences and showing the influence of the times and places where they occurred. At the same time, however, both authors' insistence on confronting readers with the explicit physical and emotional details of their bodily experiences take their stories well beyond the normal limits of academic autobiography, and indeed of autobiographical writing in general. These two narratives pose difficult questions about the relationship between the body and identity. Paul Ricoeur has written that identity is inseparable from the "absolutely irreducible signification of one's own body," [12] but Duberman's demonstration of the ways in which the body can be deployed in the interests of transgressive desire and McCloskey's narrative of the transformation of a male body into a female one raise questions about the stability of bodily boundaries and definitions.

AUTOBIOGRAPHIES IN SEVERAL VOICES

In one way or another, Carolyn Steedman, Ronald Fraser, and Luisa Passerini all set out to contest the notion of an autobiographical self whose potentialities gradually emerge from within. Instead, they emphasize the importance of the individual's interaction with the outside world and the historically situated social milieu. "It is a proposition of this book," Steedman writes, "that that specificity of place and politics has to be reckoned with in making an account of anybody's life, and their use of their own past." She combines the story of what her mother made of the social circumstances of her life with that of her own childhood because, in her view, the only way of understanding her personal experience is to understand "the disruption of that fifties childhood by the one my mother had lived before me, and the stories she told about it." [13] Fraser interweaves his own memories of his childhood with the recollections of others who lived in and around the household as a way of bringing together two conflicting visions. His "voyage of inner discovery . . . has to be combined with the account of the other voyage into the social past."[14] Passerini sees the juxtaposition of her own story with those of others of her generation as essential if her effort to recall the past is going to produce a meaningful story, one with a claim to be recognized as history.[15] All three authors also hope to have produced works that offer historical as well as autobiographical insights. The point to her book, Steedman claims, is not to retell the story of her childhood but to use that story to demonstrate how "the past is re-used through the agency of social information" and to develop the implications of that fact.[16] Fraser hopes to have demonstrated the fruitfulness of "combining two different modes of enquiry—oral history and psychoanalysis—to uncover the past in as many of its layers as possible," and Passerini talks about the "complementary nature" of her personal narrative and her investigation of others' experiences.[17]

To achieve their ambitions, all three of these authors have invented hybrid forms of narrative, clearly distinguished from both conventional models of autobiography and conventional approaches to history. Steedman mixes the narrative of her mother's life, told through her own childhood memories and recollections of the stories her mother told her, with passages of social-historical analysis in which she applies the insights of her later professional training to understand her mother's behavior and her own. Although *Landscape for a Good Woman* does not tell the story of how Steedman became a scholar, the presence of her professional persona is evident throughout the text, as when she draws on sociological insight to explain why her mother never allowed family members to answer the doorbell and admit outsiders during mealtimes. Through her subsequent study, Steedman is able retrospectively to understand this as a "reluctance to reveal the poverty of food on the table" and acknowledge the family's marginal socioeconomic situation (*Landscape for a Good Woman*, 67).

Steedman draws on her professional training in interpreting her own and her mother's lives, but her purpose is the very opposite of confirming generalizations derived from other scholarship. "The usefulness of the biographical and autobiographical core of the book lies in the challenge it may offer to much of our conventional understanding of childhood, working-class childhood, and little-girlhood," she writes. In addition, she wants to dispute stereotypes of the "psychological simplicity" and sameness of working-class life. Too much of social history, she objects, "denies its subjects a particular story, a personal history, except when that story illustrates a general thesis" (7, 10). She is at pains to demonstrate the ways her mother did not fit into the common mold of working-class women; among other things, despite her "traditional Labour background," the mother "rejected the politics of solidarity and communality, always voted Conservative, for the left could not embody her desire for things to be *really* fair" (47). What her mother wanted, Steedman believes, was the glamorous fairy-tale life she imagined rich women could lead. "When the world didn't deliver the goods, she held the world to blame" (6). Steedman's portrait of her mother thus fits uneasily into a tradition of social history that has emphasized oppression and collective resistance.

Steedman's book has had a strong attraction for feminist critics, who frequently cite it as an example of successful resistance to the standard, ego-centered male model of autobiography, but she also uses her story to counter some of the commonplaces of feminist scholarship. If she has interwoven her mother's story with her own, it is not as a gesture of gender solidarity across the generations: her mother, in Steedman's account, resented the burden of her two daughters and openly told them so: "'Never have children dear,' she said; 'they ruin your life.' Shock moves swiftly across the faces of women to whom I tell this story," Steedman reports, but she insists, "It is *ordinary* not to want your children, I silently assert; normal to find them a nuisance," and she has no patience for the "celebration" of motherhood that she finds in much feminist writing (17, 86). She is also dubious about the applicability of the notion of patriarchy to working-class life: in her own family, at least, the father was a marginal figure, and it was her mother who "dictate[d] the immediate terms of life" (80).

In its formal experimentation, Ronald Fraser's *In Search of a Past* is even more radical than *Landscape for a Good Woman*. Fraser, best known among historians for his oral history of the Spanish Civil War, applies this technique to the reconstruction of his own childhood. Much of his book consists of excerpts from interviews he conducted with the servants who worked on his parents' country estate, with his brother, and with a childhood friend. In relying on these testimonies, Fraser is careful to avoid giving the impression that he takes them as objective and reliable, in contrast to his own subjective memories: in one passage, he cuts back and forth between several informants' recollections of a single episode, dramatizing their contradictions (*In Search of a Past*, 48–50). He also contrasts such external recollections of his life with his own memories, but these are presented largely through reconstructions of dialogues with his psychotherapist, so that Fraser's own voice is itself presented in quotation marks, and his statements are subjected to critique by another voice that questions his words and probes for unconscious meanings. This technique dramatizes what Fraser sees as one of the essential aspects of his inner experience, his sense that, for him, "the first person comes hard. . . . The problem doesn't arise as an anonymous interviewer." Pronouns loom large in Fraser's text: its chapters bear the titles "We," "They," "She/He/She," "You," "We," "Us," and, as a more or less triumphant conclusion, "I," and he notes that "*you* is the pronoun I most often use about myself. I never had a clearly de-fined 'I'" (109).

The purpose of Fraser's endeavor is not only to understand himself, al-though that is an important aspect of his book, but also to demonstrate a new way of understanding the past that goes beyond both history and psy-choanalysis. Although he comes to agree with his therapist that "they're similar in reconstructing a remembered past, not the past as it actually was," Fraser is unwilling to accept that this conclusion should lead us to privilege the insights of psychoanalysis. Analysis is, he argues, "more limiting be-cause it recreates the past only in the forms in which it was internalized or repressed. The infantile aspects . . . " (119). By bringing together the two ap-proaches, he hopes to find a way to make himself, as his therapist puts it, "the subject of your history instead of the object you felt yourself to be . . . , the author of your childhood, then, the historian of your past," to which Fraser responds, "That's what I intend—to write about it from in-side and out" (187). Researching and writing about his own life offers a unique opportunity to do this, since it is only in this case that Fraser can bring internal and external memory together, but the purpose of the en-deavor is, as in Steedman's case, to clarify processes that have determined the lives of others as well as the author's own.

In Search of a Past, like *Landscape for a Good Woman*, is heavily preoccu-pied with the issue of class: its subtitle is *The Rearing of an English Gentle-man*. The paradox of Fraser's story, highlighted by his heavy reliance on in-terviews with his family's servants, is that the future gentleman was largely reared by members of the lower classes, with whom he had more contact than he did with his own parents. This serves to explain the split Fraser senses in his own personality, the fact that while "objectively a member of a privileged class I was . . . unable subjectively to fill the role into which I was born" (91). In dialogue with his therapist, who urges him to concentrate on his inner feelings, Fraser insists on the importance of these social rela-tionships. The servants "were the real human beings in my childhood whom I felt close to, sided with. Of course, it was an ambiguous alliance because I knew I was the little master. . . . A role of inherent superiority which came to me from the outside, from the servants among others" (111). He thereby demonstrates a larger historical point: the role that the subordinate classes played in perpetuating the values of those above them. The polyphonic nature of Fraser's sources brings this point out subtly, contrasting the resentment expressed by some of the servants who were driven to accept their positions by financial necessity during the Depression with the way others at times identified with their employers, such as the groom who admired Fraser's mother's skill on a horse and who told him, "It was a great honour to put her up in the saddle" (45).

Similarly, Fraser's personal experience of World War II illustrates larger points about the changes the war brought about in English society. Like many of the historian-autobiographers who were engaged in it directly, Fraser, who was still a schoolchild, emphasizes the "benefits" of the experience more than its terrors. With his distant and authoritarian father stationed overseas, his mother was free to express an independent side of her personality that had previously been concealed. She defied his father's wishes by bringing her son home from a boarding school he hated and letting him mix for the first time with the ordinary children of the local village. "Being let run was the finest thing that could have happened to you," one of his informants told him (150). His experience was symbolic of a larger movement of toward the dismantling of class barriers. "We could see that there wasn't going to be all this snobbery any more," one of his interviewees remembered. "It was the beginning of bringing them down to our level. And they never got back to where they'd been—and they never will" (143). The war, it is true, also broke up Fraser's family: his mother fell in love with an air force captain billeted in their home and divorced his father, an event about which he expresses mixed feelings. On the whole, however, the war was his route of escape from a rigidly confining environment, just as it was a moment of liberation for the English lower classes in general.

In Search of a Past is thus simultaneously a subtle psychological portrait of its author and an exploration of several critical aspects of English history during the Depression and the war years. It is also an artful demonstration of how an autobiographer and a historian both move from initial memories and discoveries to the construction of a deeper, more critical narrative. In fact, it is this search for understanding that is the real story of this autobiography: the author's childhood experiences, in and of themselves, are not that remarkable, and Fraser is not well enough known, even among historians, that readers would pick up the book just to find out more about him. The experience of reading Fraser's book reenacts one of the main themes of his narrative: the insistence that the definition of an individual's identity is in fact a collective project, carried out through interaction with others. The clearer understanding of the author's personality that emerges in the course of the book results from the collaboration not only of the author and his informants but of the reader as well: Fraser presents the pieces of the puzzle but leaves the reader some of the work of assembling them. In this, as in his polyphonic presentation of his own story, Fraser demonstrates a way autobiography can be written without positing a dominating personal ego, and simultaneously a model of how reading one person's story, written this way, can draw readers into the process of historical reconstruction.

A similar process is at work in Luisa Passerini's *Autobiography of a Generation,* which has been praised by one critic for its attempt to show that "the separation between consumers and producers of history can be . . . weakened and potentially destroyed" through an open-ended autobiographical project.[18] Passerini, like Fraser a practitioner of oral history— they both contributed to a collaborative volume on the student generation of the 1960s[19]—also mixes her own voice with that of others, but in a different manner. Unlike Fraser, she keeps control of her own narrative, which she composes, however, of distinctly varied materials: diary passages set in the present that recount a difficult search for self-definition, of which the writing of *Autobiography of a Generation* is one aspect, and in which dialogues with a therapist are an important element; a retrospective narrative of her life, from her childhood through her student years and the early part of her career; and excerpts from interviews with others, both male and female, who were part of the same cohort of student radicals.

The others who speak in *Autobiography of a Generation* did not all know Passerini personally, but all had to deal with their own variants of the same problem: growing up amid the contradictions of post-Fascist Italian society. In Passerini's view, the meaning of her own experiences becomes clear only from seeing what they shared and where they differed from those of these contemporaries. "If I had not heard the life stories of the generation of '68," she writes, "I would not have been able to write about myself; those stories have nourished mine, giving it the strength to get to its feet and speak. But I couldn't have borne them, in their alternation of being too full and too empty, if I had not confronted myself and my history with the double motion of analysis and of the exercise of remembering."[20] Like Fraser, however, Passerini does more than add her own testimony to that of others. By introducing her experience of psychotherapy into the text, sharing fragments of her analysis and even her analyst's reactions to the writing project that resulted in her book, she problematizes her authorial "I" and questions her privileged place within her own narrative. "Although the diary provides a framework," one critic has written, "it does not provide a sense of linear development, nor does it create a single vantage point from which the narrator speaks. This multiplicity of perspective can be seen as consonant with the collective nature of her project."[21]

Among other things, the structure of Passerini's book allows her to put her life story in the context of an event she did not actually participate in: during the 1968 student protests in her native Turin that form the center of her narrative, she was working with liberation movements in Africa. She nevertheless feels that she shared the fundamental experiences of her generation, the rupture with the social and political norms of their parents' generation that was paradoxically made possible only by an identification with some of the liberal and democratic values embraced by their fathers after the fall of Fascism in the 1940s. In the years after 1968, she and her contemporaries also shared the frustration of their utopian hopes and the gradual discovery that some of what they had believed was not just unrealistic but actually destructive, as some of the former student radicals turned to terrorist violence in the 1970s. Passerini's inquiry is thus an attempt not just to recover the details of what happened to her and her generation in the late 1960s but to show how their retrospective understanding of those events took shape. "What attracts me is memory's insistence on creating a history of itself, which is much less and perhaps somewhat more than a social history," she writes (*Autobiography of a Generation,* 23).

Passerini emphasizes what she shared with the generation of student radicals from the 1960s, although she could equally well have insisted on the uniqueness of her own trajectory. She had been a member of the Situationists, a group that applied its critique of the passivity engendered by modern culture not just to capitalist society but also to traditional leftist movements, and during her year in Africa, she participated in revolutionary movements in Tanzania and Mozambique. She is, however, sensitive to the differences in individual experiences; the passages in her book that deal with the author in the present—the ups and downs of the affair she was conducting with a married man during the writing and the excerpts from her analysis—underline her particular personality and the special difficulties she has had in integrating the experiences of the 1960s into her later life.

Her own case demonstrates the general proposition she advances about how "the filter of the individual biography transforms and directs the influences received from the family, from the environment, from circumstances" (125). Indeed, her fundamental conclusion is that the common element in the impact of 1968 was that it broke up the previous attachments to family and intended career that would have made its participants' lives predictable and forced them to recognize themselves as individuals with choices. "The sense of deviation from a preordained path, either taken for granted or imagined, is frequent in these lives," and therefore "there are as many 1968s as there are individual destinies." Consequently, "for this generation, what we might call the right of autobiography—to give a sense, or more than one sense, to its own past, or at least to be able to leaf through it, to unfold it—assumes a particular meaningfulness" (151–52, 154–55). Thus even Passerini's individual initiative in writing about herself can be seen as an expression of shared historical experience.

Despite this emphasis on the variety and individuality of experience, however, Passerini is not averse to all generalization. In particular, she sees differences in the experiences of men and women, and her book, like Carolyn Steedman's, has therefore been recognized as an important example of feminist autobiography. Not that Passerini, any more than Steedman, sees autobiography as an opportunity to celebrate gender solidarity or emancipation. She remembers her first engagement with women's consciousness-raising groups in the early 1970s as a difficult experience. "Participating in the leadership encouraged an image of 'exceptional woman,' which blocked the path to an awareness of the condition of women," she writes. Furthermore, in looking at her own experience and that of female contemporaries, she concludes that, in general, they had a more painful break with the past to make than the men. Radicals of both sexes were taking on an activist role that fit with existing male gender stereotypes, even when they turned their activism against their own fathers; they were rejecting the passivity and attachment to family and tradition associated with women, and this "cultural transformation was taking place, especially for women, in opposition to other women, at the expense of their relationships with one another" (112, 36). This inability to identify with feminine role models, and especially with the role of mother, was especially strong in Passerini's case, because her mother had died when she was six. The passages in Passerini's book based on her conversations with her analyst underline this connection and her difficulty in accepting "an absence that takes my breath away: why did you go away, why aren't you here, why did this happen to me?" (114). Like Steedman, Passerini rejects motherhood for herself, but, more than Steedman, she communicates the personal pain that led her to that decision.

Autobiography of a Generation thus exemplifies an original combination of collective with personal history, of research grounded in theoretical perspectives with private memory and reflection. Graziella Parati, author of the most extensive commentary on Passerini's work, underlines her deliberate contestation of the scale of values that privileges the public realm of theory and history over the private realm of personal experience: "This allows Passerini to remove theory from a public, privileged position and render it complementary to the construction of her private self. In this reverse movement from the public to the private, the public sphere becomes inscribed in a deliberately nonhierarchical structure."[22] The way Passerini shuttles back and forth between different layers of temporality is also significant. The emphasis she puts on the different perspectives generated at the time when the events discussed in the book occurred, the time of the interviews in which they were discussed, and the time when she reflects on both the events and the interviews serves to highlight the processes by which memory is constructed and then reconstructed. In this way, Passerini demonstrates connections between history and autobiography that are often obscured in more conventional autobiographical writing. Like Carolyn Steedman and Ronald Fraser, Passerini has brought something new to the writing of both history and autobiography.

FRACTURED SELVES

Like the memoirs by Steedman, Fraser, and Passerini, Saul Friedländer's *When Memory Comes,* originally published in French in 1978, deliberately departs from the conventions of autobiographical writing in an effort to communicate a deeper sense of historical experience. *When Memory Comes* has usually been read as a memoir of Jewish experience during the Holocaust, and as we have seen in an earlier chapter, it shares some important characteristics with the large body of memoirs by authors who subsequently became professional historians. These parallels remind us that there is no total division between historians whose memoirs are cast in traditional forms and those who have striven to find original ways of depicting their own past: they often have similar concerns. For that matter, other Holocaust survivors who, like Friedländer, had to disguise themselves under a false identity, have written about their experiences without feeling compelled to depart from the conventional patterns of first-person narrative.[23]

Friedländer seeks, however, to portray both his wartime experience and the subsequent process of trying to make sense of his memories of it. For this reason, he deliberately intercuts different levels of chronology. His earliest memories of his prewar childhood in Prague form a more or less self-contained unit in the narrative, but the rest of the book moves back and forth between his experiences in France during the war, his years in Israel in the 1940s and 1950s, and his perspective at the time he wrote *When Memory Comes* in 1977. In this way, Friedländer dramatizes his conviction that memory and identity are always in flux, that the present constantly changes the meaning of the past.

The core of Friedländer's story is the way the Holocaust made it impossible for him to understand his life as a unity. When he was placed in a Catholic boarding school, baptized and given a new name, "the first ten years of my life, the memories of my childhood, were to disappear, for there was no possible synthesis between the person I had been and the one I was to become. . . . It is impossible to know which name I am, and that in the final analysis seems to me sufficient expression of a real and profound confusion."[24] During the war, he embraced his new Catholic identity "body and soul. . . . Though conscious of my origins, I nevertheless felt at ease within a community of those who had nothing but scorn for Jews" (*When Memory Comes*, 120–21). Later he would be placed with a Jewish foster family, where he traded Catholicism for Zionism, an ideology almost equally removed from the assimilationist German-Jewish culture of his parents. This identification, too, proved unstable, and one of the major impulses behind the writing of *When Memory Comes* was clearly a felt need to explain why, despite his Holocaust experiences, Friedländer found himself unable to commit himself wholeheartedly to life in Israel or identification as a Jew. Pondering the political situation in the Middle East in the late 1970s, he wondered whether the Jewish state has a future or whether it would turn out to be "only a step on the way of a people whose particular destiny has come to symbolize the endless quest—ever hesitant, ever begun anew—of all mankind" (183). If this situation symbolizes the fate of humankind, it certainly symbolizes that of Friedländer himself, "destined, therefore, to wander among several worlds, knowing them, understanding them—better, perhaps, than many others—but nonetheless incapable of feeling an identification without any reticence" (155–56).

Incapable of settling into a firm identity or committing himself to a single community, Friedländer did learn one important lesson: that he needed to be able to speak about his past experience. During his post-adolescent years in Israel, he was incapable of forgetting his memories but equally incapable of communicating them to others. The result was a sort of inner paralysis: "since I could not forget the facts, I made up my mind to view everything with indifference; every sort of resonance within me was stifled." In what Paul John Eakin has identified as the key passage of *When Memory Comes*, Friedländer recalls the year he spent in Sweden, living with an uncle who ran an institute for mentally ill children. From watching them, he "realized . . . what was meant by an inner world closed off forever" (102–3). As Eakin comments, "If these cases vividly represent the failure of the autobiographical act, their muteness also speaks of its necessity in human terms."[25] Initially, Friedländer sought to recover the power of speech not through autobiography but indirectly, through committing himself to historical research on the Holocaust period. "Through the shifting prism of eyewitness accounts, stories, documents in archives, I tried to grasp the meaning of a period and reestablish the coherency of a past, my own." The process was a difficult one, however. The pursuit of historical truth obligated him, among other things, to revisit Germany and even to listen to the former Nazi leader Admiral Doenitz deny any knowledge of the Holocaust. Given his background, Friedländer found it hard to maintain the detachment of a supposedly objective scholar. But he also began to wonder whether that objectivity was necessary or even desirable. "I realized how much the essential appeared to me through a particular prism that could never be eliminated. But did it have to be eliminated?" (*When Memory Comes*, 144–45).

Infusing his scholarship with his personal perspective, however, was difficult as well. Friedländer dedicated his first book, a study of Pius XII's relations with the Jews, to his parents, thereby signaling his personal link to the subject, but it followed the canons of conventional historical scholarship. In a critique of Holocaust historiography written after the publication of his memoir, he concludes that even his own earlier works had made "little interpretive or representational advance" in the understanding of the subject.[26] Unlike Carolyn Steedman, Friedländer did not turn to writing about himself in order to challenge generalizations about collective experience. In a passage I have cited earlier, he asked himself, "Can experience as personal, as contradictory as mine rouse an echo here, in even the most indirect way? Isn't the way out for me to attach myself to the necessary order, the inescapable simplification forced upon one by the passage of time and one's vision of history, to adopt the gaze of the historian?" (*When Memory Comes*, 144). If he felt compelled to turn to the personal, it was because his contributions to the history of the Holocaust had not been enough to answer "the obscure questions of my adolescence, now returned and influencing my day-to-day outlook. [I felt] a need for synthesis, for a thoroughgoing coherence that no longer excludes anything," including his own difficulties in defining what the Holocaust meant to him personally (114). But the experience of writing from his personal vantage point convinced him that "the self-awareness of the historian of the Nazi epoch or the *Shoah* is essential." The extreme nature of these subjects "create[s] even for the professional historian a field of projections, of unconscious shapings and reshapings, of an authentic transferential situation," and a history that claims to have transcended these pressures is necessarily "giving in to the temptation of closure," of pretending to have found the fixed vantage point from with the past can be understood and its contradictions resolved.[27]

Friedländer thus generalizes the lesson of his personal experience, as pieced together in *When Memory Comes,* into a broader conclusion concerning the historical understanding of traumatic elements of the past. Although his subsequent scholarship, particularly his study *Nazi Germany and the Jews,* is less obviously experimental than his memoir—in that work Friedländer is careful, for example, to stick to a chronological framework, with none of the temporal jumps back and forth that characterize *When Memory Comes*—it does attempt to do justice to the radically different perspectives of the perpetrators and their victims. Like Passerini, Friedländer thus insists that understanding does not flow only from theory and scholarship to private experience but can also move in the opposite direction. Even in the face of an event as tremendous as the Holocaust, personal experience has lessons for the historian. The dramatization of Friedländer's fractured and dissonant sense of identity, achieved by the radical breaks in temporality in *When Memory Comes,* serves to illuminate both the effect of historical trauma on the individual and the challenge of historical reconstruction in such situations.

Inga Clendinnen's *Tiger's Eye* is also the story of a historian who lived through a traumatic experience, but her confrontation with a life-threatening medical condition lacks the collective and historical dimension of Friedländer's. The author, an Australian academic best known for her work on pre-Columbian Latin America, writes about herself as person and historian; unlike Steedman, Fraser, and Passerini, she makes no claim to have thrown much light on the experience of others in the society around her.[28] Instead, she explores the relations between history writing and other forms of narrative and the meaning of doing historical work in an individual's life. The occasion for Clendinnen's venture into autobiography was an intensely personal experience, a near-fatal disease that required a risky liver transplant. This crisis confronted her with fundamental questions about personal identity and its expressions in writing. At the outset, her disease transformed Clendinnen's sense of physical identity. "My sedate middle-aged body flung itself into a positive fandango of change. . . . I have always moved quickly. This new creature tottered and creaked, and had to be levered out of chairs. . . . My old panoply of self-representing devices was in full mutiny."[29] Later, she experienced vivid hallucinations, which brought home the fragility of her inner sense of self. "Now . . . I know what I am made of. Not sugar, not spice, not snips, not snails. Not pretty tales, either. Just a ragbag of metaphors, a hank of memories, and a habit of interrogation, held together by drugs. And if you say 'Aha! what then is this observing and commenting "I"?', I answer that it is a shred, a nothing: a sliver of shattered silk whirling in the wind, without anchor or destiny, surviving only because the wind happened to drop" (*Tiger's Eye*, 188).

Against this threat of dissolution, Clendinnen found refuge in an activity she had always treasured: writing. *Tiger's Eye* is in large part an exploration of the possibilities and pitfalls of various forms of writing and the differences between history, fiction, and the recollection of memory. In the hospital, she began by writing about her childhood, an exercise that "made me see that the marshland between memory and invention is treacherous." Converting her disordered recollections into "an ordered sequence of pages" changed their nature. "Now that they are fixed, existing as things in this world, there is no-one but me to say how true they are, and no-one but me to care. And, of course, I do care. Historians live by believing truth can be extracted from people's memories, including their written memories. Yet when I read my memories I am uneasy. I do not recognize the girl's temperament as continuous with mine" (73–74). Before long, however, the hospital experience, and particularly the interaction with other patients, made her "desire to write fiction. I wanted to feel I could change this inexorable place, these lonely, shapeless deaths, even in imagination: fiction as defiance of exigency." Fiction offered a sense of freedom that she didn't find in memoir: "Being able to make a story from nothing instead of concocting it out of elusive memories made me happy. It also relieved my fear of being trapped 'inside.' My labelled body might be lying on my labelled bed, but my mind could be anywhere, keeping whatever company I chose" (77).

At this point in *Tiger's Eye*, Clendinnen inserts several short fictional sketches, illustrating her ability to write so convincingly that only with her help are readers able to distinguish memoir from invention. She "discovered that fiction can make its own claims to truth" and that she herself believed in some of her fabricated characters "more completely than I believed in my account of myself as a girl. Fiction began to offer a balm for the obstinate opacities, the jagged inadequacies of memory" (85).

As Clendinnen confronted the fact that she might well be dying, however, she was seized by a desire to write something other than fiction, and in particular by a "need to memorialise my parents. . . . They had died close to three decades ago, but I realised, as most children come to realise, that they would not die until I was dead" (120). What she wrote taught her that the boundaries between fiction and memory are hard to define. She thought she had achieved some insight into her parents' lives but not as much as she had been able to obtain into the lives of her far more remote historical subjects. "Why was I willing to see strangers in the round—but not my parents, whom I knew intimately, if years count for anything?" The experience pointed to a general lesson: "Being ill had taught me how much of ourselves there is in all the stories we tell about the past. I had also begun to see the multiple barriers to understanding between ourselves and enigmatic others, and how fiction invites us to overleap those barriers. And I was beginning to suspect, after my drug-induced thrashings and wallowings, that we are fictions, too" (190–91).

Clendinnen's musings on the possibility of recovering the past do not stop at this point, however. As she began to recover, she undertook a new historical project. For the first time since her childhood, she interested herself in the history of her own country, "perhaps from a desire for a wider, more stable context" (192). She plunged into reading the diary of a man who had been a government-appointed agent dealing with the Australian aborigines in the early 1840s. "Mr. Robinson . . . revived the addictive pleasures of immersion in the situation, experiences and mind of a stranger dead long before I was born, with all these things lurking, waiting to be recovered, in the marks he had made on paper in life. That is the reliable miracle of history. . . . Mr. Robinson also gave me a future. He made me aware that other tragic human histories had been masked by my own" (221). After Clendinnen's unsettling lesson about the fragility of her own existence, the return to history was a return to more solid ground. She had become "tired of blundering about in the funhouse of the personal, with its multiplying images and its faces around corners. . . . I am not tired of history, because to be tired of history is to be tired of the world. It is also a refuge from one's own darker imaginings. People like Mr. Robinson do not believe themselves to be fictions. They retain their faith in agency. They believe the stories they invent about themselves, and struggle to make them real" (286).

The history Clendinnen returned to after her illness, however, was not the same discipline she had practiced before. For one thing, she had a much stronger awareness of its importance to her own psychic existence. It was her historical way of thinking that had pulled her through her crisis: "My technique for deciphering the hieroglyphs of my hallucinations was to explore my past with a professional historian's tenacity. In doing that I identified the experiences, often spread over years, which lay compacted behind certain insistent images, and uncovered connections previously unguessed at" (286). At the same time, however, her experience of illness had taught her a great deal about "the flamboyant vagaries of memory. . . . I knew I would have to think harder about the workings of memory, because it is on memory that the whole enterprise of history, along with the more anxious enterprise of sustaining a reasonably stable sense of self, depends" (221). She would not be able to think of history in the way she had been accustomed to before.

Writing her autobiography has allowed Clendinnen to communicate these insights to readers by, in some senses, putting them through a literary analogue of what she experienced. When she shifts without warning from memoir to fiction, she demonstrates the fragile boundary between truth and hallucination; when it becomes apparent that the themes of her fiction are strongly related to her own life, we learn a lesson about how truth can be expressed in fictional guise. Clendinnen's difficulties in comprehending her parents become a lesson about the hazards of reconstructing the personal past. *Tiger's Eye* puts its readers in a position comparable to the one Clendinnen occupied when she devoted herself to Mr. Robinson's diary: we are confronted with the reality of a person very different from ourselves, one who also seems, as Clendinnen wrote about Robinson, to refuse to see herself as a fiction and who retains her faith in agency, despite her ordeal. By writing a radically experimental autobiographical text, one far removed from the norms of historical narrative, Clendinnen has in fact found a way not just to affirm her own belief in the importance of history but to inculcate that conviction in others.

TRANSGRESSIVE DESIRES

Compared to the works of Fraser, Steedman, Passerini, Friedländer, and Clendinnen, the autobiographies of Martin Duberman and Deirdre McCloskey are relatively conventional in form, if not in content. Although both authors present their stories as exemplary of the experiences of the groups with which they identify themselves—gay men in Duberman's case, gender crossers in McCloskey's—neither attempts to share the privilege of narration by incorporating other individuals' voices into the telling of the story, except through the traditional device of quotation. In contrast to authors like Friedländer and Passerini, who emphasize their continuing sense of fractured and uncertain identity, Duberman and McCloskey tell stories in which the protagonist succeeds in achieving some sense of personal wholeness, and in contrast to Clendinnen, neither puts the boundary between real personal experience and imagination into question.

Duberman's *Cures* is in many ways a classic example of historians' autobiography, in which the author uses professional knowledge to contextualize personal experience and show how it was characteristic of its time. It can also be seen as a classic example of a "consciousness-raising" memoir, in which a member of an oppressed group relates his or her growing awareness of that oppression and the way he or she ultimately came to accept an identity that had previously been a source of shame and to join with others in collective action against the mechanisms of oppression. Duberman himself is quite explicit about the ways "the growing assertion by another despised minority that 'black is beautiful,' that being different was cause for celebration rather than apology," and the rhetoric of the 1960s student movement (which he, already a professor, observed from the outside) eventually influenced his willingness to accept and proclaim his homosexuality.[30] Finally, in spite of Duberman's own criticism of the "interchangeably monochromatic style" of academic historical writing,[31] *Cures* itself does not generate a truly distinctive authorial voice: despite the emotional charge of its contents, its language is the relatively flat prose of the mainstream American autobiographical tradition. The originality of Duberman's autobiography comes not from its form or style but from its bringing together in a single text different kinds of content that had generally been seen as incompatible: the story of an established professional, on the one hand, and intimate physical and emotional details of homosexual life, on the other.

McCloskey's *Crossing,* like Duberman's *Cures,* has a number of traditional features combined with some radical ones. McCloskey, who has held joint appointments in economics and history, is less insistent than Duberman on documenting the interaction between individual and historical context. She is, on the other hand, fully aware that her memoir, which ends with an evocation of the religious faith she found as part of her process of personal transformation, falls into one of the oldest categories of first-person testimony: the spiritual autobiography. On the other hand, however, in the context of Philippe Lejeune's famous definition of autobiography as a tale in which "the *author*, the *narrator*, and the *protagonist* must be identical,"[32] a personal narrative whose three sections are titled respectively "Donald," "Dee," and "Deirdre," marking the stages of the author's transit from a masculine persona to a sexually ambiguous one and finally to one clearly marked as feminine, poses a problem. McCloskey's memoir is deliberately designed to force us to ask whether the life story of someone who was born anatomically male but now writes as a woman can in fact be an autobiography, and, if so, how to classify such a text. Does *Crossing* belong in bibliographies of women's life writing? McCloskey comments repeatedly on the hostility she encountered from some radical feminists, "with their notion that a 'man is invading women's territory'"; they would presumably exclude the book.[33] In an interview she remarks, "It seems unfair that I now get to be what I have always wanted to be, and yet I have this terrifically large amount of self-confidence that comes from being a man in our society."[34]

Despite some significant differences, one of which is that McCloskey is at pains to emphasize that gender crossing has nothing to do with homosexuality—she in fact expresses a certain envy of the acceptance that homosexuals have now achieved in American society[35]—the two books have important elements in common. Both authors suffered at the hands of obtuse therapists, and both passionately condemn psychologists and psychiatrists who tried to convince them that they could and should repress desires that went against conventional social norms. Duberman's title, *Cures*, is a bitterly ironic reference to the numerous regimens he allowed himself to be subjected to in the 1950s and 1960s, ranging from an orthodox Freudian psychotherapist to a charismatic group therapy leader who turned out to be dishonest and abusive.[36] McCloskey denounces the psychiatrists who aided his sister in having him involuntarily committed to mental institutions to prevent him from undergoing sex-change surgery; on one widely publicized occasion, he was taken into custody while delivering the presidential address at a national historians' conference.[37] Both authors are also convinced that acknowledging and acting on their nonconformist desires made them better scholars, or at least opened them up to new insights. Admitting his homosexuality in print, Duberman claims, allowed him to take "a new, more honestly subjective approach to historical writing," and McCloskey found that being a woman made her less "single-minded" in her thinking than she had been as a man.[38]

The most important common feature of these two books, however, is their shared determination to bring the reality of "deviant" bodily desire into the staid precincts of historians' autobiography. As we have seen, Pierre Nora and others have justified historians' life writing as a way of exposing the fiction of the historian as a disembodied, objective student of the past. For the most part, however, the historians revealed in the *ego-histoires* written in response to Nora's call and in the other autobiographical texts analyzed here have been equally disembodied. At most, they reveal their physical self by reproducing personal photographs, in which they inevitably appear in innocent childhood poses from family albums or conventional snapshots and formal portraits from their adult years. In general, the body enters historians' personal narratives only if, as in the case of Inga Clendinnen's liver disease or Robert Hine's blindness, it threatens the author's ability to do history. Hine, a historian of the American West who kept his career going with the aid of assistants who read to him, texts in braille, and a talking computer, makes a number of thoughtful comments on the way his lack of vision affected his work during the fifteen years before surgery enabled him to see again. In his case, the state of his body was an ineluctable limitation. As he writes, "The blind are imprisoned in their bodies; the body is for them almost synonymous with their environment." He was limited to projects based on well-defined collections of sources and could not "wander freely amid his data," for example, and graduate students were reluctant to have him on their committees, since he could not easily critique their work.[39] Although Hine's story reminds his fellow historians that our ability to work as we please is dependent on the functioning of our body, it does not challenge the conventions of historical professionalism in the way that Duberman's and McCloskey's narratives do.

It is true that a surprising number of historians' autobiographies do briefly mention their author's early sexual experiences. Peter Kenez mentions an adolescent visit to a brothel, Louis Harlan a night spent with a sympathetic young woman during shore leave before D-Day, and Bernard Smith devotes four steamy pages to his initiation by a randy chambermaid. While Paul Veyne boasts of picaresque adventures with prostitutes during a youthful stay in Rome, H. Stuart Hughes admits to having been twenty-nine before losing his virginity. Gerda Lerner describes both a premarital affair and the physical passion she felt for her future husband when they first slept together.[40] Passages such as these are part of an autobiographic tradition going back to the classics of the autobiographical canon, including Gibbon's *Memoirs* with their laconic remark about the breaking off of his youthful attachment to Suzanne Curchod. Gibbon's enigmatic comment has opened the way to two centuries of speculation about his personality and sexuality. The mentions of sexuality in most historians' autobiographies, however, taken together with references to marriages and children, serve instead to show readers that these authors had normal heterosexual instincts. The point of such passages is not so much to bring the physical element of the author's life into the story as to assure readers that there is nothing interesting or unusual to be said about it. As one critic has put it, "Most autobiographers, because they belong to the heterosexual majority, tend to treat their sexual lives as something they hold in common with most of their readers rather than as clues to the uniqueness of their own experiences."[41]

By now, the general culture is sufficiently open about sexuality that a historian like George Mosse can acknowledge his homosexuality and discuss its impact on his scholarly sensibilities without much fear of shocking anyone. Mosse says more about his sex life than most historian-autobiographers, but his treatment of the subject remains fairly abstract: readers of his memoir are left free either to fill in the blanks from their own imagination or to follow Mosse's lead in treating the subject as a secondary issue. As he himself sees it, there is not much to discuss because of "the necessary suppression of that part of my personality, or rather its sublimation into work and a fantasy life." When Mosse goes on, however, to write that "I was not as closeted as I had imagined," since he discovered that younger gays had taken him as a role model long before he consciously came out of the closet, he is admitting that his sexuality was an important part of his impact on the world throughout his career.[42] In her *Promise of a Dream: Remembering the Sixties,* the pioneering women's historian Sheila Rowbotham also writes more explicitly about her sexual experiences than most scholars do. In her view, these experiences and her reactions to them are essential as part of both her attempt to reconstruct the atmosphere of the 1960s and her explanation of how she learned to recognize the possibility of writing about women and their history.

Duberman's *Cures* and McCloskey's *Crossing* break even more radically with the tradition of reticence in scholars' autobiographies and insist on confronting readers with the revelation that the colleague in the office next door may not have settled for sublimating bodily desires into academic scholarship. By implication, they suggest that any reading of history that fails to acknowledge the bodily dimension of human experience is necessarily incomplete. In contrast to Mosse, Duberman insists on taking readers through every stage of his sentimental education as a homosexual, from his first discovery of the secretive gay subculture among Harvard graduate students in the 1950s to his initiation into the world of New York "hustler hangouts" and gay sex for money in the 1960s, and then to an increasing range of practices including sadomasochism, sex with drugs, and indulgence in gay pornography. *Cures* also recounts, in exhausting detail, the long series of Duberman's mostly unhappy affairs. Initially, Duberman looked for monogamous love relationships that mirrored heterosexual norms, but by 1970, he was becoming attracting to a "queer" perspective that defended multiple partners and anonymous sex. Duberman confounded one therapist by arguing that since promiscuity seemed to be a more powerful human impulse than fidelity, "gay men are among the few who are leading natural lives."[43]

It would be easy to reject *Cures* as a self-indulgent exercise in exhibitionism and sometimes self-pity, but Duberman clearly saw it as something else: a purposeful contestation of the limits on homosexual self-expression. Those sympathetic to the cause of gay emancipation understood the importance of Duberman's autobiographical act: he insisted that it was just as legitimate to narrate the physical and emotional details of gay sexuality as to reveal those of heterosexuality. Furthermore, it was important that he did so from his position as a respected academic. Duberman's position as a well-established university professor gave him a certain protection: in 1991, when *Cures* appeared, it would have been difficult for members of most other high-status professions to publish such a book without jeopardizing their career. Duberman was thus expanding the frontiers of autobiography in general and helping to establish a precedent for a new level of gay self-revelation. Even those who have reservations about the way Duberman went about presenting his story, such as Paul Robinson, himself a gay historian and the author of a major study of gay men's autobiographies, have recognized the importance of his effort.[44] The juxtaposition of gay sexual exploration and professional success in Duberman's narrative was also important on another level: it forced academic readers to recognize that someone could be a leading scholar by day and a regular at hustler bars by night. To be sure, gay history professors have no doubt existed for a long time: Duberman mentions spotting one of his own Harvard professors at a gay meeting point along the Charles River during his student days.[45] But Duberman was determined to establish academic homosexuals' rights to speak publicly about their sexuality and even to acknowledge its influence on their scholarship.

Duberman was able to do this in part because by 1991 the historical discipline had begun to accept gay history as a legitimate subdiscipline. His memoir is cast as both an individual story and a contribution to that history. *Cures* and its successor volume, *Midlife Queer,* situate Duberman's own story in the context of a history of the changes in the American gay community, from the 1950s through the 1970s, and a critique of social attitudes toward gay sex. Duberman's personal odyssey through the changing landscape of gay America is also an explanation of how that increasingly diversified landscape developed. Unlike more academic studies of the development of gay culture, however, Duberman's book, because of its personal nature, never loses sight of the fact that to be a homosexual is to do certain things with one's body that go against the prevailing behavioral norms of heterosexual society. Like the women's movement that it paralleled in some respects, the movement for gay liberation insisted that "the personal is political"; Duberman's memoir asserts that personal experience is also historical. *Cures,* like Saul Friedländer's Holocaust memoir, claims to be a personal story that is at the same time a significant historical contribution.

Cures has not been without its critics, even within the gay community. Paul Robinson has raised questions about the inconsistency between Duberman's assertion that he recognized his sexual orientation early in life and his determination to pursue therapies designed to change him, asking "how a man of Duberman's intelligence and education could have been such a dupe."[46] Another aspect of *Cures* raises an important question about its attempt to combine autobiography and history. *Cures,* which was published in 1991, carries Duberman's story as far as the early 1970s, and its sequel, *Midlife Queer,* goes up to 1980. Only in a postscript to the latter volume does Duberman mention the first news he heard about what was initially called the "gay plague" and soon became known as AIDS. Unlike historians born in pre-Hitler Germany, who see their community's blindness to the coming danger as a major issue in their retrospective memoirs, Duberman has deliberately renounced the possibility of using his sense of historical perspective to reconsider the sexual antinomianism of the pre-AIDS years. His recollections thus capture the atmosphere of the gay community in what looks, in retrospect, like a utopian moment. Duberman's desire to preserve the memory of a time when it seemed as though gays might escape from the constraints of society and, in a sense, those of history reads curiously in light of what he already knew, when he wrote, had happened to that community. *Midlife Queer* contains a lengthy chapter on the major heart attack Duberman suffered in his late forties and reflections on other "losses"—the death of his mother, the decline of the radical current within the gay movement that he had supported—that foreshadowed a major change in his life by the end of the 1970s. "I was well aware that in my head, at fifty, I still clung tenaciously to the insatiable fantasy needs and emotional strategies of a young man starting out," Duberman concludes. For himself, "I *knew* better, having had more than a glimpse of opportunities curtailed, energies diminished."[47] But the narrative leaves it completely unclear whether his individual sense of new limits also affected the gay community as a whole.

As we have seen, *Cures* and McCloskey's *Crossing* have a similar polemical thrust, and McCloskey explicitly claims the same treatment for her category that gays now receive in most of American society. As a member of a much smaller group, she realizes she is facing even more of an uphill battle, particularly because her aim is not to achieve tolerance for an autonomous subculture but to gain acceptance of gender crossers' right to their chosen identities. The public indignity McCloskey was subjected to in 1995—being seized by the police and dragged off the podium while speaking to a major scholarly association—is the kind of treatment normally reserved for criminals, not academics; its extremity underlines the degree to which "normal" professional careers depend on conformity to accepted gender roles. And as the story of McCloskey's family's reaction to his decision to change sexes demonstrates, resistance to such decisions can be intensely personal. The instigator of McCloskey's two involuntary commitments to psychiatric hospitals was his own sister, who insisted that his plan to undergo sex-change surgery proved that he was psychologically unstable; after the surgery, his former wife and his two adult children cut off all contact with "Deirdre." That McCloskey should feel the need to do whatever she can to encourage greater understanding of people in her situation is understandable.

McCloskey was not the first gender crosser to write a memoir—she recalls reading the journalist Jan Morris's *Conundrum* early in her attempts to understand her own attraction to cross-dressing[48]—but, like *Cures, Crossing* is significant because of its author's academic status. McCloskey was, and has remained, an important figure in both economics and history, and she moved to an even more visible academic appointment shortly after the publication of her memoir. As a successful professional, with what she calls the "highest profile" of any academic gender crosser, she had a special opportunity to make a statement on behalf of others in her situation; she is certainly the only such person to be interviewed on the subject in a leading journal for professional economists.[49] There are aspects of McCloskey's memoir, such as the description of her penis-removal surgery, that are even harder for many male academics to digest than the most explicit passages of *Cures.* Deliberately violating the physical integrity of the body and the fixity of gender identity raises deep fears, and McCloskey's attempt to present sex-change surgery as an experience analogous to "foreign travel" and one perhaps less radical than the universal "crossing from child to adult" does not disarm them.[50] McCloskey's intensely physical memoir, with its graphic descriptions of the surgical procedures that transformed her body, is thus a calculatedly provocative act, meant to forcefully confront all readers, but perhaps especially academic ones, with the fact that a highly successful professor might deliberately do something that will strike most of us as completely unimaginable.

McCloskey adds to the provocation of her memoir by insisting that her transformation has made her a better, or at least more broad-minded, scholar, one less likely to accept narrowly economic explanations of human behavior. Her claim implies that all scholars, not merely gender crossers, derive some of their scholarly perspective from their personal, corporeal experiences. Like Duberman, McCloskey thus challenges not only the notion of the disembodied scholar but that of the scholar who thinks that self-reflexivity can be limited to considerations of class, generation, and public experience. Furthermore, whereas Duberman's memoir allows most academic readers to avoid identifying themselves with the author because of its insistence on his emotional neediness, his inability to form stable personal relations, his indulgence in drugs, and his strenuous efforts to escape from the confines of university life by establishing himself as a playwright, McCloskey's story is that of a scholar whose life, as she presents it, was that of an entirely normal academic. In his life as a man, McCloskey had pursued the scholarly recognition Duberman was willing to give up; in private he had a conventional lifestyle, a marriage with children, and, until those children left for college, only very occasional opportunities to indulge in secretive cross-dressing. People who feel trapped in the body of a member of the opposite sex are, as McCloskey emphasizes, a very small minority, but his memoir raises the question of what other inner secrets lie behind the masks respectable academics present to one another. In a number of ways, then, *Crossings,* like *Cures,* deserves to be included among those historians' autobiographies that challenge the usual boundaries of academic autobiography, and indeed of autobiography in general.

HISTORIANS AND AUTOBIOGRAPHICAL INNOVATION

The autobiographical texts considered in this chapter demonstrate that historian-autobiographers have made contributions as original as those of any other authors to the experimentation with the boundaries of autobiography that have characterized the last few decades. Carolyn Steedman, Ronald Fraser, and Luisa Passerini have each, in different ways, managed to combine self-portraiture with an account of others' lives and autobiography with theory and social history. All three, rather than portraying themselves as observers of a world around them, have shown how they were in fact products of it, but none has adopted Henry Adams's pose and pretended to be purely passive in the face of that history. Without making exaggerated claims for the autonomy of the individual self, all three authors have nevertheless made it clear that they remained capable of agency and of self-assertion. All three also demonstrate how the abandonment of conventional chronological narrative can, by disrupting the usual structures of historical analysis, produce new historical insights, a feature they share with Saul Friedländer's *When Memory Comes.* Of the texts considered here, Friedländer's is the most radical in its challenge to the possibility of historical understanding. Rather than defining a new space in which history and autobiography can be combined, as Passerini and Fraser do, Friedländer suggests that the impact of trauma makes it impossible to find a fixed point from which to write either an individual life story or a broader history. Inga Clendinnen's *Tiger's Eye,* although it, like *When Memory Comes,* depicts the dissolution of a self, points to a different conclusion: Clendinnen found in history an alternative to the obsession with the incoherent nature of the ego that she experienced during her illness. These two contrasting cases show us that the bringing together of autobiography and history in unconventional patterns does not necessarily lead in any particular direction.

The emphasis on the historian-author's body in the autobiographical narratives of Martin Duberman and Deirdre McCloskey links them to the feminist works of Steedman and Passerini, both of whom insist that having a female body makes a vital difference in a scholar's life. Clendinnen's narrative also highlights the significance of corporeality, though not specifically of its gender dimension. Duberman and McCloskey go further than these other authors, however, in forcing readers to confront the physical dimension of their lives and in unsettling the conventional expectations of academic autobiography. Women and sexual minorities have customarily managed to gain acceptance in the academic community by conforming to the fiction that mind can be separated from body, that disciplines such as history consist of individuals whose physical nature is irrelevant to their scholarship. *Cures* and *Crossing* deliberately challenge this proposition. If they do not unsettle the forms of historical narrative as much as the other narratives discussed here, they certainly demonstrate the power of autobiographical narrative to subvert some of the standard assumptions of the academic community of historians.

Within the larger body of historians' autobiographical literature, the texts analyzed here are exceptions. Most historian-memoirists have been more diffident about their abilities as autobiographers and less willing to exhibit ambitious literary aspirations. In most cases, these authors are scholars who have positioned themselves at the margins of the historical profession. Fraser's and Passerini's engagement with oral history, Clendinnen's controversial work in ethnohistory, and Duberman's parallel career as a playwright all indicate a willingness to question conventional historical methodology and practice; even before changing genders, McCloskey found a second home in his university's history department after challenging basic assumptions of academic economics. Nevertheless, the projects of these authors cannot be read simply as criticisms or rejections of the more conventional autobiographies written by other historians. Together with their colleagues, these authors share a common desire to show how the historian's personal experience can enrich the understanding of the past. Often the conclusions they draw from their personal narrative are not so far removed from those of other historian-autobiographers who have told their stories in more traditional ways. The women historians who contributed to the collective volume *Voices of Women Historians,* for example, often recall the impact of student radical movements in the 1960s in terms similar to those of Passerini, and we have seen in a previous chapter that Friedländer's recollections of his Holocaust experience have much in common with those of other historians. Because of their innovative and exploratory character, however, the writings of Steedman, Fraser, Passerini, Friedländer, Clendinnen, Duberman, and McCloskey highlight the contributions that historically trained authors can make to the expansion of the possibilities of autobiography. Insights derived from these texts help us appreciate the larger significance of historians' autobiography in general.

CONCLUSION

ON THE OPENING page of *Essais d'ego-histoire,* the book that inspired my interest in historians' autobiographical writings, Pierre Nora asserted that by writing about their own lives, his colleagues had provided examples of "a new genre, for a new age of historical consciousness." He thus claimed that these texts had profound implications for the understanding of history, of historians, and of autobiography. Looking back at the project fifteen years later, in an autobiographical essay of his own, Nora came to a very different conclusion: *ego-histoire,* he decided, had been "a publishing and intellectual failure."[1]

In both cases, Nora surely protested too much. As we have seen, historians' writing about their own lives was hardly the innovation Nora suggested. Even the association of such projects with claims about the inauguration of new ways of understanding history is not new. Vico, Gibbon, Henry Adams, the historians who contributed to the German collective volume *Die Geschichtswissenschaft der Gegenwart in Selbstdarstellung* in the early twentieth century, and the contributors to the Radical Historians' Organization's *Visions of History* in the 1970s, among others, all believed that they had helped articulate new forms of historical consciousness. On the other hand, even if the sales of *Essais d'ego-histoire* were a disappointment, I hope that this essay has demonstrated that the project of historians' autobiographical writing, which has flourished as never before in the years since that volume's appearance, certainly cannot be written off as an intellectual failure.

Rather than judging the importance of first-person writing by historians in terms of success or failure, I would assess it as an ambiguous supplement to the fields of history on the one hand and autobiography on the other. A supplement, as Jacques Derrida argued in his early essay *Of Grammatology,* is an addition to a structure that already exists, but the fact that something can be added suggests that there was a lack or a missing element in that structure.[2] In his justification of the project of *ego-histoire,* Nora claimed that history, as traditionally written, suffered from just this kind of lack, with the historian's individual story as the missing element. Nora did not fully comprehend the unstable nature of the supplement he proposed to add to history, however. Personal narrative, as the theoretical debates on the subject among literary scholars show, is an ambivalent genre whose truth claims are inherently contested. Ultimately, its theoreticians themselves fall back on paradoxical formulations such as Paul John Eakin's insistence on the need for a "simultaneous acceptance and refusal of the constraints of the real" or Philippe Lejeune's proclamation "In spite of the fact that autobiography is impossible, this in no way prevents it from existing."[3] The infusion of such a supplement into the bloodstream of history can hardly leave the patient unaffected.

The spread of personal writing among historians has not completely transformed or destabilized historical practice, nor is there any indication that historians who have written about their own life intended that it should. Although autobiography is inherently a subjective enterprise, as historian-memoirists acknowledge, few of them have thought that writing about themselves commits them to drawing the same conclusion about the writing of history. To date, at least, no historian has written an autobiography for the purpose of arguing that historical truth cannot be found or does not exist. As we have seen, historians' reconstructions of the reasons for their attraction to their discipline emphasize its engagement with reality, and historians' memoirs as different as Emmanuel Le Roy Ladurie's *Paris-Montpellier* and Inga Clendinnen's *Tiger's Eye* testify to the importance that the collectively defined project of historical research has had in the personal lives of scholars searching for some basis of certainty independent of ideology and more stable than the individual ego.

The fact that many historian-autobiographers have been capable of writing personal stories without rejecting standard definitions of historical truth has disappointed critics committed to postmodernist views, one of whom has criticized these authors for sticking to "a narrative of self-deception" by taking this position.[4] I have argued here, drawing especially on my reading of Paul Ricoeur, that this demand to equate history and autobiography with each other and to put both in the category of fiction reflects an oversimplification of the historical enterprise and a failure to recognize the differences between distinct genres of narrative. Understanding the special characteristics of autobiography that distinguish it from both history and fiction helps to clarify our understanding of all three of these forms of writing and what each can contribute to the project of making sense of human existence in its temporal dimension. History and autobiography do grow out of a common impulse to preserve the memory of the past by shaping it into an intelligible narrative, and both claim to tell true stories about real people; neither can be completely assimilated to the genre of fiction. But autobiography is not bound by history's requirement for documentation and its emphasis on collective, as opposed to individual, experience, and since no autobiographer can tell his or her story all the way to the end, autobiography has an open-ended character that separates it from both history and fiction. Theories of narrative, which have played such a large role in contemporary thinking about the nature of history and of fiction, need to be broadened to take into account the presence of this third genre, whose existence shows the inadequacy of any binary model based on the opposition of history and fiction.

Contemporary historical practice has in fact shown a greater understanding of the contribution autobiographical narrative can make to the understanding of the past. As we have seen, the development of subfields such as the history of everyday life and the history of memory has led historians to treat their subjects' autobiographical productions as something other than deliberately misleading testimony. New theoretical perspectives on autobiography have also enriched our understanding of the subject and made it possible to understand life writing itself as a significant cultural practice. These historiographical and theoretical developments may not represent the dawning of a radically new age of historical consciousness, but they do mark a significant inflection in the way historians understand the past. These changes have undoubtedly made it easier for historians to transform themselves into autobiographers without feeling that they are abandoning the canons of their discipline.

Even in this more tolerant climate, however, the relations between history and the shape-shifting genre of autobiography are still not entirely harmonious. Historian-autobiographers remain acutely aware that individual stories are not the same thing as history and that in telling about their own idiosyncratic experiences, they may raise the question whether *anyone* in the past lived a life fully consonant with the collective narratives that history has constructed. The ease with which autobiographical writing can come to resemble fiction also remains a concern for historians. Cuban-American historian Carlos Eire's prizewinning memoir of his boyhood in pre-Castro days, *Waiting for Snow in Havana,* is presented as a factual account. Nevertheless, its author's recollections of life with a father who claimed to be the reincarnation of Louis XVI, of paintings in the family's house whose eyes seemed to follow people in the room, and of the grotesque episodes of violence the author and his playmates engaged in evoke the "magic realism" of much recent Latin American literature and the allegorical brutality of *Lord of the Flies.* Eire clearly intends his work not just as personal testimony but as a contribution to the historical understanding of the Cuban past, and especially of the cruelty of the Castro regime. His very skill as a writer, however, may make his professional colleagues wary of citing his account as historical evidence.

The implications of autobiography, and especially historians' autobiographies, for the understanding of history are thus complex and sometimes conflicting. So are the implications of historians' autobiographical projects for historians and their profession. Although they are individual testimonies, autobiographical accounts are also one of the important ways in which the discipline of history has come to represent itself, both to its own practitioners and to the general public. Life stories serve, as psychologist Jerome Bruner has argued, both "to locate us culturally" and "to individuate us."[5] As we have seen, historians' personal narratives generally give a positive depiction of lives devoted to the study of the past; they thus tend to put more emphasis on their authors' identification with their profession than on the expression of their individuality. Even those authors who had to overcome obstacles to become historians rarely write in an angry or embittered tone. Most historians depict their vocation as a positive choice, embodying important values they are proud to represent, particularly a commitment to the study of "reality" as opposed to the more abstract or ethereal subject matter of other academic disciplines. When they write about their professional career, they imply that theirs is an occupation in which talent and hard work are duly rewarded. Just as historian-autobiographers do not set out to subvert the status of historical knowledge, the overwhelming majority of them, even those who had to overcome discrimination to enter the profession, also have no intention of denouncing or deconstructing the structures of academic life.

Although they do not usually intend to undermine their profession, however, the ways in which historians write about their lives do raise questions about some aspects of it. As we have seen, parts of a historian's life strike most of these authors as impossible or inappropriate for narration.

Historian-autobiographers say little about the routine of teaching that does so much to define the profession because to do so would be boring; they omit their memories of epic battles in committee meetings because the disproportion between the matters at stake and the emotions invested in them would be embarrassing. To avoid appearing bitter or self-pitying, they pass over the unpleasantness of personal rivalries and the oppressiveness that can result from professional hierarchies, thereby minimizing some of the less admirable characteristics of the discipline. The portrait of the historian and of the historical profession that emerges from these texts is thus a stylized one, calculated to sustain the self-esteem of both its individual practitioners and the group to which they belong. To the extent that these characteristics are shared by autobiographies from other members of other academic disciplines, they obviously raise the question whether academic autobiography requires a sacrifice of the individualizing element supposedly inherent in personal narrative.

Although historians' autobiographies tend to reinforce the collective image of the discipline, they do also highlight some of the tensions between individual expression and professional commitment. For many historian-autobiographers, writing about themselves is an opportunity to speak about things that matter deeply to them but that they have had to exclude from their professional work: personal emotions, feelings about their parents, resentment about some of the injuries that history has inflicted on them. Like Friedrich Meinecke, many historian-autobiographers are conscious that the story of their career provides a structure for their narrative, but at the price of leaving out other aspects that in fact mattered more to them. Along with its function of sustaining the structures of the history profession, historians' autobiography serves as a reminder that any professional role is a limited and sometimes confining one.

Historians' autobiographies have important implications not only for the understanding of history and of the historical profession but also for the understanding of the literary genre to which they belong. In the first place, because historians' memoirs are often, although not invariably, more historical than literary in form and tone, they remind us that autobiography is as close to history writing as it is to fiction. Because autobiography's standing as a literary genre has benefited greatly from its redefinition as a form of creative literature, this reminder may not be entirely welcome to practicing autobiographers and to some of its critics, who undoubtedly have no desire to go back to the days when the main criterion for judging an autobiographical narrative was its factual accuracy. Nevertheless, the argument I have made for insisting on autobiography's autonomy from history also separates autobiography from fiction. As a distinctive form of narrative, autobiography has to be judged by its own rules, and as critics such as Paul John Eakin and David McCooey have contended, those rules include some respect for verifiability. As we have seen, historians are somewhat more likely than the common run of autobiographers to make comments about the documentary basis for their narrative, although it would be difficult to demonstrate that their personal histories are more truthful than others'. In any event, as the example of *The Education of Henry Adams* shows, omissions and selective narration can distort a life story as badly as any misstatements of the facts: Adams's silence about his marriage and his virtual suppression of the importance that historical scholarship had for him are of greater consequence for the judging the truthfulness of his account than any factual errors he makes. The real contribution that historians' autobiographies make to the issue of truthfulness lies in their demonstration of the importance of historical context in the narration of life stories. They highlight the fact that the honesty of an autobiography depends not just on its accurately recording the emotions, thoughts, and deeds of its protagonist but also on its integrity in portraying the author's times and the way he or she interacted with them.

A second lesson about autobiography to be learned from the study of historians' life writing is the extent of the contribution that historians have made to the genre. From Vico and Gibbon through Henry Adams and down to contemporary authors such as Luisa Passerini and Ronald Fraser, historians have not merely adopted preexisting models of self-portraiture: they have made important and original contributions to the art of autobiography. Gibbon created a powerful model for the depiction of a life devoted to intellectual pursuits. Although his *Memoirs* were celebrated by the romantics and are often classified with those of his great literary contemporaries Rousseau and Goethe, Gibbon's story was not that of a man of imagination. Instead, he dramatized the value of a life dedicated to hard, disciplined work. In revolt against Gibbon, Adams invented a kind of antiheroic autobiography that emphasized the disjuncture between individual comprehension and the movement of history; he also showed that personal narrative could be used to challenge the notion of the autonomous self exemplified in autobiographical texts like Gibbon's. Contemporary historian-autobiographers such as Passerini and Fraser, among others, have demonstrated new ways to combine individual and collective perspectives on events. An understanding of how autobiography has evolved requires a recognition of the important contributions that historians, as historians, have made to the exploration of its possibilities and the definition of its forms.

A third way in which historians' autobiographies contribute to a broader understanding of the genre is by revealing how some of the classic patterns of autobiographical literature can emerge in even in seemingly prosaic stories of life in modern society. The structures of the *Bildungsroman* underlie what many historians write about the development of their vocation. Many ex-communist historians' stories are consciously told in the form of confessions and conversion narratives. Historians whose lives were reshaped because of Nazi persecution offer modern variants of classic struggles with identity and fate. The demonstration that these themes are still relevant to stories of seemingly ordinary people in the modern world is an important contribution to the study of autobiography.

Finally, historians' autobiographies are of special relevance for understanding of the phenomenon of academic autobiography and, more generally, the significance that autobiographical accounts have for the groups to which autobiographers belong. These texts are often efforts to address a general audience and questions of general interest, but they also serve specific functions within their authors' professional community. They consecrate reputations and professional status, identify their authors with particular causes and historiographical movements, and occasionally enlist readers in personal, political, or disciplinary disputes. Those that address their author's choice of vocation and professional career make implicit arguments about the importance of history as a discipline and create an image of the historical community, as well as of their author. In short, historians' autobiographies demonstrate the multiple purposes that autobiographical literature serves, for its authors and for the groups they belong to. Scholars' autobiographies are a form of literature, but a purely literary analysis of them misses important dimensions of their significance.

The recognition of the important connections between history, historians, and autobiography proposed here is not meant to claim a privileged place in the canon of academic personal narrative for the members of my own scholarly field. Rather, this case study of the relations between history and autobiography should provoke new interest in the connections between autobiography and other disciplines. Literary studies, through its concern with narrative technique and structure and with the uses of language; psychology, sociology, and anthropology, because of their interest in the formation of the self; philosophy, through its preoccupation with consciousness; and even the natural sciences—*bios* is part of both *autobiography* and *biology*—all have interactions with autobiographical writing that are potentially as interesting as those of history. History and autobiography do share a joint project, the reconstitution of the past, but that is only one aspect of life writing. Autobiography is inherently a polymorphous enterprise. It intersects not only with history but with the concerns of many other academic disciplines, and has the potential to reveal important aspects of each of them.

While historians' autobiographies thus raise important questions and offer new perspectives on history, on the historians who write and teach it, and on life writing, they are not just intellectual exercises, and it would be inappropriate to conclude an examination of many other historians' personal writings without saying something about my own reactions to reading them. Like Edward Gibbon, I have lived my research project as a grand adventure, and like many of these authors, I have enjoyed doing something quite different from any of my previous scholarly projects. Through reading other historians' life stories, I have traveled to places far removed from those that figured in my previous research on the European press in the era of the French Revolution. Vicariously, I have followed the classical curriculum in a German Gymnasium, peddled newspapers on the streets of early twentieth-century Boston, plotted the course of World War II as it unfolded, and tickled trout in Australia's Wye River. I have had the broadening experience of learning to speak the interdisciplinary language of autobiography studies, or at least some of its many dialects. This project has been, for me, a way of crafting a second professional identity, a way of defying the claim that old dogs cannot learn new tricks.

Although this project has freed me to explore new places, it has also brought me closer to home and to some unsuspected truths about myself. Each of the authors I have read has at least one thing in common with me: a commitment to history. Many have shared a good deal more with me. I recognize myself in the many stories I have read about shy, bookish youngsters; I, too, felt that my choice of discipline—history rather than the mathematics that I had also enjoyed throughout my school days—was an important personal decision. Sometimes my reading has inspired feelings of envy: many of these authors lived through events far more memorable than those I have experienced, or attained grander heights in our shared profession. At other times I recognize how relatively comfortable my early life and my career have been. As my reading in this literature has led me to think about my own life, I have come to recognize that the way I have pursued this theme has been not only a sign of an ambition to do new things but also a repetition of old habits. I have pursued historians' autobiographies as I used to collect stamps during my childhood, reveling in unusual acquisitions—a historian from Tonga![6]—and priding myself on learning to appreciate the subtle differences between specimens that look alike. Stamp collecting, like the study of these autobiographies, was a way of learning about the world but also a way of confining myself to a restricted part of it. Has this project demonstrated my ability to go boldly into unknown territories or my propensity to prefer peace and quiet to the tumult at the center of the action? At least my reading in autobiographical theory gives me the comfort of knowing that my own story is an open-ended one whose conclusion cannot be fully anticipated.

One thing I have learned in the course of carrying out this project, however, is that my fellow historians have a definite interest in the subject of historians' autobiographies. Wherever I have talked about my research, I have been greeted with questions, recommendations of new titles to read, and strong personal reactions, both to these texts and to what I have had to say about them. These experiences have strengthened my conviction that this topic speaks not only to me but to my colleagues more generally. The dreams that impelled Jean-Jacques Rousseau to write his *Confessions*—of being truly understood and acknowledged by others and of being remembered after his death—are widely shared. Like most modern professions, history requires considerable sublimation of the self. No matter how modestly they present their enterprises, historians who write about their own lives are trying to liberate themselves from that restriction. They join with Rousseau in the demand to be recognized as individuals, people whose unique thoughts and feelings matter. Few historians will actually write narratives of their lives, and even fewer will succeed in publishing such stories, but the minority who do are in some ways speaking also for the majority who remain silent. They are testifying to the powerful attraction of autobiography's ability to give meaning to individual existence.

NOTES

INTRODUCTION

1. Olney, *Metaphors of Self,* 36–37.
2. Z. Popkin, *Open Every Door.* For a summary of my grandmother's literary career, see J. D. Popkin, "Forgotten Forerunner."
3. R. H. Popkin, "Intellectual Autobiography: Warts and All," and "Introduction: Warts and All, Part 2."
4. Miller, "Introduction: Extremities," 1.
5. For an articulation of these distinctions, see Olney, "Some Versions of Memory/Some Versions of *Bios:* The Ontology of Autobiography," in *Autobiography,* 236–67.
6. John Sturrock, "Theory versus Autobiography," 23–24.
7. G. Mosse, *Confronting History,* 148.
8. Billington, *Doctor B.,* preface.

CHAPTER 1

1. Schachter, *Searching for Memory,* 308.
2. Marcus, *Auto/biographical Discourses,* 7.
3. Samuels, *Henry Adams,* 143–48.
4. E. O. Wilson, *Naturalist;* Kaplan, *French Lessons.*
5. Nora, "Memoirs of Men of State," 411.
6. Langlois and Seignobos, *Introduction to the Study of History,* 168, 171.
7. G. K. G. Clark, *Critical Historian,* 67.
8. Rousseau, *Confessions,* 5, 2.
9. Ibid., 4.
10. B. G. Smith, *Gender of History,* especially chap. 6, "High Amateurism and the Panoramic Past."
11. Dilthey, *Pattern and Meaning,* 85. Dilthey's writings on autobiography were parts of uncompleted manuscripts; they have been published in different order in his *Gesammelte Schriften,* vol. 7, and in this volume of English translations.
12. Dilthey, *Pattern and Meaning,* 111.
13. Ibid., 85–86.

14. Ibid., 86, 111.

15. Dilthey, *Gesammelte Schriften*, 278.

16. Marcus, *Auto/biographical Discourses*, 148, 154.

17. Barkin, "Autobiography and History," 89, 87, 103, 93.

18. Amelang, *Flight of Icarus*, 20–21.

19. Appleby, *Inheriting the Revolution*, viii.

20. Davis, *Fiction in the Archives;* Dekker, *Childhood, Memory, and Autobiography in Holland;* Ménétra, *Journal of My Life;* Maynes, *Taking the Hard Road.*

21. Janny Scott, "Prominent Historian Admits He Misled Students into Believing He Served in Vietnam," *New York Times*, 19 June 2001, A21; Elliott J. Gorn, "Why Are Academics Ducking the Ellis Case?" *OAH Newsletter*, August 2001, 3 (reprinted from *Chronicle of Higher Education*, 20 July 2001); Edmund Morris, "Just Our Imaginations, Running Away," *New York Times*, 22 June 2001, A21.

22. For the case against the literal accuracy of the memoir, see Stoll, *Rigoberta Menchú and the Story of All Poor Guatemalans*, 273.

23. Linda J. Craft, "Rigoberta Menchú, the Academy, and the U.S. Mainstream Press: The Controversy Surrounding Guatemala's 1992 Nobel Peace Laureate," *Journal of the Midwest Modern Language Association* 33–34 (2000–2001): 55. For two examples of the *testimonio* argument, see Beverley, "Margin at the Center," and Sommer, "Not Just a Personal Story," and for a strongly worded critique of these arguments, see Lauritzen, "Arguing with Life Stories."

24. The most thorough account of the *Fragments* affair is Maechler, *Wilkomirski Affair*, which also includes the text of *Fragments*. For one literature scholar's attempt to find some truth value in *Fragments* even after its author's claim to have experienced the death camps had been discredited, see Michael Bernard-Donals, "'Blot Out the Name of Amalek': Memory and Forgetting in the *Fragments* Controversy," *Journal of the Midwest Modern Language Association* 33–34 (2000–2001): 122–36.

25. Wievorka, *Ère du témoin*, 37, 45–48, 101, 123, 150, 165, 167, 179–80.

26. Lejeune, "The Autobiography of Those Who Do Not Write," in *On Autobiography*, 196; "Ethnologie et littérature: *Gaston Lucas, serrurier,*" in *Moi Aussi*, 275, 284.

27. Stone, "Modern American Autobiography," 108.

28. Marcus, *Auto/biographical Discourses*, 12.

29. Gusdorf, "Conditions and Limits of Autobiography," 38, 29, 41, 43, 45, 48.

30. Marcus, *Auto/biographical Discourses*, 182, 183.

31. De Man, "Autobiography as De-facement," 919, 922, 930.

32. Lejeune, "Siècle de résistance à l'autobiographie," in *Pour l'autobiographie*, 11; see also Lecarme, "Hydre anti-autobiographique."

33. Bergland, "Postmodernism and the Autobiographical Subject," 134; Friedman, "Women's Autobiographical Selves," 75.

34. Gilmore, "Mark of Autobiography," 5.

35. Smith and Watson, introduction to *Women, Autobiography, Theory*, 25–26.

36. Ibid., 32.

37. Eakin, *Touching the World*, 29.

38. Eakin, *Fictions in Autobiography*, 3.

39. Spacks, *Imagining a Self*, 310–11.

40. Olney, *Metaphors of Self*, 38–41.

41. Lejeune, "Autobiographical Pact," in *On Autobiography*, 4, 5.

42. Marcus, *Auto/biographical Discourses*, 253.

43. Bruss, *Autobiographical Acts,* 10.

44. Lejeune, "Autobiographical Pact," 22, 25–26. Lejeune's views have developed considerably since the original publication of his essay in France in 1975, but primarily in the direction of a greater recognition of the inextricable relationship between autobiography and fiction rather than in the direction of greater concern about the historicity of autobiographical narrative.

45. Laqueur, *Thursday's Child Has Far to Go,* 401. Laqueur does not mention Lejeune's name, but he is clearly responding to his argument.

46. Bruss, *Autobiographical Acts,* 10–11.

47. Eakin, *Touching the World,* 141, 144–45, 180, 181.

48. McCooey, *Artful Histories,* 7, 189.

49. Ibid., 181.

50. Ibid., 10.

51. Novick, *That Noble Dream.*

CHAPTER 2

1. Lejeune, "Siècle de résistance à l'autobiographie," in *Pour l'autobiographie,* 24; Marcus, *Auto/biographical Discourses,* 246; Eakin, *Touching the World,* 194–95.

2. Berkhofer, *Beyond the Great Story.*

3. White, *Metahistory,* 2.

4. White, "Historical Text as Literary Artifact," 42, 60, 61.

5. Eakin, *Touching the World,* 50, 177.

6. Olney, *Metaphors of Self,* 36–37.

7. White, *Metahistory,* 22–29.

8. Vann, "Reception of Hayden White," 156, 148.

9. See the essays by Holocaust historian Christopher Browning and White in Friedländer, ed., *Probing the Limits of Representation,* 22–36 and 37–53 respectively.

10. Ricoeur, *Temps et récit,* 3:224; see also Ricoeur's comments on White in "Discussion: Ricoeur on Narrative," in Wood, ed., *On Paul Ricoeur,* 185–86, and his attack on "certain English-language 'narrativist' theorists" in Ricoeur, "Intellectual Autobiography," 45.

11. Ricoeur, *Temps et récit,* 1:13. References are to the French text, and translations are my own.

12. Augustine, *Confessions,* 230.

13. Karr, acknowledgments in *Liars' Club.*

14. Bruss, *Autobiographical Acts,* 10–11.

15. Anderson, *Imagined Communities.*

16. Ricoeur, "Narrative Identity," in Wood, ed., *On Paul Ricoeur,* 188.

17. Ricoeur, "Intellectual Autobiography," 3.

18. Ricoeur, "Narrative Time," 186.

19. White, "Metaphysics of Narrativity," 146, 153, 156. In his response to White's comments, Ricoeur took exception to what he saw as White's persistent effort to blur the distinction between history and fiction ("Discussion: Ricoeur on Narrative," in Wood, ed., *On Paul Ricoeur,* 185–86).

20. It is important to note that Carr had access to only the first of the three volumes of Ricoeur's *Time and Narrative* when writing his own book; he therefore does not respond to some of the most important aspects of Ricoeur's argument, such as his effort to define the characteristics of historical and fictional narratives.

21. This insight grows out of discussions at the National Humanities Center with the anthropologist Akhil Gupta during our year together there in 2000–2001.

22. "Discussion: Ricoeur on Narrative," 182.

23. Rémond, "Contemporain du contemporain," 294; Oliver, *Looking for the Phoenix*, 2.

CHAPTER 3

1. Dodd, "Criticism and the Autobiographical Tradition," 11.

2. Eakin, *Touching the World*, 144–45, 151.

3. Freeman, *Rewriting the Self*, 186.

4. Karl Marx, *The Eighteenth Brumaire of Louis Bonaparte*, in *The Marx-Engels Reader*, ed. Robert C. Tucker, 2nd ed. (New York: W. W. Norton, 1978), 595.

5. Weintraub, *Value of the the Individual*, 368.

6. Kermode, *Not Entitled*; Harlan, *All at Sea*.

7. Harlan, *All at Sea*, 35.

8. LaCapra, *Representing the Holocaust*, 45.

9. Rémond, "Contemporain du contemporain," 294.

10. Faust, "Living History," 40.

11. Kriegel, *Ce que j'ai cru comprendre*; Williamson, "Wounds Not Scars," which is followed by the comments of seven reviewers.

12. Friedländer, *When Memory Comes*, 144.

13. Steedman, *Landscape for a Good Woman*, 7.

14. Cecil Eby, *Book World*, 19 October 1969, quoted in *Book Review Digest*, 1969, 650.

15. Lejeune, *On Autobiography*, 235.

16. G. Mosse, *Confronting History*, 5.

17. Dawidowicz, *From That Place and Time*, xiv.

18. Oliver, *In the Realms of Gold*, xv.

19. Harlan, *All at Sea*, xi.

20. Post, *Memoirs of a Cold War Son*, xvii.

21. Gay, *My German Question*, 207.

22. Eire, *Waiting for Snow in Havana*, 385; Schmitt, *Lucky Victim*, 242; Hancock, *Country and Calling*, 41.

23. Letter of 1 February 1985, in Davies, ed., *Dear Kathleen, Dear Manning*, 64.

24. Petrie, *Historian Looks at His World*, 3.

25. Lal, *Mr. Tulsi's Store*, x.

26. Hughes, *Gentleman Rebel*, 20; Kenez, *Varieties of Fear*, 36.

27. M. Clark, *Puzzles of Childhood*, 2.

28. The event is mentioned briefly in an autobiographical sketch published during Croce's lifetime, *Autobiography*, 37, but the full horror of the experience, during which Croce, unable to move, had to listen to his father's dying cries, is recorded in passages excised from that work that were published after his death: Croce, *Memorie della mia vita*, 10–11.

29. Prochasson, "Jeux de 'je.'"

30. Myerhoff and Ruby, introduction to *Crack in the Mirror*, 5–6.

31. Gay, *My German Question*, x; Lincoln, *Coming through the Fire*, 7.

32. Nora, *Essais d'ego-histoire*, 7.

33. Passerini and Geppert, "Historians in Flux: The Concept, Task, and Challenge of Ego-histoire," in *European Ego-histoires*, 8.

34. Nora, "Ego-histoire est-elle possible?" 23.

35. Novick, *That Noble Dream.*

36. For a discussion of the term *ego-document,* see Rudolf Dekker, introduction to *Egodocuments and History,* 7–13.

37. Kuczynski, *Probleme der Autobiographie,* 38–39.

38. Nussbaum, *Autobiographical Subject,* 29.

39. On the theoretical issues posed by such publications, see Popkin, "Coordinated Lives."

40. Verene, *New Art of Autobiography,* 222.

41. The overall project, which grew to nearly thirty volumes and included contributions from philosophers, professors of medicine, economists, art historians, and specialists in education, law, and religion, was conceived by a Leipzig publisher, Felix Meiner (*Felix Meiner zum 70. Geburtstag* [n.p.: n.p., 1953], 41). The two volumes of essays by historians (Steinberg, ed., *Geschichtswissenschaft der Gegenwart*) include fourteen contributions. On the overall project and its significance, see Popkin, "Coordinated Lives," 783–84.

42. Grass, ed., *Österreichische Geschichtswissenschaft der Gegenwart.*

43. Abelove et al., eds., *Visions of History* (interviews from *Radical History Review*); Adelson, ed., *Speaking of History* (interviews from the *Historian*); Greenberg and Katz, eds., *Life of Learning* (ACLS lectures).

44. Crawford, Clark, and Blainey, *Making History;* Attwood, comp., *Boundaries of the Past;* Attwood and Damousi, eds., *Feminist Histories.*

45. Passerini and Geppert, eds., *European Ego-histoires.*

46. Alter, ed., *Out of the Third Reich;* Cimbala and Himmelberg, eds., *Historians and Race;* Gallagher, ed., *Approaches to the History of the Middle East;* Boris and Chaudhuri, eds., *Voices of Women Historians;* Boles, ed., *Autobiographical Reflections on Southern Religious History;* "Reflections on Pacific Historiography," special issue, *Journal of Pacific Studies* 20 (1996); Baron and Frierson, eds., *Adventures in Russian Historical Research.* Historians have also contributed to several volumes of autobiographical essays with an interdisciplinary focus, such as Rubin-Dorsky and Fishkin, eds., *People of the Book: Thirty Scholars Reflect on Their Jewish Identity,* and Dews and Law, eds., *This Fine Place So Far from Home: Voices of Academics from the Working Class.*

47. Steinberg, ed., *Geschichtswissenschaft der Gegenwart,* 1:vi.

48. Abelove et al., eds., *Visions of History,* xi.

49. Nora, introduction to *Essais d'ego-histoire,* 5.

50. Nora, "Entre mémoire et histoire," 1:xxxiii.

51. Nora, "Ego-histoire est-elle possible?" 19; Nora, introduction to *Essais d'ego-histoire,* 5.

52. Dintenfass, "Crafting Historians' Lives," 155.

53. Dover, *Marginal Comment,* 228–30.

54. B. G. Smith, *Gender of History,* 238.

55. Hicks, *My Life with History,* viii; Ariès, *Historien du dimanche,* 26; Lal, *Mr. Tulsi's Store,* ix–x.

56. Meinecke, *Erlebtes 1862–1901,* 7.

57. Fairbank, *Chinabound,* 451–54.

58. Ibid., 450; Taylor, preface to *Personal History.*

59. Mirabal, "Que sé yo," 265–72; Feimster, "New Generation of Women Historians," 275–81.

60. Friedländer, *When Memory Comes,* 145.

61. Conway, *When Memory Speaks.*

62. For a particularly explicit expression of this point of view, see P. Smith, "What Memoir Forgets."

63. *Choice*, March 1991, quoted in *Book Review Digest*, 1991, 207.

64. Passerini and Geppert, "Historians in Flux: The Concept, Task, and Challenge of *Ego-histoire*," in *European Ego-histoires*, 14.

65. Dalziell, *Shameful Autobiographie*, 6. The texts Dalziell analyzes include the autobiographies of Australian historians Hancock, Fitzpatrick, and Clark.

66. James J. Sosnoski, "Professional Hoops," in Di Leo, ed., *Affiliations*, 78–79.

67. Dodd, "Criticism and the Autobiographical Tradition," 9.

68. Philippe Ariès and Georges Duby, eds., *A History of Private Life*, 5 vols., trans. Arthur Goldhammer (Cambridge, Mass.: Harvard University Press, 1987–92); Jürgen Kuczynski, *Geschichte des Alltags des deutschen Volkes*, 5 vols. (Berlin: Akademie-Verlag, 1982–83).

69. Ménétra, *Journal of My Life*.

70. Jonathan Spence, *The Death of Woman Wang* (New York: Penguin, 1978).

71. Conway, *Road from Coorain*, 82.

72. Duberman, *Cures*, 37, 67, 122.

73. A colleague informs me that there has been an outpouring of first-person articles in Russian historical journals since the collapse of the Soviet regime.

74. Schulze, "Vergangenheit und Gegenwart der Historiker," 72.

75. Some fragments about Heimpel's postwar career are included in Heimpel, *Aspekte*.

76. Sheringham, *French Autobiography Devices*, ix.

77. Catherine Millet, *La vie sexuelle de Catherine M.* (Paris: Seuil, 2001). Millet's memoir caused a stir not only because of its sexual explicitness and the fact that its author was a woman but because she was a well-known figure in Parisian cultural circles.

78. On French culture's generalized hostility to autobiography, see Lejeune, "Siècle de résistance à l'autobiographie," in *Pour l'autobiographie*, 11–25; and Lecarme, "Hydre anti-autobiographique."

79. Kriegel, *Ce que j'ai cru comprendre*, 743, 710.

80. Trevelyan, *Autobiography and Other Essays*, 2.

81. Cobb, *End of the Line*.

CHAPTER 4

1. James D. Watson, *The Double Helix*, ed. Gunther S. Stent (New York: W. W. Norton, 1980).

2. Carnochan, *Gibbon's Solitude*, 4.

3. For foreign readers of Henry Adams, see Ferns, *Reading from Right to Left*, 53; Hancock, *Country and Calling*, 216; Kuczynski, *Memoiren. Die Erziehung des J. K. zum Kommunisten und Wissenschaftler* (Memoirs: The Education of J. K. as Communist and Scholar), 121; for Hertzberg's comment, see Hertzberg, *Jew in America*, 43, 451.

4. Spacks, *Imagining a Self*, 102.

5. Betty Radice, "Editor's Introduction," in Gibbon, *Memoirs of My Life* (Harmondsworth, U.K.: Penguin, 1984), 16.

6. Gibbon, *Memoirs*, ed. Bonnard, 119. The emphatic statement comes from the earliest draft of this passage of the *Memoirs;* in subsequent versions he was less definite about the matter (Carnochan, *Gibbon's Solitude*, 148).

7. Porter, "Gibbon's *Autobiography*," 4.

8. Gibbon, *Memoirs,* ed. Bonnard, 2.

9. Ibid., 1–2.

10. David Womersley has argued that at the time of his death, Gibbon had come around to the idea of publishing the work while he was still alive. Womersley, "Gibbon's *Memoirs,*" 349.

11. Gibbon, letter to Sheffield, 28 December 1791, in *Letters of Edward Gibbon,* 3:240.

12. Weintraub, *Value of the Individual,* 280.

13. Gibbon, *Memoirs,* ed. Bonnard, 1.

14. On Gibbon's rejection of parallels between Rome and the eighteenth-century British Empire, see Pocock, "Gibbon's *Decline and Fall,*" 148–50.

15. Gibbon, *Memoirs,* ed. Bonnard, 185; Wuthenow, *Das erinnerte Ich,* 140.

16. Spacks, *Imagining a Self,* 110–11.

17. Adams, *Education of Henry Adams,* 91.

18. *Letters of Henry Adams,* letters of 19 May 1860 (1:149), 7 September 1860 (1:183), 16 September 1888 (3:143).

19. Quoted in Wood, "Century of Early American History," 678.

20. Among the many stimulating analyses of *The Education of Henry Adams,* Levenson's *Mind and Art of Henry Adams* remains fundamental. Other discussions that I found useful include Bové, "Giving Thought to America"; Chalfant, "Lies, Silence, and Truth"; Davidoff, *Genteel Tradition;* Harbert, ed., *Critical Essays on Henry Adams;* Hume, *Runaway Star;* Jay, *America the Scrivener;* Lesser, "Criticism, Literary History, and the Paradigm"; Levenson, "Etiology of Israel Adams"; Parkhurst, "Manikin and the Memorial Bronze"; Porter, *Seeing and Being;* Rowe, *Henry Adams and Henry James;* Rowe, ed., *New Essays on the Education of Henry Adams;* and Simpson, *Political Education of Henry Adams.*

21. Brook Thomas, "The Education of an American Classic: The Survival of Failure," in Rowe, ed., *New Essays on the Education of Henry Adams,* 38.

22. Eakin, *Touching the World,* 145.

23. Adams to William James, 11 February 1908, in *Letters of Henry Adams,* 6:118.

CHAPTER 5

1. Ménétra, *Journal of My Life;* Perdiguier, *Mémoires d'un compagnon.*

2. Gilbert, *European Past,* 69–70.

3. For a discussion of the well-known story of the new methods of historical research and training introduced in Germany in the nineteenth century, with a special attention to their gender implications, see B. G. Smith, *Gender of History,* 103–29.

4. Meinecke, *Historism,* 416.

5. Schlesinger, *In Retrospect,* 3–5; Ariès, *Historien du dimanche,* 26; Brewer, "New Ways in History," 31.

6. Goubert, *Parcours d'historien,* 21.

7. Langer, *In and out of the Ivory Tower,* 44.

8. Billington, *Doctor B.,* 44.

9. B. Smith, *Boy Adeodatus,* 174; Sinclair, *Halfway round the Harbour,* 55; Lal, *Mr. Tulsi's Store,* 83.

10. Morison, *One Boy's Boston,* 69.

11. Historians whose fathers were lawyers include the Americans John King Fairbank, John Hope Franklin (whose mother was a schoolteacher), Paul Fussell, and H. Stuart Hughes; the Czech-born historians Susan Groag Bell and Saul Friedländer; and the French-

man Pierre Vidal-Naquet. Those with fathers who were businessmen include the French historians François Bluche and Paul Veyne; the Englishman A. J. P. Taylor; the German and Austrian Jews Evyatar Friesel, Walter Grab, Jacob Katz, Gershom Scholem, Raul Hilberg, Walter Laqueur, Gerda Lerner, Hans Schmitt, and Herbert Strauss; and the Americans Arthur Schlesinger Sr. and Natalie Davis. Engineers: Philippe Ariès (France), Hermann Heimpel (Germany). Schoolteachers: Maurice Agulhon, Jacques Le Goff, Mona Ozouf (France), Gareth Stedman Jones (England), Bruce Catton and David Levering Lewis (U.S.), K. M. Pannikar (India), Russel Ward (Australia). Clergy: Manning Clark and Keith Hancock (Australia), John Hicks and Edwin Reischauer (U.S.). University professors: Jürgen Kuczynski (Germany), Arthur Schlesinger Jr., Gaines Post Jr., Carolyn Bynum, Mary Beth Norton, John Demos, William McNeill (U.S.). Doctors: Alain Besançon, Elisabeth Roudinesco, Pierre Nora, Alain Corbin (France), John Brewer (England), Walter Ullmann, Francis Carsten, Walter Goetz (Germany).

12. E. O. Wilson, *Naturalist*, 52.

13. Fairbank, *Chinabound*, 7, 9–10.

14. G. S. Jones, "History and Theory," 106.

15. Herbst, *Requiem for a German Past*, 9.

16. Conway, *Road from Coorain*, 54.

17. Franklin, *Life of Learning*, 1.

18. Pannikar, *Autobiography*, 4–7, 14.

19. Boris and Chaudhuri, eds., *Voices of Women Historians*, 90 (Offen), 159 (Keller), 176 (Strobel), 219 (Winslow); Kriegel, *Ce que j'ai cru comprendre*, 51.

20. Bell, *Between Worlds*, 17.

21. Schlesinger, *Life in the Twentieth Century*, 62–63.

22. Strauss, *In the Eye of the Storm*, 26; for other memories of Karl May, see Gay, *My German Question*, 33; Kenez, *Varieties of Fear*, 89; and Presser, *Louter Verwachting*, 34.

23. Besançon, *Génération*, 59; Bluche, *Grenier à sel*, 41; Vidal-Naquet, *Mémoires*, 1:49–51; Schlesinger, *Life in the Twentieth Century*, 70–71; Katz, *With My Own Eyes*, 130.

24. Schlesinger, *Life in the Twentieth Century*, 68, 70–71. For other mentions of Henty, see Taylor, *Personal History*, 25, and Langer, *In and out of the Ivory Tower*, 23.

25. Hughes, *Gentleman Rebel*, 27; Zinn, *You Can't Be Neutral*, 168; Roland, *My Odyssey*, 8.

26. Girardet, "Ombre de la guerre," 141.

27. Ferns, *Reading from Left to Right*, 10.

28. Perrot, "Air du temps," 244.

29. Conway, *Road from Coorain*, 140; Ariès, *Historien du dimanche*, 39; Lal, *Mr. Tulsi's Store*, 22.

30. Zinn, *You Can't Be Neutral*, 169.

31. M. Clark, *Puzzles*, 145.

32. Kanner, "Growing into History," 148.

33. Stone, "Lawrence Stone," 18; Gay, *My German Question*, 98; Laqueur, *Thursday's Child*, 73–75.

34. Hobsbawm, *Interesting Times*, 314.

35. Perrot, "Air du temps," 247; Ariès, *Historien du dimanche*, 26.

36. May, *Coming to Terms*, 43, 57.

37. Conway, *Road from Coorain*, 131–32.

38. Toynbee, *Experiences*, 89.

39. Trevelyan, *Autobiography and Other Essays*, 9.

40. Gilbert, *European Past*, 25.

41. Hughes, *Gentleman Rebel,* 20, 24.

42. Chaunu, "Fils de la morte," 69.

43. Heimpel, *Halbe Violine,* 152–71.

44. On Heidegger's influence on Heimpel, see Ernst Schulin, *Hermann Heimpel und die deutsche Nationalgeschichtsschreibung* (Heidelberg: C. Winter, 1998), 30, and Klaus Sommer, review article of publications about Heimpel, "H-Soz-u-Kult," http://hsozkult.geschichte .hu-berlin.de/rezensio/buecher/1999/SoKlo299.htm.

45. Ariès, *Temps de l'histoire,* 16, 19, 22.

46. Catton, *Waiting for the Morning Train,* 198.

47. Harrison, *Scholarship Boy,* 32.

48. Cobb, *End of the Line,* 11–12.

49. Girardet, "Ombre de la guerre," 148.

50. Stone, "Lawrence Stone," 19.

51. Rowbotham, *Promise of a Dream,* 8.

52. Heimpel, *Halbe Violine,* 186.

53. Conway, *Road from Coorain,* 99.

54. M. Clark, *Puzzles,* 188.

55. B. Smith, *Boy Adeodatus,* 165.

56. Litwack, "Making of a Historian," 18.

57. Hobsbawm, *Interesting Times,* 55.

58. Ariès's father, an engineer, wanted him to follow in his footsteps (Ariès, *Historien du dimanche,* 48). G. Mosse, *Confronting History,* 94; Perrot, "Aire du temps," 247.

59. Lal, *Mr. Tulsi's Store,* 83.

60. Scholem, *From Berlin to Jerusalem,* 36–37; Naison, *White Boy,* x.

61. Langer, *In and out of the Ivory Tower,* 45; Billington, *Doctor B.,* 88–89; Clough, *Life I've Lived,* 22–23; in *Autobiographical Reflections on Southern Religious History,* see the remarks of Hill, "Southern Religion," 4, and Flynt, "Pilgrim's Progress," 81.

62. G. S. Jones, "History and Theory," 103.

63. Schorske, *Life of Learning,* 4–5; B. Smith, *Boy Adeodatus,* 297–98; May, *Coming to Terms,* 190; M. Clark, *Puzzles,* 192.

64. Offen, "Going against the Grain," 91.

65. Vidal-Naquet, *Mémoires,* 1:218.

66. Fitzpatrick, *Solid Bluestone Foundations,* 169.

67. Kriegel, *Ce que j'ai cru comprendre,* 292.

68. Liakos, "History Writing as the Return of the Repressed," 52; Bynum, interview in *Historian,* 6.

69. May, *Coming to Terms,* 196.

70. Lake, "Taking Our Past with Us," 42.

71. Nora, conclusion to *Essais d'ego-histoire,* 366.

72. Kearns, *Psychoanalysis, Historiography, and Feminist Theory,* 116.

73. Fitzpatrick, *Solid Bluestone Foundations,* 176.

74. Ferns, *Reading from Left to Right,* 35.

75. Ibid., 36; Fitzpatrick, *Solid Bluestone Foundations,* 179.

76. May, *Coming to Terms,* 231, 228.

77. Friesel, *Days and Seasons,* 71.

78. Ariès, *Historien du dimanche,* 53–54.

79. Hughes, *Gentleman Rebel,* 311.

80. Carroll, *Keeping Time,* 63–64; Keddie, "Nikki Keddie," 132.

81. Vidal-Naquet, *Mémoires,* 1:257.

82. Le Roy Ladurie, *Paris-Montpellier,* 42–49; Besançon, *Génération,* 182.

83. Goubert, *Parcours,* 137, 139, 142.

84. Perrot, "Aire du temps," 277.

85. Kriegel, *Ce que j'ai cru comprendre,* 616–17.

86. Duby, "Plaisir de l'historien," 133; Kriegel, *Ce que j'ai cru comprendre,* 292.

87. Cobb, *Second Identity,* 1, 46.

88. FitzGerald, *Why China?* 12.

89. Snay, *"Gospel of Disunion,"* 240, 234.

90. Catton, *Waiting for the Morning Train,* 41, 128–33; Toland, *Captured by History,* 23, 44.

91. Lerner, *Fireweed,* 114.

92. G. Mosse, *Confronting History,* 95.

93. Friesel, *Days and Seasons,* 29–33, 43–63.

94. Grab, *Meine vier Leben,* 122, 140.

95. Koenigsberger, "Fragments of an Unwritten Biography," 113.

96. Hilberg, *Politics of Memory,* 42.

97. Iggers and Iggers, *Zwei Seiten der Geschichte,* 310.

98. Bell, *Between Worlds,* 208.

99. Matthews, "Learning to See with Peripheral Vision," 2.

100. N. Z. Davis, *Life of Learning,* 1–4, 12.

101. N. Z. Davis, "Natalie Zemon Davis," in *Visions of History,* 103, 106–8.

102. Conway, *Road from Coorain,* 168, 192, 193.

103. Conway, *True North,* 58–59.

104. Passerini, *Autobiography of a Generation,* 32–36.

105. Conway, *True North,* 31, 33.

106. Toland, *Captured by History,* 82, 116–17, 127, 130.

CHAPTER 6

1. Hughes, "Work and the Self," 314.

2. Gini, *My Job, My Self,* 8.

3. "The Invisible Adjunct," posting of 2 March 2003, www.invisibleadjunct.com. According to its author this website was taken down on 9 June 2004. See also Scott Smallwood, "Disappearing Act: The Invisible Adjunct Shuts Down Her Popular Weblog and Says Goodbye to Academe," *Chronicle of Higher Education,* 30 April 2004, A10.

4. Goffman, *Presentation of Self,* 46.

5. Tilly, "Blanding In," 497.

6. Reviews of *The Double Helix:* R. C. Cowen, *Christian Science Monitor,* 7 May 1968, and anonymous, *Saturday Review,* 16 March 1968. Joshua Lederberg, "Introduction: Reflections on Scientific Biography," in *The Excitement and Fascination of Science,* ed. Joshua Lederberg (Palo Alto, Calif.: Annual Reviews, 1990), 3:xvii.

7. Pyne, "Stephen Pyne," 214.

8. R. Oliver, *In the Realms of Gold,* xv.

9. Cantor, *Inventing Norman Cantor.*

10. For one brief account by a historian who was denied tenure, see Fielding [pseud.], "John Fielding." Fielding did later find another teaching position.

11. Pyne, "Stephen Pyne," 200–220.

12. Gini and Sullivan, *It Comes with the Territory*, 2, 16; Michael Bérubé, "Working for the U.," in Di Leo, ed., *Affiliations*, 33–43.

13. Ringer, *Trouble in Academe*, 38–85; Zinn, *You Can't Be Neutral*, 185–92.

14. Pipes, *Vixi*, 91–92.

15. A particularly outspoken example is the French labor and immigration historian Gérard Noiriel in his essay "Désir de vérité." For a collection of American academic life narratives that often reflect a similar sense of alienation, see Dews and Law, *This Fine Place*.

16. Toynbee, *Experiences*, 66, 68.

17. Hobsbawm, *Interesting Times*, 298.

18. Taylor, preface to *Personal History*.

19. Taylor, *Personal History*, 14–15.

20. Ibid., 63, 71, 195, 216, 225.

21. Ibid., 76.

22. Billington, *Doctor B.*, 161.

23. Ibid., 189, 194.

24. Carroll, *Keeping Time*, 125, 120, 199.

25. Le Goff, *Vie pour l'histoire*, 124, 161.

26. Kriegel, *Ce que j'ai cru comprendre*, 297; Poliakov, *Mémoires*, 207.

27. Goubert, *Parcours*, 164.

28. Stone, "Lawrence Stone," 24.

29. Hughes, *Gentleman Rebel*, 297–98.

30. Durant and Durant, *Dual Autobiography*, 368.

31. Christophe Charle, "Etre historien en France: Une nouvelle profession?" in Bédarida, dir., *Histoire et le métier d'historien*, 22.

32. Sinclair, *Halfway round the Harbour*, 167.

33. G. Mosse, *Confronting History*, 150.

34. Kriegel, *Ce que j'ai cru comprendre*, 713.

35. Katz, *With My Own Eyes*, 139.

36. Jackson, chap. 13 of "Historian's Quest" (computer printout, 1992), 8–9. This episode is included in the augmented edition of Jackson's memoir published in Spanish in 1993, but not in his earlier *Historian's Quest*. I would like to thank Professor Jackson for letting me quote from the English manuscript of the material added to the Spanish edition of his book.

37. Meinecke, *Straßburg*, 7.

38. Ibid., 133.

39. Meinecke, *Erlebtes*, 119, 169.

40. Ibid., 182, 195.

41. Meinecke, *Straßburg*, 81.

42. Ibid., 26–27. Meinecke's former student Felix Gilbert, himself from a family of Jewish origin, notes that Meinecke supervised the doctoral dissertations of many Jewish students but was willing to support the *Habilitation* or promotion to eligibility for professorships only of students who had been baptized (Gilbert, *European Past*, 75).

43. Meinecke, *Straßburg*, 114.

44. Ibid., 56.

45. Meinecke, letter to W. Steffens, 7 November 1941, in *Aüsgewählter Briefwechsel*, 201.

46. Meinecke, *Straßburg*, 90–92.

47. Ibid., 98. Among the students he mentions are the Jewish philosopher Franz Rosenzweig, the future University of Chicago historian Hans Rothfels, and the trade union leader Lothar Erdmann, who died in a concentration camp.

48. Meinecke, *Erlebtes,* 176, 175.

49. Meinecke, *Straßburg,* 39–40.

50. Ibid., 41–42, 101–2.

51. Grimshaw, "Falling into Women's History," 10.

52. Meinecke, *Straßburg,* 110.

53. Baron and Frierson, eds., *Adventures in Russian Historical Research.*

54. Faust, "Living History," 41.

55. Duby, *History Continues,* 17.

56. Farge, *Goût de l'archive,* 141.

57. Kriegel, *Ce que j'ai cru comprendre,* 677.

58. Farge, *Archive,* 25.

59. Duby, *History Continues,* 40–41.

60. Taylor, *Personal History,* 97.

61. Woodward, *Thinking Back,* 19.

62. John Baldwin, foreword to Duby, *History Continues,* xii.

63. Duby, *History Continues,* 59–61.

64. May, *Coming to Terms,* 308.

65. Kriegel, *Ce que j'ai cru comprendre,* 706.

66. Clough, *Life I've Lived,* 244; Pipes, *Vixi,* 109.

67. Katz, *With My Own Eyes,* 164.

68. R. Oliver, *In the Realms of Gold,* 328–29.

69. Hobsbawm, *Interesting Times,* 253–54.

70. Hughes, *Gentleman Rebel,* 284–85.

71. G. Mosse, *Confronting History,* 164, 166, and *'Ich bleibe Emigrant,'* 62.

72. Jackson, chap. 16 of "Historian's Quest" (computer printout, 1992), 3; chap. 15, 10.

73. Billington, *Doctor B.,* 179–80.

74. Agulhon, "Vu des coulisses," 38.

75. Iggers and Iggers, *Zwei Seiten der Geschichte,* 171–72, 175–76.

76. Schorske, *Life of Learning,* 15–18.

77. Duberman, *Cures,* 147, 151.

78. Ringer, *Trouble in Academe,* 28.

79. Passerini, *Autobiography of a Generation,* 60, 96.

80. Bridenthal, "Making and Writing History Together," 81.

81. Roudinesco, *Généalogies,* 47.

82. Passerini, *Autobiography of a Generation,* 99, 112, 120–21.

83. Roudinesco, *Généalogies,* 60.

84. Weiner, "Domestic Constraints," 211; Cooper, "Shaping of a Feminist Historian," 65–70.

85. Bynum, interview in *Historian,* 7–8.

86. Bell, *Between Worlds,* 228.

CHAPTER 7

1. Panikkar, *Autobiography,* 281. As a young man, Panikkar was active in the Indian nationalist movement; after independence, he served as India's ambassador to China.

2. Catton, *Waiting for the Morning Train,* 225.

3. Toynbee, *Experiences,* 46.

4. Perkins, *Yield of the Years,* 59.

5. Langer, *In and out of the Ivory Tower*, 85.

6. Trevelyan, *Autobiography*, 38.

7. Heimpel, *Halbe Violine*, 239.

8. Heimpel describes the circumstances in which he began the composition of *Die halbe Violine* in an autobiographical fragment, "Göttingen. 'Weihnachten' 1944," published posthumously in *Aspekte*, 236–37.

9. Meinecke, *Straßburg*, 137.

10. Le Goff, *Vie pour l'histoire*, 7; Girardet, "Ombre de la guerre," 139.

11. May, *Coming to Terms*, 12.

12. Ward, *Radical Life*, 36.

13. Hobsbawm, *Interesting Times*, 114.

14. May, *Coming to Terms*, 204–5; Schorske, *Life of Learning*, 7.

15. G. Mosse, *Confronting History*, 101.

16. Collingwood, *Autobiography*, 167.

17. Schlesinger, *Life in the Twentieth Century*, 350–51; Reischauer, *My Life*, 89, 100–101; Zinn, *You Can't Be Neutral*, 95.

18. Lincoln, *Coming through the Fire*, 38; Franklin, *Life of Learning*, 14.

19. Schmitt, *Lucky Victim*, 186, 196–97, 191.

20. Taylor, *Personal History*, 151, 171.

21. Hobsbawm, *Interesting Times*, 154, 156.

22. May, *Coming to Terms*, 272–92.

23. Harlan, *All at Sea*, 122.

24. Sinclair, *Halfway round the Harbour*, 68, 110.

25. Jackson, *Historian's Quest*, 8.

26. Conway, *True North*, 49.

27. Langer, *Ivory Tower*, 195.

28. Hancock, *Country and Calling*, 197–202.

29. Schorske, *Life of Learning*, 8.

30. Hughes, *Gentleman Rebel*, 148, 179.

31. Fairbank, *Chinabound*, 182, 312.

32. Schlesinger, *Life in the Twentieth Century*, 299, 316, 353.

33. Clough, *Life I've Lived*, 137.

34. Kuczynski, *Memoiren*, 399–400, 414; Kuczynski, '*Linientreue Dissident,*' 18–20.

35. Ferns, *Reading from Left to Right*, 162, 139.

36. Hughes, *Gentleman Rebel*, 184.

37. Reischauer, *My Life*, 109.

38. Fairbank, *Chinabound*, 340–45; Hughes, *Gentleman Rebel*, 208, 223–24; Reischauer, *My Life*, 125–26.

39. Fussell, *Doing Battle*, preface, 101, 99, 105, 124.

40. Ibid., 267.

41. Roland, *My Odyssey*, 54–55. Professor Roland's first-person recollections were among the first stimuli to my interest in the subject of historians' memoirs.

42. Manchester, *Goodbye, Darkness*, 11.

43. Colton, "Reminiscences of the War," 10, 12.

44. Rémond, "Contemporain du contemporain," 297.

45. Chaunu, "Fils de la morte," 74.

46. Grosser, *Vie de français*, 32.

47. Girardet, *Singulièrement libre*, 52, 66, 69, 73, 75.

48. Kriegel, *Ce que j'ai cru comprendre*, 179, 194, 769.
49. Harlan, *All at Sea*, 177.
50. Fussell, *Doing Battle*, 174, 262–63.
51. Palmer, *Engagement with the Past*, 87–88.
52. Thompson, "E. P. Thompson," 11.
53. Ferns, *Reading from Left to Right*, 129, 133.
54. Besançon, *Génération*, 325.
55. Le Roy Ladurie, *Paris-Montpellier*, 36–37; Agulhon, "Vue des coulisses," 24.
56. Kriegel, *Ce que j'ai cru comprendre*, 195.
57. Ibid., 381.
58. Ibid., 610.
59. Le Roy Ladurie, *Paris-Montpellier*, 164.
60. Kriegel, *Ce que j'ai cru comprendre*, 539, 388, 557, 559.
61. Besançon, *Génération*, 191.
62. Hobsbawm, *Interesting Times*, 55–56, 127, 141.
63. Ibid., 45.
64. Kuczynski, *Memoiren*, 13.
65. Kuczynski, '*Linientreue Dissident,*' 27, 42–46, 47.
66. Toland, *Captured by History*, 97–98, 107.
67. Lerner, *Fireweed*, 225, 254, 262, 347.
68. Besançon, *Génération*, 325.
69. Franklin, *Life of Learning*, 8; Hughes, *Gentleman Rebel*, 57.
70. Carter, "Reflections of a Reconstructed White Southerner," 40, 42.
71. Flynt, "Pilgrim's Progress," 81.
72. Silver, *Running Scared*, 20–21, 58, 137, 139, 118.
73. Naison, *White Boy*, 16, 37, 44, 92.
74. Horowitz's coauthorship of popular histories of the Rockefeller, Kennedy, and Ford families gives him some claim to be considered a historian-autobiographer.
75. Naison, *White Boy*, 130, 155.
76. Passerini, *Autobiography of a Generation*, 51, 126, 135.
77. Ibid., 112, 120–21.
78. Roudinesco, *Généalogies*, 60, 59.

CHAPTER 8

1. The historians' recollections discussed in this chapter are Reuben Ainsztein, *In Lands Not My Own: A Wartime Journey*; Peter Alter, ed., *Out of the Third Reich: Refugee Historians in Post-war Britain*, with autobiographical essays by thirteen German- and Austrian-born historical scholars: Julius Carlebach, Francis Carsten, Edgar Feuchtwanger, J. A. S. Grenville, E. P. Hennock, Helmut Koenigsberger, Wolf Mendl, Werner Mosse, Helmut Pappe, Arnold Paucker, Sidney Pollard, Peter Pulzer, Nicholai Rubinstein, and Walter Ullmann; Walter Arnstein, "Walter Arnstein" (interview in Adelman, ed., *Speaking of History*); Susan Groag Bell, *Between Worlds: In Czechoslovakia, England, and America*; Reinhard Bendix, *From Berlin to Berkeley: German-Jewish Identities*; Helmut Eschwege, *Fremd unter meinesgleichen: Erinnerungen eines Dresdener Juden*; Saul Friedländer, *When Memory Comes*; Evyatar Friesel, *The Days and the Seasons*; Peter Gay, *My German Question: Growing Up in Nazi Berlin*; Felix Gilbert, *A European Past: Memoirs, 1905–1945*; Walter Grab, *Meine vier Leben: Gedächtnis-*

künstler—Emigrant—Jakobinerforscher—Demokrat; Alfred Grosser, *Une vie de français;* Theodore S. Hamerow, *Remembering a Vanished World: A Jewish Childhood in Interwar Poland;* Raul Hilberg, *The Politics of Memory: The Journey of a Holocaust Historian;* Eric Hobsbawm, *Interesting Times: A Twentieth-Century Life;* Wilma Iggers and Georg Iggers, *Zwei Seiten der Geschichte: Lebensbericht aus unruhigen Zeiten;* Jacob Katz, *With My Own Eyes: The Autobiography of an Historian;* Peter Kenez, *Varieties of Fear: Growing Up Jewish under Nazism and Communism;* Annie Kriegel, *Ce que j'ai cru comprendre;* Jürgen Kuczynski, *Memoiren. Die Erziehung des J. K. zum Kommunisten und Wissenschaftler* and *'Ein Linientreue Dissident': Memoiren 1945–1989;* Walter Laqueur, *Thursday's Child Has Far to Go;* Gerda Lerner, *Fireweed: A Political Autobiography;* Moshe Lewin, "Moshe Lewin" (interview in Abelove et al., eds., *Visions of History*); Gerhard Masur, *Das Ungewisse Herz: Berichte aus Berlin—über die Suche nach dem Freien;* George Mosse, *Confronting History;* Richard Pipes, *Vixi: Memoirs of a Non-belonger;* Léon Poliakov, *Mémoires;* Jacques Presser, *Louter Verwachting: Autobiografische Schets, 1899–1919;* Hans Schmitt, *Lucky Victim: An Ordinary Life in Extraordinary Times;* Dan Vittorio Segre, *Memoirs of a Fortunate Jew: An Italian Story;* Herbert A. Strauss, *In the Eye of the Storm: Growing Up Jewish in Germany, 1918–1943;* Nechama Tec, *Dry Tears: The Story of a Lost Childhood;* and Pierre Vidal-Naquet, *Mémoires: La brisure et l'attente* and *Mémoires: Le trouble et la lumière.* The earliest of these books, the first volume of Kuczynski's memoirs, was published in 1971; the most recent, by Richard Pipes, appeared in 2003. The oldest author, Gerhard Masur, was born in 1901; the youngest, Peter Kenez, in 1936.

2. Elie Wiesel, quoted in Dinitia Smith, "Random House to Aid Holocaust Memoir Project," *New York Times,* 4 October 2000, E6.

3. Patterson, *Sun Turned to Darkness,* 12.

4. Hilberg, *Politics of Memory,* 132. The phrase "I did not interview the dead" was the title of one of the first collections of survivors' testimony, put together by David Boder immediately after the war. See Niewyk, ed., *Fresh Wounds,* 5, which reprints some of Boder's interviews.

5. Hilberg, *Politics of Memory,* 74, 83.

6. Laqueur, *Thursday's Child,* 401.

7. The Holocaust historians: Ainsztein, Eschwege, Friedländer, Hilberg, Poliakov, Strauss, Tec. Those with at least one major book on related issues—some aspect of Holocaust, German, or German Jewish history in the pre-Hitler era, or the development of anti-Semitism: Carsten, Gay, Gilbert, Katz, Laqueur, G. Mosse, Presser, Schmitt, Vidal-Naquet. Those who never wrote on the subject outside of their memoirs: Bell, Bendix, Friesel, Grab, Grosser, Hamerow, Hobsbawm, Iggers, Kenez, Kriegel, Kuczynski, Lerner, Masur, Pipes, Segre, and all but one of the thirteen contributors to the Alter volume.

8. Poliakov's *Mémoires* is a composite text: the section on the war years was apparently composed in 1946 but not published then, and it was supplemented much later with chapters covering his life before and after the Holocaust period.

9. Hart, "Historian's Past," 135.

10. The only memoirs by academics who were actually in the camps that I have encountered so far are Klüger, *Still Alive,* by a literature scholar, and Halivni, *Book and the Sword,* by a scholar of rabbinics. Halivni claims that "there are not many academicians among the survivors" (160). The only historian-memoirists whose memoirs include stories of camp confinement are Ainsztein, who was interned in Spain for several years after escaping from France, and those like Kuczynski, who were held as enemy aliens in England in 1940.

11. Bendix, *From Berlin to Berkeley,* 194.

12. Friedländer, *When Memory Comes,* 155.

13. Grab, *Meine vier Leben,* 57. After terrorizing their captives, the Nazis did give them rags to work with, and Grab managed to talk his way out of the ordeal, but the experience remained traumatic. Lerner, *Fireweed,* 94 – 113.

14. Halivni, *Book and the Sword,* 158.

15. It might be argued that the brush with the Holocaust is incidental in a few of these volumes—those whose titles do not explicitly allude to the experience and in the texts of which one finds relatively little reflection of the event in comparison to other aspects of the authors' lives. Hobsbawm's, Kriegel's, Kuczynski's, Katz's, and Presser's memoirs (which cover only his boyhood years) would be at one end of the spectrum in this regard; Tec, whose memoir is devoted exclusively to her six years in German-occupied Poland, would be at the other extreme.

16. Kenez, *Varieties of Fear,* 7.

17. Gay, *My German Question,* 21.

18. Friedländer, *When Memory Comes,* 144.

19. Ka-Tzetnik 135663, *Kaddish,* 70. On Ka-Tzetnik's autobiographical practice, see Jeremy D. Popkin, "Ka-Tzetnik 135633: The Survivor as Pseudonym," *New Literary History* 33 (2002): 343 – 55.

20. Patterson, *Sun Turned to Darkness,* 16.

21. Bell, *Between Worlds,* 19.

22. Schmitt, *Lucky Victim,* 28.

23. Friedländer, *When Memory Comes,* 6; Lerner, *Fireweed,* 32.

24. Masur, *Ungewisse Herz,* 67 – 71, 159 – 61.

25. Bendix, *From Berlin to Berkeley,* 140 – 41.

26. Kriegel, *Ce que j'ai cru comprendre,* 49.

27. Iggers and Iggers, *Zwei Seiten der Geschichte,* 60 – 63; Strauss, *In the Eye of the Storm,* 8.

28. Schmitt, *Lucky Victim,* 65.

29. Bendix, *From Berlin to Berkeley,* 170, 192 – 93.

30. Friedländer, *When Memory Comes,* 69.

31. Laqueur, *Thursday's Child,* 105.

32. Schmitt, *Lucky Victim,* 66.

33. Bendix, *From Berlin to Berkeley,* 145.

34. Segre, *Memoirs of a Fortunate Jew,* 237 – 40.

35. Tec, *Dry Tears,* 197.

36. Poliakov, *Mémoires,* 99.

37. Bendix, *From Berlin to Berkeley,* 201, 215.

38. Moshe Lewin, a historian of the Soviet period who spent the Holocaust years in Russia before emigrating to Israel, makes similar comments about Israel in the 1950s in his autobiographical interview; "Moshe Lewin," 286.

39. G. Mosse, *Confronting History,* 172.

40. Vidal-Naquet, *Mémoires: La brisure,* 112 – 14.

41. Ibid., 272.

42. Friesel, *Days and Seasons,* 180; Gay, *My German Question,* 203 – 4.

43. Pipes, *Vixi,* 55 – 56.

44. Hilberg, *Politics of Memory,* 59 – 60, 61, 74.

45. Poliakov, *Mémoires,* 186, 200.

46. G. Mosse, *Confronting History,* 176.

47. Friedländer, *When Memory Comes*, 144–45.

48. Schmitt, *Lucky Victim*, 66.

49. Bendix, *From Berlin to Berkeley*, 208.

50. Vidal-Naquet, *Mémoires*, 1:263.

51. Iggers and Iggers, *Zwei Seiten der Geschichte*, 131, 307–8.

52. Kenez, *Varieties of Fear*, 179, 211.

53. Bendix, *From Berlin to Berkeley*, 289–90, 298.

54. Ibid., 197, 212, 239.

55. Bendix, "How I Became an American Sociologist," 470–74.

56. G. Mosse, *Confronting History*, 6, 121–22.

57. Friedländer, *When Memory Comes*, 121.

58. Ibid., 155–56.

59. Foster, "Cultural Multiplicity," 210.

60. G. Mosse, *Confronting History*, 190, 197–98.

61. Iggers and Iggers, *Zwei Seiten der Geschichte*, 183.

62. Kriegel, *Ce que j'ai cru comprendre*, 761, 783.

63. Eschwege, *Fremd*, 48–50, 90–92.

64. Friesel, *Days and Seasons*, 9; Hennock, "Myself as Historian," 87.

65. Laqueur, *Thursday's Child*, 367.

66. Gay, *My German Question*, 191, 200.

67. G. Mosse, *Confronting History*, 213.

68. Alfred Grosser became France's best-known expert on German affairs, Walter Grab headed an institute of German history in Israel founded by German donors, Edgar Feucht-wanger helped create an exchange program between British and German universities, and Georg Iggers promoted a range of academic exchanges with scholars in West and East Germany.

69. Laqueur, *Thursday's Child*, 366.

70. W. Mosse, "Self-Discovery," 158.

71. G. Mosse, *Confronting History*, 194.

72. Hilberg, *Politics of Memory*, 175.

73. G. Mosse, *Confronting History*, 42, 64, 44.

74. Haffner's memoir was written in 1939, soon after he left Germany for exile in England, but was published only after his death.

75. Herbst, *Requiem for a German Past*, 228.

76. Vidal-Naquet, *Mémoires: Le trouble*, 262.

77. Bell, *Between Worlds*, 144.

78. The Library of Congress, for example, has assigned Peter Gay's *My German Question* a "DS" call number, placing it firmly in the category of Jewish history, even though its title makes no reference to Jews or Judaism.

79. Kriegel, *Ce que j'ai cru comprendre*, 753.

80. Lerner, *Fireweed*, 223–24.

81. Gay, *My German Question*, 124.

82. Lerner, *Fireweed*, 207.

83. Gay, *My German Question*, 22.

84. Hans Schmitt, criticizing historians' emphasis on elites who shaped public events, justifies autobiographies as "individual small steps toward a general upstairs-downstairs synthesis" (Schmitt, *Lucky Victim*, 2).

CHAPTER 9

1. Like Georges Gusdorf, Roy Pascal, another of the forerunners of the great explosion in autobiographical studies in the second half of the twentieth century, calls the period from 1782 to 1831 "decisive in the history of autobiography" (Pascal, *Design and Truth*, 50), and Karl Joachim Weintraub concludes that only conditions in the age of Goethe, "the great age of liberalism and individualism," had made the highest form of autobiography possible (Weintraub, *Value of the Individual*, 378). For a critique of this tendency to idealize the achievements of the first generation of "modern" autobiographers, see Marcus, *Auto/biographical Discourses*, 164.

2. Sturrock, "New Model Autobiographer," 54.

3. Sheringham, *French Autobiography*, 327.

4. Stanley, *Autobiographical "I,"* 247.

5. Simon Schama, *Dead Certainties* (New York: Alfred A. Knopf, 1991).

6. Kuczynski, *Probleme der Autobiographie*, 46, 94. On Kuczynski's passion for Henry Adams, see Kuczynski, *Memoiren*, 121. He abandons the third-person voice in the second volume of his memoirs.

7. Kuczynski, *Memoiren*, 144.

8. Marcus, *Auto/biographical Discourses*, 275, 278.

9. Scott, foreword to Passerini's *Autobiography of a Generation*, xiii.

10. Eakin, *Fictions in Autobiography*, 237–55; Ezrahi, "See Under: Memory," 366.

11. Clendinnen, *Tiger's Eye*, 286.

12. Ricoeur, *Oneself as Another*, 54.

13. Steedman, *Landscape for a Good Woman*, 6, 5.

14. Fraser, *In Search of a Past*, 118.

15. Passerini, *Autobiography of a Generation*, 36.

16. Steedman, *Landscape for a Good Woman*, 7.

17. Fraser, *In Search of a Past*, 118; Passerini, *Autobiography of a Generation*, 124.

18. Parati, *Public History, Private Stories*, 129.

19. Ronald Fraser et al., *A Student Generation in Revolt* (London: Chatto and Windus, 1987).

20. Passerini, *Autobiography of a Generation*, 124.

21. Duncan, "Corporeal Histories," 371.

22. Parati, *Public History, Private Stories*, 149.

23. Holocaust narratives that parallel Friedländer's in this regard include Frida Scheps Weinstein, *A Hidden Childhood: A Jewish Girl's Sanctuary in a French Convent, 1942–1945*, trans. Barbara Loeb Kennedy (New York: Hill and Wang, 1985), and Sarah Kofman, *Rue Ordener, Rue Labat*, trans. Ann Smock (Lincoln: University of Nebraska Press, 1996), both set in France, and Tec, *Dry Tears* (1982), a story from Poland.

24. Friedländer, *When Memory Comes*, 80, 94.

25. Eakin, *Fictions in Autobiography*, 250.

26. Friedländer, "Trauma, Transference, and 'Working Through,'" 51.

27. Ibid., 53, 44, 52.

28. For a brief sketch of Clendinnen's career, before and after her illness, see Jane Wheatley, "Stories from over the Horizon," *Sunday Times* (London), 13 January 2001, 13.

29. Clendinnen, *Tiger's Eye*, 13–14.

30. Duberman, *Cures*, 125.

31. Duberman, *Midlife Queer*, 30.

32. Lejeune, "Autobiographical Pact," in *On Autobiography*, 5.

33. McCloskey, *Crossing*, 219.

34. McCloskey, interview by Polyani, 26.

35. McCloskey, *Crossing*, xiii.

36. Duberman, *Cures*, 199.

37. McCloskey, *Crossing*, 113.

38. Duberman, *Cures*, 223; McCloskey, *Crossing*, 255.

39. Hine, *Second Sight*, 136, 41, 132.

40. Kenez, *Varieties of Fear*, 123; Harlan, *All at Sea*, 54; B. Smith, *Boy Adeodatus*, 270–73; Hughes, *Gentleman Rebel*, 163–65; Veyne, *Quotidien et l'intéressant*, 23–28; Lerner, *Fireweed*, 69, 188.

41. Finney, "Sexual Identity in Modern British Autobiography," 29.

42. G. Mosse, *Confronting History*, 118, 197–98.

43. Duberman, *Cures*, 190.

44. Robinson, *Gay Lives*, 335–63.

45. Duberman, *Cures*, 21.

46. Robinson, *Gay Lives*, 349–50.

47. Duberman, *Midlife Queer*, 226.

48. McCloskey, *Crossing*, 18.

49. McCloskey, interview by Polyani, 17.

50. McCloskey, *Crossing*, xi–xii.

CONCLUSION

1. Nora, "Présentation," in *Essais d'ego-histoire*, 5; Nora, "Ego-histoire est-elle possible?" 19.

2. Jacques Derrida, *Of Grammatology*, trans. Gayatri Chakravarty Spivak (Baltimore: Johns Hopkins University Press, 1974), 144–45.

3. Eakin, *Touching the World*, 180; Lejeune, "Autobiographical Pact (bis)," in *On Autobiography*, 131–32.

4. Dintenfass, "Crafting Historians' Lives," 165.

5. Bruner and Weisser, "Invention of Self," 133.

6. Latekefu, "Making of the First Tongan-Born Professional Historian."

BIBLIOGRAPHY

HISTORIANS' AUTOBIOGRAPHICAL PUBLICATIONS

Abelove, Henry, Betsy Blackmar, Peter Dimock, and Jonathan Schneer, eds. *Visions of History.* New York: Pantheon, 1984.

Adams, Henry. *The Education of Henry Adams.* 1918; reprint Boston: Houghton Mifflin, 1971.

Adam-Smith, Patsy. *Goodbye Girlie.* Ringwood, Aust.: Penguin, 1994.

———. *Hear the Train Blow.* 1964; reprint Adelaide, Aust.: Rigby, 1971.

Adelson, Roger, ed. *Speaking of History: Conversations with Historians.* East Lansing: Michigan State University Press, 1997.

Agulhon, Maurice. "Vue des coulisses." In *Essais d'ego-histoire,* ed. Pierre Nora, 9–59. Paris: Gallimard, 1987.

Ainsztein, Reuben. *In Lands Not My Own: A Wartime Journey.* New York: Random House, 2002.

Alter, Peter, ed. *Out of the Third Reich: Refugee Historians in Post-war Britain.* London: I. B. Tauris, 1998.

Anastos, Milton V. "Milton V. Anastos." In *The Life of Learning,* ed. Douglas Greenberg and Stanley N. Katz, 37–52. New York: Oxford University Press, 1994.

Ariès, Philippe. *Un historien du dimanche.* Paris: Seuil, 1980.

———. *Le temps de l'histoire.* Monaco: Editions du Rocher, 1954.

Arnstein, Walter. "Walter Arnstein" (interview). In *Speaking of History,* ed. Roger Adelson, 1–21. East Lansing: Michigan State University Press, 1997.

Attwood, Bain, comp. *Boundaries of the Past.* Victoria, Aust.: History Institute, 1990.

———, ed. *Labour Histories.* Caulfield East, Aust.: Monash University Printing Services, 1994.

Attwood, Bain, and Joy Damousi, eds. *Feminist Histories.* Victoria, Aust.: History Institute, 1991.

Ayers, Edward L. "Borders, Boundaries, and Edges: A Southern Autobiography." In *Shapers of Southern History,* ed. John B. Boles, 311–32. Athens: University of Georgia Press, 2004.

Badger, Anthony J. "Southern History from the Outside." In *Shapers of Southern History,* ed. John B. Boles, 203–19. Athens: University of Georgia Press, 2004.

Baron, Samuel H., and Cathy A. Frierson, eds. *Adventures in Russian Historical Research:*

Reminiscences of American Scholars from the Cold War to the Present. Armonk, N.Y.: M. E. Sharpe, 2003.

Bassett, Jan. *The Facing Island: A Personal History.* Carlton, Aust.: Melbourne University Press, 2002.

Beilharz, Peter. "Socialism by the Back Door." In *Labour Histories,* ed. Bain Attwood, 43–50. Caulfield East, Aust.: Monash University Printing Services, 1994.

Bell, Susan Groag. *Between Worlds: In Czechoslovakia, England, and America.* New York: E. P. Dutton, 1991.

Beloch, Karl Julius. "Karl Julius Beloch." In *Die Geschichtswissenschaft der Gegenwart in Selbstdarstellungen,* ed. Sigfrid Steinberg, 2:1–27. Leipzig: Felix Meiner, 1925.

Beloff, Max. *A Historian in the Twentieth Century.* New Haven, Conn.: Yale University Press, 1992.

Below, Georg von. "Georg von Below." In *Die Geschichtswissenschaft der Gegenwart in Selbstdarstellungen,* ed. Sigfrid Steinberg, 1:1–49. Leipzig: Felix Meiner, 1925.

Bendix, Reinhard. *From Berlin to Berkeley: German-Jewish Identities.* New Brunswick, N.J.: Transaction, 1986. (German edition: Bendix, Reinhard. *Von Berlin nach Berkeley: Deutschjüdische Identitäten.* Trans. Holger Fliessbach. Frankfurt: Suhrkamp, 1985.)

———. "How I Became an American Sociologist." In *Authors of Their Own Lives: Intellectual Autobiographies by Twenty American Sociologists,* ed. Bennett M. Berger, 452–75. Berkeley: University of California Press, 1991.

Besançon, Alain. *Une génération.* Paris: Juillard, 1987.

Billington, James H. Interview. *The Historian* 64 (2001): 1–18.

Billington, Monroe Lee. *Doctor B.: The Making of a History Professor.* Ruidoso, N.M.: New Mexico Historical Consultants, 2000.

Bluche, François. *Le grenier à sel.* Paris: Fallois, 1991.

Blum, John Morton. *A Life with History.* Lawrence: University Press of Kansas, 2004.

Bode, Frederick A. "Growing Up a Historian." In *Autobiographical Reflections on Southern Religious History,* ed. John Boles, 89–110. Athens: University of Georgia Press, 2001.

Boles, John B., ed. *Autobiographical Reflections on Southern Religious History.* Athens: University of Georgia Press, 2001.

———. "Coming of Age in the Bible Belt." In *Autobiographical Reflections on Southern Religious History,* ed. John Boles, 111–30. Athens: University of Georgia Press, 2001.

———, ed. *Shapers of Southern History.* Athens: University of Georgia Press, 2004.

Boris, Eileen. "In Circles Comes Change." In *Voices of Women Historians,* ed. Eileen Boris and Nupur Chaudhuri, 191–205. Bloomington: Indiana University Press, 1999.

Boris, Eileen, and Nupur Chaudhuri, eds. *Voices of Women Historians: The Personal, the Political, the Professional.* Bloomington: Indiana University Press, 1999.

Borodkin, Leonid. "From Science to History: Ego-History in the Context of Transition Society." In *European Ego-histoires,* ed. Luisa Passerini and Alexander C. T. Geppert, 75–88. Athens: Nefeli, 2001.

Braudel, Fernand. "Personal Testimony." *Journal of Modern History* 44 (1972): 448–67.

Bresslau, Harry. "Harry Bresslau." In *Die Geschichtswissenschaft der Gegenwart in Selbstdarstellungen,* ed. Sigfrid Steinberg, 2:29–83. Leipzig: Felix Meiner, 1925.

Brewer, John. "New Ways in History; or, Talking about My Generation." In *European Ego-histoires,* ed. Luisa Passerini and Alexander C. T. Geppert, 27–46. Athens: Nefeli, 2001.

Bridenthal, Renate. "Making and Writing History Together." In *Voices of Women Historians,* ed. Eileen Boris and Nupur Chaudhuri, 77–84. Bloomington: Indiana University Press, 1999.

Brown, Peter. *A Life of Learning*. New York: American Council of Learned Societies, 2003.

Buckley, Thomas E. "I Just Can't Get out of Virginia: A Personal Journey." In *Autobiographical Reflections on Southern Religious History*, ed. John Boles, 159–76. Athens: University of Georgia Press, 2001.

Burgmann, Verity. "Solving the Riddle of History." In *Labour Histories*, ed. Bain Attwood, 28–42. Caulfield East, Aust.: Monash University Printing Services, 1994.

Burton, Vernon. "Stranger in a Strange Land: Crossing Boundaries." In *Shapers of Southern History*, ed. John B. Boles, 256–83. Athens: University of Georgia Press, 2004.

Bynum, Carolyn. Interview. *The Historian* 59 (1996): 1–18.

Calhoon, Robert M. "Cusp of Spring." In *Autobiographical Reflections on Southern Religious History*, ed. John Boles, 53–72. Athens: University of Georgia Press, 2001.

Cantor, Norman F. *Inventing Norman Cantor: Confessions of a Medievalist*. Tempe, Ariz.: Arizona Center for Medieval and Renaissance Studies, 2002.

Carlebach, Julius. "Journey to the Centre of the Periphery." In *Out of the Third Reich*, ed. Peter Alter, 1–23. London: I. B. Tauris, 1998.

Carroll, Berenice A. "Three Faces of Trevia: Identity, Activism, and Intellect." In *Voices of Women Historians*, ed. Eileen Boris and Nupur Chaudhuri, 13–28. Bloomington: Indiana University Press, 1999.

Carroll, Peter N. *Keeping Time*. Athens: University of Georgia Press, 1990.

Carsten, Francis L. "From Revolutionary Socialism to German History." In *Out of the Third Reich*, ed. Peter Alter, 25–39. London: I. B. Tauris, 1998.

Carter, Dan T. "Reflections of a Reconstructed White Southerner." In *Historians and Race*, ed. Paul A. Cimbala and Robert F. Himmelberg, 33–50. Bloomington: Indiana University Press, 1996.

———. "Scattered Pieces: Living and Writing Southern History." In *Shapers of Southern History*, ed. John B. Boles, 115–36. Athens: University of Georgia Press, 2004.

Catton, Bruce. *Waiting for the Morning Train: An American Boyhood*. 1972; reprint Detroit: Wayne State University Press, 1987.

Chaudhuri, Nupur. "Bahupath Perie." In *Voices of Women Historians*, ed. Eileen Boris and Nupur Chaudhuri, 121–33. Bloomington: Indiana University Press, 1999.

Chaunu, Pierre. "Le fils de la morte." In *Essais d'ego-histoire*, ed. Pierre Nora, 61–107. Paris: Gallimard, 1987.

Cimbala, Paul A., and Robert F. Himmelberg, eds. *Historians and Race: Autobiography and the Writing of History*. Bloomington: Indiana University Press, 1996.

Clark, Manning. *Historian's Apprenticeship*. Carlton, Aust.: Melbourne University Press, 1992.

———. *The Puzzles of Childhood*. Ringwood, Aust.: Viking, 1989.

———. *The Quest for Grace*. Ringwood, Aust.: Viking, 1990.

Clark, Thomas D. "Thomas D. Clark" (interview). In *Speaking of History*, ed. Roger Adelson, 22–38. East Lansing: Michigan State University Press, 1997.

Clendinnen, Inga. *Tiger's Eye: A Memoir*. New York: Scribner, 2001.

Clough, Shepard Bancroft. *The Life I've Lived: The Formation, Career, and Retirement of an Historian*. Washington, D.C.: University Press of America, 1981.

Cobb, Richard. *A Classical Education*. London: Chatto and Windus, 1985.

———. *The End of the Line: A Memoir*. London: John Murray, 1997.

———. *A Second Identity. Essays on France and French History*. London: Oxford University Press, 1969.

———. *Something to Hold Onto: Autobiographical Sketches*. 1988.

———. *Still Life: Sketches from a Tunbridge Wells Childhood*. London: Chatto and Windus, 1983.

Collingwood, R[obin] G[eorge]. *An Autobiography*. Oxford: Oxford University Press, 1939.

Colton, Joel. "Reminiscences of the War." *Army History: The Professional Bulletin of Army History* PB-20-95-3, no. 35 (Fall 1995): 9–15. Mostly reprinted in Joel Colton, "Occupation and Affirmation," *Duke Magazine* 81 (July-August 1995): 43–45.

Conway, Jill Ker. *The Road from Coorain*. 1989; reprint New York: Vintage, 1990.

———. *True North*. New York: Alfred A. Knopf, 1994.

———. *A Woman's Education*. New York: Alfred A. Knopf, 2001.

Cooper, Sandi. "The Shaping of a Feminist Historian." In *Voices of Women Historians*, ed. Eileen Boris and Nupur Chaudhuri, 63–74. Bloomington: Indiana University Press, 1999.

Corbin, Alain. *Historien du sensible. Entretiens avec Gilles Heuré*. Paris: La Découverte, 2000.

Corris, Peter. *Sweet and Sour: A Diabetic Life*. Lismore, Aust.: Southern Cross University Press, 2000.

Crawford, R. M., Manning Clark, and Geoffrey Blainey. *Making History*. Fitzroy, Aust.: McPhee Gribble/Penguin, 1985.

Croce, Benedetto. *An Autobiography*. Trans. R. G. Collingwood. Oxford: Clarendon, 1927.

———. *Memorie della mia vita. Appunti che sono stati adoprati e sostituiti dal 'Contributo alla critica di me stesso.'* Naples: Istituto italiano per gli studi storici, 1966.

Curthoys, Anne. "Romancing the Past." In *Feminist Histories*, ed. Bain Attwood and Joy Damousi, 23–37. Victoria, Aust.: History Institute, 1991.

Daniel, Pete. "Accidental Historian." In *Shapers of Southern History*, ed. John B. Boles, 164–86. Athens: University of Georgia Press, 2004.

Davis, Mollie C. "Two Catalysts in My Life: Voter Registration Drives and CCWHP." In *Voices of Women Historians*, ed. Eileen Boris and Nupur Chaudhuri, 135–44. Bloomington: Indiana University Press, 1999.

Davis, Natalie Zemon. "Natalie Zemon Davis" (interview). In *Visions of History*, ed. Henry Abelove et al., 99–122. New York: Pantheon, 1984.

———. "Natalie Zemon Davis" (interview). In *Speaking of History*, ed. Roger Adelson, 40–59. East Lansing: Michigan State University Press, 1997.

———. *A Life of Learning*. ACLS Occasional Paper 39. New York: American Council of Learned Societies, 1997.

Davison, Graeme. "A Sense of Place." In *Boundaries of the Past*, comp. Bain Attwood, 28–35. Victoria, Aust.: History Institute, 1990.

Dawidowicz, Lucy S. *From That Place and Time: A Memoir, 1938–1947*. New York: W. W. Norton, 1989.

Demos, John. "John Demos" (interview). In *Speaking of History*, ed. Roger Adelson, 60–80. East Lansing: Michigan State University Press, 1997.

Dening, Greg. "Ethnography on My Mind." In *Boundaries of the Past*, comp. Bain Attwood, 14–21. Victoria, Aust.: History Institute, 1990.

Denoon, Donald. "An Accidental Historian." *Journal of Pacific Studies* 20 (1996): 209–12.

Dews, C. L. Barney, and Carolyn Leste Law, eds. *This Fine Place So Far from Home: Voices of Academics from the Working Class*. Philadelphia: Temple University Press, 1995.

Djordjevic, Dimitrije. *Scars and Memory: Four Lives in One Lifetime*. Boulder, Colo.: East European Monographs, 1997.

Dopsch, Alfons. "Alfons Dopsch." In *Die Geschichtswissenschaft der Gegenwart in Selbstdarstellungen*, ed. Sigfrid Steinberg, 1:51–90. Leipzig: Felix Meiner, 1925.

Dover, Kenneth James. *Marginal Comment: A Memoir*. London: Duckworth, 1995.

Duberman, Martin. *Cures: A Gay Man's Odyssey.* New York: E. P. Dutton, 1991.

———. *Midlife Queer: Autobiography of a Decade, 1971–1981.* New York: Scribner, 1996.

Duby, Georges. *History Continues.* Trans. Arthur Goldhammer. 1991; reprint Chicago: University of Chicago Press, 1994.

———. "Le plaisir de l'historien." In *Essais d'ego-histoire,* ed. Pierre Nora, 109–38. Paris: Gallimard, 1987.

Duden, Barbara. "A Historian's 'Biology': On the Traces of the Body in a Technogenic World." In *European Ego-histoires,* ed. Luisa Passerini and Alexander C. T. Geppert, 89–102. Athens: Nefeli, 2001.

Durant, Will, and Ariel Durant. *A Dual Autobiography.* New York: Simon and Schuster, 1977.

Eire, Carlos. *Waiting for Snow in Havana: Confessions of a Cuban Boy.* New York: Free Press, 2003.

Eschwege, Helmut. *Fremd unter meinesgleichen: Erinnerungen eines Dresdner Juden.* Berlin: Ch. Links Verlag, 1991.

Evans, Sara Margaret. Interview. *The Historian* 63 (2000): 1–16.

Fairbank, John King. *Chinabound: A Fifty-Year Memoir.* New York: Harper and Row, 1982.

Farge, Arlette. *Le goût de l'archive.* Paris: Seuil, 1989.

Faust, Drew Gilpin. "Living History." In *Shapers of Southern History,* ed. John B. Boles, 220–36. Athens: University of Georgia Press, 2004. (Orig. pub. in *Harvard Magazine,* May-June 2003, 38–46, 82–83.)

Feimster, Crystal. "A New Generation of Women Historians." In *Voices of Women Historians,* ed. Eileen Boris and Nupur Chaudhuri, 275–81. Bloomington: Indiana University Press, 1999.

Ferns, Henry Stanley. *Reading from Left to Right: One Man's Political History.* Toronto: University of Toronto Press, 1983.

Feuchtwanger, Edgar J. "Recovering from Culture Shock." In *Out of the Third Reich,* ed. Peter Alter, 41–54. London: I. B. Tauris, 1998.

Fielding, John [pseud.]. "John Fielding." In *American Dreams Lost and Found,* by Studs Terkel, 67–74. New York: Pantheon, 1980.

Finke, Heinrich. "Heinrich Finke." In *Die Geschichtswissenschaft der Gegenwart in Selbstdarstellungen,* ed. Sigfrid Steinberg, 1:91–128. Leipzig: Felix Meiner, 1925.

Fisher, H. A. L. *An Unfinished Autobiography.* London: Oxford University Press, 1941.

Fite, Gilbert C. "Gilbert C. Fite" (interview). In *Speaking of History,* ed. Roger Adelson, 83–103. East Lansing: Michigan State University Press, 1997.

FitzGerald, C. P. *Why China?* Melbourne, Aust.: Melbourne University Press, 1985.

Fitzpatrick, Kathleen. "A Cloistered Life." In *The Half-Open Door,* ed. Patricia Grimshaw and Lynne Strahan, 119–33. Sydney, Aust.: Hale and Iremonger, 1982.

———. *Solid Bluestone Foundations.* 1983; reprint Carlton South, Aust.: Melbourne University Press, 1998.

Flynt, Wayne. "A Pilgrim's Progress through Southern Christianity." In *Autobiographical Reflections on Southern Religious History,* ed. John Boles, 73–88. Athens: University of Georgia Press, 2001.

Foner, Eric. "My Life as a Historian." In *Historians and Race,* ed. Paul A. Cimbala and Robert F. Himmelberg, 91–110. Bloomington: Indiana University Press, 1996.

Frances, Raelene. "Fringe History." In *Labour Histories,* ed. Bain Attwood, 51–64. Caulfield East, Aust.: Monash University Printing Services, 1994.

Franklin, John Hope. "A Life of Learning." In *Shapers of Southern History,* ed. John B. Boles,

1–17. Athens: University of Georgia Press, 2004. (Orig. pub. as *A Life of Learning*. New York: American Council of Learned Societies, 1988. Reprinted in *The Life of Learning*, ed. Douglas Greenberg and Stanley N. Katz, 71–85. New York: Oxford University Press, 1994.)

Fraser, Ronald. *In Search of a Past: The Rearing of an English Gentleman, 1933–1945.* New York: Atheneum, 1984.

Friedländer, Saul. *When Memory Comes.* Trans. Helen R. Lane. New York: Avon, 1980.

Friedman, Jean E. "Personal Reflections on Community and the Writing of American Religious History." In *Autobiographical Reflections on Southern Religious History,* ed. John Boles, 177–92. Athens: University of Georgia Press, 2001.

Friesel, Evyatar. *The Days and the Seasons.* Detroit, Mich.: Wayne State University Press, 1996.

Fussell, Paul. *Doing Battle: The Making of a Skeptic.* Boston: Little, Brown, 1996.

Gallagher, Nancy Elizabeth, ed. *Approaches to the History of the Middle East: Interviews with Leading Middle East Historians.* Reading, U.K.: Ithaca, 1994.

Gardthausen, Victor. "Victor Gardthausen." In *Die Geschichtswissenschaft der Gegenwart in Selbstdarstellungen,* ed. Sigfrid Steinberg, 2:85–110. Leipzig: Felix Meiner, 1925.

Gaxotte, Pierre. *Les autres et moi.* Paris: Flammarion, 1975.

———. *Mon village et moi.* Paris: Flammarion, 1968.

Gay, Peter, *My German Question: Growing Up in Nazi Berlin.* New Haven, Conn.: Yale University Press, 1998.

Gerber, David A. "Visiting Bubbe and Zeyde: How I Learned about American Pluralism before Writing about It." In *People of the Book: Thirty Jewish Scholars Reflect on Their Jewish Identity,* ed. Jeffrey Rubin-Dorsky and Shelley Fisher Fishkin, 117–34. Madison: University of Wisconsin Press, 1996.

Gibbon, Edward. *Memoirs of My Life.* Ed. Georges A. Bonnard. New York: Funk and Wagnalls, 1966.

Gilbert, Felix. *A European Past: Memoirs, 1905–1945.* New York: W. W. Norton, 1988.

Girardet, Raoul. "L'ombre de la guerre." In *Essais d'ego-histoire,* ed. Pierre Nora, 139–71. Paris: Gallimard, 1987.

Girardet, Raoul, and Pierre Assouline. *Singulièrement libre.* Paris: Perrin, 1990.

Gluck, Carol. Interview. *The Historian* 62 (1999): 1–16.

Goetz, Walter. "Walter Goetz." In *Die Geschichtswissenschaft der Gegenwart in Selbstdarstellungen,* ed. Sigfrid Steinberg, 1:129–70. Leipzig: Felix Meiner, 1925.

Gollan, Robin. "Looking Back." In *Labour Histories,* ed. Bain Attwood, 1–12. Caulfield East, Aust.: Monash University Printing Services, 1994.

Gooch, George Peabody. "George Peabody Gooch." In *Die Geschichtswissenschaft der Gegenwart in Selbstdarstellungen,* ed. Sigfrid Steinberg, 2:111–32. Leipzig: Felix Meiner, 1925.

Gordon, Linda. "Linda Gordon" (interview). In *Visions of History,* ed. Henry Abelove et al., 71–96. New York: Pantheon, 1984.

Goubert, Pierre. "Naissance d'un historien: Hasards et racines." In *La France d'Ancien Régime. Etudes en l'honneur de Pierre Goubert,* 1:9–13. Toulouse: Privat, 1984.

———. *Un parcours d'historien: Souvenirs, 1915–1995.* Paris: Fayard, 1996.

Grab, Walter. *Meine vier Leben: Gedächtniskünstler—Emigrant—Jakobinerforscher—Demokrat.* Cologne: PapyRossa, 1999.

Graebner, Norman A. *A Twentieth-Century Odyssey: Memoir of a Life in Academe.* Claremont, Calif.: Regina Books, 2002.

Grauss, Nikolaus, ed. *Österreichische Geschichtswissenschaft der Gegenwart in Selbstdarstellungen.* 2 vols. Innsbruck: Wagner, 1950–51.

Greenberg, Douglas, and Stanley N. Katz, eds. *The Life of Learning.* New York: Oxford University Press, 1994.

Greene, Jack P. "The Making of a Historian: Some Autobiographical Notes." In *Shapers of Southern History,* ed. John B. Boles, 18–39. Athens: University of Georgia Press, 2004.

Grenville, J. A. S. "From Gardener to Professor." In *Out of the Third Reich,* ed. Peter Alter, 55–72. London: I. B. Tauris, 1998.

Grimshaw, Patricia. "Falling into Women's History." In *Feminist Histories,* ed. Bain Attwood and Joy Damousi, 10–22. Victoria, Aust.: History Institute, 1991.

Grimshaw, Patricia, and Lynne Strahan, eds. *The Half-Open Door.* Sydney, Aust.: Hale and Iremonger, 1982.

Grosser, Alfred. *Une vie de français.* Paris: Flammarion, 1997.

Guérard, Albert L. *Personal Equation.* New York: W. W. Norton, 1948.

Gutman, Herbert. "Herbert Gutman" (interview). In *Visions of History,* ed. Henry Abelove et al., 187–216. New York: Pantheon, 1984.

Haffner, Sebastien. *Defying Hitler: A Memoir.* Trans. Oliver Pretzel. New York: Farrar, Straus and Giroux, 2002.

Hamerow, Theodore S. *Remembering a Vanished World: A Jewish Childhood in Interwar Poland.* New York: Berghahn, 2001.

Hancock, W. K. [Keith]. *Country and Calling.* London: Faber and Faber, 1954.

———. *Professing History.* Sydney, Aust.: Sydney University Press, 1976.

Harding, Vincent. "Vincent Harding" (interview). In *Visions of History,* ed. Henry Abelove et al., 219–44. New York: Pantheon, 1984.

Harlan, Louis R. *All at Sea: Coming of Age in World War II.* Urbana: University of Illinois Press, 1996.

Harrell, David Edwin, Jr. "Recovering the Underside of Christian Religion." In *Autobiographical Reflections on Southern Religious History,* ed. John Boles, 39–52. Athens: University of Georgia Press, 2001.

Harrison, J. F. C. *Scholarship Boy: A Personal History of the Mid-twentieth Century.* London: Rivers Oram, 1995.

Heimpel, Hermann. *Aspekte. Alte und neue Texte.* Ed. Sabine Krüger. Göttingen: Wallstein, 1995.

———. *Die Halbe Violine: Eine Jugend in der Residenzstadt München.* Stuttgart: K. F. Koehler, 1949.

———. "Traum im November." *Geschichte in Wissenschaft und Unterricht* 32 (1981): 521–25.

Hennock, E. P. "Myself as Historian." In *Out of the Third Reich,* ed. Peter Alter, 73–97. London: I. B. Tauris, 1998.

Herbst, Jurgen. *Requiem for a German Past: A Boyhood among the Nazis.* Madison: University of Wisconsin Press, 1999.

Hertzberg, Arthur. *A Jew in America: My Life and a People's Struggle for Identity.* San Francisco: HarperSanFrancisco, 2002.

Herzfeld, Hans. *Aus den Lebenserinnerungen.* Berlin: Walter de Gruyter, 1992.

Hewitt, Nancy A. "The Emma Thread: Communitarian Values, Global Visions." In *Voices of Women Historians,* ed. Eileen Boris and Nupur Chaudhuri, 235–47. Bloomington: Indiana University Press, 1999.

Hicks, John D. *My Life with History: An Autobiography.* Lincoln: University of Nebraska Press, 1968.
Higham, Robin. Interview. *The Historian* 60 (1998): 473–86.
Hilberg, Raul. *The Politics of Memory: The Journey of a Holocaust Historian.* Chicago: Ivan R. Dee, 1996.
Hill, Samuel S. "Southern Religion and the Southern Religious." In *Autobiographical Reflections on Southern Religious History,* ed. John Boles, 1–16. Athens: University of Georgia Press, 2001.
Hinckley, Ted. C. *War, Wings, and a Western Youth, 1925–1945.* Raleigh, N.C.: Pentland, 1996.
Hine, Darline Clark. "Darline Clark Hine." In *Speaking of History,* ed. Roger Adelson, 104–23. East Lansing: Michigan State University Press, 1997.
———. "Reflections on Race and Gender Systems." In *Historians and Race,* ed. Paul A. Cimbala and Robert F. Himmelberg, 51–65. Bloomington: Indiana University Press, 1996.
———. "Up South in the Middle West: Toward a Cultural and Intellectual Autobiography." In *Shapers of Southern History,* ed. John B. Boles, 237–55. Athens: University of Georgia Press, 2004.
Hine, Robert V. *Second Sight.* Berkeley: University of California Press, 1993.
Hobsbawm, Eric. *Interesting Times: A Twentieth-Century Life.* London: Allen Lane, 2002.
———. "Eric Hobsbawm" (interview). In *Visions of History,* ed. Henry Abelove et al., 26–46. New York: Pantheon, 1984.
Hoff, Joan. "Reassertion of Patriarchy at the End of the Twentieth Century." In *Voices of Women Historians,* ed. Eileen Boris and Nupur Chaudhuri, 103–19. Bloomington: Indiana University Press, 1999.
Hogan, Michael J. Interview. *The Historian* 61 (1999): 503–17.
Holifield, E. Brooks. "The Gentleman Theologians Revisited." In *Autobiographical Reflections on Southern Religious History,* ed. John Boles, 131–47. Athens: University of Georgia Press, 2001.
Holmes, Oliver W. "Perceptions of 'Otherness': Isaac de Pinto, Voltaire, and a Personal Interpretation of Jewish Experience." In *People of the Book: Thirty Jewish Scholars Reflect on Their Jewish Identity,* ed. Jeffrey Rubin-Dorsky and Shelley Fisher Fishkin, 313–22. Madison: University of Wisconsin Press, 1996.
Horowitz, David. *Radical Son: A Generational Odyssey.* New York: Free Press, 1997.
Hourani, Albert. "Albert Hourani." In *Approaches to the History of the Middle East: Interviews with Leading Middle East Historians,* ed. Nancy Elizabeth Gallagher, 19–46. Reading, U.K.: Ithaca, 1994.
Hughes, H. Stuart. *Gentleman Rebel: The Memoirs of H. Stuart Hughes.* New York: Ticknor and Fields, 1990.
Huizinga, Johan. "My Path to History." In *Dutch Civilisation in the Seventeenth Century,* trans. Arnold J. Pomerans, 244–76. 1947; reprint New York: Frederick Ungar, 1968.
Hume, David. "Autobiography." In *Selections from "An Inquiry Concerning Human Understanding,"* ed. Eugene Freeman, v–xvi. 2nd ed. La Salle, Ill.: Open Court, 1966.
Iggers, Wilma, and Georg Iggers. *Zwei Seiten der Geschichte: Lebensbericht aus unruhigen Zeiten.* Göttingen, Germany: Vandenhoeck und Ruprecht, 2002.
Inalcik, Halil. "Halil Inalcik." In *Approaches to the History of the Middle East: Interviews with Leading Middle East Historians,* ed. Nancy Elizabeth Gallagher, 151–70. Reading, U.K.: Ithaca, 1994.
Issawi, Charles. "Charles Issawi." In *Approaches to the History of the Middle East: Interviews*

with Leading Middle East Historians, ed. Nancy Elizabeth Gallagher, 47–66. Reading, U.K.: Ithaca, 1994.

Iverson, Peter. Interview. *The Historian* 63 (2001): 491–504.

Jackson, Gabriel. *Historian's Quest*. New York: Alfred A. Knopf, 1969.

James, C. L. R. "C. L. R. James" (interview). In *Visions of History*, ed. Henry Abelove et al., 265–77. New York: Pantheon, 1984.

Japikse, Nicolaas. "Nicolaas Japikse." In *Die Geschichtswissenschaft der Gegenwart in Selbstdarstellungen*, ed. Sigfrid Steinberg, 2:133–67. Leipzig: Felix Meiner, 1925.

Jensen, Joan M. "Joan M. Jensen" (interview). In *Speaking of History*, ed. Roger Adelson, 124–41. East Lansing: Michigan State University Press, 1997.

Jones, Gareth Stedman. "History and Theory: An English Story." In *European Ego-histoires*, ed. Luisa Passerini and Alexander C. T. Geppert, 103–24. Athens: Nefeli, 2001.

Jones, Jacqueline. "Autobiography and Scholarship." In *Historians and Race*, ed. Paul A. Cimbala and Robert F. Himmelberg, 111–30. Bloomington: Indiana University Press, 1996.

Joyner, Charles. "From Here to There and Back Again: Adventures of a Southern Historian." In *Shapers of Southern History*, ed. John B. Boles, 137–63. Athens: University of Georgia Press, 2004.

Kaindl, Raimund Friedrich. "Raimund Friedrich Kaindl." In *Die Geschichtswissenschaft der Gegenwart in Selbstdarstellungen*, ed. Sigfrid Steinberg, 1:171–205. Leipzig: Felix Meiner, 1925.

Kammen, Michael. "Michael Kammen." *Contemporary Authors Autobiography Series* (ed. Shelly Andrews) 23 (1996): 133–63.

Kanner, Barbara Penny. "Growing into History." In *Voices of Women Historians*, ed. Eileen Boris and Nupur Chaudhuri, 145–57. Bloomington: Indiana University Press, 1999.

Katz, Jacob, *With My Own Eyes: The Autobiography of an Historian*. Trans. Ann Brenner and Zipora Brody. Hanover, N.H.: University Press of New England, 1995.

Keddie, Nikki. "Nikki Keddie." In *Approaches to the History of the Middle East: Interviews with Leading Middle East Historians*, ed. Nancy Elizabeth Gallagher, 129–50. Reading, U.K.: Ithaca, 1994.

Keller, Frances Richardson. "A Graduate Student's Odyssey." In *Voices of Women Historians*, ed. Eileen Boris and Nupur Chaudhuri, 159–72. Bloomington: Indiana University Press, 1999.

Kenez, Peter. *Varieties of Fear: Growing Up Jewish under Nazism and Communism*. Washington, D.C.: American University Press, 1995.

Kerber, Linda. "On the Importance of Taking Notes (and Keeping Them)." In *Voices of Women Historians*, ed. Eileen Boris and Nupur Chaudhuri, 45–60. Bloomington: Indiana University Press, 1999.

Knaplund, Paul. *Moorings Old and New: Entries in an Immigrant's Log*. Madison: State Historical Society of Wisconsin, 1963.

Koenigsberger, Helmut. "Fragments of an Unwritten Biography." In *Out of the Third Reich*, ed. Peter Alter, 99–117. London: I. B. Tauris, 1998.

Kriegel, Annie. *Ce que j'ai cru comprendre*. Paris: Robert Laffont, 1991.

Kristeller, Paul. "Paul Kristeller." In *The Life of Learning*, ed. Douglas Greenberg and Stanley N. Katz, 105–19. New York: Oxford University Press, 1994.

Kuczynski, Jürgen. *'Ein Linientreue Dissident': Memoiren 1945–1989*. Berlin: Aufbau-Verlag, 1992.

———. *Memoiren. Die Erziehung des J. K. zum Kommunisten und Wissenschaftler*. 1971; reprint Berlin: Aufbau-Verlag, 1981.

Lacouture, Jean. *Enquête sur l'auteur.* Paris: Editions Arléa, 1989.

Lake, Marilyn. "Taking Our Past with Us." In *Feminist Histories,* ed. Bain Attwood and Joy Damousi, 38–49. Victoria, Aust.: History Institute, 1991.

Lal, Brij. *Mr. Tulsi's Store: A Fijian Journey.* Canberra, Aust.: Pandanus, 2001.

Langer, Walter. *In and Out of the Ivory Tower.* New York: Neale Watson Academic, 1977.

Laqueur, Walter. *Thursday's Child Has Far to Go: A Memoir of the Journeying Years.* New York: Charles Scribner's Sons, 1995.

Latekefu, Sione. "The Making of the First Tongan-Born Professional Historian." In *Pacific Islands History: Journeys and Transformations,* ed. Brij V. Lal, 14–31. Canberra, Aust.: Journal of Pacific History, 1992.

Lavisse, Ernest. *Souvenirs.* Ed. Jacques and Mona Ozouf. 1912; reprint Paris: Calmann-Lévy, 1988.

Lavrin, Asunción. Interview. *The Historian* 61 (1998): 1–14.

Leach, Douglas Edward. *Now Hear This: The Memoir of a Junior Naval Officer in the Great Pacific War.* Kent, Ohio: Kent State University Press, 1987.

Lebsock, Suzanne. "Snow Falling on Magnolias." In *Shapers of Southern History,* ed. John B. Boles, 284–310. Athens: University of Georgia Press, 2004.

Le Goff, Jacques. "L'appétit de l'histoire." In *Essais d'ego-histoire,* ed. Pierre Nora, 173–239. Paris: Gallimard, 1987.

———. *Une vie pour l'histoire: Entretiens avec Marc Heurgon.* Paris: Editions La Découverte, 1996.

Lehmann, Max. "Max Lehmann." In *Die Geschichtswissenschaft der Gegenwart in Selbst-darstellungen,* ed. Sigfrid Steinberg, 1:207–32. Leipzig: Felix Meiner, 1925.

Lerner, Gerda. *Fireweed: A Political Autobiography.* Philadelphia: Temple University Press, 2002.

———. "Women among the Professors of History: The Story of a Process of Transformation." In *Voices of Women Historians,* ed. Eileen Boris and Nupur Chaudhuri, 1–10. Bloomington: Indiana University Press, 1999.

Le Roy Ladurie, Emmanuel. *Paris-Montpellier P.C.-P.S.U., 1945–1963.* Paris: Gallimard, 1982.

Lewin, Moshe. "Moshe Lewin" (interview). In *Visions of History,* ed. Henry Abelove et al., 281–308. New York: Pantheon, 1984.

Lewis, David Levering. "From Eurocentrism to Polycentrism." In *Historians and Race,* ed. Paul A. Cimbala and Robert F. Himmelberg, 66–90. Bloomington: Indiana University Press, 1996.

Lewis, William Roger. Interview. *The Historian* 62 (2000): 493–509.

Liakos, Antonis. "History Writing as the Return of the Repressed." In *European Ego-histoires,* ed. Luisa Passerini and Alexander C. T. Geppert, 47–58. Athens: Nefeli, 2001.

Lincoln, C. Eric. *Coming through the Fire: Surviving Race and Place in America.* Durham, N.C.: Duke University Press, 1996.

Litwack, Leon F. "The Making of a Historian." In *Historians and Race,* ed. Paul A. Cimbala and Robert F. Himmelberg, 15–32. Bloomington: Indiana University Press, 1996.

Lyerly, Lynn. "Southern Fried Grace." In *Autobiographical Reflections on Southern Religious History,* ed. John Boles, 249–70. Athens: University of Georgia Press, 2001.

Lynd, Staughton. "Staughton Lynd" (interview). In *Visions of History,* ed. Henry Abelove et al., 149–65. New York: Pantheon, 1984.

MacIntyre, Stuart. "True for the Moment." In *Labour Histories,* ed. Bain Attwood, 13–27. Caulfield East, Aust.: Monash University Printing Services, 1994.

Malone, Bill C. "'Sing Me Back Home': Growing Up in the South and Writing the History of Its Music." In *Shapers of Southern History*, ed. John B. Boles, 91–114. Athens: University of Georgia Press, 2004.

Manchester, William. *Goodbye, Darkness: A Memoir of the Pacific War.* Boston: Little, Brown, 1979.

Manis, Andres M. "Greek, Southern, and Baptist: A Southerner's Experience of Race, Religion, and Ethnicity." In *Autobiographical Reflections on Southern Religious History*, ed. John Boles, 219–32. Athens: University of Georgia Press, 2001.

Marsot, Afaf Lutfi Al-Sayyid. "Afaf Lutfi Al-Sayyid." In *Approaches to the History of the Middle East: Interviews with Leading Middle East Historians*, ed. Nancy Elizabeth Gallagher, 91–108. Reading, U.K.: Ithaca, 1994.

———. "Afaf Lutfi Al-Sayyid" (interview). In *Speaking of History*, ed. Roger Adelson, 142–63. East Lansing: Michigan State University Press, 1997.

Masur, Gerhard. *Das Ungewisse Herz. Berichte aus Berlin—über die Suche nach dem Freien.* Holyoke, Mass.: Blenheim, 1978.

Mathews, Donald G. "Crucifixion—Faith in the Christian South." In *Autobiographical Reflections on Southern Religious History*, ed. John Boles, 17–38. Athens: University of Georgia Press, 2001.

Matthews, Jill Julius. "Learning to See with Peripheral Vision." In *Feminist Histories*, ed. Bain Attwood and Joy Damousi, 1–9. Victoria, Aust.: History Institute, 1991.

May, Henry. *Coming to Terms: A Study in Memory and History.* Berkeley: University of California Press, 1987.

McCloskey, Deirdre. *Crossing: A Memoir.* Chicago: University of Chicago Press, 1999.

———. Interview by Lisa Polyani. *Challenge: The Magazine of Economic Affairs* 40 (1997): 16–29.

McDonald, Forrest. *Recovering the Past: A Historian's Memoir.* Lawrence: University Press of Kansas, 2004.

McLaurin, Melton A. *Separate Pasts: Growing Up White in the Segregated South.* Athens: University of Georgia Press, 1987.

McNeill, William H. "William H. McNeill" (interview). In *Speaking of History*, ed. Roger Adelson, 164–81. East Lansing: Michigan State University Press, 1997.

Meinecke, Friedrich. *Erlebtes 1862–1901.* Leipzig: Koehler und Amelang, 1941.

———. *Straßburg, Freiburg, Berlin 1901–1919: Erinnerungen.* Stuttgart: K. F. Koehler, 1949.

Mendl, Wolf. "A Slow Awakening." In *Out of the Third Reich*, ed. Peter Alter, 119–32. London: I. B. Tauris, 1998.

Milza, Pierre. *Voyage en Ritalie.* Paris: Plon, 1993.

Mirabal, Nancy Raquel. "Que sé yo: A Historian in Training." In *Voices of Women Historians*, ed. Eileen Boris and Nupur Chaudhuri, 265–72. Bloomington: Indiana University Press, 1999.

Molony, John. *Luther's Pine: An Autobiography.* Canberra, Aust.: Pandanus Books, 2004.

Montgomery, David. "David Montgomery" (interview). In *Visions of History*, ed. Henry Abelove et al., 169–83. New York: Pantheon, 1984.

Moorehead, Alan. *A Late Education: Episodes in a Life.* London: Hamish Hamilton, 1970.

Morison, Samuel Eliot. *One Boy's Boston, 1887–1901.* 1962; reprint Boston: Northeastern University Press, 1983.

Morrell, W. P. *Memoirs.* Dunedin, N.Z.: McIndoe, 1979.

Moses, Wilson J. "Ambivalent Maybe." In *This Fine Place So Far From Home: Voices of Acade-*

mics from the Working Class, ed. C. L. Barney Dews and Carolyn Leste Law, 187–99. Philadelphia: Temple University Press, 1995.

Mosse, George. *Confronting History: A Memoir.* Madison: University of Wisconsin Press, 2000.

———. *'Ich bleibe Emigrant': Gespräche mit George L. Mosse.* Ed. Irene Runge and Uwe Stelbrink. Berlin: Dietz, 1991.

Mosse, Werner. "Self-Discovery: A European Historian." In *Out of the Third Reich,* ed. Peter Alter, 135–60. London: I. B. Tauris, 1998.

Moyal, Ann. *Breakfast with Beaverbrook: Memoirs of an Independent Woman.* Sydney, Aust.: Hale and Ironmonger, 1995.

Mulvaney, John. "Beyond 1788: A Personal Exploration." In *Boundaries of the Past,* comp. Bain Attwood, 81–83. Victoria, Aust.: History Institute, 1990.

Munro, Doug. "My Apprenticeship and Beyond." *Journal of Pacific Studies* 20 (1996): 238–56.

Nader, Helen. "Helen Nader" (interview). In *Speaking of History,* ed. Roger Adelson, 182–99. East Lansing: Michigan State University Press, 1997.

Naison, Mark. *White Boy: A Memoir.* Philadelphia: Temple University Press, 2002.

Nichols, Roy F. *A Historian's Progress.* New York: Alfred A. Knopf, 1968.

Niethammer, Lutz. "Living Memory and Historical Practice: A Personal Tale." In *European Ego-histoires,* ed. Luisa Passerini and Alexander C. T. Geppert, 125–72. Athens: Nefeli, 2001.

Noiriel, Gérard. "Un désir de vérité." In *Penser avec, penser contre: Itinéraire d'un historien,* 249–78. Paris: Belin, 2003.

Nora, Pierre. "L'ego-histoire est-elle possible?" In *European Ego-histoires,* ed. Luisa Passerini and Alexander C. T. Geppert, 19–26. Athens: Nefeli, 2001.

———, ed. *Essais d'ego-histoire.* Paris: Gallimard, 1987.

Norton, Mary Beth. Interview. *The Historian* 60 (1997): 1–20.

Offen, Karen. "Going against the Grain: The Making of an Independent Scholar." In *Voices of Women Historians,* ed. Eileen Boris and Nupur Chaudhuri, 87–101. Bloomington: Indiana University Press, 1999.

Oliver, Roland. *In the Realms of Gold: Pioneering in African History.* Madison: University of Wisconsin Press, 1997.

Oliver, W. H. *Looking for the Phoenix: A Memoir.* Wellington, N.Z.: Bridget Williams, 2002.

Ozouf, Mona. "L'image dans le tapis." In *L'Ecole de la France,* 7–24. Paris: Gallimard, 1984.

Pannikar, K. M. *An Autobiography.* Trans. K. Krishnamurthy. Madras: Oxford University Press, 1977.

Pappe, Hellmut. "The Scholar as Businessman." In *Out of the Third Reich,* ed. Peter Alter, 161–74. London: I. B. Tauris, 1998.

Passerini, Luisa. *Autobiography of a Generation.* Trans. Lisa Erdberg. Hanover, N.H.: Wesleyan University Press, 1996. (Orig. *Autoritratto di gruppo.* Florence: Giunti, 1988.)

Passerini, Luisa, and Alexander C. T. Geppert, eds. *European Ego-histoires: Historiography and the Self, 1970–2000.* Vol. 3 of *Historein: A Review of the Past and Other Stories.* Athens: Nefeli, 2001.

Pastor, Ludwig Freiherr von. "Ludwig Freiherr von Pastor." In *Die Geschichtswissenschaft der Gegenwart in Selbstdarstellungen,* ed. Sigfrid Steinberg, 2:169–98. Leipzig: Felix Meiner, 1925.

Patrick, Alison. "Born Lucky." In *The Half-Open Door,* ed. Patricia Grimshaw and Lynne Strahan, 195–217. Sydney, Aust.: Hale and Iremonger, 1982.

Paucker, Arnold. "Mommsenstrasse to Devonshire Street." In *Out of the Third Reich,* ed. Peter Alter, 175–93. London: I. B. Tauris, 1998.

Pegueros, Rosa Maria. "Todos Vuelven: From Potrero Hill to UCLA." In *This Fine Place So Far From Home: Voices of Academics from the Working Class,* ed. C. L. Barney Dews and Carolyn Leste Law, 87–105. Philadelphia: Temple University Press, 1995.

Pelz, William A. "Is There a Working-Class History?" In *This Fine Place So Far from Home: Voices of Academics from the Working Class,* ed. C. L. Barney Dews and Carolyn Leste Law, 277–85. Philadelphia: Temple University Press, 1995.

Perkins, Dexter. *Yield of the Years: An Autobiography.* Boston: Little, Brown 1969.

Pernoud, Régine. *Villa Paradis.* Paris: Stock, 1994.

Perrot, Michelle. "L'air du temps." In *Essais d'ego-histoire,* ed. Pierre Nora, 241–92. Paris: Gallimard, 1987.

Perry, Mary Elizabeth. "Clio on the Margins." In *Voices of Women Historians,* ed. Eileen Boris and Nupur Chaudhuri, 249–62. Bloomington: Indiana University Press, 1999.

Petrie, Charles. *A Historian Looks at His World.* London: Sidgwick and Jackson, 1972.

Pipes, Richard. *Vixi: Memoirs of a Non-belonger.* New Haven, Conn.: Yale University Press, 2003.

Poliakov, Léon. *Mémoires.* 2nd ed. Paris: Grancher, 1999.

Pollard, Sidney. "In Search of a Social Purpose." In *Out of the Third Reich,* ed. Peter Alter, 195–217. London: I. B. Tauris, 1998.

Post, Gaines, Jr. *Memoirs of a Cold War Son.* Iowa City: University of Iowa Press, 2000.

Presser, Jacques. *Louter Verwachting: Autobiografische Schets, 1899–1919.* Amsterdam: Uitgeverij de Arbeiderspers, 1985.

Pulzer, Peter. "From Danube to Isis: A Career in Two Cultures." In *Out of the Third Reich,* ed. Peter Alter, 219–36. London: I. B. Tauris, 1998.

Pyne, Stephen J. "Stephen J. Pyne" (interview). In *Speaking of History,* ed. Roger Adelson, 200–220. East Lansing: Michigan State University Press, 1997.

Raboteau, Albert J. "A Fire in the Bones." In *Autobiographical Reflections on Southern Religious History,* ed. John Boles, 193–205. Athens: University of Georgia Press, 2001.

Rachfahl, Felix. "Felix Rachfahl." In *Die Geschichtswissenschaft der Gegenwart in Selbstdarstellungen,* ed. Sigfrid Steinberg, 2:199–222. Leipzig: Felix Meiner, 1925.

Rafeq, Abdul-Karim. "Abdul-Karim Rafeq." In *Approaches to the History of the Middle East: Interviews with Leading Middle East Historians,* ed. Nancy Elizabeth Gallagher, 171–86. Reading, U.K.: Ithaca, 1994.

Raymond, André. "André Raymond." In *Approaches to the History of the Middle East: Interviews with Leading Middle East Historians,* ed. Nancy Elizabeth Gallagher, 67–90. Reading, U.K.: Ithaca, 1994.

Reed, John Shelton. "Among the Baptists: Reflections of an East Tennessee Episcopalian." In *Autobiographical Reflections on Southern Religious History,* ed. John Boles, 148–58. Athens: University of Georgia Press, 2001.

Reischauer, Edwin O. *My Life between Japan and America.* New York: Harper and Row, 1986.

Rémond, René. "Le contemporain du contemporain." In *Essais d'ego-histoire,* ed. Pierre Nora, 293–349. Paris: Gallimard, 1987.

Renan, Ernest. *Souvenirs d'enfance et de jeunesse.* Paris: Calmann-Lévy, n.d.

Reynolds, Henry. "History from the Frontier." In *Boundaries of the Past,* comp. Bain Attwood, 22–27. Victoria, Aust.: History Institute, 1990.

————. *Why Weren't We Told? A Personal Search for the Truth about Our History.* Ringwood, Aust.: Penguin, 1999.

Ringer, Fritz. *Trouble in Academe: A Memoir.* San Jose, Calif.: toExcel, 1999.

Rodinson, Maxime. "Maxime Rodinson." In *Approaches to the History of the Middle East: Interviews with Leading Middle East Historians,* ed. Nancy Elizabeth Gallagher, 109–28. Reading, U.K.: Ithaca, 1994.

Roland, Charles P. "A Citizen-Soldier Remembers World War II." In *Military Leadership and Command: The John Biggs Cincinnati Lectures, 1987,* ed. Henry S. Bausum, 101–18. Lexington, Va.: VMI Foundation, 1987.

————. *My Odyssey through History.* Baton Rouge: Louisiana State University Press, 2004.

Roth, Michael S. "*Shoah* as *Shivah.*" In *People of the Book: Thirty Jewish Scholars Reflect on Their Jewish Identity,* ed. Jeffrey Rubin-Dorsky and Shelley Fisher Fishkin, 403–14. Madison: University of Wisconsin Press, 1996.

Roudinesco, Elisabeth. *Généalogies.* Paris: Fayard, 1994.

Rowbotham, Sheila. "Sheila Rowbotham" (interview). In *Visions of History,* ed. Henry Abelove et al., 49–69. New York: Pantheon, 1984.

————. *Promise of a Dream: Remembering the Sixties.* New York: Verso, 2002.

Rubenstein, Nicolai. "Germany, Italy, and England." In *Out of the Third Reich,* ed. Peter Alter, 237–45. London: I. B. Tauris, 1998.

Rubin-Dorsky, Jeffrey, and Shelley Fisher Fishkin, eds. *People of the Book: Thirty Scholars Reflect on Their Jewish Identity.* Madison: University of Wisconsin Press, 1996.

Schlesinger, Arthur M., Jr. *A Life in the Twentieth Century: Innocent Beginnings, 1917–1950.* Boston: Houghton Mifflin, 2000.

Schlesinger, Arthur Meier, [Sr.]. *In Retrospect: The History of a Historian.* New York: Harcourt, Brace and World, 1963.

Schmitt, Hans. *Lucky Victim: An Ordinary Life in Extraordinary Times.* Baton Rouge: Louisiana State University Press, 1989.

Scholem, Gerschom. *From Berlin to Jerusalem: Memories of My Youth.* Trans. Harry Zohn. New York: Schocken, 1980.

Schorske, Carl. *A Life of Learning.* New York: American Council of Learned Societies, 1988. Reprinted in *The Life of Learning,* ed. Douglas Greenberg and Stanley N. Katz, 53–70. New York: Oxford University Press, 1994.

Schulz, Constance B., and Elizabeth Hayes Turner, eds. *Clio's Southern Sisters: Interviews with Leaders of the Southern Association for Women Historians.* Columbia, Mo.: University of Missouri Press, 2004.

Scott, Anne Firor. "Chance or Choice?" In *Shapers of Southern History,* ed. John B. Boles, 40–61. Athens: University of Georgia Press, 2004.

Scott, Jonathan. *Harry's Absence: Looking for My Father on the Mountain.* 1997; reprint Sag Harbor, N.Y.: Permanent Press, 2000.

Segre, Dan Vittorio. *Memoirs of a Fortunate Jew: An Italian Story.* Bethesda, Md.: Adler and Adler, 1987.

Shineberg, Dorothy. "The Early Years of Pacific History." *Journal of Pacific Studies* 20 (1996): 1–16.

Silver, James W. *Running Scared: Silver in Mississippi.* Jackson: University Press of Mississippi, 1984.

Sinclair, Keith. *Halfway round the Harbour: An Autobiography.* Auckland, N.Z.: Penguin, 1993.

Smith, Bernard. *The Boy Adeodatus: The Portrait of a Lucky Young Bastard.* Melbourne, Aust.: Oxford University Press, 1990.

————. "History as Criticism." In *Boundaries of the Past,* comp. Bain Attwood, 1–7. Victoria, Aust.: History Institute, 1990.

Smith, Hilda. "Regionalism, Feminism, and Class: The Development of a Feminist Historian." In *Voices of Women Historians,* ed. Eileen Boris and Nupur Chaudhuri, 31–42. Bloomington: Indiana University Press, 1999.

Snay, Mitchell. "*Gospel of Disunion:* A Spiritual Autobiography." In *Autobiographical Reflections on Southern Religious History,* ed. John Boles, 233–48. Athens: University of Georgia Press, 2001.

Spitzer, Alan B. "A Historian's Memory of the Second World War." *The Palimpsest* 76 (1995): 162–73.

Steedman, Carolyn. *Landscape for a Good Woman: A Story of Two Lives.* London: Virago, 1986.

Steinberg, Sigfrid, ed. *Die Geschichtswissenschaft der Gegenwart in Selbstdarstellungen.* 2 vols. Leipzig: Felix Meiner, 1925.

Steinhausen, Georg. "Georg Steinhausen." In *Die Geschichtswissenschaft der Gegenwart in Selbstdarstellungen,* ed. Sigfrid Steinberg, 1:233–74. Leipzig: Felix Meiner, 1925.

Stone, Lawrence. *A Life of Learning.* New York: American Council of Learned Societies, 1985. Reprinted in *The Life of Learning,* ed. Douglas Greenberg and Stanley N. Katz, 17–36. New York: Oxford University Press, 1994.

Strauss, Herbert A. *In the Eye of the Storm: Growing Up Jewish in Germany, 1918–1943.* New York: Fordham University Press, 1999.

Strobel, Margaret. "Drop by Drop the Bottle Fills." In *Voices of Women Historians,* ed. Eileen Boris and Nupur Chaudhuri, 175–88. Bloomington: Indiana University Press, 1999.

Summers, Anne. *Ducks on the Pond: An Autobiography, 1945–1976.* Ringwood, Vic.: Viking, 1999.

Taylor, A. J. P. *A Personal History.* New York: Atheneum, 1983.

Tec, Nechama. *Dry Tears: The Story of a Lost Childhood.* Westport, Conn.: Wildcat, 1982.

Thompson, E. P. "E. P. Thompson." In *Visions of History,* ed. Henry Abelove et al., 5–25. New York: Pantheon, 1984.

Thornley, Andrew. "On the Edges of Christian History in the Pacific: A Personal Journey." *Journal of Pacific History* 20 (1996): 175–87.

Tindall, George. "Jumping Jim Crow." In *Historians and Race,* ed. Paul A. Cimbala and Robert F. Himmelberg, 1–14. Bloomington: Indiana University Press, 1996.

Toland, John. *Captured by History: One Man's Vision of Our Tumultuous Century.* New York: St. Martin's, 1997.

Totten, Samuel, ed. *Working to Make a Difference: The Personal and Pedagogical Stories of Holocaust Educators across the Globe.* Lanham, Md.: Lexington, 2003.

Toynbee, Arnold. *Experiences.* New York: Oxford University Press, 1969.

Trevelyan, G. M. *An Autobiography and Other Essays.* London: Longmans, Green, 1949.

Ullmann, Walter. "A Tale of Two Cultures." In *Out of the Third Reich,* ed. Peter Alter, 245–59. London: I. B. Tauris, 1998.

Vansina, Jan. *Living with Africa.* Madison: University of Wisconsin Press, 1994.

Veyne, Paul, with Cathérine Darbo-Pechanski. *Le quotidien et l'intéressant.* Paris: Les Belles Lettres, 1995.

Vico, Giambattista. *The Autobiography of Giambattista Vico.* Trans. Max Harold Fisch and Thomas Goddard Bergin. Ithaca, N.Y.: Cornell University Press, 1944.

Vidal-Naquet, Pierre. *Mémoires: La brisure et l'attente.* Paris: Seuil, 1995.

————. *Mémoires: Le trouble et la lumière.* Paris: Seuil, 1998.

Voegelin, Eric. *Autobiographical Reflections.* Ed. Ellis Sandoz. Baton Rouge: Louisiana State University Press, 1989.

Von Laue, Theodore H. "Theodore H. Von Laue" (interview). In *Speaking of History,* ed. Roger Adelson, 222–39. East Lansing: Michigan State University Press, 1997.

Wakeman, Frederic. Interview. *The Historian* 59 (1997): 505–22.

Ward, Russel. *A Radical Life: The Autobiography of Russel Ward.* Melbourne, Aust.: Macmillan, 1988.

Weiner, Lynn Y. "Domestic Constraints: Motherhood as Life and Subject." In *Voices of Women Historians,* ed. Eileen Boris and Nupur Chaudhuri, 207–16. Bloomington: Indiana University Press, 1999.

Wilbur, Clarence Martin. *China in My Life: A Historian's Own History.* Armonk, N.Y.: M. E. Sharpe, 1996.

Williams, William Appleman. "William Appleman Williams" (interview). In *Visions of History,* ed. Henry Abelove et al., 125–46. New York: Pantheon, 1984.

Williamson, Joel. "Wounds Not Scars: Lynching, the National Conscience, and the American Historian." *Journal of American History* 83 (1997): 1221–53.

Wilson, Charles Reagan. "A Journey to Southern Religious Studies." In *Autobiographical Reflections on Southern Religious History,* ed. John Boles, 206–18. Athens: University of Georgia Press, 2001.

Winkler, Allan M. "Historians and the Holocaust." In *People of the Book: Thirty Jewish Scholars Reflect on Their Jewish Identity,* ed. Jeffrey Rubin-Dorsky and Shelley Fisher Fishkin, 323–31. Madison: University of Wisconsin Press, 1996.

Winslow, Barbara. "Activism and the Academy." In *Voices of Women Historians,* ed. Eileen Boris and Nupur Chaudhuri, 219–32. Bloomington: Indiana University Press, 1999.

Womack, John. "John Womack" (interview). In *Visions of History,* ed. Henry Abelove et al., 247–62. New York: Pantheon, 1984.

Wood, Peter H. "'Hey, Man, Where Did You Come From?' Reflections on My First Three Decades." In *Shapers of Southern History,* ed. John B. Boles, 187–202. Athens: University of Georgia Press, 2004.

Woodward, C. Vann. "C. Vann Woodward" (interview). In *Speaking of History,* ed. Roger Adelson, 242–63. East Lansing: Michigan State University Press, 1997.

——. *Thinking Back: The Perils of Writing History.* Baton Rouge: Louisiana State University Press, 1986.

Wyatt-Brown, Bertram. "Neither Priest nor Poet: A Search for Vocation." In *Shapers of Southern History,* ed. John B. Boles, 62–90. Athens: University of Georgia Press, 2004.

Zinn, Howard. *You Can't Be Neutral on a Moving Train.* Boston: Beacon, 1994.

OTHER SOURCES

Adams, Henry. *The Letters of Henry Adams.* Ed. J. C. Levenson et al. 6 vols. Cambridge, Mass.: Harvard University Press, 1982–88.

Amelang, James S. *The Flight of Icarus: Artisan Autobiography in Early Modern Europe.* Stanford, Calif.: Stanford University Press, 1998.

Anderson, Benedict. *Imagined Communities.* London: Verso, 1991.

Appleby, Joyce. *Inheriting the Revolution: The First Generation of Americans.* Cambridge, Mass.: Harvard University Press, 2001.

Ashley, Kathleen, Leigh Gilmore, and Gerald Peters, eds. *Autobiography and Postmodernism.* Amherst: University of Massachusetts Press, 1994.

Augustine. *Confessions.* Trans. Henry Chadwick. Oxford: Oxford University Press, 1992.

Barkin, Kenneth D. "Autobiography and History." *Societas* 6 (1976): 83–108.

Bédarida, François, dir. *L'histoire et le métier d'historien en France, 1945–1995.* Paris: Editions de la Maison des sciences de l'homme, 1995.

Bell, Susan Groag, and Marilyn Yalom, eds. *Revealing Lives: Autobiography, Biography, and Gender.* Albany: SUNY Press, 1990.

Bergland, Betty. "Postmodernism and the Autobiographical Subject: Reconstructing the 'Other.'" In *Autobiography and Postmodernism,* ed. Kathleen Ashley, Leigh Gilmore, and Gerald Peters, 130–66. Amherst: University of Massachusetts Press, 1994.

Berkhofer, Robert F., Jr. *Beyond the Great Story: History as Text and Discourse.* Cambridge, Mass.: Harvard University Press, 1995.

Beverley, John. "The Margin at the Center: On *Testimonio* (Testimonial Narrative)." In *The Real Thing: Testimonial Discourse and Latin America,* ed. Georg M. Gugelberger, 23–41. Durham, N.C.: Duke University Press, 1996.

Bjorklund, Diane. *Interpreting the Self: Two Hundred Years of American Autobiography.* Chicago: University of Chicago Press, 1998.

Bové, Paul A. "Giving Thought to America: Intellect and *The Education of Henry Adams.*" *Critical Inquiry* 23 (1996): 80–108.

Brockmeier, Jens, and Donal Carbaugh, eds. *Narrative and Identity: Studies in Autobiography, Self, and Culture.* Amsterdam: John Benjamins, 2001.

Bruner, Jerome. "A Narrative Model of Self-Construction." In *The Self across Psychology: Self-Recognition, Self-Awareness, and the Self-Concept,* ed. Joan Gay Snodgrass and Robert L. Thompson, 145–61. New York: New York Academy of Sciences, 1997.

Bruner, Jerome, and Susan Weisser. "The Invention of Self: Autobiography and Its Forms." In *Literacy and Orality,* ed. David R. Olson and Nancy Torrance, 129–48. Cambridge: Cambridge University Press, 1991.

Bruss, Elizabeth W. *Autobiographical Acts: The Changing Situation of a Literary Genre.* Baltimore: Johns Hopkins University Press, 1976.

Canary, Robert H., and Henry Kozicki, eds. *The Writing of History: Literary Form and Historical Understanding.* Madison: University of Wisconsin Press, 1978.

Carnochan, W. B. *Gibbon's Solitude: The Inward World of the Historian.* Stanford, Calif.: Stanford University Press, 1987.

Carr, David. *Time, Narrative, and History.* Bloomington: Indiana University Press, 1986.

Chalfant, Edward. "Lies, Silence, and Truth in the Writings of Henry Adams." In *Henry Adams and His World,* ed. David R. Contosta and Robert Muccigrosso, 8–22. Philadelphia: American Philosophical Society, 1993.

Clark, G. Kitson. *The Critical Historian.* New York: Basic Books, 1967.

Clifford, James, and George E. Marcus, eds. *Writing Culture: The Poetics and Politics of Ethnography.* Berkeley: University of California Press, 1986.

Conway, Jill Ker. *When Memory Speaks: Reflections on Autobiography.* New York: Alfred A. Knopf, 1998.

Cru, Jean Norton. *Du témoignage.* 1929; reprint Paris: Editions Allia, 1997.

Dalziell, Rosamund. *Shameful Autobiographies: Shame in Contemporary Australian Autobiographies and Culture.* Carlton South, Aust.: Melbourne University Press, 1999.

Davidoff, Robert. *The Genteel Tradition and the Sacred Rage: High Culture vs. Democracy in Adams, James, and Santayana.* Chapel Hill: University of North Carolina Press, 1992.

Davies, Susan, ed. *Dear Kathleen, Dear Manning: The Correspondence of Manning Clark and*

Kathleen Fitzpatrick, 1949–1990. Carlton South, Aust.: Melbourne University Press, 1996.

Davis, Natalie Zemon. *Fiction in the Archives: Pardon Tales and Their Tellers in Sixteenth-century France.* Stanford, Calif.: Stanford University Press, 1987.

Dekker, Rudolf. *Childhood, Memory, and Autobiography in Holland.* Trans. Benjamin Roberts and Rudolf Dekker. New York: St. Martin's, 2000.

———. *Egodocuments and History: Autobiographical Writing in Its Social Context.* Hilversum. Netherlands: Verloren, 2002.

De Man, Paul. "Autobiography as De-facement." *Modern Language Notes* 94 (1979): 919–30.

Di Leo, Jeffrey R., ed. *Affiliations: Identity in Academic Culture.* Lincoln: University of Nebraska Press, 2003.

Dilthey, Wilhelm. *Gesammelte Schriften.* Bd. 7. Stuttgart: B. G. Teubner, 1914.

———. *Pattern and Meaning in History: Thoughts on History and Society.* Ed. H. P. Rickman. New York: Harper and Row, 1962.

Dintenfass, Michael. "Crafting Historians' Lives: Autobiographical Constructions and Disciplinary Discourses after the Linguistic Turn." *Journal of Modern History* 71 (1999): 150–65.

Dodd, Philip. "Criticism and the Autobiographical Tradition." *Prose Studies* 8 (1985): 1–13.

Dosse, François, et al. "Autour de l'ego-histoire." *Le Débat* no. 49 (March-April 1988): 122–40.

Duncan, Derek. "Corporeal Histories: The Autobiographical Bodies of Luisa Passerini." *Modern Language Review* 93 (1998): 370–83.

Eakin, Paul John, ed. *The Ethics of Life Writing.* Ithaca, N.Y.: Cornell University Press, 2004.

———. *Fictions in Autobiography: Studies in the Art of Self-Invention.* Princeton, N.J.: Princeton University Press, 1985.

———. *How Our Lives Become Stories: Making Selves.* Ithaca, N.Y.: Cornell University Press, 1999.

———. *Touching the World: Reference in Autobiography.* Princeton, N.J.: Princeton University Press, 1992.

Egan, Susanna. *Patterns of Experience in Autobiography.* Chapel Hill: University of North Carolina Press, 1983.

Erbe, Michael, ed. *Friedrich Meinecke Heute.* Berlin: Colloquium, 1981.

Erikson, Erik. *Childhood and Society.* Middlesex, U.K.: Penguin, 1950.

Ezrahi, Sidra DeKoven. "See Under: Memory; Reflections on *When Memory Comes.*" *History and Memory* 9 (1997): 364–75.

Finney, Brian. "Sexual Identity in Modern British Autobiography." *Prose Studies* 8 (1985): 29–44.

Folkenflik, Robert, ed. *The Culture of Autobiography: Constructions of Self-Representation.* Stanford, Calif.: Stanford University Press, 1993.

Foster, John Burt. "Cultural Multiplicity in Two Modern Autobiographies: Friedländer's *When Memory Comes* and Dinesen's *Out of Africa.*" *Southern Humanities Review* 29 (1995): 205–18.

Freadman, Richard. *Threads of Life: Autobiography and the Will.* Chicago: University of Chicago Press, 2001.

Freeman, Mark. *Rewriting the Self: History, Memory, Narrative.* London: Routledge, 1993.

Friedländer, Saul, ed. *Probing the Limits of Representation: Nazism and the "Final Solution."* Cambridge, Mass.: Harvard University Press, 1992.

———. "Trauma, Transference, and 'Working Through' in Writing the History of the *Shoah.*" *History and Memory* 4 (1992): 39–59.

Friedman, Susan Stanford. "Women's Autobiographical Selves: Theory and Practice." In *Women, Autobiography, Theory: A Reader,* ed. Sidonie Smith and Julia Watson, 72–82. Madison: University of Wisconsin Press, 1998.

Gibbon, Edward. *Letters of Edward Gibbon.* Ed. J. E. Norton. 3 vols. London: Cassell, 1956.

Gilmore, Leigh. *Autobiographics: A Feminist Theory of Women's Self-Representation.* Ithaca, N.Y.: Cornell University Press, 1994.

———. "The Mark of Autobiography: Postmodernism, Autobiography, and Genre." In *Autobiography and Postmodernism,* ed. Kathleen Ashley, Leigh Gilmore, and Gerald Peters, 3–18. Amherst: University of Massachusetts Press, 1994.

Gini, Al R. *My Job, My Self: Work and the Creation of the Modern Individual.* New York: Routledge, 2000.

Gini, Al R., and T. J. Sullivan. *It Comes with the Territory: An Inquiry Concerning Work and the Person.* New York: Random House, 1989.

Goffman, Erving. *The Presentation of Self in Everyday Life.* Garden City, N.Y.: Doubleday Anchor, 1959.

Goldman, Anne E. "Is That What She Said? The Politics of Collaborative Autobiography." *Cultural Critique* (1993): 177–204.

Gusdorf, Georges. "Conditions and Limits of Autobiography." Trans. James Olney. In *Autobiography: Essays Theoretical and Critical,* ed. James Olney, 28–48. Princeton, N.J.: Princeton University Press, 1980.

Halbwachs, Maurice. *The Collective Memory.* Trans. Francis J. Ditter Jr. and Vida Yazdi Ditter. New York: Harper and Row, 1950.

Halivni, David Weiss. *The Book and the Sword.* Boulder, Colo.: Westview, 1996.

Harbert, Earl N., ed. *Critical Essays on Henry Adams.* Boston: G. K. Hall, 1981.

Hart, Mitchell B. "The Historian's Past in Three Recent Jewish Autobiographies." *Jewish Social Studies* n.s. 3 (1999): 132–60.

Hughes, Everett C. "Work and the Self." In *Social Psychology at the Crossroads,* ed. John H. Rohrer and Muzafer Sherif, 313–23. New York: Harper and Brothers, 1951.

Hume, Robert A. *Runaway Star: An Appreciation of Henry Adams.* Ithaca, N.Y.: Cornell University Press, 1951.

Jay, Gregory S. *America the Scrivener: Deconstruction and the Subject of Literary History.* Ithaca, N.Y.: Cornell University Press, 1990.

Jellinek, Estelle C., ed. *Women's Autobiography: Essays in Criticism.* Bloomington: Indiana University Press, 1980.

Kammen, Michael. *In the Past Lane: Historical Perspectives on American Culture.* New York: Oxford University Press, 1997.

Kaplan, Alice. *French Lessons.* Chicago: University of Chicago Press, 1993.

Karr, Mary. *The Liars' Club.* New York: Penguin, 1995.

Ka-Tzetnik 135663. *Kaddish.* New York: Algemeiner Associates, 1998.

Kearns, Katherine. *Psychoanalysis, Historiography, and Feminist Theory: The Search for Critical Method.* Cambridge: Cambridge University Press, 1997.

Kermode, Frank. *Not Entitled: A Memoir.* New York: Farrar, Straus and Giroux, 1995.

Klüger, Ruth. *Still Alive: A Holocaust Girlhood Remembered.* New York: Feminist Press, 2001.

Kuczynski, Jürgen. *Probleme der Autobiographie.* Berlin: Aufbau-Verlag, 1983.

LaCapra, Dominick. *Representing the Holocaust: History, Theory, Trauma.* Ithaca, N.Y.: Cornell University Press, 1994.

Langlois, Charles V., and Charles Seignobos. *Introduction to the Study of History*. Trans. G. G. Berry. New York: Henry Holt, n.d.

Lauritzen, Paul. "Arguing with Life Stories: The Case of Rigoberta Menchú." In *The Ethics of Life Writing*, ed. Paul John Eakin, 19–39. Ithaca, N.Y.: Cornell University Press, 2004.

Lecarme, Jacques. "L'hydre anti-autobiographique." In *L'autobiographe en proces*, ed. Philippe Lejeune, 19–56. Paris: Université de Paris-X, 1997.

Lecarme, Jacques, and Eliane Lecarme-Tabone. *L'autobiographie*. Paris: Armand Colin, 1997.

Lejeune, Philippe. *L'autobiographie en France*. Paris: Armand Colin, 1971.

———, ed. *L'autobiographe en procès*. Paris: Université de Paris-X, 1997.

———. *Brouillons de soi*. Paris: Seuil, 1998.

———. *Moi aussi*. Paris: Seuil, 1986.

———. *On Autobiography*. Trans. Katherine Leary. Minneapolis: University of Minnesota Press, 1989.

———. *Pour l'autobiographie*. Paris: Seuil, 1998.

Lesser, Wayne. "Criticism, Literary History, and the Paradigm: *The Education of Henry Adams*." *Publications of the Modern Language Asociation* 97 (1982): 378–94.

Levenson, Jacob C. "The Etiology of Israel Adams: The Onset, Waning, and Relevance of Henry Adams' Anti-Semitism." *New Literary History* 25 (1994): 569–600.

———. *The Mind and Art of Henry Adams*. Boston: Houghton Mifflin, 1957.

Maechler, Stefan. *The Wilkomirski Affair: A Study in Biographical Truth*. New York: Schocken, 2001.

Marcus, Laura. *Auto/biographical Discourses: Theory, Criticism, Practice*. Manchester, U.K.: Manchester University Press, 1994.

———. "'Enough about You, Let's Talk about Me': Recent Autobiographical Writing." *New Formations* 1 (1987): 77–94.

Maynes, Mary Jo. "Autobiography and Class Formation in Nineteenth-century Europe: Methodological Considerations." *Social Science History* 16 (1982): 517–37.

———. *Taking the Hard Road: Life Course in French and German Workers' Autobiographies in the Era of Industrialization*. Chapel Hill: University of North Carolina Press, 1995.

McCooey, David. *Artful Histories: Modern Australian Autobiography*. Cambridge: Cambridge University Press, 1996.

Meinecke, Friedrich. *Äusgewählter Briefwechsel*. Ed. Ludwig Dehio and Peter Classen. Stuttgart: K. F. Koehler, 1962.

Meinecke, Friedrich. *Historism: The Rise of a New Historical Outlook*. Trans. J. E. Anderson. New York: Herder and Herder, 1972.

Ménétra, Jacques. *Journal of My Life*. Ed. Daniel Roche. Trans. Arthur Goldhammer. New York: Columbia University Press, 1986.

Miller, Nancy K. *Getting Personal: Feminist Occasions and Other Autobiographical Acts*. New York: Routledge, 1991.

———. "Introduction: Extremities; or, Memoirs at the Fin de Siècle." *A/b: Auto/Biography Studies* 14 (1999): 1.

Munro, Doug. "Looking for the Phoenix." *Archifacts*, October 2002, 61–70.

Myerhoff, Barbara, and Jay Ruby. Introduction to *A Crack in the Mirror: Reflexive Perspectives in Anthropology*. Philadelphia: University of Pennsylvania Press, 1982.

Niewyk, Donald L., ed. *Fresh Wounds: Early Narratives of Holocaust Survival*. Chapel Hill: University of North Carolina Press, 1998.

Nora, Pierre. "Entre mémoire et histoire." In *Les lieux de mémoire*, 1:xvii–xlii. Paris: Seuil, 1984–92.

———. "Memoirs of Men of State: From Commynes to De Gaulle." In *Rethinking France: Les lieux de mémoire*, dir. Pierre Nora, 1:401–51. Chicago: University of Chicago Press, 2001.

Novick, Peter. *That Noble Dream: The "Objectivity Question" and the American Historical Profession*. Cambridge: Cambridge University Press, 1988.

Nussbaum, Felicity. *The Autobiographical Subject: Gender and Ideology in Eighteenth-century England*. Baltimore: Johns Hopkins University Press, 1989.

Okely, Judith, and Helen Callaway, eds. *Anthropology and Autobiography*. London: Routledge, 1992.

Olney, James, ed. *Autobiography: Essays Theoretical and Critical*. Princeton, N.J.: Princeton University Press, 1980.

———. *Metaphors of Self: The Meaning of Autobiography*. Princeton, N.J.: Princeton University Press, 1972.

Palmer, William. *Engagement with the Past: The Lives and Works of the World War II Generation of Historians*. Lexington: University Press of Kentucky, 2001.

Parati, Graziella. *Public History, Private Stories: Italian Women's Autobiographies*. Minneapolis: University of Minnesota Press, 1996.

Parkhurst, Joseph. "The Manikin and the Memorial Bronze: The Figure of Defacement in *The Education of Henry Adams*." *Biography* 17 (1994): 144–60.

Pascal, Roy. *Design and Truth in Autobiography*. Cambridge, Mass.: Harvard University Press, 1960.

Passerini, Luisa. "Don Benedetto e l'ego-storia." *Belfagor* 44 (1989): 575–79.

———. "Giochi fuori campo." *L'Asino d'oro* no. 8 (1993): 174–83.

Patterson, David. *Sun Turned to Darkness*. Syracuse, N.Y.: Syracuse University Press, 1998.

Perdiguier, Agricol. *Mémoires d'un compagnon*. Paris: La Découverte, 2002.

Peyre, Henri. *Literature and Sincerity*. New Haven, Conn.: Yale University Press, 1963.

Pocock, J. G. A. "Gibbon's *Decline and Fall* and the World View of the Late Enlightenment." In *Virtue, Commerce, and History*, 143–56. Cambridge: Cambridge University Press, 1985.

Popkin, Jeremy D. "The American Historian of France and the 'Other.'" In *Objectivity and Its Other*, ed. Wolfgang Natter, Theodore Schatzki, and J. P. Jones, 93–110. New York: Guilford, 1995.

———. "Autobiography versus Postmodernism: Alice Kaplan and Elisabeth Roudinesco." *A/b: Auto/Biography Studies* 12 (1997): 225–42.

———. "Coordinated Lives: Between Autobiography and Scholarship." *Biography* 24 (2001): 781–805.

———. "*Ego-histoire* and Beyond: Contemporary French Historian-Autobiographers." *French Historical Studies* 19 (1996): 1139–67.

———. "Forgotten Forerunner: Zelda Popkin's Novels of the Holocaust and the 1948 Israeli War." *Shofar* 20 (2001): 37–60.

———. "Harvard's Historian-Autobiographers." *Harvard Magazine* 107 (November-December 2004): 26–35.

———. "Historians on the Autobiographical Frontier." *American Historical Review* 104 (1999): 725–48.

———. "Holocaust Memories, Historians' Memoirs: First-Person Narrative and the Memory of the Holocaust." *History and Memory* 15 (2003): 49–84.

Popkin, Richard H. "Intellectual Autobiography: Warts and All." In *The Sceptical Mode in Modern Philosophy: Essays in Honor of Richard H. Popkin*, ed. Richard A. Watson and James E. Force, 103–49. Dordrecht: Martinus Nijhoff, 1988.

————. "Introduction: Warts and All, Part 2." In *Everything Connects: In Conference with Richard H. Popkin,* ed. James E. Force and David S. Katz, xi–lxxvi. Leiden: Brill, 1999.

Popkin, Zelda. *Open Every Door.* New York: E. P. Dutton, 1956.

Porter, Carolyn. *Seeing and Being: The Plight of the Participant Observer in Emerson, James, Adams, and Faulkner.* Middletown, Conn.: Wesleyan University Press, 1981.

Porter, Roger J. "Gibbon's *Autobiography:* Filling Up the Silent Vacancy." *Eighteenth-Century Studies* 8 (1974): 1–26.

Prochasson, Christophe. "Les jeux du 'je': Aperçus sur la subjectivité de l'historien." *Sociétés et Représentations* no. 13 (2002): 207–26.

Ricoeur, Paul. "Intellectual Autobiography." In *The Philosophy of Paul Ricoeur,* ed. Lewis Edwin Hahn, 3–53. Chicago: Open Court, 1995.

————. "Narrative Time." *Critical Inquiry* 7 (1980): 169–90.

————. *Oneself as Another.* Trans. Kathleen Blamey. Chicago: University of Chicago Press, 1992.

————. *Temps et récit.* 3 vols. Paris: Seuil, 1983–85.

Riddel, Joseph. "Reading America/American Readers." *Modern Language Notes* 99 (1984): 903–27.

Robinson, Paul. *Gay Lives: Homosexual Autobiography from John Addington Symonds to Paul Monette.* Chicago: University of Chicago Press, 1999.

Rosner, Victoria. "Have You Seen This Child? Carolyn K. Steedman and the Writing of Fantasy Motherhood." *Feminist Studies* 26 (2000): 7–33.

Rowe, John Carlos. *Henry Adams and Henry James: The Emergence of a Modern Consciousness.* Ithaca, N.Y.: Cornell University Press, 1976.

————, ed. *New Essays on "The Education of Henry Adams."* Cambridge: Cambridge University Press, 1996.

Rubin, David C., ed. *Autobiographical Memory.* Cambridge: Cambridge University Press, 1986.

Ruby, Jay, ed. *A Crack in the Mirror: Reflexive Perspectives in Anthropology.* Philadelphia: University of Pennsylvania Press, 1982.

Samuels, Ernest. *Henry Adams.* Cambridge, Mass.: Harvard University Press, 1989.

Schachter, Daniel L., ed. *Memory Distortion: How Minds, Brains, and Societies Reconstruct the Past.* Cambridge, Mass.: Harvard University Press, 1995.

————. *Searching for Memory: The Brain, the Mind, and the Past.* New York: BasicBooks, 1996.

Schulze, Winfried. "Vergangenheit und Gegenwart der Historiker." *Geschichte in Wissenschaft und Unterricht* 50 (1999): 67–73.

Sheringham, Michael. *French Autobiography Devices and Desires: Rousseau to Perec.* Oxford: Clarendon, 1993.

Simpson, Brooks D. *The Political Education of Henry Adams.* Columbia: University of South Carolina Press, 1996.

Smelser, Neil J., and Erik H. Erikson, eds. *Themes of Work and Love in Adulthood.* Cambridge, Mass.: Harvard University Press, 1980.

Smith, Bonnie G. *The Gender of History: Men, Women, and Historical Practice.* Cambridge, Mass.: Harvard University Press, 1998.

Smith, Sidonie, and Julia Watson, eds. *Reading Autobiography: A Guide for Interpreting Life Narratives.* Minneapolis: University of Minnesota Press, 2001.

————, eds. *Women, Autobiography, Theory: A Reader.* Madison: University of Wisconsin Press, 1998.

Smith, Patrick. "What Memoir Forgets." *The Nation,* 27 July 1998, 30–33.

Sommer, Doris. "'Not Just a Personal Story': Women's *Testimonios* and the Plural Self." In *The Real Thing: Testimonial Discourse and Latin America,* ed. Georg M. Gugelberger, 107–30. Durham, N.C.: Duke University Press, 1996.

Spacks, Patricia Meyer. *Imagining a Self: Autobiography and Novel in Eighteenth-century England.* Cambridge, Mass.: Harvard University Press, 1976.

Stanley, Liz. *The Auto/biographical "I."* Manchester, U.K.: Manchester University Press, 1992.

Stoll, David. *Rigoberta Menchú and the Story of All Poor Guatemalans.* Boulder, Colo.: Westview, 1999.

Stone, Albert E. "Modern American Autobiography: Texts and Transactions." In *American Autobiography: Texts and Transactions,* ed. Paul John Eakin, 95–120. Madison: University of Wisconsin Press, 1991.

Sturrock, John. "The New Model Autobiographer." *New Literary History* 9 (1977): 51–63.

———. "Theory versus Autobiography." In *The Culture of Autobiography: Constructions of Self-Representation,* ed. Robert Folkenflik, 21–37. Stanford, Calif.: Stanford University Press, 1993.

Thompson, Charles P., John J. Skowrowski, Steen F. Larsen, and Andrew Betz. *Autobiographical Memory: Remembering What and Remembering When.* Mahwah, N.J.: Lawrence Erlbaum Associates, 1996.

Tilly, Charles. "Blanding In." *Sociological Forum* 8 (1993): 497.

Vann, Richard T. "The Reception of Hayden White." *History and Theory* 37 (1998): 143–61.

Verene, Donald Phillip. *The New Art of Autobiography: An Essay on the Life of Giambattista Vico Written by Himself.* Oxford: Clarendon, 1991.

Weintraub, Karl J. "Autobiography and Historical Consciousness." *Critical Inquiry* 1 (1975): 821–48.

———. *The Value of the Individual: Self and Circumstance in Autobiography.* Chicago: University of Chicago Press, 1978.

White, Hayden. "The Historical Text as Literary Artifact." In *The Writing of History: Literary Form and Historical Understanding,* ed. Robert H. Canary and Henry Kozicki, 41–62. Madison: University of Wisconsin Press, 1978.

———. *Metahistory: The Historical Imagination in Nineteenth-Century Europe.* Baltimore: Johns Hopkins University Press, 1973.

———. "The Metaphysics of Narrativity: Time and Symbol in Ricoeur's Philosophy of History." In *On Paul Ricoeur: Narrative and Interpretation,* ed. David Wood, 140–59. London: Routledge, 1991.

———. "The Value of Narrativity in the Representation of Reality." *Critical Inquiry* 7 (1980): 5–27.

Wiesel, Elie. *Memoirs: All Rivers Run to the Sea.* New York: Alfred A. Knopf, 1995.

Wievorka, Annette. *L'ère du témoin.* Paris: Plon, 1998.

Wilson, Edward O. *Naturalist.* Washington, D.C.: Island, 1994.

Womersley, David. "Gibbon's *Memoirs:* Autobiography in Time of Revolution." In *Edward Gibbon: Bicentennial Essays,* ed. David Womersley, 347–404. Oxford: Voltaire Foundation, 1997.

Wood, David, ed. *On Paul Ricoeur: Narrative and Interpretation.* London: Routledge, 1991.

Wood, Gordon S. "A Century of Early American History: Then and Now Compared; or, How Henry Adams Got It Wrong." *American Historical Review* 100 (1995): 678–96.

Wuthenow, Ralph-Rainer. *Das erinnerte Ich: Europäische Autobiographie und Selbstdarstellung im 18. Jahrhundert.* München: C. H. Beck, 1974.

INDEX

Note: Names set in italic are those of historians whose autobiographical publications are listed in the bibliography.